From Across the Sea

North Americans in Nelson's Navy

Edited by Sean M. Heuvel & John A. Rodgaard

Helion & Company Limited

Helion & Company Limited
Unit 8 Amherst Business Centre
Budbrooke Road
Warwick
CV34 5WE
England
Tel. 01926 499 619
Email: info@helion.co.uk
Website: www.helion.co.uk
Twitter: @helionbooks
Visit our blog: blog.helion.co.uk

Published by Helion & Company 2020
Designed and typeset by Mary Woolley (www.battlefield-design.co.uk)
Cover designed by Paul Hewitt, Battlefield Design (www.battlefield-design.co.uk)

Text © Sean M. Heuvel, John A. Rodgaard and contributors
Images and maps © as individually credited
Cover: Captain John Loring, 1760-1808. (Courtesy Museum of the Shenandoah
Valley, Julian Wood Glass Jr. Collection)

ISBN 978-1-913118-92-1

British Library Cataloguing-in-Publication Data.
A catalogue record for this book is available from the British Library.

For details of other military history titles published by Helion & Company Limited
contact the above address or visit our website: http://www.helion.co.uk.

We always welcome receiving book proposals from prospective authors.

Contents

List of Illustrations

List of Maps

Contributor Biographies

Matthew Brenckle holds degrees in archaeology and maritime history from Brown University and East Carolina University. For twelve years, he worked as the historian for the USS *Constitution* Museum in Boston. He is the author of numerous books and articles on naval material culture and sailor clothing and co-authored the museum's 2012 book about the everyday lives of the ship's 1812 crew. He left the museum in 2016 to open his own business reproducing historic hats for museums, historic sites, film, and reenactors, a trade he has followed for almost 20 years.

Rear Admiral Joseph Callo, USN Ret., is an award-winning author. After two years in the US Navy's Atlantic Amphibious Force, he served for more than 30 years in the US Navy Reserve. He has written three books and many articles about Admiral Lord Nelson and a wide variety of national security issues. He and his wife, Captain Sally McElwreath, USN (Ret.), were co-founders of the American Friends of the National Museum of the Royal Navy. Before his full-time writing career, Admiral Callo was an award-winning television producer and advertising agency executive. He also taught courses in writing for mass media as an adjunct professor at St John's University in New York City for 10 years.

Samantha Cavell, Ph.D. is an assistant professor in military history at Southeastern Louisiana University in Hammond, Louisiana and recipient of the Distinguished Teaching Endowed Professorship in the Humanities. She received an M.A. in European history from Louisiana State University and a Ph.D. in naval history from the University of Exeter in the UK. Dr Cavell is the author of publications on British naval history and, most recently, the Battle of New Orleans. Her publications include *Midshipmen and Quarterdeck Boys in the British Navy,* chapter contributions to *The Battle of New Orleans Reconsidered, USNA's New Interpretations in Naval History,* and *Nelson in WWII Propaganda.* A native of Australia, she is a member of the Naval Order of the United States and The 1805 Club.

Adam Charnaud was educated in South Africa and England in English literature and history, and graduated with an M.A. from St John's, Cambridge. He also flew in the Royal Navy as a conscript, and later became a qualified accountant. Over the course of his career, Mr Charnaud worked in the oil industry, the accountancy profession, and in merchant banking. The editors regret to report that Mr Charnaud passed away on 7 November 2019 prior to publication of this volume.

Andrew A. Zellers-Frederick has served as Director of the Historic Jamestowne Fund for The Colonial Williamsburg Foundation and Executive Director of the Northampton County Historical & Genealogical Society in Easton, Pennsylvania. His career within the museum and the historic site field has spanned more than three decades including several years with the National Park Service. He received a B.A. Cum Laude with History Departmental Honors from Temple University, an M.A. in History with Honors from La Salle University, and a Certificate in Historic Preservation from Bucks County Community College, Pennsylvania. He is the author of many published works primarily on the American Revolution and frequently speaks on this topic.

Caitlin McGeever Gale is a museum educator at the Pacific Aviation Museum - Pearl Harbor. She earned her B.A. in History from Christopher Newport University and her M.A. in Historical Studies from the University of Maryland, Baltimore County. Her research interests include Great Britain and the Trans-Atlantic world. She and her husband live in Ewa Beach, Hawaii.

John B. Hattendorf, D.Phil, D.Litt. is the Ernest J. King Professor Emeritus of Maritime History at the US Naval War College, having held that chair for 32 years from 1984 to 2016. Additionally, he was chairman of the College's Advanced Research Department, 1986-2003, as well as chairman, Maritime History Department and director of the Naval War College Museum for 14 years, 2003-2016. As an officer in the US Navy, 1964-1973, he saw combat action while serving on board a destroyer during the Vietnam War. He holds an A.B. from Kenyon College and an A.M. from Brown University, along with two doctorates (D.Phil. and D.Litt.) from the University of Oxford. The author, co-author, editor or co-editor of more than 50 books, he is the recipient of numerous awards, including the US Navy's Distinguished Civilian Service Award (2016) and Superior Civilian Service Award (2006, 2016), the ALA Dartmouth Medal (2007), the Caird Medal of the National Maritime Museum, Greenwich (2000), and an honorary doctorate (2016). In 2017, the Society for Nautical Research awarded him its first Anderson Medal for Lifetime Achievement.

Sean M. Heuvel, Ph.D. is a faculty member in the Department of Leadership and American Studies at Christopher Newport University in Newport News, Virginia. He holds a B.A., M.Ed., and Ph.D. from The College of William and Mary and an M.A. in History from the University of Richmond. A military historian by trade, Dr Heuvel has authored multiple naval history publications and is an active member of The 1805 Club. He also co-founded the Williamsburg-Yorktown American Revolution Roundtable in 2013 and now serves as a president *emeritus* on its executive board. Dr Heuvel and his family live in Williamsburg, Virginia.

Captain Peter Hore, RN Rtd, is an author, journalist and freelance obituarist at the *Daily Telegraph* in London. He has written over 1,200 obituaries, specialising in men and women 'with webbed feet', and also the First Aid Nursing Yeomanry (FANY) and female agents in World War II. His most recent books are *Lindell's List*, the biography of Mary Lindell, nursing heroine in World War I and MI9 agent in World War II, *Enigma: The Untold Story*, the life of David Balme who captured the Enigma machine from U-110 in May 1941, and *Henry Harwood, Hero of the River Plate*. He is an elected Fellow of the Royal Historical Society, the Society for Nautical Research, and of the Royal Swedish Society for Naval Sciences.

Andrew Lambert, Ph.D. is Laughton Professor of Naval History in the Department of War Studies at King's College, London. After completing his doctoral research in that department, he taught at Bristol Polytechnic, (now the University of West of England), the Royal Naval Staff College, Greenwich, and the Royal Military Academy, Sandhurst. Professor Lambert is a Fellow of the Royal Historical Society and Director of the Laughton Naval History Unit housed in his department. In May 2014 he was awarded the Anderson Medal by the Society for Nautical Research for his book, *The Challenge: Britain against America in the Naval War of 1812*.

Christopher P. Magra, Ph.D. is Professor of Early American History at the University of Tennessee. Cambridge University Press published both of his books on the maritime dimensions of the American Revolutionary War. He has written articles for several academic journals, including the *International Review of Social History* and the *New England Quarterly*. The Canadian Nautical Research Society awarded him the prestigious Keith Matthews Award. He has been a research fellow at the Hagley Library, the David Library of the American Revolution, the Massachusetts Historical Society, the Peabody Essex Museum, and the University of Tennessee's Humanities Center.

Thomas Malcomson, Ph.D., taught for 32 years as a professor in the School of Liberal Arts and Sciences, at George Brown College, Toronto. Thomas has produced numerous articles on naval and maritime subjects, with a primary focus on the final years of the eighteenth century and the War of 1812. He has presented papers at conferences and public forums in North America and Europe. His latest book was *Order and Disorder in the British Navy, 1793-1815: Control, Resistance, Flogging and Hanging* (Woodbridge, U.K.: Boydell Press, 2016). Current projects include tracing the stories of individual black refugees from slavery to freedom during the War fo 1812 and exploring the role of the British navy on the Great Lakes from 1813 through 1834. He is a research associate with the Nova Scotia Museum.

Judith E. Pearson, Ph.D. is a retired licensed counselor now applying her skills as an author, freelance writer/copyeditor, writing coach, and Master Practitioner/Trainer of Neuro-Linguistic Programming. While pursuing her doctoral degree and post-doctoral certifications, and building her practice, she worked as a program manager/writer in two Department of Defense contracting firms. While working as mental health therapist and employee assistance program provider, she published over 200 articles, book chapters, and reviews, as well as three books, the latest being *Improve Your Writing with NLP*. She holds a doctorate from Catholic University. Dr Pearson is a member of the Naval Order of the United States and The 1805 Club. She is also a Distinguished Toastmaster with Toastmasters International. She is married to Captain John A. Rodgaard (USN, Ret).

Chipp Reid is a former award-winning reporter, a licensed ship captain, and a US Marine Corps veteran. He is the author of *Intrepid Sailors: The Legacy of Preble's Boys and the Tripoli Campaign* and *To the Walls of Derne: William Eaton, the Tripoli Coup and the End of the First Barbary War* and the co-author of *Lion in the Bay: The British Invasion of the Chesapeake, 1813-1814*. He is currently on his fourth for the US Naval Institute, a biography of Captain James Lawrence. He works in Washington, DC and lives in Annapolis, Maryland.

Captain John Rodgaard, USN Ret., has over 41 years with the naval service of the United States, to include 12 years as a petty officer and 29 years of commissioned service as a naval intelligence officer. He is also a published author and a contributor to several Discovery Channel *Unsolved History* television programs. Captain Rodgaard co-authored *A Call To The Sea: Captain Charles Stewart of The USS Constitution*, and authored two editions of *A Hard Fought Ship: The Story of HMS Venomous*. He is the recipient of the Naval Institute's History Author of the Year for the year 1999. He is a contributor and frequent reviewer to the Naval

Institute's *Naval History Magazine*, the Society for Nautical Research quarterly, the *Mariner's Mirror*, and the Naval Historical Foundation's book review program. Captain Rodgaard holds an A.B. in History and Political Science; an M.A. in Political Science, and is also a graduate of the US Naval War College. He is the North American Secretary for The 1805 Club.

John R. Satterfield, a retired US naval intelligence officer, teaches history and business at Wilmington University in Delaware, the University of Maryland University College, and Florida Institute of Technology. He has written three books and many articles and reviews on military, naval, and aviation history. He received a B.A. from Swarthmore College, an M.Econ. from N.C. State University, an M.A. from the University of Delaware, and a D.B.A. from Wilmington University. He also is a graduate of the US Naval War College. A member of The 1805 Club and The Nelson Society, he lives with his wife in Middletown, Delaware.

Harold E. "Pete" Stark is an independent Information technology consultant. He holds a B.A. from The College of William and Mary, an M.S.L.S. from the University of North Carolina at Chapel Hill, and an M.S.A. from George Washington University. A lifelong student of the American and British sailing navies, he has been a member of The 1805 Club since 2003. He lives in Mitchellville, Maryland.

Jeremy B. Utt is a secondary school teacher. He holds a B.A. in Government and a M.A.Ed. in Curriculum and Instruction from the College of William and Mary as well as an Ed.S. in Educational Leadership from Old Dominion University. He is a member of the Sons of the American Revolution, the Society of the War of 1812, and The 1805 Club. He and his wife live in Stafford County, Virginia.

Prologue

As president of The 1805 Club I welcome the opportunity to write the prologue to *From Across the Sea: North Americans in Nelson's Navy*, which has been sponsored by the Club. The 1805 Club has grown steadily in academic credibility since the bicentenary of the Battle of Trafalgar in 2005. The Club's annual flagship publication is the *Trafalgar Chronicle*, to which experts and enthusiasts each year contribute their eclectic and quintessential knowledge of the Age of Sail and in particular of the Georgian-era Royal Navy. In this vein and following on from the 2005 publication of *Nelson's Trafalgar Captains* and the 2015 publication of *Nelson's Band of Brothers: Lives and Memorials*, the Club is pleased to support the publication of *From Across the Sea*.

As a new volume, *From Across the Sea* complements *Band of Brothers*. Under the editorship of Dr Sean Heuvel and Captain John Rodgaard USN Ret., *From Across the Sea* has been an international effort, featuring contributors from Canada, Great Britain, and the USA. Included among the contributors are world-class subject matter experts along with passionate junior scholars and enthusiastic members of The 1805 Club. It renders an insightful look into the lives of several North American-born men who served during the great Anglo-French Wars of the latter part of the eighteenth century, as well as tracing many of their lives through the post-war years leading up to Queen Victoria's accession to the throne.

Along with several biographical chapters that examine these men who served both on the quarter deck and the lower deck, the book includes thematic essays that explore topics such as impressment, the myth vis reality. It assesses North America and the Great War of 1793-1815. *From Across the Sea* also provides new insights into the post-war Anglo-American maritime relationship; a relationship that has formed the basis for the highly successful bond that the United States Navy currently enjoys with the Royal Navy, which I was privileged to be the guardian of while serving as First Sea Lord.

I congratulate the editors and the contributors on the publication of this volume. It is a testament to the strong bond that both navies, as well as the navies of Canada, Australia and New Zealand enjoy in the twenty-first century.

Jonathon Band
Admiral
President of The 1805 Club

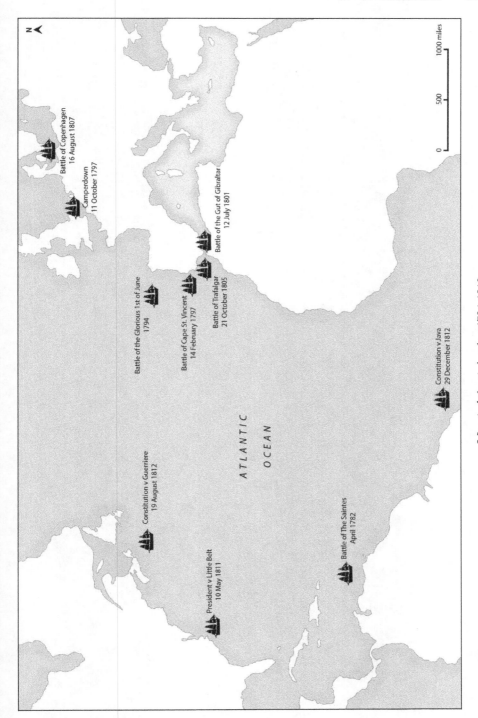

Map 1. Atlantic battles, 1794-1812.

Foreword

This is the story of an extraordinary group of seamen. They came from the United States, Canada, the West Indies, and Jamaica, and each served in the Royal Navy during the period encompassed by Admiral Lord Nelson's career. The story of each individual illuminates a unique personal narrative in a pivotal time in history.

Beyond the individual stories, however, the fact that a significant number of seafarers from the western side of the Atlantic Ocean were willing to serve in the high-tempo, high-risk Royal Navy of the Nelson era raises an intriguing question: what drew those diverse and seemingly unlikely prospects into service in 'Nelson's Navy?'

Clearly those from the largest group, the United States, had reason to actively avoid service in the Royal Navy during the last half of the eighteenth and early years of the nineteenth centuries. The bitterly-fought American War of Independence had ended with the Treaty of Paris in 1783, and the War of 1812 – fought over issues such as the impressment of US seamen by the Royal Navy – was imminent. That was hardly an environment in which US citizens would be expected to seek service in His British Majesty's Navy.

The situation for those from Canada, the West Indies, Bermuda, and Jamaica was different. Despite the distance of their homes from Whitehall, they were in fact British, and patriotism would have been an important factor for them. On the other hand, there also were significant conventional disincentives for them to join the super-active Royal Navy of the Nelson era. Those disincentives included, not only the significant physical and mental discomfort of sea-going life in the Age of Sail, but also the prospect of maimed or even an ugly death from grape shot, flying oak splinters from cannon fire, a sharpshooter's musket ball, or even a boarder's cutlass.

So the question remains, what was the extraordinary motivation that drew this special group from 'The New World' to serve in a force dominated by the spirit of Admiral Lord Nelson? Was it the expectation of prize money? Were they fugitives? Were they simply adventurers? Were they pressed men? Was it the lure of the sea?

Was it a generational thing? Was it Nelson's reputation as a winner who took care of his crews?

It is reasonable to believe that any of the above reasons, singly or in combination, could have been influential in attracting enlistment in the Royal Navy in normal times. As noted, however, service in the Royal Navy of the Nelson era was by no means normal. That reality leads us to seek a deeper, more thought-provoking attraction, something beyond the obvious – something that might be a powerful common denominator.

Based on the circumstances, there is a credible argument that it was the relatively subtle, but profoundly important, fact that those seamen from the western side of the Atlantic shared *important attitudes and values* with their counterparts from the British Isles. Those shared attitudes and values ran deep and could be traced back to Runnymede, the Magna Carta, and powerful notions of individuality and political authority derived from the will of those being ruled.

In her autobiography, *Statecraft*, former British Prime Minister Margaret Thatcher wrote about the genesis of the ideals in the Magna Carta: 'It was the insertion in the text of the document of the word "freemen," to whom its privileges were accorded, that would make the difference.' The former prime minister also pointed out that, at Runnymede, 'you… are as likely to meet American as British visitors there.'

Nelson's time was one of a changing world order, when concepts based on individualism and representative government were in conflict – literally – with Napoleon's totalitarianism. That was a fight that could be inviting for any liberty-minded person. Admiral Nelson gave us a clue about attitudes and values that reached beyond limits of traditional patriotism and the other, more conventional reasons for enlistment in the Royal Navy. In his last hours, just before the Battle of Trafalgar and in the quiet confines of his sea cabin in HMS *Victory*, Nelson wrote in his diary – not about conquest, or vengeance, or crushing a hated enemy – but about a greater good:

> May the Great God, whom I worship, grant to my Country, and for the benefit of Europe in general, a great and glorious Victory … and may humanity after Victory be the predominant feature in the British Fleet.

The outcome, for which Nelson prayed, transcended politics, adventurism, avarice, and ethnic hatred. His prayer and the values it embraced were connected to attitudes and values that ran counter to oppression. Those shared ideals could very well have added up to a deep, intuitive, and very powerful bond among seagoing warriors – a uniting factor that has survived to our own times.

Admiral Lord Nelson in the cabin of HMS *Victory* on the eve of the Battle of Trafalgar.
(Painting by Charles Lucy, Library of Congress)

Today we see that singular bond as part of 'the special relationship' between Great Britain and the United States, and as recently as World War II, it accounted for a significant number of enlistments from the western side of the Atlantic in the Royal Navy, as well as the Royal Air Force and the British Army. It was also the psychological lubricant that made it possible for the United States and Great Britain to carry out a wide variety of very difficult combined operations during that war. What Nelson prayed for in his final hours was an outcome for which sailors from the British Isles, as well as those from the United States, Canada, Bermuda, the West Indies and Jamaica, could – and did – fight.

Rear Admiral Joseph Callo, USN Ret.
New York City

Preface

We found our inspiration to compile a book about those North Americans who served in the Royal Navy between 1793 and 1837 in the book, *Nelson's Band of Brothers: Men and Memorials*,[1] sponsored by The 1805 Club.[2] The author and fellow 1805 Club member, Captain Peter Hore, Royal Navy, Rtd, had solicited the support of distinguished naval historians, some descendants of Royal Navy officers of the period, and members of The 1805 Club to write biographies of those officers who were contemporaries of Vice Admiral Lord Horatio Nelson. *From Across the Sea: North Americans in Nelson's Navy* has taken the same approach, and we were able to obtain the scholastic excellence of renowned naval historians, together with some descendants of those North Americans identified in the book, and fellow enthusiasts of The 1805 Club, who possess a variety of experience. Some are professional writers, some have had sea service experience in the US Marines, US Navy, and Royal Navy, and one has been a curator at the *Constitution* Museum. They have different styles of writing and vary in their methods of investigation. Some live in the UK and some in the US. It was our objective that this book would complement Captain Hore's book. We believe we have succeeded.

We approached Helion with our manuscript and what we thought was a catchy title, *Yankees in Nelson's Navy*. However, our editor, Andrew Bamford, suggested that our title emphasising *Yankees* would be seen by the readership, especially those from Britain, Canada, Bermuda and the Caribbean, as a bit of a stretch. We had to agree for two specific reasons.

---

1   Hore, Peter, *Nelson's Band of Brothers: Lives and Memorials* (Barnsley: Seaforth Publishing, 2015).
2   Founded in 1990, The 1805 Club is a British non-profit organisation that commemorates the Georgian sailing navy. It conserves monuments and memorials relating to the seafaring people of the Georgian era (Admiral Lord Horatio Nelson in particular), promotes and publishes research on the Royal Navy of the Georgian period, and organizes cultural and historical events for the enjoyment and edification of its membership and the public in general. The 1805 Club also has a growing presence in North America.

First, according to the *Merriam-Webster Dictionary,* the origin of the word is
'... still uncertain ... its earliest recorded use *Yankee* was a pejorative term for
American colonials used by the British military ... in a letter written in 1758 by
British General James Wolfe, who had a very low opinion of the New England troops
assigned to him.'[3] But, with the War for American Independence, American rebels
turned the pejorative word into a defiant one. Additionally, Americans born in the
southern colonies, then states of the new republic, certainly did not see themselves
as *Yankees.* They saw themselves as Virginians, Georgians, or from the colonies
of North Carolina or South Carolina. Therefore, we doubt very much that most of
the men who appear in this book, would have characterised themselves as *Yankees.*

And that leads us to the second reason. These men saw themselves as British,
especially those born in the Bahamas, Bermuda, Canada or Jamaica. Those who
were born in the former British colonies that became the United States, in all
likelihood, would have been thoroughly appalled to have been called a *Yankee.*
After all, because of their loyalty to the British Crown, they and their families
were cast out from their native land. They were the losers in the American War
for Independence. However, there were exceptions and three examples are cited
in this book. All were born as British subjects; two were from the former 13
American colonies, whilst the third was from the Bahamas. The first two lived in
the new republic. Both went to sea and had the misfortune of being impressed into
the Royal Navy. But, they managed to return to the United States. Both would
serve aboard the great fourth-rate frigate, the USS *Constitution* (44) during the
War of 1812.

These two exceptions were not really the exception in a more general sense. In his
book *A Gentlemanly and Honorable Profession: The Creation of the US Naval Officer
Corps, 1794-1815,* Dr Christopher McKee postulated that the accomplishments of
the fledgling United States Navy can be attributed to the influx of highly skilled
men who acquired their profession in the Royal Navy as petty officers, gunners,
quartermasters, etc.[4] They formed the backbone of the lower deck on most
United States Navy warships. In *The Sailor's Homer: The Life and Times of Richard
McKenna, Author of The Sand Pebbles,* biographer Dennis Noble wrote that during
nineteenth century, the United States Navy's enlisted force '... consisted mainly
of international mariners. When vacancies occurred in the ranks, the Navy put
up notices in seaports advertising for sailors with maritime experience, no matter
what nationality.'[5]

3   'Yankee', *Merriam-Webster Dictionary* <www.merriam-webster.com/dictionary/Yankee>
4   Christopher McKee, *A Gentlemanly and Honorable Profession: The Creation of the US Naval
     Officer Corps, 1794-1815* (Annapolis, Maryland: US Naval Institute Press, 1991).
5   Dennis L. Noble, *The Sailor's Homer: The Life and Times of Richard McKenna, Author of
     The Sand Pebbles* (Annapolis, Maryland: US Naval Institute Press, 2015), p.13.

Admittedly, the men we chose to profile in this book have been known to greater or lesser degree among naval historians. Paradoxically, few authors have written about them. Yes, several of the men highlighted in the following pages had direct interaction with Nelson. Some were Nelson's 'Band of Brothers,' as Captain Hore has identified in his book. Others might have been associated with Nelson, serving aboard ships that were part of a fleet/squadron that Nelson commanded, or in a fleet/squadron commanded by such men as Admiral Jervis, the Lord St Vincent, under whom Nelson also served. Regardless, all would have known of the man through his exploits and his reputation. As readers will see, this book begins with thematic chapters - ranging from the history of impressment to an examination of North Americans who fought at Trafalgar - that provide contextual background on the role that North Americans played in Nelson's Navy. As for the individual biographical chapters, they are divided into rough geographic regions. There are the New Englanders, originating from Massachusetts and Rhode Island; men from the former Middle Atlantic and Southern colonies; and finally a sampling of those from Canada and the islands of The Bahamas and Jamaica. Many of these men had strong connections to the sea and chose, or in some instances, were 'persuaded,' to join the Royal Navy.

Many of these men had a 'leg-up' as they progressed through their individual Royal Navy service. Some had fathers/grandfathers who were middle or senior Crown officials in colonial governments and/or were officers in the British Army or Royal Navy. Some had dockyard connections that placed them aboard a King's ship. With this advantage, many were placed on the crew muster books aboard Royal Navy warships operating in local waters at a very early age; an early age at which many were still tied to their mothers' apron strings. Although illegal, this was a common practice for families who had personal ties to individual commanding officers of His Majesty's Ships. These 'boys' were mustered as captains' servants, or if they were teenagers, as gentlemen volunteers. Once they physically joined their ships, they came under instruction and progressed through the ranks, accumulating the required sea time and, after passing the lieutenant's examination, acquiring the permanent rank of lieutenant. This was a turning point for young officers., Admiral Sir James Gambier entered his naval service in this manner; one far different from seamen such as Phillip Brimblecom or William Cooper.

Admiral of the Fleet James Gambier's grandfather had been a vice admiral and his son, James' father, was the Lieutenant Governor of the Bahamas. The young Gambier was placed on the rolls of his uncle's third-rate ship-of-the-line when he was 10 years old. From the time he was 11 in 1767, young James was listed successively as captain's servant, midshipman, and able seaman. On his third ship, the 16-year-old was assigned as an able seaman and then a midshipman. After three months aboard the frigate, he was transferred to a sloop, and within five months was rated as a master's mate.

With these years afloat on the West Indies Station, Gambier returned to Britain serving afloat for another year as a midshipman, before sitting for his lieutenant's examination in September 1774. He fulfilled the requirement of producing his midshipman journals and letters of endorsement from senior naval officers before the board. Additionally, in what appears to be a more common practice than not, Gambier produced a certificate that stated he was over 20 years of age; he was just 18. Gambier passed his exam, but he had to wait five months for his next promotion, until after he reached his 20th birthday in 1777.

Through his uncle's patronage, Gambier was promoted to master and commander in March 1778 and given a command of a bomb ketch operating out of New York City during the height of the American War for Independence. He lost his command to the French shortly thereafter, but was promoted to post-captain by his uncle shortly after his release. He was four days short of his 22nd birthday. Fast forward, Gambier commanded a third-rate ship-of-the-line at the Battle of the Glorious First of June in 1794. His conduct propelled him in the eyes of the Admiralty and later that year he was selected to become one of the Lords Commissioners of the Admiralty. One year later he was promoted to rear admiral. Gambier was certainly on his way, serving with honour and some controversy, before reaching Admiral of the Fleet in 1830 through King William IV's patronage.

By way of a contrast, one can see that even with Brimblecom, Cooper and Gambier, patronage, or the lack of it, did play an important role for just about all who are summarised in the pages that follow. This was especially the case for Captain John 'Jack' Perkins. Perkins came from Jamaica and was of mixed race – a mulatto. As you, the reader, will know, Perkins had extraordinary support to have been able to advance within the Royal Navy's officer corps during the time of plantations worked by black slave labour. Patronage could only go so far. It was Perkins' performance that allowed him to rise through the ranks. It was performance that made the difference for all who are summarised in this work.

Performance can be broken down into two broad categories. All of the men became masters, or at least proficient, in the sailing technology of the era. At every level of responsibility, these North Americans displayed the day-to-day proficiency required for operating a sailing ship-of-war at sea. Many had some formal education before entering the Navy, and this certainly helped in acquiring the administrative and navigational skills required of serving officers. The second category was performance under the stress of combat. All of the men profiled in this volume served in the major theatres of operations during the Great Anglo-French Wars of 1793-1815. Some saw action during the American War for Independence as well. Overwhelmingly, these men saw their first combat action in single ship actions, to include Brimblecom and Cooper, who served aboard the legendary USS *Constitution* during her first two combat actions against the Royal Navy. Many would see action in some of the great battles of the era – the battles of the Virginia Capes, The Saintes, The Glorious First of June, Cape Saint Vincent, The Nile, Copenhagen, and Trafalgar.

Additionally, we would be remiss if we did not acknowledge that there were North Americans who served in the Royal Marines during the period. Admittedly, we failed to consider addressing this area of research. What is known is that, between 1808 and 1816, the Royal Navy raised two corps (battalions) of former slaves, with the first battalion raised to operate in the Caribbean against the French. The second battalion of colonial marines was comprised, during the War of 1812, of runaway slaves from American southern plantations. They enjoyed the same quality of uniforms, weapons, and pay as their white Marine counterparts. Rear Admiral George Cockburn raised this battalion. They served with distinction in the British Chesapeake Campaign of 1814 and excelled alongside their white Marine counterparts at the Battles of Bladensburg, the burning of Washington, and the Battle of North Point, Maryland. The following year, the battalion was active at Camden County and Cumberland Island, Georgia. They also fought at the Battle of New Orleans. As Andrew Lambert wrote in his book, *The Challenge: Britain and America in the Naval War of 1812*: Cockburn's 'Colonial Marines,' recruited from former slaves, 'proved strong, loyal and highly effective at unsettling the minds of their erstwhile masters.'[6]

We are grateful to fellow contributor Chipp Reid for providing some intriguing information: 'The records are spotty…We know from the muster rolls and recruiting records that Nelson's squadron in the Mediterranean had a small but substantial number of Americans in the Royal Marines … only a few dozen to eight percent of the total [Marines assigned].' He continued: '… the records show a "surge" of US recruits in the wake of the end of the Quasi-War. Francophobia continued to run high for several years after the end of hostilities. This, coupled with the sudden demobilisation in the US Navy and, often, tardiness by the US government in paying crews and Marines, led some to join the Royal Navy or Royal Marines. Earl St Vincent, however, did his best to hide [The Royal Navy's] recruitment of foreigners for the Royal Marines. In 1800, a large contingent of "Polish" Marines entered service, having enlisted in British-held Florida, Bermuda, Jamaica, and other British possessions. As the records DO NOT identify these Marines as Afro-Caribbean (they were not allowed in the Royal Marines at this time) and there are NO records of a mass "Polish" migration to the Caribbean.

6   Andrew Lambert, *The Challenge: Britain and America in the Naval War of 1812* (London: Faber and Faber, 2012), p.233.

The supposition is these recruits were Americans who still wanted to get in a crack against the French.'[7] Finally, we admit that the men we selected for this tome represent a distinct minority of all those men who came from North America and served in the Royal Navy during the period. Unfortunately, space limitations did not permit all North American-born Royal Navy sailors and officers to be featured here. Thus, we chose to focus on those who are relatively little known and/or those who had some of the most interesting experiences while serving in His Majesty's Royal Navy during the wars with France. It is our hope that this book will act as a stimulus for others to conduct additional research on those North Americans who served on the quarterdeck as well as those who manned the lower deck.

Captain John A. Rodgaard, USN Ret.
Melbourne, Florida

Sean M. Heuvel, Ph.D.
Williamsburg, Virginia

7   Interview with Mr Chipp Reid.

Acknowledgements

From Across the Sea represents one of the first major scholarly attempts to examine the contributions of North American-born officers and sailors in the Royal Navy during the wars with Revolutionary and Napoleonic France. As one would expect with a project of this magnitude, we are immensely grateful to many individuals for their invaluable support. First, our team of contributors was first-rate and provided the heart and soul of this book through their informative and compelling entries. Their work and dedication are appreciated and their biographies may be found elsewhere in this book.

Second, as members of The 1805 Club, we wish to thank our fellow club members for their support. Many of them were contributors to the book. Their enthusiasm for the Georgian-era of the Royal Navy was infectious, and it showed in the individual articles and biographies they submitted to us. We are most appreciative to Admiral Sir Jonathon Band GCB, DL, RN, Rtd, President of The 1805 Club, and the late Mr Peter Warwick, Chairman of The 1805 Club from 2004 to 2019. Because Admiral Band and Mr Warwick are regarded as leaders of one of the premier scholarly organisations dedicated to the study of the Georgian-era Royal Navy and Nelson's memory, we are grateful for their endorsement.

We are also grateful to a number of faculty colleagues at Christopher Newport University (CNU) – Dr Sheri Shuck-Hall, Dr Phil Hamilton, and Dr Sarah Chace specifically – for offering useful scholarly resources as well as critical guidance and support. CNU colleagues Emily Gingrich and Emily Munson were also active in helping to transcribe key primary source materials and their efforts are much appreciated. Staff at the Mariners' Museum, the USS *Constitution* Museum, the Museum of the Shenandoah Valley, and the Massachusetts Historical Society were also helpful in guiding us during the project's early stages, so we appreciate their support as well.

Most importantly, we are immensely grateful to our spouses, Dr Judy Pearson and Katey Heuvel. Judy was our vital 'secret weapon' over the course of this project, serving as a contributor, copy editor, and as a key member of our senior editorial team. This book is all the better because of her active involvement. Katey was also an active supporter of the project and spent countless days tending to her young family, allowing her husband to concentrate his efforts on helping to complete this book. For the many others who supported the creation of this book and were not named specifically, we ask your forgiveness and wish to say thank you!

North America and the Great War, 1793-1815

1

North America and the West Indies in the Great War, 1793-1815

Dr Andrew Lambert

The American Revolution shattered the political cohesion of the Anglophone North Atlantic, but it did not break old commercial ties, or the human connections that saw British cultural output flood into the new republic, and cultured Americans hasten across the Atlantic. Britain retained a relatively strong position in the Caribbean, courtesy of the Royal Navy, and a less impressive grip on Canada. While the emergence of a new state to the south forced the British to think about land borders, the scale of the problem and the lack of settled population beyond the St Lawrence Valley meant the defence of Canada and the West Indies would be a combination of limited, local defences and small peacetime garrisons all aligned against the threat of an overwhelming naval counterstroke.

Under the first two Presidents, Washington and Adams, Anglo-American relations were dominated by a pragmatic recognition of shared interests that ameliorated the inevitable tensions after the new wars began. From 1800, the very different ideological and strategic ambitions of Democratic Republican administrations, led by Thomas Jefferson and James Madison, stressed division and difference. They imposed the Embargo and the Non-Intercourse Acts; measures that deliberately crippled American export business in an attempt to create an agrarian republic of citizen farmers, free from the contamination of foreign trade and foreign ideas. These measures divided and polarised American society with serious consequences for the national war effort in 1812. Jefferson wanted America to be a new society, free from the evils of Europe, but he could not carry the country with him. He and Madison presided over an era in which

America began shifting from a maritime to a continental culture; a process that would require many years, profound economic change, and much bloodshed.[1]

Tory Refugees on their way to Canada by Howard Pyle 1901. (Open source)

At the human level, the American Revolution prompted a dramatic refugee movement among settlers in the New World. American Loyalists left in large numbers, crossing the border into Canada, or going to the West Indies or Britain. Among the displaced were many servants of the imperial system: tax collectors, customs officials and administrators. They and their sons found work in the British system. Several prominent British naval officers of the era were *American born*; among them Ben Hallowell, Ralph Miller, and the brothers Jahleel and Edward Brenton. Others, British born, harboured deep personal resentments: Admiral Sir

---

1   Alex Roland, W.J. Bolster & A. Keyssar, *The Way of the Ship: America's Maritime History Re-envisioned, 1600-2000* (Hoboken, New Jersey: John Wiley & Sons Inc. 2008).

Alexander Cochrane never forgave the Americans for the death of his elder brother; sentiments that shaped his strategy in 1814. Nor was he alone; many British officers looked forward to teaching the Americans a 'lesson'. Others viewed the War of 1812 as a 'stab in the back' in the context of the war in Europe. Ordinary sailors and soldiers were less scrupulous. Modern notions of national identity had yet to harden, and a common language made it easy to start a new life. Desertion from British forces in North America remained stubbornly high throughout the era, undermining the national war effort. America simply ignored well-founded British requests for the return of these men. A particularly blatant refusal to return known deserters led to the *Leopard-Chesapeake* incident of 1807.

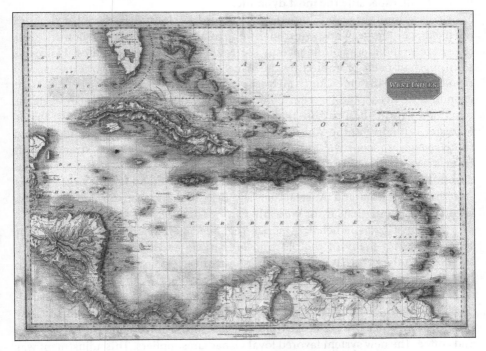

1818 Map of the West Indies, Antilles and the Caribbean Sea by John Pinkerton. (Public Domain)

The West Indies after the American Revolution

In 1793, the Americas, North and South, along with the Caribbean, remained political, economic, and strategic appendages of Europe. With one exception; the entire Western Hemisphere constituted a collection of colonies belonging to

Spain, Portugal, France, Britain, Holland, and Denmark; colonies that provided raw materials and foodstuffs, from silver to sugar, to the dominant Eurocentric world, fueling an economic boom and the creation of a truly global trading system, as North American otter pelts and Mexican silver opened the markets of China. While control of American trade had been a great prize in a succession of eighteenth century conflicts, by 1793, new ideas were entering the world system; ideas as revolutionary as those that prompted the overthrow of British rule in America and Bourbon rule in France. The old mercantilist measures that had denied foreign powers access to colonial economies had been challenged by Adam Smith's argument that reducing barriers increased commercial activity, to the benefit of all, especially the most dynamic.

British economists and imperial theorists like John Baker Holroyd, Lord Sheffield, saw the way ahead through 'informal empire'; using economic levers to secure preponderant influence in the trade of other nation states. Holroyd's thinking had been prompted by the American Revolution; in large measure a revolt against British mercantilism by the large settler population. He believed that economic tariffs should be adjusted to ensure the newly independent Americans remained within the British Atlantic economy. Between 1783 and 1801, Prime Minister William Pitt the Younger's economic reforms lowered taxes and released funds for naval reconstruction. At the same time, he oversaw a geo-strategic shift from a Western Hemispheric imperial system of mercantilism and territorial dominion towards an Eastern axis of oceanic command and market access stretching to China and Australasia. The British abandoned the idea of ruling large settler populations from Westminster.[2]

As Holroyd had predicted, America remained part of the British system for some time, and many of the old trades, markets and relationships continued. In addition, the tax system was used to shift the economic balance. The British persuaded Nantucket whalers to move their business to the United Kingdom by slapping a heavy import duty on their oil, and offering a bounty for British produce.[3] US merchants were now cut out of trade with the West Indies. They could no longer legally exchange timber, grain, and fish for sugar, molasses, rum and coffee. The new system favored loyal Canadian suppliers. This adjustment was significant. In 1790, 30 percent of British trade was with North America and the West Indies – clearly something worth fighting for.

---

2   V. Harlow, *The Founding of the Second British Empire 1763-1783* (London: Longman, 1964); John Ehrman, *Pitt the Younger* (London: Constable, 1969).

3   Edouard A. Stackpole, *Whales and Destiny: The Rivalry Between America, France and Britain for Control of the Southern Whale Fishery, 1784-1825* (Amherst, Massachusetts: University of Massachusetts Press, 1972).

Despite the loss of the American colonies, Britain remained the dominant power in the Atlantic world, with a strong position in the Caribbean. Here, large amounts of capital were invested in the plantation system, generating significant profits and providing a political power base for regional interests. British governments needed the support of the West Indies interest in the House of Commons; support that had to be purchased by providing substantial naval and military defences for West Indies shipping and territory. In Canada and Newfoundland, an influx of Anglophone settlers after 1782 was beginning to open new economic activities, but the key trades remained fish and fur.

Britain's long-standing alliance with Portugal provided a vital link in the Atlantic system; access to Lisbon and the Azores secured the westward passage, while Portuguese trade provided a steady supply of Brazilian gold. Britain had long sought direct commercial access to Brazil and Spanish America but had been unable to break the mercantilist command economies of the continentally-minded Iberian Empires. It was no accident that when Napoleon invaded both states, the British exploited the opportunity to secure new markets, not new imperial possessions. They preferred the indirect imperialism of capital and trade to the costly, counter-productive effort to sustain local government.

The emergence of the United States, an independent republic created by a settler population, challenged the core assumptions of the European states and encouraged the political ambitions of settler populations in other continental regions. The new country was, as yet, relatively restricted. It stretched south from the Canadian border to Georgia, while Florida, Louisiana and Texas remained in Spanish hands, along with the mouth of the Mississippi. The new state posed little threat to its neighbours while Europe was at peace: it had no naval or military forces worthy of note, and limited political cohesion. It was struggling to deal with the challenge of Native American peoples and the armed resistance of frontier settlers. Revenues were minimal, states disputed the legitimacy of Federal structures, and regional splits between the maritime northeast and agrarian plantation economies of the south and west were slowly morphing into political form. It was not clear where the new republic was going.

The boom element of the economy was the dynamic commercial shipping sector of the northeast; exploiting cheap timber and plentiful export crops, with a substantial seafaring population to secure new markets that replaced the now closed British Caribbean region, where the exchange of timber, fish and grain for sugar, coffee and molasses had been a staple trade. By 1793, American merchant ships were active in the Mediterranean, the Far East, and much of Western Europe, and along with whaling and fishing shipping, provided excellent returns on capital. No longer under the protection of the British flag or the Royal Navy, American shipping was exposed to the attentions of Barbary Corsairs, pirates, and unprincipled states. This obliged the new nation to establish a navy in March 1794, albeit reluctantly.

In 1790, the French West Indies provided 33 percent of French external trade and was by far the most dynamic sector. St Domingue had become the most profitable of all Caribbean possessions, creating a shipping boom; more ships, sailors, and support services. British visitors to France noted the prosperity of Bordeaux.[4] British strategists recognised the opportunity to cripple the French Navy and the French economy; always a key target in the long cycle of Anglo-French wars that began in 1688. By taking the French islands, they could hurt the enemy and secure their own possessions. Fleets based at Port Royal, Martinique, the main French naval base in the region, had seized seven British sugar islands between 1778 and 1782. With their economic power and political consequence, West Indian planters formed a significant parliamentary voting bloc, making their protection a serious concern for any administration. Between 1782 and 1793, Britain had spent half a million pounds on local defences and maintained substantial garrisons throughout the region.[5]

On the surface, Imperial Spain appeared to be in a strong position in the New World; vast continental territories stretching from Florida to Tierra de Fuego fed specie and produce into the Bourbon system, along trade routes guarded by imposing fortress/arsenals at Havana, Cartagena and Veracruz. The Spanish Navy had a large new fleet of powerful warships; many built of Cuban timber at Havana. But, like the state it served, the Spanish Navy lacked the money and skilled manpower to sustain the illusion of great power, while the monarchy, fixated on European issues, largely ignored the New World and the sea. Behind the imposing façade of Havana lay a moribund system, whose bluff had been called in 1762, when British had taken and ransacked the 'Pearl of Antilles.' Spain must have hoped for a long period of peace in which to rebuild a shattered economy and a moribund state. Instead, it faced dynamic challenges from creole societies tired of metropolitan rule and inspired by the revolutionary example of America, which Spain had encouraged, and the dynamic economic activity of the expansive new republic to the north, which wanted to send its trade down the Mississippi and extend its land holdings.[6] Smaller European powers, the Dutch and the Danes, held West Indian Islands on the sufferance of the major regional powers. Unable to provide effective security, Dutch possessions would be seized by France and

4   Michael Duffy, *Soldiers, Sugar and Seapower: The British Expeditions to the West Indies and the War Against Revolutionary France* (Oxford: Oxford University Press, 1987), pp.10-11.
5   Duffy, *Soldiers, Sugar and Seapower*, pp.15-23.
6   Larrie Ferreiro, *Brothers at Arms: American Independence and the Men of France and Spain who Saved it* (New York: Knopf, 2016).

Britain. The Danes fared little better: Britain occupied Iceland, the key to the Artic whale fishery.

War

The American War of Independence, 1776-1783, having been the epicentre of the previous global conflict, the New World would be far less important in the wars of the French Revolutionary and Napoleonic era. Furthermore, the wars that began in 1793 would be very different. While they stretched around the globe, they were total wars, dominated by the mobilisation of millions of men on the European continent. Events outside Europe were peripheral. From the beginning of the Anglo-French wars in 1793, both Britain and France recognised the existential nature of the conflict. The French openly compared the conflict to the Punic Wars of the ancient world; wars in which Rome, the dominant military power, utterly destroyed the Carthaginian sea power state, removing Carthage from the map and the pages of history. French statesmen from Danton to Bonaparte constantly referred to the British as 'Carthaginians', anticipating that history would repeat itself while France, as republic and empire, consciously and overtly modelled itself on the Roman Universal State. Napoleon had studied the fate of Carthage in Livy's *Roman history* and adopted all the trappings of Roman power: eagles, imperial pretensions, and endless ambition. Ultimately, the British would accept the analogy, and their victory was built on the strategic weight of sea power.[7]

Throughout the long cycle of wars, Britain relied on sea power; the strategic use of sea control to counter the striking military successes of France. French armies repeatedly crushed the military forces of the other European great powers, dominating Western Europe, Iberia, and Italy. Large French armies in Flanders and Holland, the obvious bases for an invasion, posed an existential threat to Britain. French war aims included the destruction of the British state, removing the king and the constitution, along with the dissolution of the Empire. Unable to counter French aggression by symmetrical means of mobilising mass armies, Britain operated a limited maritime strategy, relying on sea control and economic warfare to weaken France, and to fund a succession of coalitions and alliances with other *status quo* powers. This strategic choice required a dominant navy, and in 1793 this was the weak point in Britain's global position. The entire system of commerce, colonies, and economic growth depended on the ability to use the sea. Sea control had to be secured by a dominant battle fleet, able to defeat any challenger.

---

7   For the art that captured this identity see: John Gage, *J.M.W. Turner: A Wonderful Range of Mind* (New Haven, Connecticut: Yale University Press, 1987), p.216.

In 1793, the Royal Navy was outnumbered by the combined fleets of France and Spain. Furthermore, the effective exploitation of sea control for the defence of trade and the prosecution of economic war against rivals initially required a large cruiser fleet and Britain had neither the ships nor the sailors for both missions. It would take six years, large scale shipbuilding, the impressments of thousands of seafarers and a series of titanic victories in European and Middle Eastern waters for the Royal Navy to achieve maritime dominance. By 1800, Howe, Duncan, St Vincent and Nelson had captured, sunk, or destroyed enough hostile line-of-battle ships to restore British dominion at sea and the strategic sea power needed to counter the overwhelming land power of Republican France.

Earl Howe breaking the French Line of Battle on the First of June 1794. (NHHC 66159)

As a relatively small, insular sea power state, Britain had the luxury of waging limited, maritime war. It did not mobilise mass armies. Instead it created and exploited a world economy to sustain the war effort. Although effectively invulnerable to invasion, while it retained command of the sea, it depended on the import of food and strategic raw materials, and the profits created by international trade, making it vulnerable to naval and privateering attacks on floating trade. France, Spain, the Dutch Republic, the Armed Neutrality and lastly, America, tried to defeat Britain by maritime economic warfare. British counter-measures, combining a convoy system, shipping insurance, and the Royal Navy ensured that their efforts all ended in failure.

By contrast, the impact of British economic warfare, which had devastated French war efforts of 1744-48 and 1756-63, was markedly increased by the mobilisation of massive French armies that stripped men away from agriculture. By 1794, France was already feeling the effect, as famine and shortages undermined the war effort. A large convoy of American grain reached France after the Battle of the Glorious First of June 1794, but further American attempts to profit from servicing this exceptional French demand were blocked. The Royal Navy upheld Britain's legal interpretation of belligerent and neutral rights at sea. Britain contended that enemy goods carried on neutral ships were lawful prizes. By contrast, Britain licensed neutral ships to trade with Britain, drawing them into the British economic and strategic system, where they replaced British merchant tonnage diverted to carry expeditionary forces to Europe, the West Indies, and other distant theatres. Economic warfare would be a constant element throughout the era, the rules constantly revised to meet evolving strategic needs. In 1813, American merchant ships, registered in a state at war with Britain, were licensed to carry New England grain to feed British troops in Iberia.

This licensed trade had devastating political consequences in the United States, deepening divisions between the northeast and the south and west. Neutral ships operating without a licence were closely watched and often harassed. Even those engaged in lawful trade were often detained for long periods, to deter any thought of trading with France. The law was a key strategic weapon for Britain. Neutral ships attempting to carry French and later Spanish colonial produce between the New World and the Old, were prime targets. Danish protests were crushed at the Battle of Copenhagen in 1801, along with the Armed Neutrality that had been formed to back their position. By the time the Peace of Amiens was signed in 1802, Britain controlled the trade in colonial produce, sugar, spices, coffee, tea, and much more besides, and taxed the profits of that trade to sustain the Royal Navy, the national war effort, and allied powers. This system was, as Alfred Thayer Mahan observed 'illustrative of the natural workings of so great a force as the sea power of Great Britain then was.'[8] Seizing key offshore islands enabled Britain to blockade whole continents, Trinidad being especially useful in the southern Caribbean.

Although the outbreak of war between Britain and Revolutionary France brought large scale maritime warfare back to the Caribbean only a decade after the American Revolutionary conflict had ended, the North American continent

---

8   Alfred T. Mahan, *The Influence of Sea Power upon the French Revolution and Empire 1793-1812*, Vol. 2 (London: Sampson and Low, 1892), pp.353-411. See also James Davey. *In Nelson's Wake: The Navy and the Napoleonic Wars* (New Haven, Connecticut: Yale University Press, 2016) for a modern discussion of the role of sea power.

would see little warfare for another two decades. Instead, the war affected the maritime economy and seafaring labour in familiar ways. Anglo-French economic warfare provided powerful incentives for American merchants and ship owners to challenge blockades and embargoes, including those of their own government, in search of windfall profits. However, the United States quickly discovered that interfering with the declared political and strategic aims of great powers engaged in a life and death struggle was a risky business. Many American ships were seized for breaking blockades, and many sailors were impressed into the Royal Navy or detained in France. At the same time, the Democratic-Republican administrations of Jefferson and Madison found little support in the leading maritime economic centres, the power base of their Federalist rivals. The War of 1812 would expose the cultural fractures between the Atlantic commercial vision of the Federalists and the agrarian continentalism of the Republicans.

At the start of the Anglo-French Wars of 1793–1815, Britain had a commanding presence in the Caribbean. Superior base facilities at Port Royal in Jamaica, Antigua, Carlisle Bay at Barbados, Bermuda, and Halifax in Nova Scotia ensured that whenever Britain wished to send suitable forces, it would dominate the region. Britain opened the war in the New World in 1794 by reprising the successful strategy of the Seven Years War (1756-63); that of Pitt the Elder, striking hard at French overseas colonies, shipping, and trade, while supporting allies on the European mainland.[9] Seizing French Caribbean possessions, Martinique, Guadeloupe, and St Domingue, would disrupt the French Atlantic economy, reduce state revenue, and lock up many of the French sailors needed to man the French fleet. Not only was Martinique the major French naval base in the Caribbean, but restricting the production of the French islands, which were major producers of sugar, coffee, and other tropical crops, would benefit the less productive British possessions, and ensure West Indian planter Members of Parliament backed the war effort. Furthermore, French commerce raiders would be deprived of regional bases, reducing the threat to British trade.

For Britain, the ultimate objectives of the West Indies campaigns were to protect the British islands and floating trade, while seizing French islands as diplomatic leverage for a European peace. Britain expected to exchange them for the Austrian Netherlands, modern Belgium, in an echo of the Peace of Aix la Chappelle of 1748. By the time the British campaigns began, the French position in the Caribbean had already suffered a massive blow. Slave uprisings in St Domingue/Haiti had annihilated the planter population and devastated the plantations. For the British, the Franco-Spanish Bourbon alliance had been replaced by something far worse.

9   Julian S. Corbett, *England in the Seven Years War: A Study in Combined Strategy* (London: Longman, 1907).

The existence of St Domingue was a standing menace to the British islands, increasingly anxious about security. Planters pressed for action. The security of the West Indies dominated British strategy in the early years of the French Revolutionary War.

The British campaigns proved costly, and controversial, heavily criticised by those, including Britain's allies, who believed that wars are won on the 'decisive theatre' by mass armies. The French managed to recover some of their colonies, although the greatest prize, Haiti, eluded both sides. Servile uprisings swept away the settler population and deliberately destroyed the plantations, effectively removing the islands from the global economy, rendering them unattractive to both France and Britain. Furthermore, lurid accounts of savage slave uprisings terrified planters from Brazil to Virginia, leading them to demand ever greater levels of local defence, in the form of white soldiers. These were a distinctly perishable asset in a region devastated by malaria, yellow fever, and other tropical diseases. On the other hand, anxious French planters were easily reconciled to British rule, because it offered protection. Others escaped to the American South, bringing their slaves and their fears with them: some of these men fought at the Battle of New Orleans in January 1815, in defence of plantation slavery as an economic model and a social system.

The British amphibious force despatched in 1794 seized Martinique and the French naval base at Port Royal. These forces were moved and supplied by merchant ships, hired from Britain's dynamic shipping sector by the newly created Transport Board. The operations were conducted along the same lines as those in two previous wars, in 1756-83 and 1776-82.[10] Guadeloupe was taken in 1795. The French occupation of the Netherlands in 1795 enabled the British to take Curaçao and Demerara without a fight, preventing their use as French bases. Similar concerns prompted the occupation of Spanish Trinidad. Just as the British began to run down their campaign, French reinforcements, relatively small forces, turned the tide. French leader Victor Hugues exploited the rhetoric of revolution and rising disenchantment with British occupation to motivate locally-raised men. British garrisons, decimated by disease, were defeated and withdrawn: Port au Prince in St Domingue/Haiti had to be abandoned, and a fresh wave of British amphibious forces had to be despatched before the smaller French islands could be secured. By 1797, French Atlantic trade was effectively at an end. To fund his war, Hugues resorted to large scale privateering, careless of the rights of neutrals. While his campaign caused major political problems for the British government, already hard-pressed on many fronts, it backfired in the Caribbean. The lawless violence of French privateers was another factor that forced the United States to create a navy.

10   Robert K. Sutcliffe, *British Expeditionary Warfare and the Defeat of Napoleon, 1793 -1815* (Woodbridge, Suffolk: Boydell Press, 2016).

Quasi-War

Unable to contest control of the Atlantic or the Caribbean, for want of ships, bases, and sailors, the French resorted to a violent and illegal campaign against commerce, ignoring the protests of neutrals. This forced the United States to take action.[11] By 1798, US shipping was heavily engaged in Caribbean trade, where it replaced the merchant fleets of France, Holland and finally Spain, which were at war with Britain. US merchants carried this colonial produce, sugar, coffee, indigo, and spices to the United States, but much of it was swiftly reloaded and sent to Europe. US merchants were exploiting their neutrality to conduct a profitable carrying trade, acting for powers that did not allow them to carry these goods in peace time. The British 'Rule of 1756' established that this was a deliberate violation of US neutrality, undermining the British blockade, and therefore illegal. As the dominant naval power in the region, the British could enforce this rule, sending many US ships with French cargoes to local Vice Admiralty Prize Courts for condemnation.

However, President John Adams' Federalist administration was more alarmed by other issues: the lawless violence of Hugues' privateers and the French decree of 27 January 1798 that declared all vessels trading with Britain were liable to capture. These measures threatened US lives and economic activity, prompting Adams to create the Navy Department and purchase ships. In May 1798, the US took action in the undeclared 'Quasi-War.' US Navy warships defended US trade, while 365 American privateers attacked France shipping. By the time the Quasi-War ended in September 1800, with France agreeing to compensate American owners for their losses, the new United States Navy had taken 85 French ships, including two frigates. Adams' Navy of two new frigates, armed merchant ships, and hurriedly commissioned officers functioned well, demonstrating that the United States was still very much part of the British Atlantic world. The Americans took part in joint operations with the Royal Navy against privateers and shared convoy duty with the erstwhile imperial power. Clearly loss of life and property outweighed republican ideology.

Sailors, Trade, and Impressment

However, there were limits to that co-operation. Throughout the 22 years of war, the Royal Navy would remain desperately short of sailors; seafarers with the professional skills to work aloft. In 1792, there were only 16,000 men serving in the Royal Navy; it reached a maximum manpower of just over 147,000 men by

---

11   The similarities with the US declaration of war in 1917 are obvious and consistent.

1814.[12] As Britain's total seafaring population was little more than 150,000 men, and the nation depended on merchant shipping for food and economic survival, additional men were needed. Furthermore, wastage rates were stubbornly high: in the eight years of French Revolutionary Wars, the Royal Navy lost 24,000 men, mostly to disease, in the West Indies alone.[13]

'The Neglected Tar': a press gang seizing a seaman. (NMM PAD4772)

The scale of demand reflected a massive naval arms race that raged in the decade that followed American independence. After 1783, France and Spain pushed ahead with programmes that had doubled their battle fleets by 1790. This left the hitherto dominant Royal Navy outnumbered in capital ships, and critically so in

12   N.A.M. Rodger, *The Command of the Ocean: a Naval History of Britain 1649-1815* (New York: W.W. Norton & Company, 2004), p.639.
13   N. Frykman, 'Seamen on Late Eighteenth Century European Warships', *International Review of Social History,* (2009), pp.67-93.

the largest classes. The new ships were larger and carried heavier artillery, which increased the demand for seafaring labour, both skilled and unskilled. By 1793, the Royal Navy would have required almost the entire British seafaring population of approximately 150,000 to man the fleet, leaving no sailors for merchant ships. This was never going to happen.

Instead, the British diluted their skilled resources with easily raised unskilled landsmen and paid recruitment bounties to skilled volunteers, took on Irish and foreign labour, and used impressment to encourage sailors to volunteer. These measures kept both naval and merchant fleets at sea and developed new reserves of skilled manpower. The most controversial aspect of this programme was and remains impressment; the time-honoured legal right of the British Crown to the labour of its seafaring population in time of war. The only alternative was the naval conscription system used by France, Spain, and Denmark. Impressment was not, as has so often been argued, illegal, or arbitrary. The Royal Navy rarely impressed landsmen, and while mistakes were made, the image of the press gang sweeping up non-seafaring men from port towns is a caricature, largely created by political opponents of the war, and sustained thereafter as part of a campaign to abolish impressment in the 1820s and 1830s. In reality, the Royal Navy carefully picked out the best men; those who could handle the sails and yards of large warships. These men understood that wartime service in the Navy was an occupational hazard of deep-water seafaring. Most accepted their fate and volunteered, taking the bounty that was offered.[14] Between 1793 and 1814, Britain waged virtually continuous war with most of the world's navies. Furthermore, the principal conflict, with Revolutionary and then Napoleonic France, was existential. Defeat would entail the destruction of the British state. So long as wars lasted, the Royal Navy's need for men was endless. While disease and shipwreck decimated crews, battles were far less costly for the dominant Royal Navy.

Once the cycle of wars began, the space for neutral shipping in the Atlantic quickly disappeared. The British had maximised their manpower base by licensing neutral ships to carry British cargoes, a policy which also kept those ships from aiding France. By 1796, only Denmark-Norway, Sweden, the North German ports, and the United States were still at liberty. From 1803, America was the only significant neutral carrier. As the Anglo-French conflict evolved into an economic total war after Trafalgar, the US was caught between two powers, both of which were ready to use force to stop US merchants from trading with the other.

14   J. Ross Dancy, *The Myth of the Press Gang: Volunteers, Impressments and the Naval Manpower Problem in the Late Eighteenth Century* (Woodbridge, Suffolk: Boydell Press, 2015); M. Salmon, 'More Talk of Peace than Prize Money: The letters of common or 'lower deck' seamen from the Revolutionary and Napoleonic Wars 1793-1815' (Master of Arts Thesis, National Maritime Museum, University of Greenwich, 2016).

Napoleon, who never fully understood the difference between Britain and the US, seized and burnt US ships and cargoes, leading to long-standing US claims against the French government. These were only settled in the 1830s. British Prize Courts condemned US-flagged ships that broke the blockade of France, denying them the right to carry goods between the West Indies and France.

In the process of imposing the blockade, British warships frequently stopped US merchant ships, inspected their papers, and mustered their crew. Skilled men were impressed, and some of them were US citizens. However, the definition of an 'American' (a US citizen) was in dispute. Britain did not recognise any transfer of allegiance. British-born equalled British in the eyes of the law; furthermore, many of the men taken were British in both senses. Many 'American' sailors carried printed forms that stated they were either American-born or naturalised US citizens. These forms, and they came in an infinite variety of shapes and sizes, typefaces, and wording, were sold for a small fee by US consuls in most seaport towns around the Atlantic world. They had no legal status, and short-handed British captains were unlikely to find them persuasive. Critically, impressment exposed the political divide in the United States. The Federalist states of New England, those which were profiting heavily from the neutral carrying trade, tolerated it: the slave-owning southern states, which had nothing to do with seafaring, objected that it was a form of white slavery, and therefore degrading to the nation.

While the impressment of sailors from US merchant ships became a major source of complaint and played a part in 'War Hawk' propaganda leading up to the outbreak of the Anglo-American War of 1812, the underlying reality is that the US seafaring communities who traded on the Atlantic between 1793 and 1815 did not object to impressments. Like the sailors who were impressed, they accepted it, if reluctantly, as an occupational hazard of a lucrative business. US objections came from southern and western states, which had no shipping, or sailors, where the system was commonly compared to slavery. Furthermore, the explosive growth of US commercial shipping after 1793 was fueled by foreign seamen, many of them British. This was understood by the US, who rejected requests to keep British seafarers off their ships. Consequently, many of the prime seamen on US ships, naval and commercial, were British, a reality that was not affected by printed claims of US nationality that had no legal status in US Federal Statutory Law, let alone British.[15]

15   See: Andrew D. Lambert, *The Challenge: Britain Versus America in the Naval War of 1812* (London: Faber & Faber, 2012) for the origins and conduct of the conflict.

A Return to War, 1803

At the Peace of Amiens, France recovered Martinique and Guadeloupe, and Napoleon used the former as the staging post for an attempt to recover St Domingue/Haiti from the black insurgents. Unable to overcome local resistance and appalling losses to disease, the effort had faltered before the renewal of hostilities with Britain, when the remaining French warships in the region were quickly swept up. With his regional ambitions thwarted, Napoleon hastily sold Louisiana, which he had taken from Spain, to the United States at a knock-down price, fully intending to return when he had settled his account with the British. The funds were used to rebuild the French Navy.

Whilst Britain secured control of the Caribbean in 1803, it lacked the disposable military forces needed to conquer the major French islands: while sea control, convoys and strong island garrisons were enough to keep the region under control, French privateering remained a significant problem. Spain's entry into the war in 1804 did not alter that situation. However, the importance of the Caribbean in the British grand strategy would be highlighted in the 1805 campaign. Napoleon's idea that a Franco-Spanish incursion into the region would panic the British into detaching major forces from Europe was sound. When Villeneuve and Gravina passed the Straits of Gibraltar, Nelson, despite his command authority being restricted to the Mediterranean, was quick to follow. A combination of incisive analysis and superior seamanship ensured Nelson's fleet reached the Lesser Antilles before Villeneuve could achieve any strategic impact, although he did take a rich British convoy.

Having been unable to even attempt an invasion of Britain between 1803 and 1806, and then having seen his fleet annihilated at Trafalgar, Napoleon switched to continental warfare. At Austerlitz and Jena, his Grand Army smashed the forces of Austria and Prussia and drove Russia out of central Europe. Having secured dominion over the continent, Napoleon launched a total war of economic attrition, beginning with the Berlin Decree of 21 November 1806, which prohibited all trade with Britain, excluding Britain from European markets. As Alfred Thayer Mahan observed, the Berlin Decree forced Britain to act. If the US was free to trade with France, the British war effort would be undermined.

The British responded with the Orders in Council of 11 November 1807, which extended the licensing system to all neutral ships wishing to trade with the Continent. Napoleon responded with the Milan Decree of 11 December, which made any neutral ship carrying a British license an enemy that could be seized and sold as a lawful prize. The Anglo-French economic total war left no space for neutral shipping, and the biggest loser would be the United States, the last neutral carrier. US commercial profits had threatened the survival of Britain; they had to be curbed, and Napoleon's decrees provided the perfect opportunity.

Napoleon backed up his decrees with a return to the classic *guerre de course* methods adopted by Louis XIV and other French leaders. Recognising that he could not defeat the Royal Navy, browbeat the British into surrender, or launch a serious invasion, he deployed battle squadrons and frigates from Brest and Rochefort to raid the central Atlantic and Caribbean. His target was the economic system that underpinned the British war effort: trade, taxation, capital, and, above all, confidence. The first French sortie to the West Indies ended in disaster off St Domingue/Haiti on 6 February 1806, when Admiral Sir John Duckworth took or destroyed all five of Admiral Leisségues' capital ships. There would be no more fleet actions in the region.

The British responded to the threat of squadron warfare by seizing the bases that the French needed to operate in the West Indies. On New Year's Day 1807, they secured the strategic island of Curaçao from the Dutch in a surprise naval attack. Anything more depended on mobilising military resources and detaching significant naval and transport fleets from the hard-pressed European theatre, where major operations at Copenhagen and Portugal in 1807, and on Walcheren Island in 1809, had first call on scarce resources. In addition, the need to defend vital food and shipbuilding supplies coming through the Baltic between 1807 and 1812 limited the cruiser force that could be sent to the west. The Spanish Uprising shifted the strategic balance: with the Spanish fleet no longer a threat, Britain could release ships to the wider world, ending the cruiser war in the West Indies by blockading the French islands.

In 1808, Admiral Sir Alexander Cochrane, a combined operations expert, prepared to capture Martinique and Guadeloupe, for a third time since 1793. Martinique, and the key naval base at Port Royal, surrendered to a major amphibious force on 24 February 1809; Guadeloupe a year later, followed shortly afterwards by the naval rendezvous at the Saintes. Without secure bases in the region, French cruiser and privateer activity collapsed, leaving Cochrane to administer Guadeloupe in the British interest. He kept the production of 'French' sugar at a low level to benefit the British islands, and the West India interest in the House of Commons. Continuing anxiety about servile uprisings made his job relatively easy. While Britain retained significant garrisons in the region until 1815, this had more to do with the domestic anxieties of the planters than any external threat. Throughout the Anglo-American War of 1812, there would be more British troops in the West Indies than in Canada. After 1809, British naval forces on the North America, Leeward Islands, and Jamaica Stations were reduced to very low levels, mostly comprised of over-age or worn out craft, often with unimpressive officers and weak crews. The region had become a backwater, as the war had moved to the East Indies, the Mediterranean, and elsewhere. Consequently, Britain was ill-prepared when the United States declared war in June 1812. Two crack frigates sent to the theatre earlier that year had been a gesture of deterrence, not a fighting force.

America and the War of 1812

The US economy had been profoundly affected by the two-decades long cycle of wars. The US soon discovered that in a total war there was no space for neutral trade. The Peace of Amiens, which removed American shipping from Caribbean trade, halved American imports, but the renewed war soon increased that level three times. Neutral US ships resumed the carriage of French West Indies produce to Europe, a trade closed to them in peace time. President Thomas Jefferson recognised that trading openly with either belligerent would draw the United States into the European war. US shipping was undermining British strategy, weakening the blockade, and reducing the financial resources needed to continue a war for national survival. Britain would have to stop the US, or lose the war, enabling Napoleon to extend his empire from Europe to the New World, beginning with a renewed offensive against Haiti. Napoleon should have been the ally of the United States, as supportive neutrals, but instead his decrees embroiled them in the war and enabled the British to defeat the threat they posed.

The British Orders in Council were enforced by naval patrols stretching from US coastal waters to the open ocean. British warships stopped and searched US merchant ships for French cargoes and frequently impressed skilled sailors, who were predominantly, but not entirely, British. These patrols sparked a serious clash between British and US warships on 22 June 1807 when HMS *Leopard* stopped the USS *Chesapeake*. US naval authorities ashore had refused to return men who were known to have deserted from the Royal Navy and allowed them to insult their former officers on shore with impunity. Vice Admiral Sir George Berkeley ordered the *Leopard* to stop the US Navy warship, on which the deserters had enlisted. Four Americans were killed before the deserters were surrendered. One deserter was subsequently hanged.

Despite public outrage at this insult to the US flag, Jefferson recognised reality. The US could not defend neutral trade with Europe. His Embargo Act of 22 December 1807 ended the problem by banning foreign trade, a measure that proved deeply unpopular with ship-owners and exporters alike. Enforcement was limited by the weakness of the federal state. Despite devastating the US economy, Jefferson's measure had little effect on Britain: US goods continued to arrive. In an attempt to reduce domestic objections, newly installed President James Madison replaced the Embargo Act with the Non-Intercourse Act on 1 March 1809, restricting the trade ban to Britain and France, and promising to revoke the measure if either side revoked their measures against US trade. Napoleon promised to do so, but continued to seize and destroy US merchant ships, leaving the United

USS *Chesapeake* v HMS *Leopard*, 22 June 1807. Sketch by Fred S. Cozzens reproduced from his 1897 book *Our Navy, its Growth and Achievements.* (NHHC NH 74526)

USS *President* vs HMS *Little Belt* by J. Cartwright. (NHHC KN-10868)

States without legal recourse. Britain refused to act unless France actually revoked the Berlin and Milan Decrees. This never happened, although Madison acted as if Napoleon had lived up to his promise.

Tension between Britain and the United States remained high: on 16 May 1811, the USS *President* fired on HMS *Little Belt*, in international waters off the New Jersey coast, killing 13 men in a night encounter sparked by the impressment of US sailors. The incident did not lead to war – neither side was anxious to fight about 'Free Trade and Sailor's Rights.' Britain finally revoked the Orders in Council that applied to the United States when Napoleon invaded Russia in the summer of 1812, only to discover that the US had invaded Canada. The 1807 Embargo Act had reduced US economic activity back to peacetime levels, and after a small increase following Madison's Non-Intercourse Act, the British wartime blockade and US export restrictions annihilated national commerce. This slashed the customs revenue on which the federal system depended. As a result, the War of 1812 doubled the US national debt, inflation and debt interest, and left the country bankrupt.[16]

US naval strategy was dominated by economic considerations. Lacking the naval power, even with large scale privateering, to cut Britain's Atlantic trade links, the US opened the war by sending out a large force of frigates and sloops to look for a West India convoy. Commodore John Rogers chased one across the Atlantic but failed to capture it. Thereafter, US warships and privateers operated singly or in small groups, unable to tackle major convoys, which were usually escorted by a battleship, a frigate, and some smaller craft. The combination of convoys, excellent intelligence work, and secure shipping insurance enabled Britain to endure heavy losses in 1812 and 1813. By 1814 the threat had been mastered.

Once again, Napoleon provided the key to British success. The overstretched British were rescued by his invasion of Russia, which followed Russia's departure from the Continental System, rather than be reduced to bankruptcy. In a matter of days, Russia went from enemy to ally, and by the autumn of 1812, the British could dispense with their Baltic fleet, the second largest British fleet of the period. This released ships and men for the North American and West Indies Stations and, more significantly, allowed the British to send some of their best officers.

These reinforcements enabled the British to secure command of the Atlantic in the early summer of 1813. Two engagements on June 1st completed the process. In the late morning, two US frigates were driven into New London and blockaded there until the war ended. Then the frigate USS *Chesapeake* was taken in a single

16   Brian Arthur, *How Britain Won the War of 1812: The Royal Navy's Blockade of the United States, 1812-1815* (Woodbridge, Suffolk: Boydell Press, 2012), pp.222-229; Lambert, *The Challenge.*

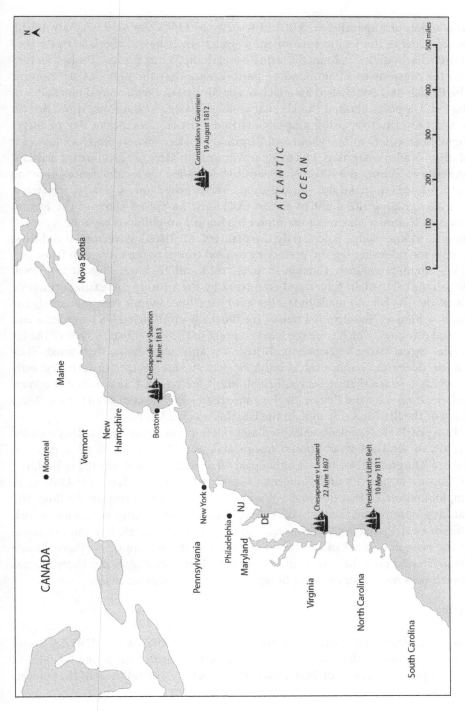

Map 2. North Americans fighting in Royal Navy and US Navy frigate actions 1807–1813.

ship action of unparalleled skill and ferocity by HMS *Shannon*. Captain Philip Broke became the iconic hero of the conflict when he led the US frigate into Halifax harbour, her colours fluttering beneath the White Ensign. Broke's victory was the capstone to a commanding performance over the previous six months. The British had established an effective convoy system, while naval blockades of the key US ports blunted the US maritime offensive. At the same time, Britain seized the initiative, using amphibious raids in the Chesapeake Bay to target Republican voters in Maryland and Virginia; the slave owners who had voted for Madison's administration. Led by Rear Admiral Sir George Cockburn, a brilliant protégée of Nelson, the Royal Navy steadily degraded the local defences, moving quickly by sea to strike at depots, arsenals, and exposed towns, seizing privateers, and encouraging the flight of slaves. Cockburn mobilised some of the former slaves as 'Colonial Marines' to reinforce his limited amphibious capability, exploit their local knowledge, and terrify the planters. Madison's government did little to help the tidewater region, preferring to send troops to the Canadian frontier.

US attempts conquer Canada in 1812, 1813 and 1814 were blocked by local British and Canadian forces and countered by the steadily increasing economic blockade. The US was made to feel the hard hand of economic war in precisely the same fashion as Napoleonic France. The blockade annihilated US commerce and federal revenues, which were the weakest point of the war effort. In view of the far greater threat posed by Napoleon, British war aims were distinctly limited. They had no desire to conquer the country or occupy vast swathes of territory; only to secure a peace that preserved British maritime power, Canada, and the West Indies. At no stage did Britain deploy more than seven percent of either the Royal Navy or the British Army to fight the US: this was a sideshow.

In April 1814, Napoleon abdicated and the European war ended. This enabled Britain to send a few additional troops and warships to the North American theatre. The great majority were either paid off or deployed to secure the re-building of Europe at the Vienna Congress. George Cockburn's dynamic 4,000-man amphibious strike that destroyed Washington, DC led to a run on the domestic banking system, and the flight of American capital into British securities. British offensives at Plattsburg, Baltimore, and New Orleans failed, but the extension of the economic blockade to New England and the seizure of northern Maine demonstrated how the war would be won. By November 1814, the United States government had defaulted on debt repayments. Peace was inevitable.

Peace

Sea power enabled Britain to survive and prosper in the wars of 1793-1815, and it was no accident that the first order of business for Britain at the Ghent and Vienna peace processes of 1814-15 was to uphold the critical tools of that power:

maritime belligerent rights and impressment. The Anglo-American Treaty of Ghent and the Congress of Vienna upheld British interpretations of maritime law: Britain refused to allow them onto the agenda in either forum. 'Free Trade and Sailor's Rights' – the putative US war aims of 1812 – were abandoned by a bankrupt Republican administration desperate for peace. France and Russia fell into line at Vienna. Having secured the legal basis for a highly effective sea power strategy, Britain readily conceded mere terrestrial issues. This diplomatic victory secured British command of the Atlantic in the nineteenth century by isolating and defeating the three greatest contemporary opponents of Britain's sea power: Napoleon, Tsar Alexander, and James Madison.

The great cycle of wars ended with Britain at the heart of a grand European coalition; one that removed Napoleon from power, reduced France to its pre-1793 borders, but restored most, although not all, of its Caribbean colonies. While Britain returned Martinique, which enabled France to operate significant naval forces in the region, it retained St Lucia, which strictly limited its strategic value. The French dream of recovering St Domingue/Haiti slowly withered: the former French side of the island had been destroyed as an economic resource. When British troops occupied Bordeaux in April 1814, this boom town of the late eighteenth century French Atlantic economy had become a desert; grass grew in the streets. Napoleon's Continental System had annihilated France's Atlantic economy, and it would be many years before it recovered.

Elsewhere, the war had bankrupted Spain and wrecked her threadbare ability to control the vast American empire of 1793. The French Revolution had provided another example of dramatic political change, and Napoleon's overthrow of the Bourbons deprived regional governors of legitimacy, prompting fresh waves of revolutionary war and independence movements. After 1815, the restored Bourbon monarchy in Madrid had little chance of recovering the mainland colonies. Florida fell to the US in 1817 and by 1830 only Cuba and Puerto Rico remained of a once commanding empire. A miniscule fleet was assembled, just enough to secure the islands, but without a large army, Spain was powerless to act against the mainland provinces. In desperation, Spain and her revolted colonies resorted to privateering, which only served to emphasise their mutual weakness and draw a heavy Anglo-American naval presence into Cuban coastal waters.[17]

British capital, demobilised British soldiers, and surplus weapons were important factors in the South American Wars of Liberation. The contribution of British naval expertise was, if anything, more significant. Britain blocked any attempt by France or Russia to support a Spanish re-conquest, which would have damaged

---

17   Matthew McCarthy, *Privateering, Piracy, and British Policy in Spanish America 1810-1830* (Woodbridge, Suffolk: Boydell Press, 2013).

British economic interests in the new republics, while naval veterans, including the legendary Lord Cochrane, led fleets that denied Spain and Portugal the opportunity to recover their lost provinces. Sea power secured the independence of Latin America but left the Caribbean Islands under European control.

By 1815, the Atlantic was firmly Anglophone, and strategic power was equally firmly in British hands. The physical manifestations of increased British control could be seen in the major dockyard developments at Bermuda and Halifax; developments prompted by the War of 1812. New facilities and improved defences secured the pivot points of any future Anglo-American conflict against a pre-emptive *coup de main*. These bases were the key to blockading the US eastern seaboard, enabling a superior fleet to control US commerce. They were also the staging posts for military power projection. The British made no effort to fortify the Canadian frontier; too costly in men and treasure and impossible to protect against a far larger population south of the border. They put their faith in sea power and the blockade; a strategic tool that had been upheld at Ghent and Vienna.

The United States emerged as the main beneficiary of the dramatic changes that had occurred in North America and the Caribbean after 1793. Through the Louisiana Purchase and the occupation of East Florida, it had become a fully-fledged Caribbean power, with its sights firmly set on Cuba and the remainder of Florida. That strategic advance reflected the dramatic expansion of the US population, and the rapid spread of settlement, rather than military or naval prowess. While the War of 1812 exposed the fundamental weaknesses of the US as a military power possessing a trivial army and navy, her internal disunity, latent servile uprisings, and profound sectional divisions, it was equally clear that the country had become too large to be conquered. No European state had the political will or the strategic and economic resources to attempt such an undertaking. The question for the other major powers was which direction the United States would take.

In 1815, it stood at the cross-roads between maritime expansion and continental imperialism, with a growing navy competing with westward expansion for funds and attention. US enthusiasm for a serious navy stalled in the late 1820s, as continental expansion and looming sectional division dominated political agendas. US aspirations to become a great sea power faded before the lure of cheap land and westward expansion. Meanwhile, British admirals and statesmen digested the lessons of a war that had exposed the Achille's heel of the United States: anxieties about slave uprisings. The bitter legacy of St Domingue/Haiti resulted in massive programmes to fortify the US Atlantic and Gulf coasts against British fleets carrying black soldiers in red jackets.[18] The longer-term consequences of the war also included a steady shift away from the sea. By 1813-14, industrial production was absorbing much of the capital that had been locked up in shipping, transforming port cities such as Baltimore into major processing and manufacturing centres.[19] The contribution of ocean-going shipping to the US economy steadily declined. Only the protected coastal and inland sectors remained buoyant.[20]

At the same time, the British learned to appreciate Canada. As the delegates were assembling for Anglo-American peace talks in Ghent, Foreign Secretary Lord Castlereagh read the colonial reports, and recognised that the colonies could be a major source of timber and grain, hitherto largely supplied from the Baltic at great strategic cost. Post-war British tariff policies achieved those objectives, leading to the dynamic growth of Canadian ports such as Quebec, St John in New Brunswick, and Halifax, spurring Canadian shipbuilding and maritime labour. British policy created an imperial Atlantic synergy, opened a new outlet for emigrant populations, and reinforced the nascent Canadian identity that had been forged in adversity in the War of 1812.

Britain controlled the Caribbean in 1815 and spent much of the next 50 years maintaining a broad equilibrium by enabling the decaying Spanish Empire to hold Cuba, keeping Havana, key to the entire Caribbean region, out of US hands. Localised upsurges of piracy and privateering, driven by the Latin American Wars of Liberation, were controlled jointly, in the interests of British and US trade and shipping. The Monroe Doctrine, which reflected growing US anxiety about the regional ambitions of France and Russia, provided a text that would be sustained by British sea power.

Secure and effective bases remained the key to projecting sea power in the North Atlantic and Caribbean, as they had been before and during the Wars of the French Revolution and Empire, but only as long as these bases were linked to a dominant fleet. The fates of Louisbourg, Havana, and the Washington Navy Yard were stark reminders that bases without fleets were mere targets. Bermuda and Halifax enabled a dominant Royal Navy to control the US Eastern seaboard any time it chose. Long after 1815, Britain would retain that unique position, updating base and communications capabilities to connect the region to the metropole, and facilitate the deployment of large fleets.

18   The classic study is Emanuel Raymo Lewis, *Seacoast Fortifications of the United States* (Annapolis, Maryland: US Naval Institute Press, 1993).
19   Jerome R. Garitee, *The Republic's Private Navy: The American Privateering Business as Practiced by Baltimore during the War of 1812* (Mystic, Connecticut: Wesleyan, 1977).
20   Roland, *The Way of the Ship*.

Conclusion

British success in North America and the West Indies between 1793 and 1815 was based on sea power; a strategy that focused all elements of national power on securing and exploiting command of the sea, for war and trade. In contrast to its continental rivals, Britain was a sea power state; one that depended on, and identified with, the sea. France, Spain, and the United States were continental powers that used the sea: they did not depend upon it for their food supply, nor did they prioritise naval force over military. British strategy reflected the reality of being a maritime state, together with the powerful financial and commercial sector that helped it to sustain naval dominance. Lloyds of London, the leading shipping insurers, worked with the Admiralty to organise convoys, and funded prestigious awards for naval officers who won the great battles, and those who distinguished themselves in combat in defence of trade. Such indications of esteem, alongside the sustained investment in bases, shipbuilding, logistics, and victuals ensured the war was won.

In the age of sail and horse transport, North American conditions greatly favoured the defensive: neither the United States nor Britain made any significant gains with land-based invasions between 1812 and 1814. Dependence on sailing ships and horses placed severe limits on the size of military forces that could be moved to and sustained in the Americas. As the British had learnt in 1776-82, such forces could not hold down local populations. In sharp contrast to the conflicts in Western Europe, local resistance only had to endure to succeed. The British had taken that lesson to heart, especially after a fiasco at Buenos Aires in 1807-08, and made no attempt to conquer any large state in the region. They had a different mechanism to extract profit; the 'Informal Imperialism' of British capital replaced the stultifying mercantilist dominion of the Iberian powers. Access to these markets, the great prize for British statesmen since the Tudors, had been achieved as a by-product; a series of total European conflicts, in which Britain harnessed sea power to help defeat France, and open up long-closed trading opportunities. Those markets had helped sustain the Napoleonic wars, and they would generate far more profit than the formal empire.

By 1793, the Royal Navy had developed a powerful and coherent doctrine covering the full range of naval operations, from fleet battle and amphibious landings, to oceanic cruiser warfare and convoy defence. While the impact of tactical doctrine in battle is obvious, it was only a trifling element of the whole. Any professional navy would have suitable tactical doctrine. Far more significant was Nelson's politico-strategic decision to pursue Villeneuve to the Caribbean in 1805. He willingly violated his orders to serve a higher purpose: the defence of a massive floating trade and colonial commerce upon which the economic well-being of the nation depended. At another level, every officer escorting a merchant convoy who fought a superior foe, in order that his charges might escape, reflected the same inexorable logic. He could also expect a reward from Lloyds of London. Without the ability to use the sea for food supply and trade, Britain would be defeated.

Between 1793 and 1815, British overseas trade doubled.[21] Together with the related growth in manufacturing industry, this expansion enabled the state to sustain the enormous economic demands of prolonged high level mobilisation, the support of allies, and the expansion of imperial control. In the Western Hemisphere, British possessions were secured; Canada and the extensive range of West Indian Islands, even extending territorial control at the expense of France, Spain, and Holland. Attacks on floating trade, which persisted across 22 years, were defeated, while the maritime economic activity of rivals was crushed. Throughout the war, successive governments improved Britain's strategic position, upgrading bases, adding new facilities, and removing others from hostile control. It was the mark of that success that the next hundred years passed without a single challenge to British dominion on the ocean, or invasion of imperial territory.

Between 1793 and 1815, the strategic weight of sea power in the New World had been greatly reduced by the growth of settler populations, and the spread of settlement inland. In 1815 the Americas had emerged as a distinct politico-strategic factor in world politics. The Americas were the 'New World' that Prime Minister George Canning famously called into existence to balance the Old. The new American states could act in their own interests.

In the Western Hemisphere, the United States had risen to the fringes of great power status, while the end of the Iberian continental empires left European territories on the mainland restricted to Canada. While Canada and the Caribbean remained under British control, the rest of the two continents would soon be independent as large settler populations threw off colonial rule and shaped their own political and cultural futures.

The wars in the Americas had exposed the limits of sea power in the Western Hemisphere. Sea power could not overcome the essentially negative strength of the new republics, a reality which inspired James Monroe's famous 'Doctrine.' The United States did not have the power to stop the Europeans' attempt to recover these colonies, nor did it need to while Britain controlled the Atlantic and retained a large financial stake in the success of the new republics, including the United States. Informal imperialism replaced formal control, and Britain would use sea power to restrain US expansionism after 1815, retaining Canada, and keeping Cuba Spanish, but Britain recognised new limits, avoiding entanglement in continental affairs that were not direct British concerns.

21   Arthur, *How Britain Won*, p.242.

2

The Anglo-American Naval Relationship, 1815-37

Captain John Rodgaard & Adam Charnaud

Words such as admiration, contempt, cooperation, hostility, respect and rivalry come to mind when thinking about the Anglo-American naval relationship that existed after The Napoleonic War. A synopsis of that relationship follows, and it is hoped the reader will see that the naval relationship formed the framework for today's partnership. Examining the Anglo-American naval relationship between 1815 and 1837 must begin with the culture and values that both navies share.

On 27 March 1794, the US Congress authorised the construction of six frigates under the auspices of the War Department. Four years later, on 30 April 1798, Congress authorised the establishment of the US Navy. In July, the Department of the Navy formally established the Marine Corps, and the first six frigates mandated by Congress were completed and commissioned.[1] But there was more to these actions than creating an organisation and building the ships. It required the creation of an officer corps and the recruitment of seamen to man the Navy's ships. With recommendations from President John Adams and Captains John Barry, Samuel Nicholson, Thomas Truxton and Richard Dale, the Secretary of War, James McHenry, was directed to select 'six captains, 15 lieutenants and 21 midshipmen, three sailing masters, four surgeons, five surgeon's mates, and five pursers ... ' to form the Navy's first naval officer corps.[2] The enlisted personnel would be obtained through a two-year volunteer enlistment contract – impressment was forbidden.

---

1   Christopher McKee, *A Gentlemanly and Honorable Profession: The Creation of the US Naval Officer Corps, 1794-1815* (Annapolis, Maryland: US Naval Institute Press, 1991), p.3. The first three frigates, the *Constellation, Constitution* and the *United States* were built by the War Department. The other three frigates were built by the newly-formed Department of the Navy; Christopher McKee, 'Foreign Seamen in the United States Navy: A Census of 1808', *The William and Mary Quarterly*, Vol. 42, No. 3 (July 1985), pp.383-393.
2   McKee, *A Gentlemanly*, p.xi.

Portrait of Commodore John Barry, USN by Gilbert Stuart. (NHHC K-18537)

In *A Gentlemanly and Honorable Profession, The Creation of the US Naval Officer Corps, 1794-1815,* Christopher McKee posed the question regarding how the United States had so quickly developed into a 'highly professional naval force … in eighteen years?'[3] Of the five elements that composed a navy (ships, shore establishments, civilian administration, seamen, and officers), McKee stated that the critical element toward such rapid success was the United States Navy's officer corps. The question he then raised was, 'How did that happen?'[4] There were several mature navies to mirror. But, which navy should the US Navy turn toward? As McKee stated, 'The question was never even asked; the choice was predetermined. The navy of Great Britain was part and parcel of the American colonial heritage.'[5] For one, the seamen of both countries had a shared language and cultural heritage

---

3   McKee, *A Gentlemanly*, p.xi.
4   McKee, *A Gentlemanly*, p.210.
5   McKee, *A Gentlemanly*, p.210.

that had spanned centuries. As Benjamin Stoddert, the first Secretary of the Navy said, 'We must imitate [the British] in things which tend to the good of the services.'[6]

In 1804, Lieutenant Arthur Sinclair, USN made a deep-rooted observation; something that he and his fellow officers recognised: that '... the customs of the British sea services, in cases not embraced by our laws, have usually been the criterion by which we have been guided.'[7] McKee wrote: 'The historian is struck by the speed with which the transfer was accomplished, by the early date at which the fledgling navy of the Quasi-War and the Tripolitan War required the professional polish and established methods characteristic of a far more mature organisation.'[8] McKee also explained how Royal Navy operations were adopted by the US Navy. He wrote that it was not through the colonial Continental Navy, because '... the naval side of the American Revolution was a past they [in the US Navy] were eager to forget.'[9]

As with the Continental Army of the American War for Independence, foreign officers had their imprint on the formation of the US Army. However, for the United States Navy that was not the case. Acquiring experienced officers from other countries was rejected outright.[10] As McKee wrote, 'Pride and confidence precluded that approach.'[11] The pride and confidence came first with the knowledge that the captains had combat-at-sea experience and the lieutenants selected were masters of sailing technology. All knew sail, ships, and the sea.

Besides being at sea and knowing the intricacies of the sailing world, US naval officers felt a strong need to expand their professional development in the naval arts through self-education. As McKee observed: 'American naval officers owned, borrowed, read, and internalised the professional British naval literature – *The Naval Chronicle* and *A System of Naval Tactics* ...' of the period.[12] While at sea, they also had opportunities to observe the Royal Navy, especially at its operational nexus – Gibraltar. Beginning in 1800, several US naval squadrons, ordered to the Mediterranean to fight the Barbary States, used Gibraltar as a major communication and supply base. The use of Gibraltar would continue through the

---

6   McKee, *A Gentlemanly*, p.210.
7   McKee, *A Gentlemanly*, p.210.
8   McKee, *A Gentlemanly*, p.211.
9   McKee, *A Gentlemanly*, p.211.
10   Although, as McKee's research discovered, one out of 15 junior naval officers and or sailing masters selected for the United States Navy officer corps had been previously impressed into the Royal Navy. See McKee, *A Gentlemanly*, p.214.
11   McKee, *A Gentlemanly*, p.212.
12   McKee, *A Gentlemanly*, p.214.

mid-nineteenth century, and by default, US and British naval professionals rubbed elbows.

McKee also gave another example of how Royal Navy culture was transferred to the US Navy. It was through those sailors who volunteered to serve. In a letter written in 1798 by Midshipman John Roche, Jr., USN, whilst aboard the US Frigate *Constitution*, to his father, he said, 'Our petty officers are very good men. Most of them, such as quartermasters, master's mates, gunners, master-at-arms, etc., are either English or Irish who have sustained the same berths on board British men-of-war.'[13] Thus, the lower deck could have fitted into either navy without too much difficulty. As with a British warship, Usher Parsons observed 'the crews of US warships were perceived by their officers as "a rough and rugged class of men," accustomed to and requiring severe physical punishment for their management.'[14] This theme was evident in the written law governing the US Navy; its 'dire language ... resonated, too, with a long tradition of naval justice inherited from the British role model; the pedagogical and conservative roles of tradition were not to be ignored. As aboard ships of the Royal Navy, the "rough and rugged class of men" manning US warships experienced instant justice.'[15] Minimum infractions were punished with men being denied their grog or being clapped in irons with reduced rations and no grog. Then there was flogging. Although the death penalty was on the books, it was the extreme exception that a sentence of death was awarded to an offence that stipulated such in the regulations.

Concerning regulations governing the fledgling navy, the *US Naval Regulations of 1802* and the corresponding *US Marine Corps Rules of 1798* relied heavily on the *Regulations & Instructions Relating to His Majesty's Service at Sea*. However, as McKee wrote: 'It would be wrong to think of either set as simply the product of a copy to the British *Regulations and Instructions*, scissors, paste, and a printing press.'[16] Yes, senior US Navy officers did assemble the new regulations by borrowing and excluding those from the British example as they saw fit. But, they also incorporated their own, and they compiled them within the guidelines of the US Constitution and Federal Statutes.

The men selected to form the first officer corps for the US Navy became known as Barry's Boys; named for Commodore John Barry. Unknown at the time, these first officers would pilot the Navy's course for the next 60 years. Names such as Bainbridge, Barren, Decatur, Porter, Somers, and Stewart would place the US

13   McKee, *A Gentlemanly*, p.213.
14   McKee, *A Gentlemanly*, p.234.
15   McKee, *A Gentlemanly*, p.252.
16   McKee, *A Gentlemanly*, p.174.

Navy on a solid foundation. But, domestic politics would hold considerable sway. As John B. Hattendorf wrote in a 2014 article for the Naval War College:

> Americans were having a serious debate as to the 'purpose and function of the navy'. There were two political camps: One, the Federalists who believed 'the new navy should be the most effective expression and symbol of the nation's power, honour, and prestige as well as a potent and capable and effective fighting force that played a major role in the world balance of power as an instrument of political influence.'[17]

The second group were the Republicans; the anti-navalists. While they did recognise a need for a navy, they argued that the Federalists aims were unrealistic and too costly. Their vision was of a small, militia-type navy, consisting mostly of gunboats for coastal protection but with a few large ships that could operate on distant stations – just enough to protect US commerce. Except for the Navy's expansion during the War of 1812 and the US Civil War, the Republican vision held sway through most of the nineteenth century. According to Hattendorf, the Republican vision held sway because of the recognition that:

> British maritime superiority was a political and naval fact ... Freed from this burden, the US Navy could concentrate on a more select range of tasks. What it could and did do was bounded, by both its capabilities and interests, as well as the political compromises necessary in the creation of practical naval policy and strategy.[18]

The US Navy concentrated on supporting and defending US maritime activities. These activities fell into four broad categories. The first was trade. Second was the evangelical missionary movement that took US citizens across the world to include the broad expanse of the Ottoman Empire. The third was a corresponding missionary spirit of spreading the US concepts of freedom, neutral rights and self-determination. Fourth was scientific exploration which took US citizens around the world.[19] All four categories would also be the Royal Navy's mission during the post-Napoleonic period and through the nineteenth century.

---

17   John B. Hattendorf (ed.), *Changing American Perceptions of the Royal Navy Since 1775* (Newport, Rhode Island: US Naval War College, 2014).

18   John B. Hattendorf (ed.), 'The US Navy's Nineteenth-Century Forward Stations', *Talking about Naval History: A Collection of Essays* (Newport, Rhode Island: Naval War College Press, 2011), pp.233-234.

19   James A. Field, Jr, *America and the Mediterranean World 1776-1882* (Princeton, New Jersey: Princeton University Press, 1969).

A Visit to America

In the years after 1815, the relationship between the two navies reflected a more subdued appreciation for the qualities and limitations of each. One example can be seen through the eyes of a young Royal Navy officer who arranged leave from his duties in Halifax, Nova Scotia to visit the United States. In a book published in 1827,[20] Lieutenant F. Fitzgerald De Roos wrote about his one-month-long whirlwind tour. He was 22 years old at the time of his travels and assigned to the Royal Navy's North American Station based at Halifax. De Roos was granted a month's leave to visit the United States. His insights into the US, its people, and its navy opened a door into aspects of life in the early republic, especially since it was soon after the war. He was extremely keen to see how the US Navy had built the exceptional warships, famous for impressive exploits during the War of 1812.

In the company of Major Yorke, he sailed to New York City with the intent to travel to Washington City. From New York, he travelled again, by steam boat and horse-drawn coaches, to Philadelphia, which, De Roos said, '... Has the appearance of a well-built old English town of the time of Queen Anne.'[21] Staying just long enough to drop off correspondence to the British consular, the two young officers travelled to Baltimore and Washington. Reaching Washington, he first delivered dispatches to the British minister, Mr Vaughan, who then took both officers to the Capitol. De Roos was 'struck by its immense size ... the senate-room and the chamber of representatives ... remind me strongly of the Chamber of Deputies at Paris.'[22] Vaughn then took De Roos and Major Yorke to the Washington Navy Yard; the primary reason for visiting the town. De Roos was surprised by the Marine guard's the lack of interest in the foreign visitors. The Marine said that, 'he guessed we were at liberty to see any part of it we pleased.'[23]

However, walking through the yard, they were prevented from seeing the store houses. De Roos did see three frigates in various states of construction or repair. He provided a succinct description of them. The one that he identified as the *Susquehanna* was on the building way:

> She was constructed on the latest and most approved principles of the American builders and was to mount 60 guns. Her timbers were close together, and her shape remarkable for a very full bow, and a perfectly

20   F. Fitzgerald De Roos Royal Navy, *Personal Narrative of Travels in the United States and Canada in 1826 with Remarks on the Present State of the American Navy* (London: William Harrison Ainsworth, 1827).

21   De Roos, *Personal Narrative*, p.10.

22   De Roos, *Personal Narrative*, p.15.

23   De Roos, *Personal Narrative*, p.16.

straight side. She had a round stern, but its rake and flatness, combined with judicious construction of her quarter galleries, gave it quite the appearance of being square.[24]

US Frigate *Congress*: Nineteenth Century photograph of a painting by Vandenburg.
(NHHC NH 590)

Describing the second ship under construction, the US Frigate *Potomac* (44), he wrote that she was 'another heavy and clumsy-looking 60-gun frigate, was hauled up on ways ... called Commodore Porter's inclined plane.' The third frigate, the USS *Congress* (38), was newly overhauled, and he was allowed to go aboard. He must have recognised the ship's pedigree.[25] As De Roos, Major Yorke and Minister Vaughan left the yard, they came across a monument:

24   De Roos, *Personal Narrative*, p.17.
25   The young lieutenant was mistaken about the name of the ship on the building way. The first US warship with the name *Susquehanna* was a steam-power warship, which did not see service until 1850. See *Dictionary of American Naval Fighting Ships*: '*Susquehanna* I (Side-wheel Steamer)', *Naval History and Heritage Command*, <https://www.history.navy.mil/research/histories/ship-histories/danfs/s/susquehanna-i.html> (accessed 11 July 2017).

... which was erected to the memory of some officers, and bore an inscription declaring it to have been mutilated by Britons at the taking of Washington. At the capture of this city, many excesses were undoubtedly committed, but I have been assured that there are no grounds for this particular accusation. Let it, however in justice be observed, that this is the only public inscription of memorial which I saw in the United States, of a nature calculated to wound the feelings of a stranger.[26]

The monument that De Roos saw was the oldest military or naval monument in the United States. It honoured those US naval officers who were killed during the Barbary Wars.[27] After spending a thoroughly enjoyable evening in '... George's Town, which had all the agreeable characteristics of a European assembly,' he and Major Yorke were invited to attend the only Episcopal church in the city. Present at the service were President Monroe and the recently returned ambassador to the Court of St James, Richard Rush.[28] One wonders if the preacher's sermon was targeted at the two British officers:

> The sermon was worthy of the preacher; it treated of the oppression which the United States formerly endured while under the yoke of England, whose downfall, discomfiture, and damnation he confidently predicted ... I strongly suspect that the blasphemous absurdity was the produce of his own brain. I was sorry to learn that this man was considered much superior to American preachers in general.[29]

Following the church service, De Roos was invited to a Virginia household, and during his visit: 'Politics and travelling form the usual topics of conversation ... The events of the last war, and the capture of Washington in particular, I found to be a frequent topic ...' De Roos compared the American experience of the war with his own and that of Europe in general when he wrote: 'The attention of Europe was so completely engrossed by the mighty conflict, which decided its fate on the

As for the *Congress*, she was one of the original six frigates authorised by the United States Government.

26   De Roos, *Personal Narrative*, p.19.
27   This monument is known as the Tripoli or Navy Monument. It presently sits on the grounds of the United States Naval Academy, Annapolis, Maryland.
28   Rush had demilitarized the Great Lakes with the successful negotiations that led to the Rush-Bagot Convention in 1818. While ambassador to Britain, he acquired expertise in the Royal Navy. Rush became Secretary of State.
29   De Roos, *Personal Narrative*, pp.26-27.

plains of Waterloo, that the Washington campaign was regarded with comparative indifference.'[30]

Travelling back to New York from Washington, De Roos stopped at Baltimore. He had an opportunity to visit '... a port justly celebrated for its shipbuilding.' Walking down to the shipyards he noted that, '... I saw a schooner building ... Everything was sacrificed to swiftness, and I think she was the most lovely vessel I ever saw.' Meeting one of the builders, he was shown a book containing architectural ship drawings; '... drafts of all the fastest-sailing schooners built in Baltimore, which had so much puzzled our cruisers during the war. It was everything I wanted; but after an hour spent ... I could not induce him to part with one leaf of the precious volume.'[31] De Roos wrote: 'I could not help admiring the public spirit which dictated his conduct, for the offer I made him must have been tempting to a person in his station of life.'[32] So much for De Roos' attempt at gathering intelligence.

Arriving in Philadelphia, he called upon the British consul, who took him to the birth place of the US Navy; the Philadelphia Navy Yard. Upon arriving, he was presented to the commandant of the yard. There he saw, on stocks, the incomplete hull of the first-rate, USS *Pennsylvania* (136), the largest sailing warship ever built by the United States. He had the following impression: 'A mistaken notion has gone abroad as to the Americans calling such ships ... seventy fours [third-rate], which, at first sight, and to one unacquainted with the reason, bears the appearance of intentional deception.'[33] However, he knew that Congress had only authorised the building of third-rate ships-of-the-line, but it was the Navy Commissioners who took the liberty to build *Pennsylvania* and others 'on a more extended scale.'[34]

On his return to New York, De Roos visited the Brooklyn Navy Yard and was struck by the level of activity as well as the warships he observed. The yard was busy building the US Frigate *Brandywine* (60) and fitting out the sloop-of-war, USS *Boston* (20). Aboard the *Boston,* he noted an ingenious improvement:

> To avoid the weakness ... which is always made in the after-part of the lower-decks of vessels of this description, in order to give greater accommodation to the officers, it was laid so as to form a plane inclining toward the stern, and by this method, strength was united with convenience. So roomy was her hold, that there was sufficient space to

---

30   De Roos, *Personal Narrative*, pp.27-28.
31   De Roos, *Personal Narrative*, p.38.
32   De Roos, *Personal Narrative*, p.38.
33   De Roos, *Personal Narrative*, pp.41-42.
34   De Roos, *Personal Narrative*, p.42.

pass between them and the lower-deck. By this means, she was enabled to dispense with hatches.[35]

Photograph of the USS *Ohio*. (NHHC NH 60676)

He next went aboard the first-rate USS *Ohio* (102) which was lying in ordinary. 'A more splendid ship I never beheld.' However, he '… was filled with astonishment at the negligence which permitted so fine a ship to remain exposed to the ruinous assaults of so deleterious a climate … and … is already falling rapidly into decay.' De Roos later found that as with other American warships, the *Ohio*:

> … was an instance of the cunning, I will not call it wisdom, which frequently actuates the policy of the Americans. They fit out one of the finest specimens of their shipbuilding in a most complete and expensive style, commanded by their best officers, and manned with a war-complement of their choicest seamen. She proceeds to cruise in the Mediterranean, where she falls in with the fleets of European powers, exhibits before them her magnificent equipment, deploys her various

35   De Roos, *Personal Narrative*, p.61.

perfections, and leaves them impressed with exaggerated notions of the maritime powers of the country which sent her forth.[36]

After New York City, De Roos travelled to Boston to visit the Charlestown Navy Yard, and he was able to visit the facility. He was impressed with its size and the large ship storage houses. At the yard he was told that the:

> Americans propose to divide their ships into five classes, namely, three-deckers, two-deckers of 102 guns, frigates of 60 guns, corvettes of 22 guns, and schooners. On the model of every ship a committee is held – the draft determined on and transmitted to the builders of the dockyards; and as periodical inspections take place, no deviation from the original model can occur. This system of classification and admirable adherence to approved models have been attended by the most beneficial results, which are visible in the beauty and excellent qualities of the ships of the United States.[37]

As with many a young man, he reveled in his interaction with American men and women whom he met during his travels. However, De Roos chided those fellow Englishmen who considered American men as being rough and coarse in manners. This 'aroused my indignant disagreement ...' finding American men 'cordial, frank and open ...' and American women 'so easy and natural that being in their company was a constant pleasure, although some of the expressions and metaphors they used in conversation were so nearly unintelligible ...' At times he could not understand them. He said that he was taken by American good will and regarded Americans as 'a brave, intelligent, kind-hearted, unprejudiced ...' people who took great pride in their country.[38]

With his tour at an end, De Roos reflected upon his experience on seeing the United States: 'Everything in America is upon a gigantic scale. How enormous are its resources! How boundless its extent! ... From the energies she has displayed in her infancy, to what powers may not her maturity aspire?'[39] However, his observations about the US Navy were to be less than prophetic:

> My humble lucubrations were directed, during my tour, to points more immediately connected with my own profession; and I took my leave of America, with the satisfactory conviction that the naval strength of the

---

36   De Roos, *Personal Narrative*, p.63.
37   De Roos, *Personal Narrative*, p.62.
38   De Roos, *Personal Narrative*, p.64.
39   De Roos, *Personal Narrative*, p.190.

United States has been greatly exaggerated – that they have neither the power nor the inclination to cope with Great Britain in maritime warfare – far less to presume to dispute with her the Dominion of the Seas.[40]

The Mediterranean

With the end of the War of 1812, the US Navy re-entered the Mediterranean. We can see aspects of the relationship between the two former enemies through the eyes of two men who left their respective journals to future historians. One journal, by George Jones, was written during his time with the Mediterranean Squadron between 1825 and 1827.[41] Although the second was written just after the end of the Georgian Era (between 1843 and 1845), Francis Schroeder's account would still be relevant.[42] Besides writing about their experiences with the squadron throughout the Mediterranean, both men provided insights into the Anglo-American relationship as a whole.

In 1825, Jones acquired a berth aboard the US Frigate *Brandywine* (54) as a school master to the ship's midshipmen. *Brandywine*, together with the second-rate USS *North Carolina* (90) and the sixth-rate sloop-of-war USS *Erie* (20), comprised the Mediterranean Squadron. Before entering the Mediterranean, *Brandywine's* crew had the honour of returning the Marquis de Lafayette to France after the hero's grand tour of the United States. The trip to France was so arduous that the frigate required emergency repairs. Instead of re-caulking the ship's hull in France, *Brandywine's* captain sailed across the Channel to Portsmouth. Jones wrote that he was shocked by this decision, as it was only seven years since the war. 'I should have thought him [the captain] foolishly jesting or mad.'[43]

However, Jones' shock turned into admiration during *Brandywine's* stay. Of the port and naval dockyard, he wrote what a 'beautiful sight … it is a noble enemy to cope with …'[44] He visited HMS *Victory* as well as sailing across to the Isle of Wight and was very much impressed by the Royal Navy and the beauty of the island. At the same time he wrote, 'Our ship has had a great many visitors of late,

40   De Roos, *Personal Narrative*, p.191.
41   George Jones, *Sketches of Naval Life with Notices of Men, Manners and Scenery on the Shores of the Mediterranean in a Series of Letters from the Brandywine and Constitution Frigates, Vol. 1*, (London: Forgotten Books, 2017; originally published London: H. Howe, 1856), p.4.
42   Francis Schroeder, *Shores of the Mediterranean With Sketches of Travel: 1843-45* (New York: Harpers & Brothers, 1846), digitized on *The Internet Archive*, 2009 from the collection of Harvard University, <https://archive.org/details/shoresmediterra03schrgoog/page/n13> (accessed 31 March 2019).
43   Jones, *Sketches of Naval Life*, p.9.
44   Jones, *Sketches of Naval Life*, p.9.

and I understand has been greatly admired.[45] A similar experience occurred to then-Midshipman Charles Wilkes, USN. In his autobiography, Rear Admiral Wilkes wrote about his visit to the heart of British sea power in 1818. 'At Cowes the ship was much frequented by officers & men who seemed desirous of gratifying their curiosity by inspecting the American frigate who had celebrated the naval victories over them. The *Guerriere* ...was equipped well for a fighting one and as such did credit to our country.'[46] However, his opinion of the Royal Navy Base at Portsmouth was in marked contrast to that of Jones who visited seven years later:

> I was much [struck] at the want of system in the English dockyard and the want of arrangement. The wooden walls of Old England did not impress me with much respect. The *Victory* & other ships of note were laid up dismantled and, of course, it is difficult to impress one with much veneration for a small, dismantled hull. The *Victory* was of small dimension in our eyes, and the impression was how inferior to that of our own ship, both in size and armament...showing the progress that naval architecture and efficiency for combat had made within the last 20 years.[47]

When Jones visited Gibraltar on 2 November 1825, he wrote: 'It is difficult to get admittance [to Gibraltar], but our character as officers was sufficient passport; they told us that an order had been given, to admit all officers, and particularly Americans ...'[48] Walking about the rock, he observed how large the presence of the British Army was: 'Numerous soldiers are pacing the walls.' He was especially taken by one regiment – The Black Watch. He wrote that they 'are conspicuous, the brave "forty twa's" in their fantastic highland dress. They are fine looking fellows, with muscular limbs, stout frames and national features.'[49]

Six months later, Jones and the rest of the American squadron returned to Gibraltar for the purpose of picking up spring dispatches from the Navy Department and State Department. The day the squadron arrived (17 April 1826) was on King William IV's birthday. He observed that the 'Rock' was celebrating in grand style. The regiments of the garrison were in full dress, fired volleys, and then marched in review past the governor. 'Nowhere, probably, can troops be found, in better order: their precision in exercise, is astonishing to one accustomed to the militia parades.

45   Jones, *Sketches of Naval Life*, p.9.
46   William James Morgan, David B. Tyler, Joye L. Leonhart, Mary F. Loughlin, (eds), *Autobiography of Rear Admiral Charles Wilkes, US Navy, 1798-1877* (Washington, DC: Naval History Division, Department of the Navy, 1978), p.52.
47   Morgan, et al, *Autobiography*, p.53.
48   Morgan, et al, *Autobiography*, p.15.
49   Morgan, et al, *Autobiography*, p.17.

The Scots were there with their bagpipes and drew particular attention.'[50] He also noted that all the ships in the bay and harbour dressed ship, with the ships of the American squadron flying the Union Flag from their foremasts.

Similar sentiments about Gibraltar and the British military and naval presence were expressed 17 years later by Francis Schroeder, who was the secretary to the US Mediterranean Squadron's commodore, Captain Joseph Smith, USN, aboard the flagship, the US Frigate *Cumberland* (50). 'We received the salutes of sentinels at every turn ... I should again exclaim in admiration of the English soldier.'[51] Schroeder and the squadron spent Christmas 1843 in Gibraltar. In a letter to a friend, he expressed his admiration for British engineers in the 'extent, and ingenuity and immense labour with which they have been contrived. I was filled with amazement.'[52]

Greek Pirates attack a merchantman by Alexandre Gabriel Decamps. (Open source)

50   Jones, *Sketches of Naval Life*, p.30.
51   Shroeder, *Shores of the Mediterranean*, p.4.
52   Shroeder, *Shores of the Mediterranean*, p.5.

As for Jones, in June 1826, the US squadron was on its summer cruising cycle and it had entered the Aegean Sea, arriving at the island of Sifnos. This was during the Greek War for Independence against the Ottoman Empire. One aspect of the revolution was the scourge of Greek piracy. The squadron was escorting US merchant ships trading with the Ottoman Empire as well as working with the Royal Navy squadron in anti-piracy operations. At Sifnos, the British flagship of the squadron, HM Frigate *Cambrian,* had arrived and the US Navy commodore visited with his British counterpart. Jones wrote:

> We meet the vessels of that nation frequently and I am much pleased to see harmony and good feeling subsisting between their officers and our own. Dinners and visits exchanged from Captains to Midshipmen; picnics are made for each other; and speaking the same language, with common objectives of esteem and antipathy, they appear much like officers of the same nation; and so it should be.[53]

On 30 April 1827, the American squadron arrived at the ancient Greek port of Smyrna (Izmir, Turkey) to show the flag. Smyrna was the major trading port between the United States and the Ottoman Empire. In his writings, we see another instance of cordial Anglo-American naval relations: 'We received the usual compliments on anchoring: visits have been frequent between the officers and ours: our midshipmen are giving a dinner to those of HM Frigate *Seringapatum* and the cries of "Hip, Hip, Hip – Huzza, etc." among them, are beginning to be thick and indistinct.'[54]

Then again, there were instances of arguments and slights between the two navies. When the *Constitution* arrived at Piraeus, Greece, there were several British, French and Austrian warships anchored. HMS *Cambrian* was there and the Royal Navy flagship rendered honours to 'Old Ironsides.' Jones wrote that as the *Constitution* passed by, *Cambrian's* band played *Hail Columbia*. *Constitution's* band responded with *God Save the King.* Then they played *Yankee Doodle*. Jones wrote that he did not like the way the British ship played it. 'They "rattled it off" … I am sure it must have produced a general laugh there as it did with us. To me … it produced mortification.'[55]

53   Jones, *Sketches of Naval Life*, p.51.
54   Jones, *Sketches of Naval Life*, p.64.
55   Jones, *Sketches of Naval Life*, p.70.

Combating Slavers

After the defeat of Napoleonic France, both navies waged another kind of war
– the war of combating the African slave trade. Over the next three decades,
they operated off the coast of West Africa and throughout the Caribbean against
the slave trade. Their shared mission was truly ironic in that, for both US and
British, the wealth from human trafficking had formed the foundation of each
country's economic prosperity. However, each country approached the slave
trade differently. The United States had tried, since the inception of its federal
government, to suppress slavery in the Caribbean. During President John Adam's
administration, the Act of 1794 was passed, which prohibited US citizens from
transporting anyone to another country for the purpose of selling them as slaves.
Heavy financial penalties, to include the confiscation of vessels, were imposed
on those found to be conducting such activities. While the law originally had
no enforcement provisions, fines and possible imprisonment were added during
the last year of Adams' administration as possible punitive options. Further, US
Navy warships were authorised to seize US slavers operating in the Caribbean as
prizes. However, along the US coastline:

> ... the enforcement of foreign trade regulations was the provenance of
> the Revenue Cutter Service of the Treasury Department ... the Revenue
> Cutter Service and federal marshals ... were active, though with varying
> rates of success, in suppressing the trade as it occurred on the American
> coast and in its harbors.[56]

However, with the Jefferson Administration in 1801, interdiction by the Revenue
Cutter Service and by federal marshals at the source of interdiction (harbours and
ports) dropped off precipitously. The Jefferson Administration's anti-navalism
severely cut back the size of the US Navy's larger warships as well as the number of
Revenue Service cutters. As a result, the percentage of US flagged ships operating
in the slave trade almost doubled.[57]

---

56   Donald L. Canney, *Africa Squadron: The US Navy and the Slave Trade, 1842-1861*
     (Washington, DC: Potomac Books, 2006), pp.xi-xii.
57   In Ned and Constance Sublette's book, *The American Slave Coast: A History of the Slave-
     Breeding Industry,* (Chicago, Illinois: Lawrence Hill Books, 2016), p.348, they quote
     Seymour Drescher's assessment found in his book, *Econocide: British Slavery in the Era of
     Abolition, 2nd edition* (Chapel Hill, North Carolina: University of North Carolina Press,
     2010), that the percentage of American ships engaged in the slave trade had only been nine
     percent during the Adam's administration. But under Jefferson, it expanded to 16 percent.

The purchase of the Louisiana Territory fed the demand for slaves. This vast amount of land, together with the invention of the cotton gin and improved methods of cultivating and processing Louisiana sugar cane, required thousands of slaves. Although the absolute ban on importation of slaves commenced in 1808, the illicit importation of Africans did continue, but at a reduced rate. However, the demand for slaves was increasingly being satisfied by a:

> ... new class of American traders ... supplied with home-grown captives born into slavery on Virginia and Maryland farms. The conditions were right for a massive forced migration of enslaved Chesapeake labourers down South, and it did not have to be a one-time drain: a continuing domestic slave-breeding industry was possible.[58]

After the Napoleonic War, the US Navy became more active in enforcing the law. The illegal slave trade conducted by US-flagged ships, with the rise of piracy in the Gulf of Mexico and on the east Florida coast, saw the operation of the first squadron ordered to combat piracy and the slave trade. By the 1820s, the Navy had established a permanent West Indies squadron consisting of two frigates, a sloop-of-war, and five schooners. However, the squadron could seize only US-flagged slave ships.[59] It did not take long for US slavers to reflag their ships and avoid being stopped by the US Navy.

This action was followed by sending the first US Navy squadron to Africa's west coast in 1819, under the command of Commodore Matthew C. Perry. But Perry's squadron, and subsequent squadrons sent out for the next 20 years, did not have enough ships to patrol the vast African coastline and the slave routes across the Atlantic. In fact, the Navy did not have a consistent presence until 1842. The result was that very few slavers were caught, compared to the effectiveness of the Royal Navy's West Africa Squadron. Britain abolished all aspects of the slave trade by British subjects in 1807, and that included seizing ships fitted out for slave transportation and not having slaves aboard. During the height of the Napoleonic War, the Royal Navy dispatched the first tactically-paired warships to Africa's west coast.[60] Also, the Crown offered letters of marque to stimulate private ventures in seizing slavers. However, during the first decade of the law's enforcement, the Royal Navy had to tread lightly so as not to confiscate slavers from those countries fighting Napoleon, such as those flying the Portuguese flag.

58 Sublette, *The American Slave Coast*, p.362.
59 Canney, *Africa Squadron*, p.16.
60 The tactical pair consisted of a frigate and a brig-sloop. The latter could cruise in shallower waters for scouting and capturing slavers operating inshore.

The Royal Navy's West African Station was organised with a naval station established at Freetown, Sierra Leone in 1819. The first squadron consisted of six ships, with the flagship ironically named *Creole,* under the command of Commodore Sir George Ralph Collier, RN. The squadron's composition was far from able to cover the entire expansive west coast of Africa ranging north of Sierra Leone down through the Gulf of Guinea toward modern day Nigeria. During the succeeding two decades, the squadron was enhanced to the point that it eventually consisted of nearly one in 20 Royal Navy commissioned warships. Additionally, special courts were established, consisting of judges from the various countries who signed the provisions of the Congress of Vienna that pertained to ending the practice. Throughout the remaining decades of the nineteenth century, British governments expanded the anti-slavery operations of the Royal Navy beyond the west coast of Africa, to include the Mediterranean, Red Sea, and the Indian Ocean.[61]

It would take the ratification of the Webster-Ashburton Treaty of 1842, and specifically the provision to end the slave trade on the high seas, to validate the US Navy's contribution to the Africa Squadron. However, as Donald Canney's book, *Africa Squadron: The US Navy and the Slave Trade, 1842-1861,* states, the US squadron's operations failed in its objectives. He wrote that, '... the squadron was unsuccessful, even though it was [ironically] the Navy's only permanent squadron with a specific, congressionally mandated mission: to maintain a quasi-blockade on a foreign shore.'[62]

Science & Exploration

The early nineteenth century brought about an explosion in maritime-oriented scientific and surveying endeavours by both navies. For the United States, much of this exploration was oriented toward the country's continental expansion, although there were significant oceanic accomplishments supporting expansion and overseas trade. The Royal Navy's achievements during the period were in response to Britain's rapid post-war global economic expansion. The foundations for the noteworthy accomplishments in maritime science occurred prior to the period covered by this book. These advances resulted in improved navigational and time-keeping instruments and the creation of new supporting organisations that made possible the scientific accomplishments of the period covered by this book.

61   Robert Moore and John Rodgaard, *A Hard-Fought Ship: The Story of HMS Venomous,* *3rd edition* (St Albans, England: Holywell House Publishing, 2017). The destroyer HMS *Venomous* became part of the Royal Navy's anti-slavery patrol on the Red Sea during the immediate post Great War years of the 1920s.
62   Canney, *Africa Squadron.*

Britain's Hydrographer to the Admiralty and subsequent Admiralty's Hydrographic Department was one such result. On the order of King George III, Alexander Dalrymple was appointed as the Hydrographer to the Admiralty in 1795. The King charged Dalrymple and the organisation under his guidance to bring together existing charts from private chart publishers and foreign sources to be catalogued and centralised under his auspices. The first mass-produced Admiralty chart eventually appeared in 1800, which supported the Royal Navy's blockade of France's Brittany coast. Subsequent charts were created and published to support naval operations in the Mediterranean, followed by charts of the North Sea and the English Channel.[63] Prior to his death in 1808, Dalrymple also produced sailing directions and notices to mariners' journals.[64]

Dalrymple's successor was Captain Thomas Hurd, RN, who '… brought considerable surveying experience, having spent nine years making a detailed survey of Bermuda.'[65] He organised a system of routine surveying and developed the specialised field of Royal Navy hydrographic surveyors. He improved the efficiency of Admiralty mass-produced charts and had production costs become part of the Admiralty's annual budget. Hurd also made Admiralty charts available to merchant mariners. In 1819, Hurd negotiated with the Royal Danish Navy what is believed to be the first bilateral agreement with a foreign government to exchange charts and supporting publications.

In 1823, Rear Admiral Sir W. Edward Parry, RN was appointed the third Hydrographer to the Admiralty. Parry, together with the Royal Society, organised scientific and surveying expeditions to the South Atlantic in a first time in cooperation with French and Spanish hydrographers.[66]

Parry was succeeded by Rear Admiral Sir Francis Beaufort in 1829, who introduced a wind intensity scale named for himself –The Beaufort Scale – as well as a tide tables in 1833. He also continued Parry's programme of scientific and surveying expeditions, of which the most famous were those conducted by Captain FitzRoy, commanding HMS *Beagle*.[67] It is safe to state that the United

63   Andrew David, 'The Emergence of the Admiralty Chart in the Nineteenth Century', a paper presented at the International Cartographic Association Symposium on 'Shifting Boundaries: Cartography in the 19th and 20th Centuries', Portsmouth University, Portsmouth, United Kingdom, September 10-12, 2008, p.3, *ICA Commission on the History of Cartography* <http://history.icaci.org/wp-content/uploads/2016/09/David.pdf> (accessed 31 March 2019)
64   'United Kingdom Hydrographic Office', *Wikipedia* <https://en.wikipedia.org/wiki/United_Kingdom_Hydrographic_Office> (accessed 30 March 2019)
65   David, The Emergence of the Admiralty Chart, p.5.
66   'United Kingdom Hydrographic Office'.
67   It was Beaufort who introduced FitzRoy to Charles Darwin; 'United Kingdom Hydrographic Office'.

States Navy, as well as America's merchant mariners purchased and benefitted from Admiralty charts. In 1830, the US Navy established the Depot of Charts and Instruments (the forerunner the Navy's Hydrographic Office).[68] In 1833, the 35-year-old Lieutenant Charles Wilkes, USN was placed in charge of the Depot of Charts and Instruments. During his naval service, he had shown considerable aptitude for coastal survey work along the US Atlantic and Gulf coasts after the War of 1812.

In 1836, The US Congress authorised the formation of a US Navy Exploration Squadron with Charles Wilkes in command. It was a global interdisciplinary scientific expedition directed to 'exploring and surveying the Southern Ocean.'[69] It departed in 1838. Following Wilkes as one of the US Navy's prominent hydrographers and scientists was Lieutenant Matthew Fontaine Maury, USN. Although his accomplishments occurred after the period covered by this book, his formative experience took place between the time he received a midshipman's warrant at the age of 19 in 1825, and 1837, when he studied navigation, meteorology and the world's oceans. He eventually became the superintendent of the US Naval Observatory and the head of the Depot of Charts and Instruments. He made major contributions to humankind's understanding of the world's oceans, its currents, and winds. Maury became known as the Father of Modern Oceanography. After the US Civil War, the United States Hydrographic Office was established under the Navy's Bureau of Navigation in 1866.[70]

Conclusion

Indeed, words such as admiration, contempt, cooperation, hostility, respect and rivalry do come to mind when describing the Anglo-American naval relationship that existed between 1815 and 1837. This synopsis has shown that the relationship was indeed complicated. It is hoped the reader will see that this relationship, forged during war and peace, was fundamental in developing the framework of today's partnership between the two navies; a partnership that now includes the other navies of the Queen; Australia, Canada, and New Zealand. This greater partnership will continue to have major consequences across the world's oceans during the twenty-first century.

68   'Naval Oceanographic Office', *Wikipedia* <https://en.wikipedia.org/wiki/Naval_
     Oceanographic_Office> (accessed 30 March 2019)
69   'Naval Oceanographic Office'.
70   'Naval Oceanographic Office'.

Impressment – Myth vs. Reality

3

Thralls in Nelson's Navy: Impressment and American Mariners

Dr Christopher P. Magra

Captain Lucius O'Brien of the fifth-rate frigate HMS *Juno* (32) sailed out of Portsmouth, England bound for New York City, New York in the summer of 1764. Even though the Seven Years War had recently ended, the Royal Navy still had to safeguard a seaborne empire that stretched around the globe. The navy needed seamen to accomplish this daunting task. O'Brien crossed an ocean and came to America to get these men. The *Juno* anchored off Sandy Hook on 29 March after a relatively quick transatlantic journey. O'Brien then made liberal use of the press warrants the British Admiralty had given him. These warrants authorised him to press Americans into the Royal Navy. O'Brien pressed a total of 80 Americans between 30 June and 28 July. He sailed for home on 29 July. At Spithead, O'Brien distributed 53 of the pressed men to other needy warships between 12 November and 15 November.[1] The entire roundtrip transatlantic journey exclusively involved securing American mariners to meet the needs of the Royal Navy.

1   For Captain Lucius O'Brien's logbook, see The National Archives (TNA), Kew, London, Records of the Navy Board and the Board of Admiralty, 51/496. On 30 June he recorded in his log that he was 'Moored in the North River' near New York City, and had 'received from the *Harlequin*, tender, 25 Impressed men.' O'Brien continued to send press gangs into the colonial seaport and onto commercial vessels in its harbour. On 6 July he 'received from out [the] tender 17 Impressed Men.' Two days later, he 'Received on board 13 impressed Men from the Tender.' On 13 July he 'Received from the tender 15 Impressed Men.' On 24 July he 'Discharged the *Harlequin* Tender' at Sandy Hook and 'Impressed 2 Men out of a Brig.' The next day, he 'Impressed 4 Men out of a schooner.' Last, on 28 July, he 'Impressed 4 Men out of a Brig at 1/2 past 4 am.'

There never were enough stout hearts of oak to man British fleets entirely with volunteers. The British government habitually relied upon impressment to mobilise for wars and to expand the size of its fighting force. Impressment involved elements of coercion and negotiation. Press gangs rounded-up potential recruits and naval officers offered the fresh men incentives including advance pay and extended shore leave to get them to volunteer to serve. Press gangs physically forced the unwilling onto warships. Naval recruiters used carrots and sticks to man fleets around the world in the eighteenth and nineteenth centuries.

British press gangs did not discriminate when shorthanded warships had orders to set sail. They did not restrict their efforts to Englishmen with nautical skills and experience.[2] Naval officers and administrators preferred these sorts of mariners, of course. But, they were never readily available in large numbers because of demographic constraints and competition from commercial shipping. This meant that there were Britons from Ireland, Scotland, and Wales in the Royal Navy, and there were landlubbers as well. It also meant that there were Britons from the North American colonies who served in the Royal Navy before the Revolution. There were even Americans who fought alongside Nelson and other Jack Tars during and after the birth of the United States. The Royal Navy pressed many of these Americans into service, and they resented the state appropriation of their labour.

American mariners viewed British impressment as a form of slavery. Christopher Prince, for example, was pressed into the Royal Navy at the start of the American Revolution. He referred to his service as 'thralldom.'[3] Historians have dismissed such first-hand observations in journals and memoirs and diaries.[4] Certainly, naval impressment was not the full equivalent of slavery. Yet, we should pause and consider why American mariners perceived British impressment in this way. It

---

2   For arguments that British fleets were fairly homogenous, as naval administrators and government officials passed formal regulations restricting the service to Englishmen with seafaring experience, see Nathan Perl-Rosenthal, *Citizen Sailors: Becoming American in the Age of Revolution* (Cambridge, Massachusetts: Harvard University Press, 2015); Denver Brunsman, *The Evil Necessity: British Naval Impressment in the Eighteenth-Century Atlantic World* (Charlottesville, Virginia: University of Virginia Press, 2013), pp.2, 9, 58, 60; Denver Brunsman, 'Subjects vs. Citizens: Impressment and Identity in the Anglo-American Atlantic', *Journal of the Early Republic*, Vol. 30, No. 4 (Winter 2010), pp.557-586; and Nicholas Rogers, *The Press Gang: Naval Impressment and Its Opponents In Georgian Britain* (London: Continuum, 2007), pp.93, 99.

3   Michael J. Crawford (ed.), *The Autobiography of A Yankee Mariner: Christopher Prince and the American Revolution* (Washington, DC: Brassey's, 2002), p.59.

4   Denver Brunsman flatly stated that mariners who referred to impressment as slavery were 'wrong.' Brunsman, *Evil Necessity*, p.7. For more along these lines, see J. Ross Dancy, *The Myth of the Press Gang: Volunteers, Impressment and the Naval Manpower Problem in the Late Eighteenth Century* (Woodbridge, Suffolk: Boydell Press, 2015); and N.A.M. Rodger, *The Wooden World: An Anatomy of the Georgian Navy* (London: Collins, 1986).

was common for people around the world to resent British press gangs.[5] Maritime wage earners in various locales resented being removed from the free market. They typically believed impressment violated their individual liberties. But, there were certain ideological and material grievances that were unique to North America. The labour markets were exceptionally strong in this part of the world. Parliament had also banned impressment in North America, and this made the activities of press gangs particularly egregious to American colonials. There were regionally specific and historically consequential explanations for American bitterness about British impressment.

Impressment Explained

Horatio Nelson lived through some of the largest military conflicts the world had ever known. He was born in war and he died in battle. The Seven Years War is now considered the first global conflict. Great Britain and France fought each other on land and at sea around the world. They were still locked in combat on multiple fronts by the time of the Battle of Trafalgar. Though much had changed over the course of Nelson's life in regard to the Royal Navy, much remained the same. The British government expanded the size and scope of its navy between the middle of the eighteenth century and the beginning of the nineteenth century. In large part, this growth was due to the imperial rivalry that existed between Great Britain and France. Both European powers fought for control of overseas colonies and access to resources such as sugar fields and fishing waters. Religious antagonisms only spurred the rivalry.

Members of Parliament and naval administrators developed a blue water strategy to bring about a balance of power in Europe over the course of the 1700s. This strategy involved using the navy to nurture and sustain overseas trade and colonization. Mercantilist heads of state believed that a seaborne empire would provide the mother country with raw materials and solid specie. At the same time, securing these resources would keep them from European competitors. The strategy aimed, in essence, to use the navy to build up Great Britain and to knock down her rivals, chiefly France.[6] The British government spent public funds on

---

5   For more on popular forms of resistance to press gangs, see Rogers, *Press Gang*; and Jesse Lemisch, *Jack Tar vs. John Bull: The Role of New York's Seamen in Precipitating the Revolution* (New York: Garland Publishers, 1997).

6   Jeremy Black, *The British Seaborne Empire* (New Haven, Connecticut: Yale University Press, 2004), pp.97-106; Eliga Gould, *The Persistence of Empire: British Political Culture in the Age of the American Revolution* (Chapel Hill, North Carolina: The University of North Carolina Press, 2000), pp.35-71; Daniel A. Baugh, 'Great Britain's Blue-Water Policy, 1689-1815,' *International History Review*, Vol. 10 (February 1988), pp.33-58.

naval expansion in response to the adoption of this strategy. In 1710, at the height of the War of Spanish Succession, there were 180 warships and 48,072 seamen in the Royal Navy.[7] When Nelson was born, the Royal Navy maintained 250 warships and 86,626 seamen.[8] At his death, there were 285 warships and 126,192 seamen in the Royal Navy.[9] These floating fortresses became the bulwark of an island nation and a seaborne empire. The British government did not pour enough public funds into naval expansion, however. Naval wages remained at the same rate for the 144-year period between 1653 and 1797.[10] In peacetime or wartime, during the eighteenth century, the Royal Navy paid its most skilled, able-bodied seamen 24 shillings per month. An ordinary seaman earned 19 shillings per month, and a landlubber earned 18 shillings per month.[11]

Not only was this rate low, it was uncompetitive. Mariners stood to earn less in the Royal Navy than they could in commercial shipping and far less than they could make in privateering and whaling. In shipping, highly skilled mariners could earn 30 shillings per month during periods without conflict, and peace was rare during the eighteenth century. British armed forces were at war one in every two years between 1690 and 1815. Between 1739 and 1815, they were active two in every three years.[12] During these years of conflict, skilled mariners could earn as much as 70 shillings, or £3.10.0, per month in commercial shipping.[13] Wages for officers on commercial vessels typically increased 67 to 133 percent during wars.[14] Wages for common tars usually increased by 50 percent.[15] Whaling

---

7   N.A.M. Rodger, *The Command of the Ocean: A Naval History of Britain, 1649-1815* (New York: W.W. Norton & Company, 2004), p.608, Appendix II.

8   Rodger, *Command of the Ocean*, p.637, Appendix VI.

9   Rodger, *Command of the Ocean*, p.639, Appendix VI.

10   Brunsman, *Evil Necessity*, p.57; Bernard Capp, *Cromwell's Navy: The Fleet and the English Revolution, 1648-1660* (Oxford: Oxford University Press, 1989), p.259; Rodger, *Wooden World*, p.126; Daniel A. Baugh, *British Naval Administration in the Age of Walpole* (Princeton, New Jersey: Princeton University Press, 1965), p.493.

11   Rodger, *Wooden World*, p.125.

12   Rogers, *Press Gang*, p.5.

13   Rodger, *Wooden World*, pp.126-127; Stephen F. Gradish, *The Manning of the British Navy During The Seven Years War* (London: Royal Historical Society, 1980), p.75; Ralph Davis, *The Rise of the English Shipping Industry In the 17th and 18th Centuries* (London: Macmillan & Company, 1962), pp.135-137.

14   Davis, *Rise of the English Shipping*, p.140. Davis calculated wages for gunners, boatswains, doctors, pursers, cooks, carpenter's mates, and boatswain's mates in peace and war between 1660 and 1776. Boatswain's mates experienced the smallest wage increase during wartime; 30 shillings per month to as little as 50 shillings per month, or a 67 percent increase. Gunners experienced the largest increase, 30 shillings per month to as much as 70 shillings per month, or a 133 percent increase.

15   Marcus Rediker, *Between the Devil and the Deep Blue Sea* (Cambridge: Cambridge University Press, 1987), p.124, pp.304-305, Appendix C, Wages in the Merchant Shipping

captains and mates averaged monthly earnings of £7 and £5.5 respectively during the 1770s.[16] Deckhands earned less than higher-ranking officers did. During lean periods in the eighteenth-century whaling business cycle, when prices were not good, deckhands earned profit shares that amounted to as little as £1.5 per month. During boom periods, however, such as the period just prior to the American Revolution, common labourers could earn shares that amounted to £3 for each month's work.[17] The proceeds from privateering during the 1740s were often more than double the average wages in commercial shipping and six times British naval wages.[18]

It was widely known that naval wages were low and uncompetitive. Benjamin Franklin summed up the differences between maritime labour in the navy and work on merchant vessels during the eighteenth century. He wrote:

> Under the Merchant…[the mariner] goes in an un-arm'd Vessel not obliged to fight, but only to transport Merchandize. In the King's Service he is oblig'd to fight, and to Hazard all the Dangers of Battle. Sickness on board King's Ships is also more common and more Mortal. The Merchant's Service too he can quit at the End of a Voyage, not the King's. Also the Merchant's wages are much higher.[19]

The Royal Navy experienced chronic problems getting skilled mariners to volunteer for naval service as a result of these issues. It also had problems keeping men in the service. Desertion was rampant throughout the early modern era.[20] Impressment was the only means by which Britannia could continually man her warships and rule the world's waves.

Industry, 1700-1750. For more along these lines, see Rodger, *Command of the Ocean*, pp.316-317; and Capp, *Cromwell's Navy*, p.259.

16   Daniel Vickers, 'The First Whalemen of Nantucket,' *The William and Mary Quarterly* 40:4 (October 1983), p.284.

17   Vickers, 'The First Whalemen,' p.295.

18   Carl E. Swanson, *Predators and Prizes: American Privateering and Imperial Warfare, 1739-1748* (Columbia, South Carolina: University of South Carolina Press, 1991), p.219.

19   Benjamin Franklin, "Remarks on Judge Foster's Argument in Favor of the Right of Impressing Seamen," (c. 1762-1781) *The Papers of Benjamin Franklin* <http://franklinpapers.org/franklin/> (accessed 30 March 2019)

20   See Nick Slope, 'Discipline, Desertion and Death: HMS *Trent*, 1796-1803,' in Philip MacDougall and Ann Veronica Coats (eds.), *The Naval Mutinies of 1797: Unity and Perseverance* (London: Boydell & Brewer, Ltd., 2011), pp.226-242; and Martin Hubley, 'Desertion, Identity and the Experience of Authority in the North American Squadron of the Royal Navy, 1745-1812,' (PhD Dissertation, University of Ottawa, 2009).

British press gangs were active in every major conflict that occurred between the Seven Years War and the Napoleonic Wars.[21] We will never know precisely how many pressed men served in the Royal Navy. It was simply impossible for the Admiralty then, and the historian now, to count every man who was pressed. The most concerted academic effort to quantify impressment concludes that nearly 40 percent of the 405,000 men the Royal Navy recruited had been coerced into military service between 1740 and 1815.[22] For his part, John Nicol believed most of the men who served on his warship had been pressed into service. Nicol was a mariner who served in the Royal Navy in 1776 at the start of the American Revolutionary War. In his words, 'I was surprised to see so few who, like myself, had chosen [naval service] for the love of that line of life. Some had been forced into it by their own irregular conduct [i.e. they were convicts or vagrants] but the greater number were impressed men.'[23] Some of Nicol's pressed shipmates may have been Americans.

Parliament attempted to regulate impressment in North America on three occasions prior to the American Revolution. The first piece of legislation enacted in 1708, known in America as 'the Sixth of Anne,' for it took effect in the sixth year of Queen Anne's reign, banned all naval impressment in all British territorial possessions in the Western Hemisphere. This was done to stimulate maritime commerce in the colonies. Naval administrators and officers complained about having to defend an entire seaborne empire with one hand tied behind their backs. They pleaded the necessity of using impressment to man their fleets. They pointed out the rising number of maritime labourers in North America. And so, in 1746, Parliament tacitly allowed the British navy to press men in this region. This act mandated that impressment was banned only in the Caribbean. Naval administrators and officers continued to push for full government support for impressment in North America and they got it in 1775. That year, not coincidentally, just before Americans issued a Declaration of Independence that included impressment as a major grievance, the British government officially repealed the Sixth of Anne's prohibition pertaining to North America. This act gave press gangs full authority and legal sanction to conduct impressment activities in this corner of Britain's seaborne empire.

---

21   Brunsman, *Evil Necessity*; Rogers, *Press Gang*. For a counter argument that impressment was used sparingly and most naval seamen were volunteers, see Dancy, *The Myth of the Press Gang*; and Rodger, *Wooden World*, p.182.

22   Rogers, *Press Gang*, pp.5, 40.

23   Tim Flannery, (ed.), *The Life and Adventures of John Nicol, Mariner* (New York: Atlantic Monthly Press, 1997; originally published 1821), p.26.

Press Gang, by Howard Pyle, 1879. (Editors' collection)

Though British impressment of American mariners is most commonly associated with the War of 1812, press gangs coerced and convinced Americans to serve in the Royal Navy during every major conflict that occurred over the course of Nelson's lifetime.[24] Although press gangs were not allowed to operate in North America prior to 1775, there was a large loophole in the 1708 ban. The legislation allowed the navy to use impressment in North America in cases of desertion to retrieve runaway seamen. This loophole provided British press gangs with a pretext they would use for over a hundred years prior to the War of 1812.

Press gangs were most active in America during the military mobilisation phase of the start of wars. There were 21 warships on the North American station at

---

24 For more on British naval impressment and the origins of the War of 1812, see Paul A. Gilje, *Free Trade and Sailors' Rights in the War of 1812* (Cambridge: Cambridge University Press, 2013); Troy Bickham, *The Weight of Vengeance: The United States, the British Empire, and the War of 1812* (Oxford: Oxford University Press, 2012); and Andrew Lambert, *The Challenge: Britain Against America in the Naval War of 1812* (New York: Faber & Faber, 2012).

the start of the Seven Years War. They arrived on station in the summer and left before winter. The Admiralty subdivided this command into nine zones. A frigate and a sloop or two typically defended each zone.[25] These warships were in chronic need of fresh men. Death, disease, and desertion habitually depleted British fleets. Commodore Richard Spry, commander of the North American Station, reported to the Admiralty in 1756 that he had had to resort to impressment in and around Boston, Massachusetts for manpower 'as all the ships here are short of [their] Complement and Numbers of our People are so weak and sickly that they cannot be taken on Board.'[26]

The American Revolution complicated British naval impressment in North America. The conflict pitted the Royal Navy against former British subjects. Naval officers had to be careful in pressing Americans for military service against their fellow Americans. Vice Admiral Samuel Graves maintained command of the North American station at the start of the war in 1775. He reported to the Admiralty that his officers had 'by means of their Press Warrants picked up a few Men from the Merchant Ships' in the area. He had 'avoided as much as possible entering American Seamen on board the King's Ships, knowing from Experience they will seize every Opportunity of making their Escape or of assisting their Countrymen in Rebellion.' He optimistically hoped that in the future 'we shall be able to complete the Ships [complements] without being obliged to take Americans.' 'But,' he pragmatically resolved for the present to 'put on board the Kings Ships going home as many Americans as can be conveniently carried.' Graves believed that draining North America of rebellious mariners would help the British war effort. He 'humbly propose[d]' that the Admiralty should send these rebels 'to the East Indies [or the] Coast of Africa; but on no account to be sent back again to America.'[27] One year later, the Declaration of Independence stated that impressment was one of the chief reasons Americans were forming their own government. The Royal Navy had 'constrained our fellow Citizens.' These citizens had been 'taken Captive on the high Seas.' American mariners were compelled to serve in the Royal Navy at the start of the Revolution, and they were made 'to

25   Neil R. Stout, *The Royal Navy in America, 1760-1775: A Study of Enforcement of British Colonial Policy in the Era of the American Revolution* (Annapolis, Maryland: US Naval Institute, 1973), p.29.

26   TNA, ADM 1/480, Letters from Admirals on the North America station from 1745-1777, Part V. 702 Letter from Commodore Richard Spry, commander of the North American Station, to John Cleveland, Admiralty Secretary dated onboard the *Fougueux*, at Halifax Harbor, 18 April 1756.

27   Samuel Graves, *Samuel Graves Journal, 1774-1776*, Vol. 2 (Boston, Massachusetts: Massachusetts Historical Society), Graves to Stephens, 20 November 1775, pp.299-300.

bear Arms against their Country, to become the executioners of their friends and Brethren, or to fall themselves by their Hands.'[28]

The Royal Navy continued to press US citizens even after the United States secured independence. The French Revolution and the Napoleonic Wars generated further conflict between Great Britain and France, and, as before, this conflict inevitably led to naval expansion and impressment. American business owners then lobbied their government to take action to protect commerce. On 28 May 1796, the United States Congress authorised the president to appoint consuls in foreign ports to find 'American citizens or others sailing ... under the protection of the American flag' who had been 'impressed or detained by any foreign power.' It was the consul's job 'to endeavour by all legal means to obtain the release of such American citizens or others.' To assist them, Congress mandated that all masters of US registered ships file 'a protest' with the consuls against impressment that occurred within the jurisdiction of a foreign port. If the impressment occurred on the high seas, then US masters had to file the protest with a customs agent at the first United States port they entered. Masters then needed to send a copy of the protest directly to the Secretary of State. In order to provide the government with ammunition to use in diplomatic negotiations with foreign powers, each and every protest needed to state 'the manner of such impressment or detention, by whom made, together with the name and place of residence of the person impressed or detained; distinguishing also, whether he was an American citizen; and if not, to what nation he belonged.'[29] The United States government compiled all of this data in an effort to halt the impressment of US citizens into foreign navies and to return pressed men. The problem was so widespread that on 2 March 1799, Congress passed a second act that required the Secretary of State to present an abstract of this data to the House of Representatives each and every year.[30]

Captain David Cook submitted his protest to the US consul in Trinidad on 22 July 1797. This was just two days before Nelson lost his arm in an assault on Santa Cruz de Tenerife. Cook and his mate, Bradford Taber, testified they were sailing the schooner *Hope* from Charleston, South Carolina on a trade voyage bound for Trinidad. They left Charleston on 14 May. The British sloop-of-war *Frederick*

28   Thomas Jefferson, et al, The Declaration of Independence, Washington, DC: *Library of Congress* <http://www.loc.gov/rr/program/bib/ourdocs/DeclarInd.html> (accessed 31 March 2019)
29   Acts of the Fourth Congress of the United States: An Act for Relief and Protection of American Seamen, April 28, 1796, p.477. *Library of Congress* <https://www.loc.gov/law/help/statutes-at-large/4th-congress/c4.pdf> (accessed 30 March 2019)
30   Acts of the Sixth Congress of the United States: An Act for Relief and Protection of American Seamen March 2, 1799, p.731. *Library of Congress* <https://www.loc.gov/law/help/statutes-at-large/6th-congress/c6.pdf> (accessed 30 March 2019)

stopped them near St Lucia on 21 June. A press gang boarded the *Hope* and took John Dore, who was a common sailor 'sailing before the mast.' Dore was born in the Netherlands. But, by the time Cook recruited him in New York City early in 1797, Dore had become an US citizen. Once the *Hope* reached Trinidad, a press gang from the third-rate HMS *Dictator* (64) boarded her and took another US mariner, John Gale. Cook 'remonstrated' against both cases of impressment. He informed British naval officers of the 'injury' the trade voyage would suffer for the want of his sailors, but they refused to listen. The *Hope's* owners lost the freight rates they were charging merchants to ship tropical goods back to the United States. The merchants lost out on the profits they hoped to gain from the sale of those goods. Cook lamented the 'costs, losses, hurts, prejudices, detriments and inconveniences' that were sure to result from the British navy 'forcibly seizing and taking possession of [the] said two foremast men.'[31]

That same year, Captain James R. Dennis submitted his protest to the customs collector at Newburyport, Massachusetts. Dennis was master of the Newburyport brig *Tryall* in 1797. But, the previous year he had sailed as first mate on a voyage to Martinico (now Martinique) in the West Indies. The *Tryall* and her crew reached the island in November. The captain succumbed to an unnamed tropical fever and quickly died. More bad luck followed. On 18 December, a press gang from a 74-gun British warship boarded the brig 'and demanded the chest and clothes of George Gay, one of the *Tryall's* mariners, whom they had previously impressed.' The naval officer in charge of the gang stated that Gay 'was an Englishman by birth and had no legal protection.' Another gang, from a second 74-gun, then pressed John Davis, another of the *Tryall's* mariners, into service while he was on shore. They also claimed Davis was an Englishman by birth. On behalf of himself, 'the owner or owners, freighters, insurers, and all others concerned in the said brig *Tryall*,' Dennis protested against 'the commanders of the said two ships of war of 74 guns' for 'impressing and taking by force the two mariners as aforesaid, and detaining them to the injury and damage of him the said deponent, for all damages, injuries, disappointments and expenses whatsoever, had borne suffered and sustained, or to be had borne suffered and sustained.'[32]

In both protests, US masters made the point that British naval impressment caused a harmful ripple effect on the US economy. The appropriation of maritime manpower did not simply result in a few men being taken from a couple of

---

31   National Archives and Records Administration, College Park, Maryland, microfilm M1839, *Captain Cook's Protest, 22 July 1797, Miscellaneous Lists and Papers Regarding Impressed Seamen, 1796-1814, Protests and Lists of Impressed Seamen, 1796-1810.*

32   National Archives and Records Administration, College Park, Maryland, microfilm M1839, James R. Dennis' *Protest Relative to the Impressment of Two of His Seamen, 8 March 1797, Miscellaneous Lists 1796-1814, Protests and Lists, 1796-1810.*

commercial vessels. For the masters, men who worked directly for the ship owners, and men whose interests more closely aligned with those who controlled the means of production, the heart of the matter was not the national identities of the pressed men.[33] Whether or not Gay and Davis were well and truly British subjects or US citizens mattered less to Dennis and others like him than the financial repercussions associated with the loss of workers. For Dennis and Cook, and all the other protests of US masters in the entire data set the United States government collected between the Revolution and the War of 1812, the main thrust of their protests was that British naval impressment was bad for US businesses. It jeopardised 'the owner or owners, freighters, insurers, and all others concerned in' overseas trade.

Fluctuations in maritime commerce impacted the US by the turn of the nineteenth century. A consumer culture had emerged in this part of the world over the course of the eighteenth century. Americans imported Chinese tea in large quantities. They drank this tea in porcelain cups manufactured in England. They dunked sugar in their tea that came from Caribbean plantations.[34] The United States was not an isolated agrarian society populated by few merchants and mariners. British naval impressment was not a fringe subject that only truly mattered to a small demographic. The US economy was affected every time a British warship slowed or prevented commercial vessels from crossing the Atlantic Ocean.

In 1747, shortly after the famous Knowles Riot, in which Americans reacted violently to the appropriation of local mariners, Massachusetts governor William Shirley complained that people in Boston and in the surrounding countryside suffered 'great Difficulties' as a result of British impressment. They received a 'great Part' of their 'Supplies of Provisions' from overseas, and press gangs were slowing and halting the flow of these provisions, 'cutting 'em off from these Supplies.' Shirley worried that the absence of a continual, timely flow of imports 'might endanger the starving of the poorer Sort' throughout Massachusetts.[35] In 1765, a Rhode Island newspaper told a similar tale. British warships had been stationed along the New England coastline, and they had been pressing American mariners

---

33   For more on ship captains' bourgeois mentalities, see Rediker, *Between the Devil and the Deep Blue Sea*. For more on the importance of national identities in the run-up to the War of 1812, see Perl-Rosenthal, *Citizen Sailors*.

34   T.H. Breen, *The Marketplace of Revolution: How Consumer Politics Shaped American Independence* (Oxford: Oxford University Press, 2004); Benjamin L. Carp, *Defiance of the Patriots: The Boston Tea Party and the Making of America* (New Haven, Connecticut: Yale University Press, 2010).

35   TNA ADM 1/3818/285-94: Governor William Shirley to the Admiralty, 31 December 1747.

'for four or five Weeks.' As a result, the 'Wood Wharves' in Newport's waterfront, where poor and wealthy Americans got fuel to heat their homes and cook their food, was 'almost clear of Wood.' Coasting vessels carrying kindling from nearby colonies were 'shunning our Port, to escape the hottest Press ever known in this Town.' This artificial dearth would have caused the price of the remaining wood in Newport to skyrocket. The presence of press gangs 'greatly distressed' the coastal community's fish market, as 'few of the Fishermen dare venture out, it being reported none shall escape the Impress.' Food prices rose as a result.[36] Impressment continuously hurt American consumers. In the fiery 1814 words of Samuel Young, a New York legislator, British press gangs 'sweep our commerce from the ocean' and 'commit spoliations upon us, boundless in extent and endless in duration!'[37]

American business owners, consumers, and workers had a special disdain for British naval impressment. There were ideological and material reasons for this. In terms of principles, Americans never stopped believing that all British naval impressment was illegal in North America because of the Sixth of Anne. In a letter to the Admiralty, Governor Shirley stated his belief that: 'the persuasion all over the Continent that the Impressing of Seamen within any of his Majesty's Plantations is illegal by a Virtue of a Clause in a Statue of the [Sixth] of Queen Anne, which they conceive to be perpetual.'[38] What is more, Americans were jealous about the 1746 act that expressly banned impressment in the Caribbean, but said nothing about North America. In Samuel Adams' words: 'Every One of the Plantations suffer' from impressment 'except the Sugar Islands.' These islands were 'protected by a special Act.' 'Why,' Adams asked, should the Caribbean sugar plantations have

---

36   TNA ADM 1/3818/285-94: Governor William Shirley.

37   Samuel Young, *Speech of Mr Young* (New York: E. Conrad, 1814), p.5.

38   TNA ADM 1/3818/292: Governor Shirley to the Admiralty, 1 December 1747. John Adams stated in 1769 that 'It has been reported as the Opinion of Sir Dudley Rider and Sir John Strange that this Statute [the Sixth of Anne] expired with the War of Queen Anne. These are venerable Names, but their Opinions are Opinions only of private Men. And there has been no judicial Decision to this Purpose in any Court of Law.' Regarding these venerable opinions, Adams wrote, 'I have taken Pains to discover what Reasons can be produced in Support of them; And I confess I can think of none. There is not the least Color for such an Opinion. On the Contrary, there is every Argument for supposing the act [to be] perpetual.' L. Kinvin Wroth and Hiller B. Zobel (eds.), *Legal Papers of John Adams* (Cambridge, Massachusetts, 1965), 2:324. Wroth and Zobel explained: 'Dudley Ryder (1691-1756) was attorney general of England, 1737-1754; John Strange (1691-1754) was solicitor general, 1737-1742 ... In 1740, they signed a joint opinion: "We have perused the several clauses in the American Act, and by comparing the several clauses together, it seems to us, that the act is not now in force, but expired at the end of the war."' They further noted that 'In 1716, Sir Edward Northey, the attorney general, had given an identical opinion.'

such 'a Special Protection?' Why were Members of Parliament not attending to American interests?[39]

Americans witnessed exceptional economic growth over the course of the eighteenth century. Between 1650 and 1770, the overall economy of the 13 British mainland North American colonies increased by an annual rate of 3.5 percent.[40] By comparison, the economy in Great Britain expanded at an annual rate of only 0.5 percent over the same range of dates.[41] American entrepreneurs who became ship owners or maritime insurers and businessmen who took risks shipping goods to and from overseas markets could reasonably expect exceptional profits from these ventures. Isaac Wikoff, a merchant in Philadelphia, Pennsylvania, stated in 1774: 'The Design of Trade is to make a profit in the End. I am sure I would have Quit a business immediately in which no Evident profit should arise.'[42] Stopping commercial vessels and depleting their manpower put American business owners' pursuit of profits at risk.

The exceptional economic development in North America also meant that job opportunities and wage rates were particularly good for workers in this part of the world. A mariner testified to this fact before the members of the Massachusetts Court of Admiralty in 1731. He explained, 'One great inducement why Sailors' commonly jumped ship in North America was that 'the Wages given from hence are greater than out of Great Britain.'[43] There was great demand for mariners in North America's expanding economy. By the American Revolution, there were

39   Evans' Early American Imprints, Series 1, #5900: Amicus Patriae/Samuel Adams, 'An Address to the Inhabitants of the Province of the Massachusetts-Bay in New England, More Especially, To the Inhabitants of Boston; Occasioned by the late Illegal and Unwarrantable Attack Upon their Liberties, and the unhappy Confusion and Disorders consequent thereon.' (Boston: Printed and sold by Rogers and Fowle in Queen-Street, 1747). For more on the authorship of this essay, and the fact that Amicus Patriae was Samuel Adams, see Rogers, *Press Gang*, p.90; Benjamin L. Carp, *Rebels Rising: Cities and the American Revolution* (Oxford: Oxford University Press, 2007), p.37; Peter Linebaugh and Marcus Rediker, *The Many-Headed Hydra: Sailors, Slaves, Commoners, and the Hidden History of the Revolutionary Atlantic* (Boston, Massachusetts: Beacon Press, 2000), p.216; and Gary B. Nash, *The Urban Crucible: Social Change, Political Consciousness, and the Origins of the American Revolution* (Cambridge, Massachusetts: Harvard University Press, 1979), p.224.

40   John J. McCusker and Russell R. Menard, *The Economy of British America, 1607-1789* (Chapel Hill, North Carolina: University of North Carolina Press, 1985), p.57.

41   McCusker and Menard, *Economy of British America*.

42   Isaac Wikoff to Peter Ewer, 4 May 1774, quoted in Sheryllynne Haggerty, 'Merely for Money?': *Business Culture in the British Atlantic, 1750–1815* (Liverpool: Liverpool University Press, 2012), p.9.

43   Guy vs. Skinner (1731), Records of the Court of Admiralty of the Province of Massachusetts Bay, 1718-1747, Manuscript Division, Library of Congress, quoted in Rediker, *Between the Devil*, p.103.

an estimated 10,000 to 30,000 coastal traders, commercial fishermen, merchant mariners, privateers, and whalers in America.[44] This was fully one-third the number of mariners in Great Britain, an island nation with no hinterland to draw off manpower. But even this number was not enough to meet the growing needs of America's maritime enterprises.

The North American labour market was a particularly bad place for the Royal Navy to recruit mariners. American maritime employers had a great need for workers, and there were high-paying employment opportunities for labourers in this part of the world. It was also well-known in this part of the world that the Royal Navy did not adequately compensate its seamen. Captain Housman Broadly, commander of HM Sloop *Oswego*, informed Vice Admiral Edward Boscawen in 1755 that 'there will be no getting Seamen at New York or Boston ... upon the Wages allowed in the Navy.'[45] That same year, Governor William Shirley stated he was 'not encouraged to expect' that the navy could recruit volunteers in Massachusetts 'for the King's usual Pay.'[46] In 1764, Captain Archibald Kennedy informed the Admiralty that it was 'not in the power of Man ... to prevent Seamen from running away' in North American ports. 'Especially considering,' he explained, 'the high Wages and other inducements the Merchants give them.'[47] In Kennedy's words, 'not one of His Majesty's Ships who are stationed at any of the trading ports in North America would ever be able to proceed on service after laying up for one winter if they did not impress.'[48]

Impressment Case Studies

In this economy, mariners especially valued occupational mobility and the ability to maximise earning potential. These were highly prized American economic freedoms. In the words of James Durand, an eighteenth-century New Hampshire mariner, he and his mates desired to 'follow fortune's paths where ever they lead.'[49]

44   Denver Brunsman, *Evil Necessity*, p.95.
45   TNA ADM, Records of the Navy Board M 1/480, Part IV, p.647. Captain Housman Broadly to Vice Admiral Edward Boscawen, 15 February 1755.
46   TNA, ADM 1/480. Part IV, p.488. Governor William Shirley to Commodore Augustus Keppel, 20 May 1755.
47   TNA, ADM 1/2012: Kennedy to the Admiralty, 18 February 1765.
48   TNA, ADM 1/2012: Kennedy to the Admiralty, 18 February 1765.
49   James Durand, *The Life and Adventures of James R. Durand, From the Year One Thousand Eight Hundred and One, Until the Year One Thousand Eight Hundred and Sixteen. Written by Himself. His First Leaving His Parents: How He Was Cast Away, and the Hardships He Underwent; His Entering the American Service; Together With the Particulars of His Impressment and Service On Board a British Man of War, Seven Years and 1 Month, Until 1816* (Bridgeport, Connecticut: Printed By Stiles Nichols & Son, 1817), p.6.

Mariners were not all 'giddy young bachelors' who were unable to 'rationally assess their future prospects.'[50] These were sober, mature mariners who actively pursued well-paying vocations and careers.

Ashley Bowen was one such sober American mariner. He was born in Marblehead, Massachusetts in 1728. His father was a notary and justice of the peace and he taught navigation on the side.[51] Bowen's working life began in 1739, when he was 11 years old. Four mariners who had been learning navigation with his father in order to pursue career advancement in commercial shipping convinced their captain, Edmund Gale, to 'persuade my father to let me go to sea with them.' Bowen most likely worked as a cabin boy for Gale on the snow *Diligence*. Gale and his crew were supposed to ship a load of dried, salted cod from Boston to Bilbao, Spain, but they learned that Britain and Spain had gone to war. So, the *Diligence* transported tar from Cape Fear, North Carolina to Bristol, England in September.[52]

It was at Bristol that Bowen first encountered press gangs. In the midst of military mobilisation, the Royal Navy 'pressed' most of Bowen's shipmates. With a skeleton crew, the *Diligence* limped to Swansea, Wales, picked up a load of coal, and then returned to Boston in August 1740. Bowen's older brother, Edward, then went to work as a mariner on a commercial voyage to London, where he 'was impressed.'[53] Over the course of his life, Bowen experienced much occupational mobility. He worked at sea and on land as a cabin boy, fisherman, merchant mariner, naval seaman, plasterer, privateer, ship rigger, surveyor, and wood cutter.[54] Near his death in 1813, he was working as a sail maker.

50   Rodger, *Wooden World*, p.118. Rodger went on to write: 'The common thread of every informed description of the sailor's character is imprudence.' Bernard Capp concurred on this point. He wrote: 'It was generally agreed that sailors lived for the moment. Most of them were young, single, and carefree. Moreover, a life of perpetual uncertainty and danger almost inevitably produced a short-term, feckless outlook.' Capp, *Cromwell's Navy*, p.245. For more along these lines, see E.P.Hohman, *Seamen Ashore: A Study of the United Seamen's Service and of Merchant Seamen in Port* (New Haven, Connecticut: Yale University Press, 1952), pp.254-255.

51   Phillip Chadwick Foster Smith (ed.), *The Journals of Ashley Bowen (1728-1813)* Vol. l. (Portland, Maine: Anthoensen Press, University of Maine, 1973), pp.5-6.

52   Smith, *The Journals*, p.7.

53   Smith, *The Journals*, p.7.

54   For additional information on Ashley Bowen, see Daniel Vickers, *Young Men and the Sea: Yankee Seafarers In the Age of Sail* (New Haven, Connecticut: Yale University Press, 2005), pp.96-130; Daniel Vickers, 'Ashley Bowen of Marblehead: Revolutionary Neutral,' in Nancy & Ian Steele (eds.), *The Human Tradition in US History: The Revolutionary Era* (Wilmington, Delaware: Scholarly Resources Inc., 2000), pp.99-115; and Daniel Vickers, 'An Honest Tar: Ashley Bowen of Marblehead', *New England Quarterly* 69:4 (December, 1996), pp.544-553.

Bowen also achieved career advancement. When he was thirteen years old, he went to work as a captain's apprentice and cabin boy in 1741.[55] Four years later, he began working as a common mariner, or a man who worked the foremast near the ship's bow, or a foremast hand, on various commercial vessels that sailed between Atlantic ports. He 'learned navigation' while between jobs at Bristol, England in 1748. This skill enabled him to sign on to be 'a-coming to Boston as Second Mate.'[56] In 1752, Bowen became a sailing master.[57] In commercial shipping, this was a position that either replaced the duties of a mate, or it represented an intermediate step between mate and captain. A year later, an 'agent from a company of whalemen' approached Bowen about working as the captain of a vessel on a whaling expedition.[58] After a long and fruitless expedition, Bowen decided to return home to Marblehead, Massachusetts in 1754. He worked 'as a [foremast] hand' just to get home as quickly as possible. At Marblehead, he could find work only 'as a foremast man,' because local employers insisted he work up through the ranks.[59] It took two years before Bowen could work his way back up to mate.[60] He reached the pinnacle of work in commercial shipping and became a captain in 1756, 15 years after he first went to sea as a young lad.[61]

Elijah Cobb was another American mariner who experienced occupational mobility and career advancement in America's expanding economy. He was born in 1769 in Cape Cod, Massachusetts. In 1783, at age 14, he began working as a cabin boy for a commercial shipping firm based in Boston. The green hand worked as a cabin boy.[62] He then 'shipped as a common sailor' on commercial voyages to the West Indies.[63] In 1787, he began working as a foremast hand for his uncle's shipping firm on trade voyages between Boston and Philadelphia.[64] 'I continued in the employ of B.C. & Sons,' Cobb wrote, 'about a year, when they promoted me to the office of mate – and in that capacity I served them, under many different captains, between 6 & 7 years.' Cobb felt his uncle was unfairly denying him a position as captain. He must have repeatedly sought such a position. 'Seeing no disposition on their part to indulge me,' he wrote, 'I left the employ' of B.C. & Sons. He went to Baltimore, Maryland and 'made two voyages to Europe, in the capacity

55   Smith, *The Journals*, p.9.
56   Smith, *The Journals*, p.29.
57   Smith, *The Journals*, p.33.
58   Smith, *The Journals*, p.33.
59   Smith, *The Journals*, p.42.
60   Smith, *The Journals*, p.44.
61   Smith, *The Journals*, p.44.
62   Ralph D. Paine (ed.), *Elijah Cobb, 1768 – 1848; A Cape Cod Skipper* (New Haven, Connecticut: Yale University Press, 1925), p.21.
63   Paine, *Elijah Cobb*, p.21.
64   Paine, *Elijah Cobb*, p.25.

of 1st mate of a ship.' With experience outside his family's business under his belt, he returned to Boston 'and got the command of a Brig, in the employ of Edward & William Reynolds.' As captain, Cobb made regular 'voyages to Virginia, & one to the West Indies.'[65] He captained a merchant vessel on a voyage to Cadiz, Spain.[66] Then, he proudly wrote, 'In October 1799 I took charge of the Brig *Mary*, went to Savannah, in Georgia, from that to Lisbon, from thence to London, to Rotterdam, Copenhagen, St Petersburg, and back to Boston – and performed the voyage, in 8 months & 4 days.'[67]

Christopher Prince also found employment options and gainful employment as an American mariner. Prince was born in Massachusetts in 1751. On coming of age, Prince went to sea as a fisherman in the New England commercial cod fishing industry. He then moved into commercial shipping and became a merchant mariner. He switched to privateering during the Revolutionary War. He also served on American warships. In 1779, he transferred back into commercial shipping.[68] He had a brief stint as a ship rigger in 1780.[69] Then, he went back into shipping.[70]

Prince advanced up the ranks in commercial shipping. He worked as a fifteen-year-old common seaman on trade voyages between Massachusetts and the West Indies over the course of 1766-67, and then he earned promotion to able-bodied seaman.[71] After three years, Prince learned the art of navigation and earned promotion to mate.[72] Nine years later, having had experience on privateers and American warships during the Revolutionary War, he was promoted to captain of a merchant vessel.[73] At the same time, in 1779, Prince placed one foot firmly outside the ranks of maritime labourers and into the ranks of capitalist ship owners. He used some of his privateer earnings to purchase a third share of a trade vessel 'loaded for one of the West India Islands,' for 'eighteen thousand dollars continental money.' The trade ship 'was loaded with a valuable cargo and 48 horses.'[74] The profit from this voyage catapulted Prince into an entirely different social stratum. Wealth and status brought political success. Prince served as Secretary of the Marine Society for 25 years. From 1813 to 1831 he worked as agent for the United States Marine Hospital in New York.[75]

65   Paine, *Elijah Cobb*, p.26.
66   Paine, *Elijah Cobb*, p.26
67   Paine, *Elijah Cobb*, p.49.
68   Crawford, *The Autobiography*, p.184.
69   Crawford, *The Autobiography*, p.185.
70   Crawford, *The Autobiography*, p.186.
71   Crawford, *The Autobiography*, pp.19-20.
72   Crawford, *The Autobiography*, p.20.
73   Crawford, *The Autobiography*, p.124.
74   Crawford, *The Autobiography*, p.184.
75   Crawford, *The Autobiography*, p.222.

American mariners such as Bowen, Cobb, and Prince resented British naval impressment for reasons that were unique to North America. Because of the Sixth of Anne, they did not believe the Royal Navy had the legal authority to appropriate manpower in this region. The exceptional economic development made maritime jobs both plentiful and comparatively high-paying. The Royal Navy took men out of this work environment and compelled them to risk their lives for little compensation. Impressment limited American economic freedoms. American mariners associated British naval impressment with what was the antithesis of liberty in their minds – slavery. They viewed pressed men as not merely dependent, but as having no control over their labour. They saw the Royal Navy as an extremely exploitative environment with limited or no earning potential. They perceived it as a workplace that sharply curtailed their occupational mobility.

What is more, men of letters and men of means in America echoed and amplified workers' correlation of slavery and impressment. Benjamin Franklin stated that 'if impressing seamen is of Right by Common Law, in Britain, Slavery is then of Right by Common Law; there being no Slavery worse than that Sailors are subjected to.'[76] Eight years later, he wrote a treatise on slavery in which he defined a slave as 'a human Creature, stolen, taken by Force, or bought of another or of himself, with Money; and who being so taken or bought, is compelled to serve the Taker, or Purchaser, during Pleasure or during Life.' Franklin went on to state his belief that based on this definition, 'Many Thousands' of American mariners who had been pressed into service in the British navy could be considered slaves.[77] Americans, business owners and workers alike, viewed press gangs with extreme distaste.

Conclusion

The American perception of impressment was exceptional. To be sure, mariners and merchants in other parts of the world condemned the state appropriation of labour. But, American business owners and free wage labourers had reasons for being particularly resentful of this practice. The British government banned impressment in North America in 1708. The Royal Navy continued to press men in this region, however. Then, in 1746, Parliament appeared to encourage the Caribbean islands at American expense. Moreover, by 1775, North America was the only region in the entire Western Hemisphere where the Royal Navy could legally press men into service. What is more, North America was a region in which there was exceptional economic growth. Businesses were expanding overseas trade and importing and exporting more and more goods across the seas. Workers grew

76   Franklin, 'Remarks on Judge Foster's Argument'.
77   Franklin, 'Remarks on Judge Foster's Argument'.

up in a thriving economy in which jobs were plentiful and wages were relatively high. They were free labourers in a free market. They valued having employment options and being able to maximize their earning potential. For all these reasons, Americans developed an exceptional aversion to British naval impressment over the course of Nelson's lifetime.

4

North Americans at Trafalgar

Captain Peter Hore

In order to comprehend the role played by North Americans in the Royal Navy during its sea battles against Revolutionary and Napoleonic France, a most compelling place to begin is the Battle of Trafalgar, the most legendary maritime battle of the Nelsonic era. Professor N.A.M Rodger in *Command of the Ocean* gives the number of Americans at the Battle of Trafalgar as 373,[1] but, despite this being based on the Ayshford Trafalgar Roll (ATR),[2] this number is suspiciously precise. In fact the ATR gives the names of 535 North Americans, comprising 478 Americans and 57 Canadians, and even these numbers need to be qualified and adjusted by several factors. First, Pam and Derek Ayshford, who compiled the ATR, did so from the ships' muster books which were extant and in use on the day of the battle. These books were opened each time a ship was newly commissioned and show who was on board at each monthly muster of the crew. In some cases the books cover several years and, for example, names of men who were marked 'R' (meaning 'run,' i.e. they had deserted) or 'D' (meaning they been discharged to another ship) were carried forward from muster to muster. Only men who were marked 'DD' meaning they were 'discharged dead' (i.e. died or killed) had their names removed from the muster books. So, the compilers of the ATR listed all the names that were in the books, including men who, before the battle, had been lent to other ships, discharged for various reasons, and some who had died. The

---

1   N.A.M. Rodger, *The Command of the Ocean: a Naval History of Britain 1649-1815* (New York: W.W. Norton & Company: 2004), p.498 and fn. 63.

2   Pam Ayshford and Derek Ayshford, *The Ayshford Complete Trafalgar Roll* (Brussels, Belgium: SEFF, 2004). Pam and Derek Ayshford spent several years compiling this complete list of Royal Navy personnel present (and/or on the ships' books) at the Battle of Trafalgar, based on ships' muster books and other primary source materials.

ATR therefore includes some 21,500 names of whom some 18,000 were present at the battle on 21 October 1805. Of the 535 North Americans in the ATR, 89 were Americans whose names appear in the books but who were not present at the battle. Three were Canadians whose names are given but who were not at the battle. Thus, the total were reduced to 389 Americans and 54 Canadians who fought in the battle.

Second, in 1805, the concept of the United States of America – not least in the mind of ship's clerk responsible for keeping the muster books – was still new and even somewhat hazy. Also, the country now known as Canada consisted of several separate colonies. An early nineteenth century ship's clerk could not be expected to have a clear grasp of this geography when writing entries in his muster book. Some place names like Boston, Halifax, and Northampton are suffixed 'America' to distinguish them from eponymous towns in England, and the modern reader can guess from the context whether in these cases 'America' meant the USA or modern Canada. However, in 103 entries, the place of birth is simply given as 'America' and there is little clue as to whether this means the USA or the territories of the British Empire in mainland North America which had been known formally since 1783 as British North America. It is possible that some of those men shown as being from America, with no further place name to clarify which part of America, were in fact from Canada.

Third, the ATR comprises some 21,500 names of which some are without any place of birth and it is likely that a proportion of these also came from North America. Fourth, there are some small errors and duplications that have inevitably crept into the ATR. The following table shows all the North Americans, i.e. those identified as Canadians, those coming from the USA, and those North Americans who might be from either country, numbering in total 535, in the ships' muster books on 21 October 1805:

	Canada	'America'	USA	All North America
Officers	3	-	4	7
Royal Marines	2	-	2	4
Seamen – volunteers	34	55	188	277
Seamen - 'prest'	11	18	81	110
Substitute		1	2	3
Not known	7	27	100	134
Total	57	101	377	535
At Trafalgar	54	79	310	443
Not at Trafalgar	3	24	65	92

The table also endeavours to show what number of men were volunteers and who were pressed, but just as there were many men with no clear place of origin from an amorphous 'America,' so there were many men with no notation against their names to indicate whether they were freemen or no.

Controversy

Nevertheless the ATR represents the first large scale analysis of the personnel of the Royal Navy. Laird Clowes gave the strength of the Royal Navy as voted by Parliament as 120,000 seamen and marines,[3] so the sample covered by the ATR is approximately one-fifth of the Royal Navy, a sample so large that, besides being fully representative of the men at the battle, may be held to be representative of the Georgian navy as a whole in 1805. Thus the ATR and further detail contained within the muster books enable the researcher to look beyond the usual 'quarterdeck histories' that study the lives of the ships' officers and to examine in some detail the men of the lower deck.

Of the grand number of Americans at Trafalgar, 535, between 81 (15 percent) and possibly 99 (18 percent) were pressed men. Controversially, this suggests that by extrapolation there were only about 500 pressed Americans in the entire Royal Navy in 1805. Most of these were skilled seamen, and fewer than 10 percent were landsmen, or unskilled hands. The largest number of American seamen came from just five ports; New York (87), Philadelphia (62), Boston (26), Rhode Island (17) and Baltimore (12). Of the New Yorkers, 52 seamen were volunteers, and an unusually high portion of them, 16, or 30 percent, were pressed men: the status of 19 men has not been recorded. However, only one of the pressed New Yorkers was unskilled. Indeed, of all the pressed men from North America, only 13 (10 Americans and three Canadians) were unskilled. All the others were ordinary seamen and able-bodied seamen and higher rates, indicating clearly that the Royal Navy was in want of skilled men.

Young and Old

An example of a pressed man is Quartermaster John Donaldson. At age 57, Donaldson was also the second oldest American in the fleet off Cadiz in October 1805. Where and how he was pressed is not clear, but from the receiving ship *San Salvador* he was transferred to the second-rate HMS *Prince* (90) on 27 April 1804 and entered in the books as an able seaman. He was evidently an experienced

---

3   William Laird Clowes, *The Royal Navy: a History from the Earliest Times to the Present*, Vol. V (London: Chathan, 1997; reprint of 1899 edition), p.9.

seaman and became reconciled to his lot because on 1 October 1805 he was rated quartermaster, and he served on in the Royal Navy to receive his petty officer's share of the prize money of £10.14.0 and the Parliamentary Award of £26.6.0. He hailed from 'New Ratchel, America'.[4] 'New Ratchel' most likely refers to New Rochelle, New York, situated on the western shore of Long Island Sound.

The oldest American at Trafalgar was 59-year-old Ordinary Seaman Ralph Henry from 'America' who received his prize money and Parliamentary Award, and we know he was illiterate because he 'made his mark' (i.e. he placed a cross against his name) instead of signing his name when he collected his seaman's share of prize money, £1.17.6 and the Parliamentary Award of £4.12.6.[5] At age 55, the oldest American in HMS *Victory*'s books was Ordinary Seaman John Scott from Philadelphia. Some evidence indicates he was serving in the fifth-rate frigate HMS *Resistance* (32) when she was wrecked on the Portuguese coast near Cape St Vincent on 31 May 1803. His name was entered in the muster book of *Victory* on 14 June 1803. He was discharged sick to the hospital on Gibraltar on 24 July after Nelson's great chase to the West Indies and back. He did not return on board before the Battle of Trafalgar.[6] The youngest American in the fleet off Cadiz was Boy Third Class Robert Holbrooke who volunteered at the Gosport rendezvous (a rendezvous in this sense was a recruiting station). More precise information as to his place of birth is not given, but he joined the third-rate HMS *Orion* (74) as she prepared to sail for Cadiz on 2 August 1805. He too 'made his mark' when he collected his prize money and Parliamentary Award.[7]

Pressed Men

A pressed man in the third-rate HMS *Leviathan* (74) was Richard Baker who was entered in the books on 26 September 1800. Baker too was from 'America' (no other place name given), and he served three years as an ordinary seaman before being advanced to able seaman on 24 November 1803. He received his £1.17.6 of prize money after Trafalgar and was discharged to the second-rate HMS *Formidable* (90) in Plymouth on Christmas Day 1805.[8] Another pressed man who was subsequently marked as a volunteer was 19-year-old Landsman Onore Rogue. Does his name suggest that he was French or a slave by origin? He hailed from

4   TNA 36/16274, 36 and 37: Records of the Navy Board and the Board of Admiralty contain ship musters books for HM Ships from 1688-1842. See Discovery National Archives, Kew, London. <http://discovery.nationalarchives.gov.uk/details/r/C1745>
5   TNA ADM 37/18.
6   TNA ADM 36/15900.
7   TNA ADM 37/18.
8   TNA ADM 37/18.

New Orleans and joined the third-rate HMS *Belleisle* (74) on 24 September 1805 from the prison ship *San Ysidro* in Plymouth in one of the last drafts of men to reinforce Nelson's fleet off Cadiz. He was not entitled to the King's bounty as a volunteer, but he did receive his £1.17.6 of Trafalgar prize money. His career was short, and he was sent to man the hospital ship *Prince Frederick* on 9 January 1806.[9] Amongst other pressed men from America was 26-year-old Ordinary Seaman Antonio Marino whose place of birth was given as 'Carthergenia [sic], America', which seems likely to be a reference Cartagena on the Spanish Main, i.e. in South America. He was sent into the Royal Navy 'from civil power' i.e. jail, but nevertheless gave four years' service in the third-rate HMS *Agamemnon* (64) from 1804, and he pocketed his prize money from the battle. His name suggests that he might have been of Spanish origin and perhaps is it not surprising that he deserted in Maldonado Bay, Uruguay on 27 December 1808.[10]

John Davis

There are 39 'John Davises' in the muster books. There were so many that one suspects the name may have been a pseudonym or epithet: four of them came from North America (There were 68 John Smiths). One more pressed-man-turned-volunteer was John Davis, a 22-year-old ordinary seaman from Boston, America who was taken in Barbados on 20 December 1800. He soon volunteered and received the King's bounty of £2.10.0. Davis served at least five years in *Leviathan* and received his Trafalgar prize money of £1.17.6.[11] Another American, John Davis, a 21-year-old from Harlem, presumably New York, who joined *Leviathan* on 13 January 1804, had volunteered at the Gosport rendezvous, and received the King's bounty of £5. His destiny is unknown.[12] There were two other men from America also called John Davis. A 21-year-old Ordinary Seaman John Davis (no place name given) received the King's bounty of £2.10.0, and entered the second-rate HMS *Temeraire* (98) on 10 February 1804 from the brig-sloop HMS *Seagull* (16), but his Trafalgar prize money of £1.17.6 and his Parliamentary Award of £4.12.6 were paid to his father, Joseph, in England on 9 June 1807.[13] *Seagull* disappeared without trace in the Channel in February 1805. The fourth John Davis was a boatswain's mate in the third-rate HMS *Achille* (78), also from 'America' without further definition of his place of birth. He came from the second-rate HMS *Windsor Castle*

9   TNA ADM 36/15814.
10   TNA ADM 36/16520.
11   TNA ADM 36/15837.
12   TNA ADM 36/15837.
13   TNA ADM 36/15851.

(98) on 5 May 1805, and, as a petty officer, he received £10.14.0 in prize money after Trafalgar, but when he saw his chance he deserted in Madeira on 22 May 1807.[14]

Other Volunteers

The volunteer Americans include three men who initially were shown in the muster books as pressed men but who subsequently received the King's bounty as volunteers. Others may have decided, once they were pressed, to make the best of their situation by volunteering. They included the 41-year-old Landsman Prymus Hutchinson, from New York, who served at least five years in *Leviathan*, joining on 29 July 1800 and who received £1.17.6 in prize money after Trafalgar. His age, his lack of advancement in over five years, and that he was pressed in St Kitts, suggest something unique about him, but ship's muster books do not include any physical descriptions that would enable us to know if he was a freed slave.[15] Amongst the genuine volunteers was 18-year-old Landsman William Brown Connor who joined the third-rate HMS *Polyphemus* (64) on 5 March 1805, fought at the great battle, but deserted in Portsmouth on 11 February 1806 while his ship was under repair. Thus, he did not collect the prize money and award due to him and this was forfeited to Greenwich Hospital.[16] Another volunteer was a 30-year-old landsman from 'Mexico, North America', who nevertheless, judging from his name, William Morris, was an Anglo-Saxon. Morris had previously served in the fourth-rate HMS *Adamant* (50) in the West Indies, entered in the third-rate HMS *Ajax* (74) on 22 August 1804 and received his prize money from the battle and £10 from the Lloyd's Patriotic Fund for wounds sustained.[17]

American Midshipmen

In the ship muster books were several American midshipmen, among them two brothers, Richard Augustus Yates (1788-1867) and Robert Winthrop Yates (1789-1827) from New York. Their father was Adolphus Yates and their mother was Margaret Shirreff nee Winthrop.[18] The boys' uncle was Vice Admiral Robert Winthrop (1762-1832) who, though born in New London, Connecticut, died at Dover, Kent. Young Richard was christened in the Church of St Paul the Apostle, New York on 23 March 1790, served under his uncle in the third-rate HMS *Ardent*

---

14   TNA ADM 37/5.
15   TNA ADM 36/15837.
16   TNA ADM 36/16507.
17   TNA ADM 36/16538.
18   Robert C. Winthrop.*A Short Account of the Winthrop Family* (Cambridge, England: J. Wilson & Son, University Press, 1887). See also TNA ADM 36/16545.

(64), and joined the third-rate HMS *Revenge* (74) on 28 April 1805, before being appointed to HM Brig-sloop *Prospero* (14) on 20 June; thus, he missed the Battle of Trafalgar. He subsequently rejoined his uncle in the fifth-rate frigate HMS *Sybille* (44), became a lieutenant in 1809, and after an active career in war and peace, he became an admiral in 1864.[19] His younger brother Robert Winthrop accompanied him in their early services. He became a lieutenant in 1810 and died, unmarried, in 1827.[20]

Another US-born midshipman was James Pearl, who was baptised on 27 September 1783, at St Paul's, Hertford [i.e. New Hartford], Connecticut.[21] Pearl was a master's mate of three years standing when he was advanced to midshipman in the second-rate HMS *Neptune* (98) on 1 August 1805. He signed for £10.14.0 of prize money and £26.6.0 of Parliamentary Award. Later he obtained a large land grant in Newfoundland and the city of Mount Pearl is named after him.[22] A 17-year-old Elias Symes hailed from somewhere in America,[23] and came as a volunteer from the prison ship *San Damaso*[24] in Portsmouth to join *Orion* on 2 July 1805. Symes fought at Trafalgar and signed for his £10.14.0 of prize money and £26.6.0 of Parliamentary Award. Nothing more is known of his birthplace or of his subsequent career except that, as a midshipman, he was not commissioned as a lieutenant into the Royal Navy. Thomas Mcgill from Virginia is unusual for his age: he was 39 years old at Trafalgar.[25] He had volunteered three years before at the Portsmouth rendezvous, and was rated able seaman when Thomas Bladen Capel commissioned the fifth-rate frigate HMS *Phoebe* (36) on 21 September 1802. Capel evidently valued Mcgill's seamanship because he advanced Mcgill to midshipman on 1 December 1803, even though Mcgill could not read or write, and had no hope of promotion. He made his mark when he collected his £10.14.0 of prize money and £26.6.0 of Parliamentary Award.

The Captain's Cook

At the Battle of Trafalgar, 31-year-old George Sullivan was the captain's cook in the third-rate HMS *Belleisle* (74).[26] He volunteered at the Plymouth rendezvous

---

19   Richard Augustus Yates' portrait is in the National Portrait Gallery, London.
20   TNA ADM 36/16545 and TNA PROB 11/1736/22.
21   TNA ADM 6/104/246 and ADM 107/35/423-425 Lieutenants' Passing Certificates.
22   Mount Pearl, *Wikipedia* <https://en.wikipedia.org/wiki/Mount_Pearl> (accessed 2 April 2019)
23   TNA ADM 37/18 and TNA ADM 36/16244.
24   Formerly the Spanish *San Dámaso* (74), taken by Captain John Harvey at Chaguaramus Bay, Trinidad on 17 February 1797.
25   TNA ADM 36/16809.
26   TNA ADM 36/15814.

and entered the ship on 21 September 1802: *Belleisle* had various short-term commanders until William Hargood took command December 1803.[27] Sullivan's rating implies some degree of personal connection to the captain. However, there is nothing to link him with any of them except perhaps that they were all veterans of the American War, and perhaps they had met then. Sullivan left *Belleisle* on 14 January 1806, being discharged to the depot ship in Plymouth, *Salvador del Mundo*, while Hargood stayed in *Belleisle* until 1809. Where in America Sullivan was born is unknown, but he settled in the West Country of England. From November 1802 onwards he remitted 14 shillings per month to his wife, which was paid at Plymouth,[28] where he also collected his £1.17.6 of prize money for Trafalgar, but not, apparently, his Parliamentary Award.

HMS *Pickle*: A Case History

The history of HM Schooner *Pickle* (10) and her people is better known than that of many other ships.[29] On 9 March 1805, in Jamaica, one George Almy was appointed acting second master and pilot of *Pickle*. Almy had previously been shown in the HM Schooner *Superieure*'s (14) muster book as aged 29 and from Newport, America, and he had joined *Superieure* as a supernumerary in February 1804;[30] he had been rapidly advanced from able seaman to gunner's mate in June, and by August 1804 he was her acting second master. Almy's age was not shown on entry in *Pickle*'s muster list, but in subsequent entries he is shown under 'age on time of entry in this ship' as 30, which would indicate he was born in about 1775. He again gave his place of birth as Newport, America. Almy is a common name in the Newport area, but the records of the town of Newport were taken by the British forces when they evacuated Newport in 1779 and the ship carrying them sank in New York Harbour; what survived was returned and has now been conserved, but researchers have, as yet, been unable to find a surviving birth or

27   'Admiral Sir William Hargood (1762-1839)' in John Marshall, *Royal Naval Biography*, Vol. VIII (London: Longman, Hurst, Rees, Orme, and Brown, 1823-30), p.260; William R. O'Byrne, *Naval Biographical Dictionary: Containing the Life and Services of Every Living Officer in Her Majesty's Navy*, Vol. I (London: John Murray, 1849), p.463. See also Peter Hore, *Nelson's Band of Brothers* (Barnsley, England: Seaforth, 2015).
28   TNA ADM 27/7/19: Allotment registers recording the sending of wages to next of kin by warrant officers, ratings and Royal Marines.
29   Peter Hore, *HMS Pickle: The Swiftest Ship in Nelson's Fleet at Trafalgar* (Stroud: History Press, 2015).
30   TNA ADM 36/15794: Ship muster book, HM schooner *Superieure*, December 1803 to June 1805. *Superieuse* is the name given in the muster book, but evidently she was the *Superieure*, a 14-gun French privateer captured at San Domingo and purchased into the Navy in 1803.

Newport, Rhode Island-born George Almy served as second mate and pilot of HMS *Pickle* until he incurred serious wounds against a French privateer. Painting by Gordon Frickers (Editors' Collection)

baptismal record to identify George Almy's parents' names.[31] The master's logs that the American Almy kept from 10 March 1805 to early 1807 are the principal source of information about *Pickle*'s movements in the months before and after the Battle of Trafalgar.[32]

On sailing from Jamaica, there was no wind when *Pickle*'s crew used the sweeps in order to leave harbour and to recommence the beat to windward towards the Mona Passage. It took two weeks to reach New Providence, Bahamas, and another 10 days to reach Bermuda. There, on 23 April 1805, while at anchor in St George's Harbour, Able Seaman Thomas Bascombe from New York, who had been a pressed man in *Pickle* since 22 July the previous year, was discharged 'per order'. There were Bascombes living in New York and Bermuda, and maybe they were involved in getting Bascombe's American citizenship acknowledged, or perhaps Bascombe

---

31   The author is grateful to Professor John B. Hattendorf for this information.
32   TNA ADM 52/3669: Master's log, *Pickle*, 10 March 1805 to 10 March 1806 and TNA ADM 52/3786, master's log, *Pickle*, 11 March 1806 to 5 January 1807. The dates are taken from Almy's journal in which, though each day's entry runs from midnight to midnight, the date changed at midday.

had waited until he was in a port where he could take an easy passage home to New York. On 25 April, Almy was able to close his log entry for that day with 'made sail for England.'[33]

Somewhere in the vastness of the Atlantic, in April and May, *Pickle* missed both the Combined Fleet and the fleet of Admiral Lord Nelson. However, on 12 May, some 700 miles southwest of Cape Clear in Ireland, *Pickle* did sight a strange sail and gave chase:[34]

> At 8.26 saw a sail to eastward at nine set the main topmast staysail and flying jib … at 1 fired a gun and brought to the *Augusta* of New York from Antigua to Belfast out boat and boarded her … at four the boat returned and in boat and made sail imprest four seamen.

All four were skilled seamen. One of these seamen was a John Oxford, like George Almy, also from 'Newport, America'. Presumably Almy and Oxford recognised each other and Almy persuaded Oxford to volunteer, which he did, and next day he was rated able seaman in *Pickle*'s muster book and received his bounty. The remaining three were not so lucky: Peter Strong, John Bines (?) and William Hogan were transported to Plymouth, where they were sent into the receiving ship HMS *Salvador del Mundo* to begin their service as pressed men in the Royal Navy. Hogan and Strong, both rated as able-bodied seamen, were sent on to other ships on 25 and 28 May respectively. However, by some means, Bines was able to prove that he was indeed an American and was discharged on 11 June 1805: the muster book of *San Salvador* showing 'per Admiralty order being an American'. No correspondence has yet been found as to these circumstances.

Trafalgar

Pickle was the second smallest ship on the British side when, on 21 October 1805, the wind fell to light airs from the northeast and haze. At 0800, Villeneuve had ordered the Combined Fleet to reverse course to the north, but the light airs and lack of sea experience of his captains resulted in a long, broken, curved line. Nelson attacked from the west in two columns, the lee column led by Collingwood in *Royal Sovereign* aimed at the enemy's rear, and himself in *Victory* leading the weather column towards the enemy's centre. As *Pickle* tacked gently between the two fleets, Almy noted, 'At 8 the enemy bore east distance 4 or 5 leagues, the Commander-in-Chief W.S.W. 2 or 3 leagues.' Of Nelson's famous signal ('England

33 TNA ADM 52/3669 and ADM 52/3669.
34 TNA ADM 52/3669 and TNA ADM 52/3669.

expects that every man will do his duty'), Almy laconically entered in his log, 'at ten the Commander-in-Chief made signal to prepare for action with a no. of other signals.'[35]

HMS *Pickle* did not fire her guns in anger at the Battle of Trafalgar, but as the British fleet sailed slowly across the gap that separated it from the Combined Fleet, Lapenotiere and his crew had a grandstand view. A midshipman in *Euryalus* wrote: 'How well I remember the ports of our great ship hauled up, and the guns run out, and as from the sublime to the ridiculous is but a step, the *Pickle*, schooner, close to our ship with her boarding nets up, her tompions out and her four [sic] guns about as large and formidable as two pairs of Wellington boots, "their soul alive and eager for the fray," as imposing as Gulliver waving his hanger before the King and Queen of Brobdingnag.'[36] The battle was succinctly recorded in *Pickle*'s log:

> Log of HM Schooner *Pickle*, from Noon on the 21st to Noon of the 22nd of October, 1805. P.M. Light airs and clear. At 1/2 past 12 the *Royal Sovereign* commenced her fire on the Enemy and broke through the enemy's line the Enemy directed a warm fire on the abovementioned Ship, until she was covered by the *Victory* and two or three other Ships. At 1/2 past 2, we discovered four of the enemy's ships dismasted. The wind being light our ships were not all got in action. At 4 we discovered several of the enemy making their escape. At ½ past 4 the enemy ceased their firing, except four ships, which were trying to effect their escape to windward, and were attacked by two of our ships, but their rigging being damaged, the enemy got off. Nineteen of them struck and one took fire and blew up. Out boats to save the men. At 6 the boats returned. In cutter and made sail. Saved one hundred and twenty or thirty men. At 8, moderate breezes and hazy. Employed assisting the disabled ships. At 12 [i.e. midnight] ditto weather. The Commander [Lapenotiere] went onboard the *Victory*.

There was no mention in Almy's log of the death of Nelson.

On the morning of 22 October, Lapenotiere began to offload his prisoners to other ships, including some to *Revenge* and the second-rate HMS *Dreadnought* (98) and 18 men to the fifth-rate HMS *Euryalus* (36). By the afternoon, the wind had settled into a westerly gale and Lapenotiere began to reduce his sail, double-reefing *Pickle*'s main and foresails and taking in jib sails. At 1800, Almy noted in

35   TNA ADM 52/3669.
36   Rear Admiral Hercule Robinson, *Sea Drift* (Portsea: Hinton & Co., 1858), p.206. The old admiral is showing off his classical education with a misquotation from the *Iliad*.

his log that the wind was strong and squally, the fleet widely separated, and several prizes and injured ships that had been in tow were drifting out of control. There was a storm after the battle and Almy must have played a large part in *Pickle's* survival and in racing her home to Falmouth and Plymouth with the despatches of Vice Admiral Cuthbert Collingwood who assumed command after the death of Nelson. After Lapenotiere was promoted for this feat, Almy and Oxford stayed on in *Pickle*, until January 1807, when Almy was severely wounded in action. *Pickle's* new captain described the action: [37]

His Majesty's Schooner *Pickle*, Plymouth, 5th Jan. 1807
Sir, I beg leave to acquaint you, that on the morning of the 3d instant, the Lizard bearing N. five leagues, I saw a cutter in the S.E. steering to the westward, under press of sail, and a brig in chase of her, which proved to be His Majesty's brig *Scorpion*: all sail was immediately made to close with the cutter, which was effected about ten o'clock. We exchanged a few broadsides. Finding he was pushing hard to get to leeward of us, I laid him on board; and, in a few minutes, was in possession of *La Favorite* French cutter privateer, E.J. Boutruche, Commander, of 14 guns, with a complement of seventy men, one of whom was killed, and two wounded. She left Cherbourg on the 1st instant; has made no capture; is well found, and only two months off the stocks. I am sorry to add, that Mr George Almy, acting Master, and one seaman, are badly, and Mr Charles Hawkins, Sub-Lieutenant, slightly, wounded in boarding ...

However, for Almy the consequences of his wounds in the fight with *Favorite* were more serious. Whatever George Almy's loyalties as an American were, he had been one of the boarders of *Favorite* and taken part in some bitter hand-to-hand fighting. The College of Surgeons examined him later that year and reported that his wounds were 'of equal prejudice to the habit of Body with the loss of a limb and independent of such wounds, he upon the same occasion totally lost the use of an eye.' The Navy Board recommended and the Admiralty approved, 'that as by the New Naval Instructions (Page 393) Mr Almy is entitled under either of these circumstances to the Gratuity of a year's Pay', and on 5 November 1807 he was awarded a year's pay for each injury.[38] Nevertheless, Almy also had to petition for his pay for his time as *Pickle's* second mate and pilot. No captain's certificate was

37   *The Naval Chronicle*, Vol. 16, (1807) p.76.
38   National Maritime Museum (NMM) ADM 354/229/20, 'G Almy, late acting Master of the Pickle Schooner, was injured whilst taking a French privateer. Propose he should receive a gratuity, as was awarded Lieutenant William Cook of the Cerberus the previous May', 5 November 1805.

available, but his master's logs were record enough to show that he was owed some two years' pay, and, with the small sum of prize money owed to him, he became a relatively wealthy man. He is not shown as superseded in the ship's muster list until July 1807, but he was discharged from *Pickle* on 22 February 1807, and William Rourke's master's log was opened on 27 February.

In fact, Almy found a sinecure as a gunner in the dockyard at Plymouth, where he served until September 1814, and it was not for a further few months, until April 1815, that he was found unfit for duty at sea or ashore on the grounds that he had lost the use of his right arm and right eye.[39] Almy married Susanna Easton in St George's, East Stonehouse, on 7 September 1807 and seems to have settled there. The Almys in the USA originated from Devon and Cornwall, and Almy may have found cousins still living around Plymouth. Without his townsman in *Pickle*, John Oxford seems to have lost heart and on 25 April 1807 he was marked 'R' in the ship's muster book. What happened to him is unknown, but he disappeared with a large sum in wages and prize money owing to him. Perhaps he had been swept up by the press gang and placed on another ship, or he may have smuggled himself on a merchant ship bound for America.

Flotsam on a Sea of Information

The preceding information about the Americans in Nelson's Royal Navy is the flotsam on the sea of information which is available to the curious and scholarly researcher in the ATR and in its companion database, the Complete Navy List.[40] As has been demonstrated by the examples given, much needs to be done to analyse these databases. From this preliminary study we can say that there were at least 377 Americans (meaning from the US) at the Battle of Trafalgar and there were also at least 57 Canadians (meaning British North Americans), but that these numbers must be enhanced by whatever portion of another 101 men who are simply shown in the muster books as coming from 'America' or 'North America.'

We can also say that the proportion of pressed men was at least one in five, but that this proportion is increased by the number of pressed men who subsequently volunteered in order to be paid a bounty, and by a large number of men whose status as volunteers or pressed men is not known. And it can be shown that the men who were impressed were predominantly experienced seamen and that landsmen or unskilled men were only about one in ten of those impressed. Finally,

---

39   NMM ADM 354/228/236: 'G Almey [sic] has asked for payment for his time in the *Pickle* schooner. No Captain's certificate is available but records show he acted as 2nd Master and Pilot of the Pickle from 1805–1807. Recommend payment', dated 16 October 1807.

40   Patrick Marioné, Jean-Marie Pâques, and N.A.M. Rodger, *The Complete Navy List of the Napoleonic Wars 1793-1815* [Electronic Resource] (Brussels, Belgium: SEFF, 2003).

we can say that, if the large sample of seamen in the Royal Navy, about one-sixth, as represented by the ATR, is representative of the Royal Navy in 1805, then that there were about some 360 Canadians and some 3,200 Americans in the Royal Navy as whole. Furthermore, that, of these Americans, between 20 percent and 45 percent were pressed men. These numbers are generally far less than contemporary, especially American, sources have reported. However, the reader and researcher must remember the caveats given at the beginning of this chapter. Much work remains to establish how many of these men were pressed or truly volunteers, how many would have claimed American (US) citizenship, and how many were Loyalists, and what were their origins and their destinies.

Biographical Portraits

Mid-Atlantic and South

5

Rear Admiral Sir Robert Barrie, KCB, KCH (1774-1841) – St Augustine, Florida

Dr Thomas Malcomson

Surgeon Robert Barrie, 31st (Huntingdonshire) Regiment of Foot, was posted to Pensacola, West Florida, in 1767.[1] West Florida had been ceded to Britain after the Seven Years War and the 31st was replacing the regiment originally stationed there. The 31st was garrisoned in Pensacola, West Florida, but also served at St Augustine, East Florida, until 1772, when most of the regiment was sent to St Vincent, to suppress the Carib revolt. Surgeon Barrie, who had brought his wife Dorothea (Dolly) [nee Gardner] with him to Florida, stayed in St Augustine. On 5 May 1774, Dolly gave birth to a son who was named after his father.[2] The infant's Scottish father died the following year, most likely of yellow fever. Dolly took her son, Robert, and returned to Preston, Lancashire.

Dolly married George Clayton, a successful merchant, in 1784. Robert Barrie attended schools in Neston, Cheshire and Dedham, Lancashire until the age of 14, when his life took the bearing it would hold for its remainder. His mother's brother, Captain Sir Alan Gardner, took him into the third-rate HMS *Goliath*

---

1   Richard Cannon, *Historical Record of the Thirty-First or the Huntingdonshire Regiment of Foot* (London: Parker, Furnival, Parker, 1850), pp.33-35.
2   John Marshall, *Royal Naval Biography: or Memoirs of all the Flag-Officers, Superannuated Rear-Admirals, Retired Captains, Post-Captains, and Commanders*, Vol. II, Part 2 (London: Longman, Hurst, Rees, Orme & Brown, 1823-1825), p.721. Robert Barrie is listed as a post-captain of 1802.

Rear Admiral Sir Robert Barrie. (© Friends of Point Frederick, Kingston, Ontario)

(74), as a midshipman, after carrying his name in the muster book of the third-rate HMS *Europe* (64) – (formerly HMS *Europa*) – for four years as a servant. This act of familial patronage was a common way for boys to enter the navy. In another act of nepotism, Gardner had Robert placed as a midshipman in Captain George Vancouver's 1790 expedition to the northwest coast of North America. Aboard HMS *Discovery* he took part in the onerous task of surveying the countless inlets, rivers, and islands. Vancouver valued his relentless effort and great skill at surveying, naming Point Barrie, British Columbia, after the young midshipman for his work in that particular area.[3]

Barrie was frequently placed in command of one of *Discovery's* launches and sent, often for days at a time, to survey the coast line.[4] During one such sojourn in June 1793, Barrie and some of his men ate mussels laying along the shoreline at low tide. Back to work in the boat, they found their limbs becoming numb and

3   George Vancouver, *A Voyage of Discovery to the North Pacific Ocean, and Round the World* (London: G.G. and J. Robinson, Paternoster Row, and J. Edwards, Pall Mall, 1798).
4   Vancouver, *A Voyage of Discovery*, pp.285-286.

were dreadfully sick. Barrie had had this experience before, in England, and had found relief after extreme physical exertion. Recalling the memory, he ordered his men to grab an oar and row as hard as they could to shore. Once there, unaffected members of the boat crew helped the men to shore. Barrie recovered quickly, most of the others more slowly, but one man died from the tainted mussels.

When *Discovery* returned to England in 1795, Robert Barrie was promoted to lieutenant and served the next five years in the second-rate HMS *Queen* (90).[5] After a year ashore, he was placed in Captain Thomas Manby's brig HMS *Bourdelois* (24), a former French privateer taken into British service.[6] Manby knew Barrie from the Vancouver expedition. The vessel's low, long and narrow build made it a constantly wet and sickly member of the squadron blockading Flushing, Holland.[7] The Admiralty later sent the brig to the West Indies. On the way out, two strange sails were sighted off the Island of La Palma in the Canary Islands, Spain. With *Bourdelois* 'in a calm,' First Lieutenant Barrie was sent with two boats to board them.[8] After a 14-hour chase, with only his boat left, Barrie boarded a French prize, the captured British merchant ship *Adventure*. Manby re-captured the second ship, another French prize, off Santa Cruz, Tenerife.

Barrie's first ship-to-ship action occurred off Barbados, when *Bourdelois* fought two French brigs and a schooner on 29 January 1801.[9] When the three French vessels were observed bearing down on the *Bourdelois*, Manby shortened sail to let them catch up. At six in the evening, he wore round to engage all three. The largest brig, the *Curieuse* (18), was within 10 yards, while the other two kept a safe distance, as the British worked both broadsides. After a 30-minute engagement, *Curieuse* surrendered with fifty casualties. Manby lost one dead and seven wounded. The badly damaged *Curieuse* sank, taking two of Manby's midshipmen and five sailors with it. The other two vessels fled, though sufficiently damaged to require a return to Cayenne, French Guiana. Wounded during the engagement, Barrie was forced to go below for treatment.

On 23 October 1801, Lieutenant Barrie was made a commander and placed in HM Sloop *Calypso* (16), followed by 12 months in HM Sloop *Shark* (16).[10] Little is

5   Cy Harrison, 'Sir Robert Barrie (1774-1841).' *Three Decks* <https://threedecks.org/index. php?display_type=show_crewman&id=3125> (accessed 2 April 2019)

6   This spelling reflects contemporary documents rather than modern references, *Bordelois*.

7   Flushing and its environs had been a province of Austria when, in 1794, the armies of the French Revolution annexed the Austrian Netherlands and incorporated it into the French Republic

8   Manby to Duckworth, 16 January 1801. *The London Gazette* No. 15351, 4-7 April 1801, p.373.

9   Manby to Duckworth, 1 February 1801, *The London Gazette* No. 15351, 4-7 April 1801, pp.373-374.

10   Marshall, *Royal Naval Biography*.

known of his time aboard these vessels. Being made post-captain 29 April 1802 he left the *Shark*.[11] He spent the next two years ashore. He gained command of the Enterprise class, sixth-rate HM Frigate *Brilliant* (28), from December 1804 to May 1806, sailing in the English Channel and along the Scottish coast. In January 1805, while off the Firth of Clyde, some seamen deserted. Firing several guns, to alert other vessels in the area about the deserters, Barrie alarmed nearby Greenock, where locals thought the French had landed.[12]

Captain Robert Barrie assumed command of the Leda class, fifth-rate HM Frigate *Pomone* (38), in May 1806. His time aboard the frigate demonstrates his zeal for action against the enemy and his reputation for running a tightly ordered ship. Serving under Rear Admiral Sir Richard J. Strachan, in the Bay of Biscay, on 6 June 1807, Barrie destroyed 17 of 27 French merchant ships, escorted by three gunboats off Sables d'Olonne, France.[13] Barrie joined Vice Admiral Lord Collingwood in the Mediterranean in 1808. On 13 June 1809, he captured a three-gun French privateer, the *Lucien Charles*, off Cap Bon (now Watan el-kibli, in Tunisia).[14] On board was Chevalier Charles Lucien Prevost de Boissi, Adjutant General of France. Nothing on the ship revealed why an important member of the French government was in a small craft, sailing off the coast of North Africa. It was surmised that he had been in negotiations with the Barbary Coast pirates. *Pomone* served as the eyes of the squadron blockading Toulon in 1809, warning Collingwood of the French departure on 22 October. The following day, while the British squadron chased the French, Barrie destroyed five transports carrying food for the French forces in Spain. In 1810, *Pomone* captured another prominent Frenchman, Napoleon's brother, Lucien Bonaparte. In response to the civil treatment Lucien and his family received, he offered his captors £300. Barrie declined the offer, but the ship's company gladly enjoyed a round of porter instead.[15]

On 1 May 1810, HM Frigate *Pomone*, together with another fifth-rate frigate, HM Frigate *Unité* (36), and the sloop-of-war, HM Sloop *Scout* (18), fought two French Brigs *la Giraffe* and *la Nourrice*, an armed merchant ship and a shore fortification in Sagone Bay, Corsica.[16] The French position included 200 soldiers, a number of local men under arms, a shore battery of five guns and a mortar, plus

---

11   Thomas L. Brock, 'Robert Barrie', *Dictionary of Canadian Biography Vol. 7, 1836-1850*, para 2 <http://www.biographi.ca/en/bio/barrie_robert_7E.html> (accessed 2 April 2019); Marshall, *Royal Naval Biography*, p.721.
12   Michael Phillips, 'Brilliant' (entry dated 2007), *Michael Phillips' Ships of the Old Navy* <http://www.ageofnelson.org/MichaelPhillips/info.php?ref=0389> (accessed 19 June 2016).
13   Barrie to Gardner, 6 June 1807, *The London Gazette* no. 16040, 6-20 1807, pp.834-838.
14   Untitled, *The London Gazette*, no. 16295, September 9, 1809, pp.1438-1439.
15   Marshall, *Royal Naval Biography*, pp.726-727.
16   Marshall, *Royal Naval Biography*, pp.724-725.

the broadsides of the three ships covering the approach into the bay and the shore around the fortified tower. With no wind, Barrie ordered the three British vessels towed into position. The 90-minute action commenced at 1800. The *Giraffe* caught fire, which spread to the other two ships. Pulling themselves away, the British watched as each of the French ships blew up. Some of the wreckage of *la Nourrice* rained down on the fortified tower, bringing about its total destruction. At the end of the day, Barrie's little squadron had sunk three enemy ships and destroyed a shore fortification.

The *Pomone* was sent to England in September 1811. On the night of 14 October, Barrie left instructions for the ship's master to use the Hurst Lighthouse for entering the narrow western approach to Portsmouth. Unfortunately, the master failed in this task and the frigate was wrecked in Alum Bay, just off the Needles, a notable rock formation at the west end of the Isle of Wight.[17] In the court martial that followed, the master was censored for not obeying Barrie's instructions, while Barrie was acquitted. The *Pomone* archives include the captain's order book.[18] He created this book to ensure that his junior officers were in step with how he wanted the ship and crew to operate. Barrie's orders covered activities such as hoisting and reefing various sails, casting off and hauling in the anchors, and working the great guns. The very words the officers were to use were written out, with the expectation they would be memorised. The book included an order of absolute silence above deck, at all times so that the crew could hear such commands.

Patronage for Robert Barrie went beyond his uncle, who died Admiral Lord Alan Gardner, in 1809.[19] Barrie knew some of Britain's nobility, including Lord and Lady Grenville. His correspondence with the Grenvilles is that of a protégé. He sent them oranges from the Mediterranean, plant seeds, rooted flowers, and even trees from North America.[20] After the wreck of *Pomone*, Lord Melville, First Lord of the Admiralty, personally promised Barrie a new command and a posting in the Mediterranean.[21] But it was not until the fall of 1812 that Captain Barrie was assigned to the fourth-rate 'great' frigate HM Frigate *Grampus* (50). He

---

17   HMS *Pomone, Maritime Archaeology Trust* <http://www.maritimearchaeologytrust.org/ alumbay1> (accessed 2 April 2019).
18   National Maritime Museum, Royal Museums Greenwich, England, MS 80/170 WQB/49, Robert Barrie, *HMS Pomone Establishment and Order Book*.
19   William Stewart (ed.), 'Gardner, Baron Alan (1742-1809)', *Admirals of the World: A Biographical Dictionary 1500 to the Present* (Jefferson, North Carolina: McFarland & Company Inc., 2009), p.139.
20   British Library, Robert Barrie, The Dropmore Papers, Add. 59004 vol. Cl ff 173-265v, Barrie to Lord Grenville, January 12, 1814; Barrie to Lord Grenville, August 19, 1814; & Barrie to Lord Grenville, May 16, 1815.
21   William L. Clements Library, University of Michigan, Robert Barrie File, Melville to Barrie, 12 October 1812.

carried Commodore George Cockburn to Cadiz, to mediate between Spain and its colonies. Barrie then cruised the Straits of Gibraltar, five months after the United States declared war on Britain.

HM Frigate *Grampus* captured six American merchant ships carrying food to the British fighting the French on the Iberian Peninsula.[22] The Americans were sent into the Prize Court at Gibraltar; their agents protested their capture, producing protections from the British Council in Boston, Andrew Allen and from Rear Admiral Sir Herbert Sawyer at Halifax. The Prize Court referred the matter to the British government, who ordered the release of the merchant ships, without explanation.[23] After the ships were released, the Prize Court assessed that they were legal prizes, but to no avail. In a letter to his mother, Barrie wrote that the government's decision cost him £20,000 in prize money.[24]

On 6 November 1812, he was informed he would have a new ship, the third-rate HMS *Dragon* (74), the flagship of Rear Admiral Francis Laforey, commander of the Leeward Islands.[25] In the war against America, the *Dragon* had been assigned to reinforce the British squadron on the North American Station. Barrie wrote to his mother that he did not like the feel of this advancement, being too junior for a 74-gun ship. He saw it as a possible compensation for the loss of his prizes.[26] But this was not the case. Lord Melville issued the order before the prizes were an issue. The assignment was quite likely another stroke of patronage. Lord Melville indicated that this was not the placement into the Mediterranean that Barrie had requested, but promised that the warfare on the North American coast could provide much activity and reward.[27] Even with this monetary incentive, Barrie did not relish the North American Station and told his step-father that he would work to be replaced and sent home.[28] Captain Barrie arrived in Barbados on 11 January 1813, after an agonisingly long seven-week voyage. Barrie shifted his belongings into the third-rate HMS *Victorious* (74) for the trip to Bermuda, where

22   William Perkins Library, Durham, North Carolina, Duke University, Robert Barrie Correspondence, James Brook to Barrie, October 23, 1812; J. Brook to Barrie, October 24, 1812; J. Brook to Barrie, 25 October 1812; J. Brook to Barrie, 1 November 1812; Barrie to George Clayton, 6 November 1812 and Barrie to G. Cutforth, 9 November 1812.

23   William Perkins Library. Robert Barrie Correspondence, Wm. Ingram to Barrie, 14 January 1813.

24   Clements Library, Robert Barrie File, Barrie to George Clayton, 5 April 1813.

25   William Perkins Library. Robert Barrie Correspondence, Barrie to George Clayton, 17 November 1812.

26   William Perkins Library. Robert Barrie Correspondence, Barrie to G. Clayton, 14 January 1813.

27   Clements Library, Robert Barrie File, Melville to Barrie, 12 October 1812.

28   William Perkins Library. Robert Barrie Correspondence, Barrie to G. Clayton, 17 November 1812.

Third-rate, HMS *Dragon* (74), by Antoine Roux 1823. (Open source)

Dragon awaited. As Barrie handed the *Grampus* over to her next commander, Rear Admiral Laforey made it clear to Barrie that he saw the swap as inappropriate.[29]

When Barrie entered the War of 1812, the British, under the command of Admiral Sir John B. Warren, were beginning to blockade the American east coast. From the first arrival of the British off Lynnhaven Bay, Virginia, in the Chesapeake, in late February 1813, African-American slaves began running to the British ships.[30] For the remainder of the war, African-American men, women and children freed themselves from the bondage of slavery by going to the British. Slave owners came out to the ships to convince their former slaves to return. Barrie, as did other officers, always allowed such communication, that is, if the

---

29   William Perkins Library. Robert Barrie Correspondence, Barrie to G. Clayton, 14 January 1813.
30   Thomas Malcomson, 'Freedom by Reaching the Wooden World: American Slaves and the British Navy during the War of 1812.' *The Northern Mariner/le marin du nord*, 22:4 (October 2012), pp.361-392.

African-Americans wanted to speak to the slave owners.[31] Barrie made sure coercion was never used and people did not return to slavery against their will. By the end of November, *Dragon* had 120 men, women and children, all escaped slaves, on board seeking freedom.[32]

In June 1813, the *Dragon* sailed to Halifax, its foremast sprung and the crew reduced by scurvy. Repairs took three weeks, during which time Captain Barrie visited nearby Aboriginal camps, fished, and acquired furs for a coat for his mother. He also spent time with the young women of Halifax. Barrie wrote home of the HM Frigate *Shannon*'s defeat of the US Frigate *Chesapeake*, which he felt was the first American encounter with a professional British officer and a well-trained crew.[33] Barrie worked to have his midshipmen, some with him since the *Pomone*, promoted by the station commander-in-chief, first by Admiral Warren, then by Vice Admiral Sir Alexander Cochrane. These attempts at promotion met with limited success because Barrie's midshipmen had to compete with the midshipmen sent out by the Admiralty. As for his new crew, Barrie often saw them as a 'most troublesome set of black guards.'

The *Dragon* was back in the Chesapeake by September. Barrie was given command of the British forces in the bay, as Cockburn and Warren withdrew for the winter.[34] Left with his 74-gun ship, two frigates, two brigs and three schooners, Barrie's mission was to ensure the blockade of the US Frigate *Constellation* (44), in Norfolk, Virginia, harass local inshore trade, and prevent American merchant vessels and privateers from leaving the bay. Overstretched to accomplish these goals, Barrie watched in frustration as the fast American schooners slipped through the meagre blockade at night, or in strong northerly winds. None of the British ships could catch them. Warren praised Barrie's performance in the bay, but Barrie would rather have been off New York with hopes that the American frigates there would attempt to come out.[35] In January 1814, Barrie bragged of capturing more ships in the previous three months than did 'Warren's fleet last year.'[36] Subsequently, the *London Gazette* published a list of 79 vessels captured or

31   Clements Library, Robert Barrie File, Galye to Barrie, 10 March 1814.
32   Clements Library, Robert Barrie File, Pedlar to Barrie, 5 November 1813, p.395.
33   Clements Library, Robert Barrie File, Barrie to D. Clayton, 23 June 1813.
34   William S. Dudley, (ed.) *The Naval War of 1812: A Documentary History*, Vol. 2, 1813 (Washington, DC: Naval Historical Center, 1992), pp.384-385, Barrie to D. Gardner Clayton, 4 September 1813.
35   Warren to Barrie, 21 December 1813, Barrie Correspondence; Clements Library, Robert Barrie File, Barrie to D. Clayton, September 4, 1813.
36   Clements Library, Robert Barrie File, Barrie to D. Clayton, 12 January 1814.

destroyed by the squadron under Barrie's command, between 6 September 1813 and 12 January 1814.[37]

The extreme winter weather of early 1814 was a hardship for both men and ships. Food was scarce, at times, causing rationing, which Barrie wrote of as 'rough usage.' Captain Barrie allowed his men as much tobacco as they could carry from any of the inshore vessels captured transporting the stuff, in order to offset the hunger. At times it was so cold he could barely hold pen to paper.[38] Still, Barrie managed to send home sheep found on the Chesapeake's Smith's Island, for study by the Board of Agriculture.[39] Barrie's opinion of the war with America was mixed. He was glad not to have been involved in the debacle at Craney Island on 22 June 1813, nor the despicable attack on the town of Hampton, which witnessed former French prisoners of war, serving as independent companies under British command, murder and rape the town's citizenry. He saw the need to restore Britain's reputation as the one true global maritime power, and remind the Americans, whom he referred to as Nathan, of their 'insignificance as a maritime power.'[40]

Admiral Cockburn returned in April 1814, and sent the *Dragon* and the schooner *St Lawrence* up the Chesapeake, in search of the US Baltimore-based flotilla of gunboats under the command of Captain Joshua Barney, USN.[41] Using the ships' boats to get inshore, with the *Dragon* and *St Lawrence* more than a mile south, Barrie was searching for Barney's flotilla along the west coast of the Chesapeake, above the Potomac River. On 31 May, the Americans appeared to the north.[42] With the wind in his favour, Barney pounced on the seven British boats, driving them south. The wind changed, giving the *Dragon* and *St Lawrence* a chance to close with the Americans. Out-gunned, Barney slipped into the Patuxent River. Barrie blockaded the Patuxent and asked Cockburn for reinforcements to attack the flotilla. With the arrival of the fifth-rate HM Frigate *Loire* (44) and the Sloop *Jaseur*, Barney took the flotilla into St Leonard's Creek. On 10 June, the British

37   Robert Barrie, Vessels captured, burnt, or destroyed by His Majesty's Ships and Vessels under the Orders of Captain Barrie, *The London Gazette*, no. 16853 (8 February 1814), pp.307-309.
38   British Library, The Dropmore Papers, Barrie to Lord Grenville, 9 January 1814.
39   M. J. Crawford (ed.), *The Naval War of 1812: A Documentary History, Vol. 3, 1814-1815* (Washington, DC: Naval Historical Center, 2002), pp.17-18, Warren to Barrie, 19 January 1814.
40   Crawford, *Naval War*, Barrie to D. Clayton, 4 February 1814, pp.17-18.
41   Barney was originally an Acting Master Commandant but was raised to a Captain in April 1814. His flotilla varied in size from 18 to 25 vessels.
42   Crawford, *Naval War*, pp.77-79, Barrie to Cockburn, 1 June 1814, Cockburn to Barrie, 3 June 1814; Clements Library, Robert Barrie File, Cockburn to Barrie, 5 June 1814; 21 June 1814.

enticed the Americans (with a bombardment of rockets) to come down the creek and attack the British boats.[43] As the flotilla approached, it came within range of the *Loire* and *St Lawrence*. Barney retreated up St Leonard's Creek. Barrie attempted to lure him out again by raiding villages along the Patuxent, all the way up to Lower Marlborough, burning several tobacco fields and several customs houses. Barney did not take the bait. Cockburn wrote Vice Admiral Cochrane that Barrie's raids in the Patuxent cost the Americans upwards of a million dollars.[44]

Recalled to Lynnhaven Bay, the *Dragon* headed for a refit in Halifax after 12 months at sea. In September, Barrie took part in the British attack on Castine, Maine.[45] This was one of several British offensive initiatives in 1814, including the August raid on Washington, and the attacks at Baltimore and Plattsburg, and the later assault on New Orleans. Led by Lieutenant General Sir John C. Sherbrooke, Lieutenant Governor of Nova Scotia, and Rear Admiral Griffiths, commanding at Halifax, the expedition arrived off Castine, Maine in the morning of 1 September. The invasion force was carried in 10 transports accompanied by HMS *Dragon* and eight other warships. As they approached their target, the British learned that the former frigate, now a sloop-of-war, USS *Adams* (28) was in harbour at Castine; an unexpected bonus. The American fort at Castine opened fire on the British fleet, but before Sherbrooke's soldiers could land, the Americans blew up the magazine, decimating the fort, and disappeared across the Penobscot River. Sherbrooke secured the area, dissuading the local population from assembling their militia. The British possessed Castine with relatively little effort.

The *Adams* escaped and sailed up the Penobscot River to Hampden, nearly 25 miles inland from Castine. The ship's guns were removed and placed on the riverbank to cover the vessel from attack by the river or by land. American soldiers, numbering 1400, were positioned south of the *Adams*, crossing the only road into Hampden from Castine, on the high ground, just north of a bridge that the British had to cross. The dense forest made it impossible for the British to leave the road and sweep around the Americans' flank. At either end of the line were two hills; the one on the east side within cannon range of the river. The Americans placed field pieces on the hills and in the centre of their line. It was a nearly perfect defensive position.

43   Crawford, *Naval War*, p.88, Barney to Jones, 11 June 1813, pp.89-91, Barrie to Cockburn, 11 June 1813.

44   Crawford, *Naval War*, pp.117-120, Cockburn to Cochrane, 25 June 1814. Barney slipped by a becalmed British force on June 26, 1814, going up the Patuxent to greater safety.

45   The narrative is based on Sherbrooke to Bathurst, 18 September 1814; John to Sherbrooke, 3 September 1814; Griffith to Cochrane, September 9, 1814; and Barrie to Griffith, September 3, 1814. *The London Gazette* no. 16944 (8 October 1814), pp.2025-2032.

In command of a naval contingent, including 80 of *Dragon*'s men, Captain Barrie ferried 600 soldiers, under Lieutenant Colonel Henry John, and several field pieces up the Penobscot on 1 September. He landed the soldiers and marines at Bald Head Cove, three miles south of Hampden, late the next day. Drenched by an overnight rain, the soldiers and marines were engulfed in fog as they marched to Hampden. Barrie landed the field pieces and a rocket apparatus before heading up river. British soldiers drove back the American advance pickets. Coming out of the fog at the foot of the bridge, Lieutenant Colonel John ordered his men across, with little loss, formed them up on the other side, and carried the American line as Barrie enfiladed the American position from the river. As their defences crumbled, the Americans set the *Adams* ablaze and headed for Bangor, Maine, pursued all the way by Barrie and John. Barrie reported to Griffith the capture of 25 cannons, of which 11 were destroyed, and the burning of eight vessels, besides the *Adams*. Apart from the raid on Washington, the Castine expedition was the only other success of the British 1814 offensive.

The *Dragon* returned to the Chesapeake in October, where Barrie assumed command of a reduced British naval force as Sir Alexander Cochrane (now the station commander-in-chief) left to begin preparations for operations against New Orleans.[46] Hearing that the American militia had been disbanded for the winter, Barrie decided to conduct shore raids to make the American government recall them.[47] He raided Tappahannock, along the Rappahannock River, on 2 December, taking away tobacco and army equipment and burning the local jail and customs house. Four days later, he landed a force of 600 marines, soldiers and sailors, along with two field pieces at Seven Mile Head. The local militia assembled inland at Farnham Church, and Barrie became determined to give them a fight. Marching overland, he found the American force drawn up across the road outside of Farnham, with three field pieces on a hill behind them. While his skirmishers occupied the front and right flank of the Americans, Barrie took the main force through the forest, around the American left flank, and attacked. The Americans reformed to meet the assault, fired a volley, and ran. Only one of the American field pieces was captured. The other two, along with the militia, disappeared in the thick brush. Barrie returned his force to the boats, gathering in slaves seeking freedom, and left the Chesapeake shore for the last time.

Barrie was then ordered to seize Cumberland Island off the coast of Georgia and harass the mainland. This act was a feint to draw potential American reinforcements away from New Orleans. Barrie sailed on 19 December, heading

---

46   William Perkins Library. Robert Barrie Correspondence, Malcolm to Barrie, 6 October 1814.

47   Crawford, *Naval War*, pp.341-344, Barrie to Cockburn, 7 December 1814.

south to rendezvous with Rear Admiral George Cockburn off Charleston, South Carolina, but Cockburn was delayed at Bermuda.[48] Without the Rear Admiral, Barrie continued south and seized Cumberland Island on 11 January 1815. With 650 Royal Marines and sailors, Barrie pushed over to the mainland and assailed the Fort on Point Petre, which protected the town of St Mary's. Moving through dense underbrush to access the rear of the fort, the Americans ambushed the British. Barrie declared, 'The fire was as smart as any I remember to have been in for about two minutes when Nathan ran and we had no chance of overtaking him.' Without defense, St Mary's capitulated. Approximately 1,000 slaves ran to the British from slave holders in the area. All who had reached British lines by 17 February 1815 (the date the United States ratified the Treaty of Ghent, ending the war) were taken away to freedom. Those who came after that date were returned. With the arrival of Cockburn, Barrie was relegated to coordinating activity on Cumberland Island, his North American assignment at an end.

With the *Dragon* 110 men short of complement, he told his mother that his ship had twice been ordered home but was kept on the station by Cochrane (a compliment to Barrie). 'But,' he wrote, 'I am sadly tired of the lay.'[49] He asked his mother to send documents concerning land ceded to his father in West Florida, which he hoped to reclaim. The question of ownership remained unresolved through 1831, when short mention of it appears in a letter from Julia Barrie (Robert's wife) to her mother-in-law.[50] How this matter finally evolved is unknown.

With the war over, Robert Barrie was recalled home. His junior officers gave him a gift of a silver plate as a mark of their respect.[51] Cochrane wrote to the Admiralty praising Barrie's service in the Chesapeake, noting his 'high sense of the gallantry and indefatigable zeal and devotion to the service which appears at all times to have been manifested by the officer.'[52] Robert Barrie was made a Companion of the Most Honourable Military Order of the Bath, third class on 4 June 1815.[53] Back in England, Barrie put his attention to other matters. He wrote his mother in October

---

48   William Perkins Library. Robert Barrie Correspondence, Barrie to D. Clayton, 22 January 1815.
49   William Perkins Library. Robert Barrie Correspondence, Barrie to D. Clayton, 22 January 1815.
50   Massey Library Archive, Royal Military College, Kingston, Ontario, Barrie Letters from Kingston. FC441.B3A3 1818, J. Barrie to D. Clayton, 3 August 1831.
51   Clements Library, Robert Barrie File, Officers of *Dragon* to Barrie, 24 May 1815; 'Sir Robert Barrie, Obituary', *The Gentleman's Magazine*, (September 1841), p.320.
52   William Perkins Library. Robert Barrie Correspondence, Cochrane to Croker, 7 April 1815.
53   'Whitehall,' *The London Gazette*, no. 17061 (4 June 1815), 1877.

1815, that the 'rain and the girls have kept me pretty much within doors.'[54] He mentioned, 'I am not sure that I am not half in love with one of the misses – when I am certain I shall cut and run.' Cut and run, he did not. The young woman was Julia Wharton Ingilby (age 23), daughter of Sir John Ingilby, whom he married on 24 October 1816. The couple moved to France. Barrie was 42 years old, and with peace, further naval employment seemed unlikely.

But the Admiralty had one last assignment for Barrie. At the end of the War of 1812, Britain and the United States agreed to limit their naval forces on the Great Lakes. The 1818 Rush-Bagot agreement allowed each nation to have two warships on the upper Great Lakes; one on Lake Ontario and one on Lake Champlain, each with one gun. The Admiralty needed a dock yard commissioner to tend the warships in ordinary, keeping them unarmed but ready for any renewal of hostilities. The first commissioner, Sir Robert Hall, died in February 1818. After a lengthy negotiation, Barrie accepted the posting, arriving in Kingston, Ontario in July 1819.[55] Barrie commanded the main dock yard at Point Frederick, opposite the town of Kingston, Upper Canada, where the Cataraqui River enters Lake Ontario, and small naval establishments on Lake Erie, Georgian Bay, and Isle aux Noix, in the Richelieu River. He also oversaw the storehouse at Montreal and a depot at Lachine, on the St Lawrence River. At Point Frederick, two unfinished first rates stood in their stocks, two ships were drawn up on shore, with six others housed over at anchor, or kept by the wharfs.[56]

Decay had rendered the ships nearly useless. The only saving grace was that the American lake ships were just as dilapidated.[57] The British government's poor financial state greatly affected Barrie's tenure. The situation was impressed upon Barrie as the Admiralty, taking the opportunity of his appointment, lowered the pay of the officers and men on the Great Lakes. Not only did they remove a stipend paid to compensate the seamen for working on the lakes, they asked the men to pay back what they had received since May 1817. The Admiralty rejected Barrie's plea to, at least, not seek repayment.[58] Barrie enlarged the commissioner's residence at Point Frederick and added an ice house. Both projects drew censorship from the Admiralty due to the costs. His wife Julia, and their two children, William and

54   William Perkins Library. Robert Barrie Correspondence, Barrie to D. Clayton, 21 October 1815.
55   Massey Library Archive, RMC, Barrie to D. Clayton, December 5, 1818; Barrie to D. Clayton, 27 January 1819; Thomas L. Brock, 'H.M. Dock Yard, Kingston under Commissioner Robert Barrie, 1819-1834.' *Historic Kingston*, no. 16, 1968, pp.3-22; see p.6.
56   T. L. Brock, 'H.M. Dockyard', p.8.
57   Massey Library Archive, RMC, Barrie to D. Clayton, 31 October 1819.
58   Queen's University Archive, Kingston, Ontario, 2160.2, box 1 file 2, J. Barrow to Barrie, 18 January 1820 and Barrie to Montresor, 14 May 1820.

Julia (ages unknown), arrived in mid-1820.[59] Three more children were born at Kingston; Dorothea (Dolly) in 1821, Eliza in 1823, and Georgiana in 1825.[60] Barrie was a strict yet, loving father, who pushed the children to engage in their studies. Letters exchanged with his grown daughters reflect a positive relationship, though he still commented on spelling errors.[61]

Robert and Julia Barrie were part of Kingston's social elite, hosting large dinners and dances on Point Frederick, arranging hunting trips and boat outings among the local islands, and celebrating the Royal births, deaths and coronations with banners and illuminations.[62] Charity to the needy and encouragement of local farmers to breed better livestock were part of their contributions to the community at large. They socialised with the Governor General and Lieutenant Governors of Upper and Lower Canada. Barrie promoted the first Welland Canal, allowing ships to move from Lake Ontario across the Niagara Peninsula to Lake Erie, and the Rideau Canal linking Lake Ontario with Montreal via the Ottawa River.[63]

Barrie planted a sizable garden and built a greenhouse at Point Frederick, growing fruit and vegetables, even pineapples; a first in Canada.[64] His pineapples adorned the tables of the Lieutenant Governor in York (now Toronto) and the Governor General in Quebec. He bred horses and fox hounds.[65] They lived on his commissioner's salary (£1,425 per annum) and though money was tight, he paid his creditors.[66] Commissioner Barrie also oversaw the building of a large stone warehouse to store ship rigging, sails, and other material. The four-story structure was called the 'Stone Frigate' and serves today as a residence for cadets at the Royal Military College, which occupies the former dockyard site.

In 1824, an outbreak of cholera raged in Upper Canada. Barrie ordered every building at Point Frederick, including the privies, to be cleaned and whitewashed and the privies' contents to be treated with lime.[67] When the contagion cut a swath of death through Kingston, not a person perished on Point Frederick. Barrie,

---

59   Massey Library Archive, RMC, Barrie to D. Clayton, 28 February 1820.
60   Georgiana became a nun and served as a nurse with Florence Nightingale in the Crimea. William entered the Royal Navy and retired as a Captain.
61   Massey Library Archive, RMC, Barrie to J. Barrie [daughter], 13 March 1828,
62   T. L. Brock, 'Commodore Robert Barrie and his Family in Kingston, 1819-1834.' *Historic Kingston*, No. 23 (1975) pp.1-18; see pp.7, 9-10.
63   Massey Library Archive, RMC, Barrie to Peregrine, 17 March 1828.
64   Massey Library Archive, RMC, Barrie to D. Clayton, 19 December 1824.
65   'Daghee – Property of Commodore Barrie, commanding British Naval Forces in Canada', *American Turf and Sporting Magazine*, 5:5 (January 1834), pp.225-227; 'That beautiful full bred horse ...'; *American Turf and Sporting Magazine.*, 5:8 (April 1834), inside back cover; 'Valuable Dogs', *American Turf and Sporting Magazine*, 5:2 (November 1813), p.150.
66   Massey Library Archive, RMC, Barrie to D. Clayton, 27 January 1819; & Barrie to Fannie Lyon, 18 April 1824.
67   T. L. Brock, "H.M. Dock Yard", pp.14-15.

frustrated with the continual cut backs, and fearing for his family's health, returned to England, on leave, in the summer of 1825.[68] After two years, the Admiralty convinced him to continue by making him a commodore. Barrie returned to Kingston but left his family in England for the next three years. He returned to England for nine months in 1830 to retrieve his family. Only fear of a war with the US and Barrie's own advocacy kept the Great Lakes naval establishment active.[69] The budget dissolved from £12,000 in 1822 to £8,000 by 1834.[70] Barrie passed austerity measures on to the officers in charge of the various establishments under his command. He warned against over-expenditure and promoted the keeping of accurate accounts. He dismissed the Lake Erie clerk for failure to provide timely and accurate accounting reports.[71]

Finally, in 1834, the British government could no longer justify the expense and ordered Commodore Barrie to dispose of the remaining vessels and supplies.[72] Julia Barrie and the four girls left Kingston at the end of May. With another outbreak of cholera, no official dinner was given for the Barrie family who had contributed so much to the town.[73] Robert and William stayed to see the sale of the items they were not taking back to England, leaving on 12 July 1834 with little fanfare.[74] Back in England, the Barrie family lived at Ripley Castle where Julia died November 23, 1836, at the age of 43.[75] There is no information as to what took her life. Barrie left Ripley Castle and moved to Swarthdale, Lancashire.

Upon his return to England from Canada, Robert Barrie was made a Knight Commander of the Royal Hanoverian Guelphic Order, in October 1834. In July 1838, he was promoted to the rank of Rear Admiral of the Blue.[76] He received his Knight Commander of the Bath, on 4 July 1840.[77] Sir Robert Barrie died in his home in Swarthdale at age 67, on 7 June 1841. No cause of death was stated in his

68   Massey Library Archive, RMC, J. Martin to Barrie, 27 January 1825,
69   E. Laws to Barrie, 20 February 1822. Massey Library Archive, RMC, Terry McDonald, "'It is Impossible for His Majesty's Government to withdraw from these Dominions" Britain and the Defence of Canada, 1813 to 1834', *Journal of Canadian Studies* 39:3 (Fall 2005), pp.40-59.
70   Massey Library Archive, RMC, J. Martin to Barrie, March 7, 1822; J. B. Pickett to Barrie, 9 January 1834.
71   Queen's University Archive, 2160.2, box 1 file 2, Barrie to E. Burton, 1 October 1820.
72   Massey Library Archive, RMC, J. Barrow to Barrie, 11 January 1834; Barrow to Barrie, 10 January 1834.
73   McDonald, 'It is impossible', p.53.
74   Brock, 'Commodore Robert Barrie', p.16.
75   'Deaths'. *The Nautical Magazine and Naval Chronicle*, London: Simpkin, Marshall and Co., (1837), p.63.
76   'Admiralty, June 28, 1813', *The London Gazette*, No. 19631 (3 July 1838), p.1491.
77   'Downing Street', July 4, 1840, *The London Gazette*, No. 19872 (7 July 1840), pp.1599-1600.

obituary.[78] He was laid to rest, next to his wife, in All Saints Church, on the grounds of Ripley Castle. Apart from Vancouver naming a point of land after Barrie, there is a Barrie Creek and a Barrie Reach in British Columbia, and Barrie Island in Lake Huron.[79] The small community of Barriefield, just outside the former dock yard, was named by John Marks, Barrie's secretary while at Kingston. The city of Barrie, Ontario, was named in honour of Barrie's service at Kingston.

Rather than fleet actions, Sir Robert Barrie's career was primarily one of cutting out, shore raids and independent commands. Throughout his service, from his days as a midshipman under George Vancouver, through those as a frigate captain under Strachan and Collingwood, into the War of 1812, Sir Robert's reliability to complete his assignment, and his leadership of those serving under him, were the two characteristics upon which his superior officers came to rely. His talent for organisation and creating order made him suitable as commodore in charge of HM Dock Yard at Kingston, Upper Canada. For four decades Sir Robert Barrie served King and Country with dedication and determination, leaving behind him an example to those who followed in the Royal Navy.

78   'Obit, Sir Robert Barrie', *Gentleman's Magazine*, (September 1841), p.320.
79   Brock, 'Robert Barrie', *Dictionary of Canadian Biography*, para 5.

6

Captain Nicholas Biddle (1750-1778) – Philadelphia, Pennsylvania

Chipp Reid

Her name was Elizabeth Elliott Baker. She might have had one of the biggest impacts on the war at sea during the American Revolution, even though few would know about her involvement. Elizabeth was the 18-year-old daughter of Thomas Bohun Baker, a wealthy South Carolina plantation owner who lived just outside of Charleston. By all accounts, Elizabeth was one of the prizes of Charleston society. She could speak French, Italian and Latin, knew mathematics, and as the eldest child, stood to inherit a considerable fortune.[1] No one knows how many suitors she had, but in mid-1777, she forgot them all when a dashing 27-year-old Continental Navy captain, regarded by many as the Horatio Nelson of the America's Revolutionary War, arrived in South Carolina. He was Captain Nicholas Biddle.[2]

The comparison is no mere hyperbole. Biddle was arguably the most talented and best trained captain in the fledgling Continental Navy, even more so than John Paul Jones. He had served with Nelson in the Royal Navy and was, by most accounts, a close friend of the future British hero.[3] Biddle's adventures as a young mariner likely caught Nelson's attention, strengthening their bond when they were midshipmen on the same ship. And, just as Nelson's life changed when he

---

1   Edward McCrady, *The History of South Carolina in the Revolutionary War, 1775-1778* (New York: MacMillan & Co., 1901), pp.282-285.

2   Library of Congress, Washington, DC, Edward Biddle Memorial, Nicholas Biddle Papers, Manuscript Division.

3   Washington Irving, 'Nicholas Biddle', in John H Frost (ed.), *American Naval Biography* (New York: John Low, 1821), p.90.

Portrait of Captain Nicholas Biddle, by Orlando Lagman. (NHHC NH 51535)

met Lady Emma Hamilton,[4] so, too, did Biddle's when he met Elizabeth Baker. His arrival in Charleston and relationship with Elizabeth was the catalyst for a series of decisions that would have tragic consequences for both Biddle and the Continental Navy.

The romance with Elizabeth and command of the Continental Frigate *Randolph* was the culmination of what had already been an adventurous and, at times, an arduous life for Biddle. Born in Philadelphia on 10 September 1750, he was the eighth child of nine born to William Biddle and Mary Scully. Though his family was once prosperous, by the time he was four, his father's failed investments and subsequent death in 1754 left the family destitute. Nicholas grew up watching his mother struggle just to keep her brood clothed, fed and housed.[5] As adults, his four

4   Tom Pocock, *Horatio Nelson* (New York: Alfred A. Knopf, 1988), p.172.
5   Charles Biddle, *Autobiography of Charles Biddle: President of the Executive Council of Pennsylvania* (Philadelphia: E. Claxton & Co., 1855), p.3.

oldest siblings, James, born in 1731, Lydia, born in 1734, John, born in 1736 and Edward, born in 1738, all supported their mother. Lydia lived in the British colony of Antigua, as the wife of a retired Royal Navy officer, William McFunn.[6] The five youngest children – Charles, Abigail, Mary, Nicholas and Thomas – grew up feeling an obligation to work at an early age to help support their mother.[7]

At age 16, Charles found a job as a deckhand on a merchant ship his sister's husband, William McFunn, owned. Two years later, in 1764, Nicholas asked his mother for permission to follow his brother. Nicholas had grown up near the Wharton Shipyard in Philadelphia and yearned to go to sea. After some argument, his mother relented and Nicholas signed on as a cabin boy on the snow *Ann and Almack*, in which McFunn had a one-third ownership interest. By this time, Charles was second mate.[8] Leaving Philadelphia on 11 October 1764, the little vessel carried a load of pig iron, barrel staves and flour bound for Antigua.[9] The voyage south took nearly a month. From Antigua, the *Ann and Almack* sailed to British Honduras (modern-day Belize), and then Jamaica, before pointing again toward Philadelphia, where she arrived on 2 September 1765.[10]

The nearly year-long voyage did little to dull Nicholas' desire for the sea. He signed on for a second cruise and shipped out on 20 October 1765, bound for Jamaica, which the *Ann and Almack* reached in early November.[11] After picking up a cargo of flour and iron, Captain McFunn, who commanded the voyage, sailed once more for the British Honduras. On 2 January 1766, the snow was in the eastern Caribbean, sailing just off the Northern Triangles, a particularly dangerous chain of reefs, when a sudden gale drove the *Ann and Almack* onto a reef. She stuck fast and was in danger of being smashed by towering waves when McFunn ordered the crew to abandon ship. However, the crew could not abandon ship because a wave had carried away the ship's longboat, leaving just a small yawl in which to escape. McFunn put Nicholas in charge of the craft. Biddle calmly launched it and expertly kept it away from the wrecked snow. 'He did everything he was ordered with as much coolness as he would have done alongside a wharf,' his brother said.[12]

The 10-man crew remained on the wreck for a day, when McFunn ordered the crew to put provisions into the little yawl and make for an island eight miles

6   William Bell Clark, *Captain Dauntless: The Story of Captain Nicholas Biddle of the Continental Navy* (Baton Rouge, Louisiana.: Louisiana State University Press, 1949), pp.16-18.
7   Clark, *Captain Dauntless*, pp.16-18.
8   Clark, *Captain Dauntless*, p.19.
9   Clark, *Captain Dauntless*, p.20.
10   Biddle, *Autobiography*, pp.4-5.
11   Biddle, *Autobiography*, pp.4-5.
12   Biddle, *Autobiography*, pp.4-5.

away. Once there, the crew spent two days making trips back and forth to the wreck, salvaging as many supplies as possible. McFunn decided to sail the yawl to Antigua for help but could take only five others with him. The crew drew straws to see who would remain behind. Nicholas was one of the four who stayed on the island.[13] McFunn promised to send a rescue party back for the stranded men once he reached safety, although none of the four castaways believed McFunn could reach Antigua in the tiny lifeboat.[14] Nicholas and his companions spent 13 days on the island, surviving on lizards, a bit of ship's bread, and salt pork. Their only water came from a pair of brackish pools. Although it slaked their thirst, the water caused mild dysentery, which added to the castaways' misery.[15]

On 18 January 1766, a small ship appeared off the island. The castaways at first feared the newcomers were Spaniards – and they were correct – but leading them was Nicholas' brother, Charles. The brothers had a tearful reunion and remained on the small island, this time fully supplied, while they salvaged the cargo from the *Ann and Almack*.[16] The brothers remained with McFunn, sailing the Caribbean, and did not return to America until July 1766.[17] On their return, Charles bought his own ship while Nicholas continued sailing for McFunn. In 1769, Biddle parted company with his brother-in-law to become the first mate on the merchant ship the *Rotterdam*, which made three trips to Europe. During this period, Biddle began to acquire some wealth, buying 200 acres of land in Bucks County, Pennsylvania, a prosperous agricultural area north of Philadelphia. He also supported his mother.[18]

By 1770, Biddle had grown weary of merchant service and cast his eyes toward service in the Royal Navy. He was 20 years old and his reputation as a mariner had spread throughout the colonies. A contemporary described him as possessing a 'temper [that] was uniformly cheerful, and his conversation sprightly and entertaining ... [he was] remarkably handsome, strong and active, with the most amiable mildness and modesty of manner. A sincere Christian, his religious impressions had a decided and powerful influence upon his conduct.'[19] Biddle's family connections had grown just as steadily. His older brother, Edward, was a judge and politician who convinced Joseph Galloway, Speaker of the Pennsylvania House of Representatives, to write to Benjamin Franklin, asking the famed

13   Biddle, *Autobiography*, p.7.
14   Biddle, *Autobiography*, p.7.
15   Biddle, *Autobiography*, pp.9-10.
16   Clark, *Captain Dauntless*, p.32.
17   Clark, *Captain Dauntless*, p.32.
18   Irving, *American Naval Biography*, p.95.
19   Description from a portrait by Charles Wilson Peale (1741-1847), National Portrait Gallery, Washington, DC.

colonial representative to petition for a warrant for Biddle. Franklin agreed. The two met in June 1771 in London. The meeting left a lasting impression on Biddle, who wrote to his brother James that Franklin, 'Made a long speech full of advice and encouragement,' and that he was struck by Franklin's 'kind and free manner with which he delivered it.' On 22 June 1771, Biddle received his appointment as a midshipman and reported for duty to Captain Walter Sterling on board the sixth-rate HM Frigate *Seaford* (20).[20]

Biddle spent six months on the *Seaford* before transferring with Sterling, and a select group of *Seafords*, to the fourth-rate HM Frigate *Portland* (50). This 'great' frigate was bound for the West Indies. War with Spain loomed over the far-away Falkland Islands, breathing excitement into Biddle's service. However, the war rumours soon proved false and Biddle settled into the monotonous routine of the peacetime Royal Navy.[21] The *Portland* spent a year in the West Indies, returning to England before going into ordinary on 13 October 1772. He spent that winter in London, waiting for a lieutenant's commission and orders to report for duty.[22] By March 1773, news swirled around London of an expedition to find an Arctic passage.

Constantine Phipps, later Lord Mulgrave, a noted Royal Navy captain and explorer, was in charge of the expedition. Biddle sought out his former captain, Walter Sterling, and asked for his help in securing a place on the expedition. Sterling demurred, telling Biddle that Phipps had already selected his officers and midshipmen.[23] The old captain, however, failed to cool Biddle's enthusiasm. Biddle decided to enlist as a seaman on either HMS *Racehorse* or HMS *Carcass*, the two bomb ketches that were being specially fitted out at Deptford and Sheerness for the Arctic expedition. Biddle went first to Sheerness, where he learned the *Racehorse* already had its full complement of 90 sailors. He then went to Deptford, where on 4 May he enlisted on the *Carcass*, keeping secret that he was a midshipman in the King's naval service. [24] A former sailor from the *Portland* was also among the crew and he recognised Biddle from their days together. Believing Biddle had been demoted, the sailor "was greatly affected" and approached Biddle to ask what happened. Biddle explained why he had enlisted as a seaman and the sailor, 'was equally surprised and pleased when he learned the true cause of the young officer's

20   Library of Congress, Biddle Papers, Nicholas Biddle to James Biddle, 17 July 1771.
21   Clark, *Captain Dauntless*, pp.46-50.
22   Library of Congress, Biddle Papers, Nicholas Biddle to Lydia McFunn, 20 October 1772.
23   Library of Congress, Biddle Papers, Edward Biddle Memoir.
24   The National Archives (TNA), Kew, London, ADM 36/7567: Records of the Navy Board and the Board of Admiralty, Ships' Muster Rolls: HMS *Carcass* 1773. Biddle's name is spelled 'Beddle' in the muster books. He was rated 'AB' and from 11 May as 'Coxswain'. He received his £3 bounty as a volunteer.

disguise, and he kept his secret as he was requested to do.'[25] Phipps accepted Biddle as an able seaman before rating him as a coxswain based on Biddle's stated experience.[26]

At 23 years old, Biddle reported aboard *Carcass* on 7 May and shortly after his arrival, he met the young midshipman who came aboard as a coxswain, the 16-year-old Horatio Nelson.[27] Despite their age difference, Biddle and Nelson were kindred spirits. Both possessed a desire for adventure and an innate quality of leadership. Biddle likely enthralled Nelson with tales from his merchant marine service and the two became fast friends.[28] The expedition set out on 4 June 1773 and by 24 July, was off Svalbard Island in the northern Greenland Sea. Ice abounded and within days, it had trapped both vessels. Captain Skeffington Lutwidge, commander of the *Carcass*, sent Biddle and Nelson out in long boats to scout the few passages through the ice while sailors tried to cut the ships loose.[29] As the ice continued to encase the vessels, the sailors took the opportunity to frolic on the ice. This moment of abandon probably gave Nelson the idea of disobeying Lutwidge's orders and striking out on his own trip of exploration. He needed an accomplice and found a ready one in Biddle.[30]

The identity of Nelson's companion on his adventure is disputed, but according to a biography of Biddle published in 1949, one night while the *Racehorse* and *Carcass* remained trapped, the two coxswains sneaked past the mid-watch and set out across the ice for Svalbard Island. [31]A heavy fog covered their escape, although it lifted by 3 a.m. Lutwidge soon realised he was missing two men and a sharp-eyed lookout spotted Biddle and Nelson traipsing over the ice in pursuit of a bear. Lutwidge called out for both to return to the *Carcass* immediately. Biddle hesitated, looking toward the ship, and called on Nelson to return with him. Nelson, however, refused and while Biddle made his way back, Nelson continued his hunt. His musket, however, misfired, leaving him at the mercy of the bear. Only a large chasm in the ice prevented the animal from getting at the future admiral and a shot from one of *Carcass*' great guns frightened the bear off. A chagrined

25   Irving, *American Naval Biography*, p.93.
26   Library of Congress, National Biddle Papers, Nicholas Biddle to Lydia McFunn, 23 October 1773.
27   TNA ADM 36/7567: 'Admiralty Ships'.
28   Irving, *American Naval Biography*, pp.94-95.
29   Constantine John Phipps, Baron Mulgrave, *A Voyage Towards the North Pole Undertaken by His Majesty's Command, 1773* (Dublin: Sleater, Williams, Wilson, Husband, Walker & Jenkin, 1775), p.63.
30   Clark, *Captain Dauntless*, pp.66-68.
31   Clark, *Captain Dauntless*, pp.66-68.

Nelson returned to the *Carcass* where both Biddle and Nelson received an earful from their captain.[32]

Biddle and Nelson served together for the remainder of the expedition. They returned to England in October 1773, and parted company, although neither would forget the other. Biddle spent the winter in London, waiting for assignment to a warship. In a letter to his sister, Lydia, he expressed the lesson he learned from his adventure with Nelson on the ice while espousing an outlook that embraced the boldness that defined his and Nelson's character and future service. He told her, 'not to credit idle tales; for you must know I have been so frightened, so terrified at hearing of the surprising difficulties we encountered, the dreadful dangers we were in, that I am positive my hand shakes while I write, and what astonishes me most of all is that during the whole voyage, I did not apprehend danger.'[33] Biddle remained in London and submitted an application to take part in an expedition to the Antarctic, but events in the American Colonies scuttled his plans. By December 1773, the situation between England and her North American colonists had deteriorated to the point that bloodshed appeared inevitable. Biddle, unwilling to turn his hand against his own family, submitted his resignation to the Royal Navy and returned to Philadelphia.[34] Before he left England, his mentor, Captain Sterling, and 'many others' attempted to persuade Biddle to remain loyal to King George III. Whether Nelson was one of those who spoke with Biddle is unknown.[35]

Biddle spent a year in Philadelphia, watching as the colonies and their mother country moved closer to war. It marked the longest period of time he had spent with his family since he first shipped out as a cabin boy nearly 10 years earlier. Following Lexington and Concord, the Committee of Safety in Philadelphia decided to build and equip several sail galleys to defend the Delaware River. The committee put Biddle in command of the largest, a 65-foot vessel named the *Franklin*. The ship was part sailing ship, part row galley and designed for riverine warfare, with a shallow, somewhat flat bottom. He commanded the galley for four months, when he accepted a commission in the fledgling Continental Navy and took command of the brig *Andrea Doria*, a converted merchantman Congress purchased in October 1775.[36]

---

32   Robert Southey, *The Life of Horatio Lord Nelson* (no location indicated; Astounding Stories 2017 reprint of 1813 edition), pp.7-8; Irving, *American Naval Biography*, p.95.

33   Library of Congress, National Biddle Papers, Nicholas Biddle to Lydia McFunn, 23 October 1773.

34   Clark, *Captain Dauntless*, p.70.

35   Clark, *Captain Dauntless*, p.73.

36   Worthington C. Ford, et al. (eds.), *Journals of the Continental Congress, 1774-1789* (Washington: Government Printing Office, 1904-37), Electronic Edition, Vol. 3, p.443. The

Biddle's new ship carried 14 four-pounder guns and a crew of 112 men.[37] She was part of the small flotilla Commodore Esek Hopkins led in an attack on Nassau in the Bahamas. The Continental Marines, under Captain Samuel Nicholas, stormed the town, marking the first time American troops captured a foreign town. Biddle and the *Andrea Doria* played only a small part in the raid, the crew remaining on board the *Doria* while marines and sailors from the *Cabot, Columbus* and *Alfred* carried out the attack.[38] It proved fortuitous, as did his insistence that his crew receive vaccinations against small pox, which had broken out in the American squadron. The sailors on the *Doria* were the only ones not infected and soon the sick from other ships crowded on board the brig, which became a hospital ship to the flotilla, returning to New London, Connecticut on 14 April 1776, where Biddle unloaded war material captured at Nassau.[39]

Biddle returned to sea with the brig *Andrea Doria* on 4 May. Seventeen days later, he captured his first prize: a brigantine laden with rum, salt, and molasses bound for Liverpool. On 29 May, he captured a pair of British ships transporting a group of 42nd Royal Highland Regiment (The Black Watch) officers and men to Halifax. Biddle sailed to Newport, Rhode Island, arriving 21 June 1776, and again set out on a cruise on 10 July, capturing four ships carrying Loyalist refugees from Virginia and their supplies as well as a large schooner carrying rum and sugar bound for England. All told, he took 14 prizes in his cruises before relinquishing command on 17 September 1776 and transferring to the fifth-rate frigate *Randolph* (32).[40] His tally was the top among all Continental Navy captains.[41]

Throughout his time in command of the *Andrea Doria*, Biddle forged a reputation as a bold mariner and as a compassionate captain. He trained his crew daily in gunnery and ran his ship as though it was in the Royal Navy. When Congress authorised the construction of 13 frigates, ranging in size from 28 to 36 guns, Biddle was at the top of the list to command. At 26 he was the youngest of the 13 captains and ranked fifth in seniority.[42] His reputation in the colonies and beyond was even greater. When his brother Charles fell into English hands during

---

Andrea Doria was also known as the *Andrew Doria*.

37   *Dictionary of American Naval Fighting Ships* Vols. 1-8, 1952-1991 (Washington, DC: Naval History Division, 1992), Digital edition on *Dictionary of Naval Fighting Ships* <http://www.hazegray.org/danfs/> (accessed 2 April 2019)

38   Nicholas Biddle, *Journal of the Andrea Doria*, March 4, 1776, Vol. 4, p.171 in William Bell Clark (ed.), Naval Documents of the American Revolution, OCLC 426774 (Naval History Division, Dept. of the US Navy, Washington, DC, Government Printing Office, 1964).

39   Naval History Division, Dept. of the US Navy, Report of Captain Samuel Nicholas, Continental Marines, April 10, 1776, *Naval Documents*, pp.748-752; 14 April 1776, p.818.

40   Clark, *Captain Dauntless*, p.148.

41   Clark, *Captain Dauntless*, p.148.

42   Ford, et al, *Journals of the Continental Congress*, Vol. 5, p.412.

a voyage to the West Indies, his captor pointed to an article in the *Pennsylvania Gazette* extolling the virtues of the young captain and asked Charles whether he was related to 'Captain Biddle.' Charles told the Briton somewhat proudly that the captain was his brother and his captor immediately put Charles in irons.[43]

Bad luck, or so it seemed, plagued Biddle's initial time in command of the *Randolph*. The first purpose-built, keel-up warship launched for the Continental Navy, the ship, Biddle said, 'Is the very best vessel for sailing that I ever knew.' That was, when she could sail. After her launch in October 1776, the British blockade and an early winter kept the frigate trapped in the Delaware until late January 1777. Thaw finally allowed her to slip past the Delaware Capes into the Atlantic. She cleared the capes on 6 February 1777 and appeared ready for a cruise.[44] The sojourn in open water lasted barely a day. A gale sprang up that shattered the fore and mainmasts, forcing Biddle to make for Charleston, South Carolina, under a jury rig. She arrived on 12 March and immediately drew crowds, despite her appearance.[45]

Although he had been to the city twice before while in the merchant service, and his brother, Charles, had contacts there, Biddle was a relative newcomer to the city. However, his reputation as a fearless sea warrior was well-known in the Palmetto City and he had many admirers. One of them was a young militia lieutenant who lived in a palatial home along the Hobcaw River called Archdale Manor – Thomas Bohun Baker – who invited Biddle to see the house and meet his family, including his four sisters, one of whom was the 18-year-old Elizabeth Elliott Baker. Named for her mother, Elizabeth captivated Biddle. The first visit led to many others and the *Randolph's* captain's barge became a common sight on the Hobcaw.[46]

Biddle had plenty of time to get to know Elizabeth. A fever and desertions had reduced Biddle's crew to less than 100 men, and repairs to the *Randolph* proceeded slowly. The new masts did not arrive until 14 May and the sailors and shipwrights began the laborious process of stepping in the masts to restore *Randolph* to duty. Despite the difficulty, the repairs were finished on 10 June. Two days later, a freak bolt of lightning hit the new mainmast, shattering it 'from cap to deck.' Once more, sailors and shipwrights went through the process of removing the broken mast and replacing it. They finished on 2 July but just eight days later, another storm and another bolt of lightning shattered the third mainmast. It would be another three weeks before the *Randolph* would be ready for sea.[47]

43   Biddle, *Autobiography*, pp.90-91.
44   Naval History Division. Dept. of the US Navy, Robert Morris to Commissioners in France, February 15, 1777, *Naval Documents*, Vol. 7, p.1229.
45   Clark, *Captain Dauntless*, pp.182-186.
46   Biddle, *Autobiography*, p.107.
47   Biddle, *Autobiography*, p.189.

Biddle occupied his time with two tasks. The first was to find enough crew to man his ship. Unfortunately for him, privateers operating from Charleston had claimed most of the able seamen in the port, including several men from Biddle's crew. Biddle appealed to Governor John Rutledge for help, but there was little the powerful Rutledge could do to convince seamen or anyone else to accept the lower wages the Continental Navy offered. The *Randolph* remained only partially manned throughout the summer.[48]

Biddle's second task was likely far more agreeable, as he continued wooing Elizabeth Baker. The two spent the Fourth of July together on the *Randolph*, which is when several biographers say he proposed to the planter's daughter.[49] By late July, Biddle also spent some of his time explaining to his betrothed the purpose of what was then a new-fangled instrument that he installed on the *Randolph*. After lightning did indeed strike twice in the same place – namely, the frigate's mainmast – Biddle decided to install a lightning rod, an invention of his Royal Navy sponsor Benjamin Franklin. Although in use on buildings, Biddle was the first naval officer to install the apparatus on a warship.[50] Charleston residents came out in droves to see what, to them, was a novelty. Among the crowds was Elizabeth, who was a near-daily visitor to the frigate.[51] The time with Elizabeth taught Biddle one major lesson about his betrothed – he could not support her on a navy salary. She was a child of privilege and while he was a successful and increasingly well-known naval commander and a moderate land owner, Biddle believed it would not be enough to convince Thomas Baker to part with his daughter. He would need a successful cruise to increase his holdings.[52]

Although he did not know it, both Congress and the governor of South Carolina had hatched plans that would give Biddle the opportunity to greatly increase his personal wealth. Governor John Rutledge in Charleston and Robert Morris in Philadelphia wanted to hit the British where it would hurt them the most and boost both the local and national economies. Both men cast their eyes on the rich Jamaica sugar convoys that sailed for England carrying the wealth of the Caribbean to Britain. For Morris, the potential to capture part of it was a risk worth taking.[53] For Rutledge, the reason was far more immediate. British ships

48   Naval History Division, Dept. of the US Navy, John Dorsius to Robert Morris, 28 August 1777, *Naval Documents*, Vol. 9, p.821.
49   Irving, *American Naval Biography*, p.97.
50   Naval History Division, Dept. of the US Navy, John Dorsius to Marine Committee, 28 August 1777, *Naval Documents*, Vol. 9, p.821.
51   Library of Congress, National Biddle Papers, *Edward Biddle Memoir*.
52   Biddle, *Autobiography*, p.105.
53   Marine Committee to Nicholas Biddle, 29 April 1777, *Journals of the Continental Congress 1775-1789*, Letters of Delegates, Vol. 6, p.681 (Library of Congress, Washington, D.C.:

operating out of Jamaica and Antigua had stifled the South Carolina economy. He had to do something to bring money into Charleston. Rutledge also dreamed of controlling the wealth that flowed in and out of the British West Indies and saw in Biddle and the *Randolph* the perfect weapon with which to accomplish both.[54]

Despite his orders from Congress and pleas from Rutledge, Biddle was unable to recruit men to man the frigate. He asked Rutledge to provide money for bounties, but the governor at first refused, saying he did not have the available cash. The two men met in early September, and Major General William Moultrie, the hero of the defence of Charleston the previous year, also attended. Moultrie argued against the bounties, citing the same reasons Rutledge presented. The governor and Biddle then went into a room and had a private talk. Moultrie never recorded what the two men discussed. When they returned to the main meeting, however, Rutledge had agreed to advance Biddle money to offer bounties and would recoup the cash from any prizes Biddle took with the *Randolph*, which would come only into Charleston.[55] It did not take long for Biddle to make good on his promise to the governor.

The *Randolph* slipped out of Rebellion Row in Charleston Harbour on 10 September 1777. One week later, *Randolph* lookouts spied five ships – one larger than the rest – on the horizon. Biddle expertly steered his frigate toward the ships and quickly came up on the bigger vessel, a ship pierced for 20 guns. She was the armed merchantman *True Briton* out of Jamaica and was the escort to four ships ranging in size from the *True Briton* to a small sloop. The *True Briton* opened fire on the *Randolph* the minute her captain spotted the Grand Union flag flying from the American frigate. The *Randolph* made no reply, instead closing ominously and silently on the British vessel. The *True Briton* fired three more broadsides, striking the Randolph but causing no real damage or casualties. Still, Biddle held his fire. He was parallel to the *True Briton* and within pistol shot when he ran out his guns and demanded the surrender of the British ship. The captain of the *True Briton* promptly hauled down his colours. Biddle quickly corralled three of the remaining vessels, with only the small sloop escaping. Combined, his four prizes carried more than 600 puncheons of rum, tons of sugar and other material.[56] It was a huge haul and Biddle escorted his prizes back to Charleston, where the governor and

---

Manuscript Division). Order instructions prevented Biddle from opening them until 10 July.

54   William Moultrie, *Memoirs of the American Revolution So Far as It Related to the States of North Carolina, South Carolina, and Georgia*, Vol. 1 (New York: David Longworth, 1802), p.100.
55   Moultrie, *Memoirs*, p.102.
56   Naval History Division, Dept. of the US Navy, Nicholas Biddle to Robert Morris, 12 September 1777, *Naval Documents*, Vol. 9, pp.919-920.

the people greeted him as a hero.[57] An Admiralty Court condemned the prizes and their cargoes, which sold for more £90,000.[58] Biddle's cut was 10 percent – £9,000 or more than $1.3 million in 2014 dollars.[59]

In spite of all the problems with weather, freak lightning strikes, rotted masts, and lack of crew, Biddle's captures earned the *Randolph* the reputation as a lucky ship and increased Biddle's fame. Rutledge wanted him to immediately lead a cruise to Jamaica, but the *Randolph* needed a refit. Although there was no doubting her sailing qualities, the long refit and time in harbour had allowed barnacles and other marine growth to foul her bottom and Biddle wanted to have the frigate's bottom cleaned and coppered.[60]

At the same time, news reached Charleston that the British had captured Philadelphia and the Royal Navy was on its way to renew its southern blockade. By October 1777, the fifth-rate HM Frigates *Carysford* (20) and *Lizard* (20), together with the sixth-rate HM Sloop *Perseus* (20) and HM Brig *Hinchinbrook* (8), were patrolling off Charleston. Within a month, the British had again choked off the seaway into the city, alarming Rutledge, who turned to Biddle and the *Randolph* for help. Rutledge asked Biddle to take command of a flotilla that included the South Carolina state ships *General Moultrie* (20), *Volunteer* (18), and *Notre Dame* (16) and drive off the British.[61] Biddle hesitated, pointing out that the state ships were barely manned. Rutledge appealed to the state and Continental forces in the area for volunteers but found none. Moultrie suggested it would be easier to recruit men if Rutledge announced that Biddle would lead a naval force on a cruise against the Jamaica convoy, which held the lure of rich prize money. Moultrie made a powerful argument and Rutledge agreed to equip the *General Moultrie* (20), and the brigs *Notre Dame* (16) and *Fair American* (16) and *Polly* (14), all under Biddle's command. The Continental Navy captain, sensing this was his moment, agreed.[62]

Weather and the blockade stranded Biddle and his flotilla in Charleston throughout the winter. It was not until 12 February 1778 that Biddle and the *Randolph* cleared the bar off Charleston and slipped into open waters of the Atlantic. The British blockade had lapsed, allowing the five American ships to begin their cruise. At first, it was uneventful. The Americans did not see another

57   Naval History Division, Dept. of the US Navy, John Dorsius to Robert Morris, 12 September 1777, *Naval Documents*, Vol. 9, pp.920-921.
58   Naval History Division, Dept. of the US Navy, John Dorsius to Robert Morris, 12 September 1777, *Naval Documents*, Vol. 9, pp.920-921.
59   Lawrence H. Officer and Samuel H. Williamson, 'Computing "Real Value" Over Time With a Conversion Between UK Pounds and US Dollars, 1774 to Present', *Measuring Worth* (2016) <https://www.measuringworth.com/> (accessed 2 April 2019)
60   Clark, *Captain Dauntless*, p.228.
61   Moultrie, *Memoirs*, p.195.
62   Biddle, *Autobiography*, p.106.

ship until 6 March, when the *Polly* captured an English schooner.[63] Late the next day, 7 March 1778, lookouts spotted several sail on the horizon. One of the shapes was larger than others and it headed for the American flotilla. Biddle knew that his old ship, the fourth-rate HMS *Portland* (50), was patrolling out of Antigua. What he did not know was that the third-rate HMS *Yarmouth* (64) was also on station, and it was the larger *Yarmouth* that was approaching Biddle's squadron.[64]

Captain Nicholas Vincent, commander of HMS *Yarmouth* could see that the approaching ships were armed but could not tell in the dwindling daylight whether they were friend or foe. He brought the *Yarmouth* to bear on the second largest of the ships and slowly closed the distance.[65] Biddle, from *Randolph's* quarterdeck, watched the British ship manoeuvre toward the *Notre Dame*. He turned his frigate into the wind, but instead of tacking, kept her in the wind, backing her sails, stopping the frigate. The captains on the *General Moultrie* and *Notre Dame* followed, but not the *Fair American* and *Polly*, which tacked through the wind and had to sail in a large circle to come back up on the wind.

Even in the fading light, it was clear the approaching ship was a two-decker. Biddle, however, believed he could outgun any one opponent unless it was a ship-of-the-line. Only the 20-gun *General Moultrie*, however, carried artillery to match the *Randolph* – nine-pound cannons. The other four ships had six or four-pounders, which would do little damage unless the gunners could get into a raking position. The *Randolph* had 12-pounders on her gun deck and six-pounders on her foredeck.[66] By 7 p.m., HMS *Yarmouth* was within hailing distance of the *Norte Dame* and demanded her captain identify himself and his ship. The American claimed to be a merchant ship out of British-held New York. Vincent was about to demand the same information from the skipper of the *General Moultrie* when the *Randolph* suddenly hove into view. Her lines and gun ports betrayed her as a warship. Biddle let the *Yarmouth* come up. His gunners had loaded their 12-pounders with bar and chain shot, while on the foredeck they had grape and canister to sweep the enemy deck. Biddle refused to answer repeated hails from Vincent, who hailed for a last time threatening to fire on Biddle unless he answered. Biddle's answer was concise. He ran up the Grand Union flag and let loose a broadside that swept over the *Yarmouth*.[67]

63   Biddle, *Autobiography*, p.107.
64   Biddle, *Autobiography*, p.107.
65   Naval History Division, Dept. of the US Navy, Nicholas Vincent to James Young, *Naval Documents*, Vol. 11, p.684.
66   Naval History Division, Dept. of the US Navy, Notre Dame Letter, *Naval Documents*, Vol.11, p.562.
67   Naval History Division, Dept. of the US Navy, Nicholas Vincent to James Young, *Naval Documents*, Vol. 11, p.684.

The *Randolph* and the *Yarmouth*.

Continental Frigate *Randolph* vs HMS *Yarmouth*, by J.O. Davidson. (NHHC NH 1102)

The American broadside completely surprised Vincent and his crew. The British replied, but their first shots went over the *Randolph*. On board the *Randolph*, the American gunners went about their work with grim precision. The two ships were barely 30 yards apart and blasted away at one another, but it was the Americans who made their shots count. The *Randolph's* crew fired three broadsides for every one broadside from the *Yarmouth*. The British ship was quickly a wreck. The American gunners shot off the British ship's bow sprit, shattered her mizzen and shredded most of her lower rigging, endangering her fore and mainmasts. Above deck, 50 men selected from the crack 1st South Carolina Regiment, many armed with rifles, poured fire onto the deck of the *Yarmouth*. Vincent, and his first and second lieutenants all went down with wounds while a rifle shot killed the quartermaster at *Yarmouth's* helm. Biddle had also gone down with a wound as a splinter tore open his left thigh. Nevertheless, he ordered his men to bring him a chair and he continued to direct the battle.

The *General Moultrie* and *Notre Dame* joined the fight, firing three broadsides, although the wind forced both vessels to break off. The *Notre Dame* actually fired on the *Randolph* by accident. Both ships attempted to get into a raking position, the *Notre Dame* on the bow and the *General Moultrie* at the stern. It appeared to the captains of both American vessels that Vincent was ready to strike his colours. Just as they managed to get into position, a massive explosion illuminated the night sky. When the smoke and debris cleared, the *Randolph* was gone. Out of a crew of 302 sailors and marines, only four men survived. Nicholas Biddle was dead. American naval icon John Paul Jones reportedly wept on hearing the news of Biddle's death, while Horatio Nelson is also reported to have mourned the loss of his friend.[68]

Biddle's career was tragically short. In the few months he commanded ships of war, he displayed the same courage and audaciousness that would characterize the service of his former messmate, Horatio Nelson. In one of his last letters to his brother Charles, Biddle embraced a philosophy that could have come from Nelson: 'I fear nothing but what I ought to fear,' Nicholas wrote. 'I am much more afraid of doing a foolish action than of losing my life. I am for character of conduct as well as courage and hope to never throw away the vessel and crew merely to convince the world that I have courage. No one has dared to impeach it yet. If any should, I will not leave them a moment of doubt.'[69] Although his life and career were short, Captain Nicholas Biddle left a memorable mark on both the Royal and Continental Navies. His legacy has also been secured in the US Navy, which later christened four warships in his honour.[70]

68 Account of the battle from Clark, *Captain Dauntless*, pp.237-242; Biddle, *Autobiography*, pp.107-109; Irving, *American Naval Biography*, pp.97-101; Naval History Division, Dept. of the US Navy, *Notre Dame* Letter, *Naval Documents*, Vol. 11, p.562; Vincent to Young, Vol. 11, p.684.

69 Library of Congress, National Biddle Papers, Nicholas Biddle to Charles Biddle, 16 June 1776.

70 These warships were (1) USS *Biddle* (TB-26), a torpedo boat in service from 1901-19 (2) USS *Biddle* (DD-151), a destroyer commissioned 1918 and in use through 1945 (3) USS *Biddle* (DDG-71, a guided missile destroyer commissioned in 1962 and renamed *Claude V. Ricketts* in 1964 (4) USS *Biddle* (CG-34), a guided missile cruiser in service from 1967-93.

7

Ordinary Seaman William Cooper (1784-1812) – Brookhaven, New York

Matthew Brenckle

Unfortunate events have a way of raising from obscurity men and women who otherwise would have vanished into the recesses of history. The misfortunes of William and Dorothea Cooper ensured their lives were documented in a way rivalled by few of their contemporaries. Born in 1784 at Poospatuck, a Unkechaug tribal reservation near Brookhaven on the southern shore of Long Island, New York, William Cooper was described as 'a man of large stature and more than ordinary elegance and agility.'[1] As with many members of the tribe, he hired himself as a labourer to local landowners. In 1806, while working on the nearby farm belonging to the Robert family, he met and married Dorothea (Dolly) Smith, a servant who had worked in the Robert household for more than 20 years.[2] The marriage ceremony took place on the reservation and was officiated 'by a person professing to be a minister of the gospel, and who was a coloured man or an Indian, … whose name was Paul [Cuffee] and who was well-known among the colored people and Indians in Suffolk County by the appellation of minister Paul, and who was also known by that appellation among the white people in said county.'[3]

Cooper worked on the 'lay' system. He earned wages, but also received foodstuffs and other goods from his employers. These items were deducted from his pay, and as time went on, he began to accrue larger and larger debts. After

1   John A. Strong, *The Unkechaug Indians of Eastern Long Island, A History* (Norman, Oklahoma: University of Oklahoma Press, 2011), p.166.
2   National Archives, Washington, DC, War of 1812 Pension files, File no. 272, RG 15, Dorothea Cooper Pension Application.
3   National Archives, Washington, DC, Cooper Pension Application.

three or four years of working on the Robert's farm, as well as the nearby property of US Senator John Smith of New York, Cooper 'at the time or soon after, ran away and went to sea', leaving Dorothea and their two young daughters to fend for themselves.[4] Cooper shipped aboard a merchant vessel called the *Salvadore* as a seaman.[5] During a European voyage in 1809, he was impressed into the Royal Navy. Cooper sent letters home to Dorothea asking her to obtain 'certain papers,' most likely a seaman's protection certificate or proof of citizenship and send them to the American Consul at Liverpool or London. According to US State Department records, however, Cooper was detained on board the floating battery, HMS *Princess* (26).[6] The British refused to discharge him because he had 'a spurius [sic] Protection.'[7] Before Dorothea could obtain the documents, word came that William had been lost at sea: 'That being on board his Britannic Majesty's ship the *Defence* he was cast away in the Baltic somewhere in the year 1810 or 1811, that the ship with all her officers and crew including said Cooper, were totally destroyed and had perished.'[8] In one of the more tragic incidents in Royal Navy history, the third-rate HMS *Defence* (74) and the second-rate HMS *St George* (98) ran ashore on the coast of Jutland on Christmas Eve, 1811 with a tremendous loss of life.

In a remarkable case of good timing, William Cooper was not among the drowned. In March or April 1812, Dorothea received a letter from Senator Smith (for whom Cooper had previously worked), informing her that, to his surprise, he had discovered William Cooper among the crew of the fourth-rate US Frigate *Constitution*, then refitting at the Washington Navy Yard. Apparently, Cooper swam from the *Defence* while the ship lay at anchor in the Thames in February 1811 and had enlisted aboard the fifth-rate US Frigate *Essex* (32), which was

4   National Archives, Washington, DC, Cooper Pension Application. John Smith (1752-
      1816) was an American politician from New York. He served in the US House of
      Representatives from 1800 to 1804 and the US Senate from 1804 to 1813. Smith also
      served as a major general in the New York State Militia.
5   Strong, *Unkechaug*, p.166.
6   J.J. Colledge and Ben Warlow, *Ships of the Royal Navy: The Complete Record of all Fighting
      Ship of the Royal Navy from the 15th Century to the Present* (London: Chatham Publishing,
      2006), p.227. HMS *Princess* was a former Dutch East Indiaman, *Williamstadt en Boetzlaar*,
      that was captured by the Royal Navy when the British took the Dutch colony at the Cape
      of Good Hope in 1795. Taken into the Royal Navy as a sixth-rate frigate of 28 guns, the
      Princess had been converted to a floating battery in 1800. She was sold at Liverpool in
      1816.
7   National Archives, Washington, DC, Department of State Records Relative to Impressed
      Seamen, RG 59, 'A Return or List of American Seamen and Citizens who have been
      Impressed and held onboard His Britannic Majesty's Ships of War from 1st October to 31st
      December 1809 inclusively'.
8   National Archives, Washington, DC, Cooper Pension Application.

visiting England at the time.[9] After the ship's return to the United States, Cooper was transferred to the *Constitution*. According to the ship's muster roll, Cooper joined *Constitution*'s crew on 4 August 1811 as an ordinary seaman. A few months after Smith's letter, one or two letters arrived from Cooper (written for him by someone else because Cooper was 'unable to write') confirming this explanation of events. One of these letters may have been dated around 12 October 1812 and informed Dorothea that William was still serving aboard *Constitution*, then in Boston Harbour, and that he had survived unscathed the battle with the fifth-rate HMS *Guerriere* (38). Cooper also indicated that it was 'his intention to return to her as soon as his term of service should expire.'[10]

USS *Constitution* vs. HMS *Guerriere*. (NHHC NH 118645)

9   Strong, *Unkechaug*, p.167.
10   National Archives, Washington, DC, Cooper Pension Application.

The ship soon sailed from Boston on another cruise, this time under the command of Commodore William Bainbridge. According to the ship's quarter bill, Cooper served as the first sponger for gun number nine on the quarterdeck.[11] This was an exposed position, and during the engagement with the fifth-rate HMS *Java* (38), on 29 December 1812, Cooper was killed by enemy shot. When the ship returned to the United States in February 1813, a list of killed and wounded appeared immediately in newspapers nationwide, and that was how Dorothea learned her husband had been killed. Senator Smith wrote letters on Dorothea's behalf requesting the pay and prize money owed Cooper, which, according to Daniel Robert, came to approximately $200 after Cooper's debts were paid.[12] Dorothea survived William by many years and became a fixture of the Unkechaug community. She eventually remarried. Her second husband drowned in a fishing accident and her third died in 1847. In the 1850s she successfully applied for a bounty land grant and was able to reinstate her pension. She died sometime between 1865 and 1870.[13]

11   National Archives, Washington, DC, Bainbridge Battle Bill, Series 464 Box 222 Subject Files 1775-1910, RG 45.
12   Strong, *Unkechaug*, pp.168-169.
13   Strong, *Unkechaug*, p.178.

8

Admiral Sir Francis Laforey, 2nd Baronet of Whitby, KCB (1767-1835) – Virginia

Harold 'Pete' Stark

Sir Francis Laforey, 2nd Baronet of Whitby, KCB, Admiral of the Blue, had a long and distinguished career with the Royal Navy, including serving as one of Vice Admiral Lord Nelson's captains at the Battle of Trafalgar. Through birth and service, his life and career were closely linked with North America. Not only was Laforey born in the first English colony of what would become the United States, making him a native-born American, he also successfully served on various North American stations, predominantly in the Caribbean, and as Commander-in-Chief of the Leeward Islands Station during the War of 1812. Laforey was well-respected in his profession, and although his ship, the third-rate HMS *Spartiate* (74), was one of the last to engage at the Battle of Trafalgar, he was instrumental in turning away a late attempt at attack on the heavily damaged British fleet by the French van, and provided much needed relief service during the severe storm that followed. While greatly benefiting from the patronage of his father in his early career, Laforey created his own reputation and legacy through his very capable actions and personal merit.

Sir Francis Laforey was descended from significant military ancestry. His grandfather, Lieutenant Colonel John Laforey, Governor of Pendennis Castle at Falmouth in Cornwall, was the only son and heir of Louis Laforey, brother of the Marquis de la Forest, who had crossed to England with King William III.[1] However, it was his father, Admiral Sir John Laforey, 1st Baronet of Whitby, who

---

1   John Marshall, *Royal Naval Biography or Memoirs of all the Flag-Officers, Superannuated Rear-Admirals, Retired Captains, Post-Captains, and Commanders,* Vol. 1, Part II (London: Longman, Hurst, Rees, Orme and Brown, 1823), p.446.

Coat of Arms of Sir Francis Laforey, KCB, 2nd Baronet of Whitby. (Heraldry Online)

set his son on the naval path upon which he moved so successfully. To understand Laforey, we must also understand something of his father, whose service in the Royal Navy provided an excellent example for him to follow. His influence was critical to his son's early progression in the Royal Navy. Sir John served under Admiral Keppel on the North American station in 1755. He was present at the capture of Lewisburg under Admiral Boscawen and was with Admiral Sir Charles Saunders at the capture of Quebec. Assigned to the West Indies, he was at the reduction of Martinique under Admiral Sir George Rodney. During this time, Sir John became closely tied to the island of Antigua, which in turn led to his stay in the Virginia colony.[2]

In 1763 at Antigua, Sir John married Eleanor, daughter of Colonel Francis Farley, Royal Artillery, member of the Council of Antigua, and one of the judges of

2   *New Monthly Magazine and Literary Journal*, Part 3, London: Henry Colburn (1835), pp.131-132.

that island.[3] After their marriage, and the birth of their first daughter in London in March 1764, John took a leave of absence from the navy and lived for several years with the Farley family in Virginia at Maycock's (Maycox) Plantation. Maycock's was located on the south side of the James River, directly across the water from Westover plantation, home of the very influential William Byrd, with whom the Farleys frequently interacted. While Maycock's Plantation no longer exists, the site survives as Maycocks Point, part of the James River National Wildlife Refuge.

During his leave of absence, Sir John moved within colonial Virginia society, taking some part in the management of the plantation. His name appears as the subscriber for an advertisement in Williamsburg's *Virginia Gazette*, 16 May, 1766, offering a three-pound reward for the apprehension and delivery to Maycock's of a 22-year-old runaway slave named Jemmy.[4] It was likely at Maycock's that Francis was born on 31 December, 1767, giving him his Virginia roots.[5] Sir John had returned to the service by 1770, when he commanded the fifth-rate frigate HMS *Pallas* (36), for a short time. In September 1776, he commanded the second-rate HMS *Ocean* (90), and was present in the action off Ushant on 27 July 1778. Sir John returned to the West Indies as Commissioner of the Navy at Barbados and the Leeward Islands, residing at Antigua and acting as commander-in-chief when no flag officer was present.[6] In 1789, Sir John Laforey was created 1st Baronet of Whitby, and appointed Rear Admiral of the Red on 10 November 1789. He took command of the Leeward Islands Station shortly thereafter and was still in command when the war with France broke out in 1793. He captured Tobago soon after the wars with revolutionary France began. At his death, he had reached the rank of Admiral of the Blue. Francis' service would mirror that of his father in many ways.

Francis' early naval service benefited directly from his father's influence; yet, throughout his career Francis demonstrated that he possessed his own significant ability in his chosen profession. He entered the navy early in his life, as was customary, and in 1791 at age 24 he was made commander and appointed to HM Sloop-of-War *Fairy* (16), on the Leeward Islands Station under command of his father. Upon the capture of Tobago in spring 1793, Sir John sent Francis home with dispatches to the Admiralty concerning the action.[7] As the bearer of the

---

3   *New Monthly Magazine*, pp.131-132.
4   *Virginia Gazette*, Issue 782, Williamsburg, Virginia (16 May 1766,), p.3.
5   Charles D. Rodenbough, *History of a Dream Deferred: William Byrd's Land of Eden* (Raleigh, North Carolina: Lulu, 2009), p.86.
6   Sidney Lee (ed.), *Dictionary of National Biography*, Vol. 11 (New York: Macmillan, 1909), p.396.
7   Tom Wareham, *The Star Captains: Frigate Command in the Napoleonic Wars* (Annapolis, Maryland: US Naval Institute Press, 2001), p.170.

dispatches, he was rewarded, as was the practice at that time, with promotion, and was made post-captain on 5 June 1793, four days after *Fairy's* arrival in England.

Author Tom Wareham considers Laforey a 'star captain' because of his successful frigate commands.[8] Appointed to the sixth-rate frigate, HMS *Carysfort* (28), on 29 May 1794, he captured the French frigate *Castor* (32), which, in the action, had 16 killed and nine wounded out of 200 aboard. *Carysfort* had one killed and six wounded out of 198. However, the capture of *Castor* put Laforey in an unanticipated legal bind. *Castor* had previously been captured from the Royal Navy and placed into French service. Following her arrival in port as Laforey's prize, the Lord Commissioners of the Admiralty made the claim that the ship be considered a recovered prize and restored to the service, with payment only on customary salvage, a considerably smaller amount of money than if it had been declared a legitimate prize. Laforey successfully protested this ruling, even calling the French captain of the captured prize to testify. The French captain stated that he had been appointed to the command of *Castor* by the French admiral, by whose orders and commission he took possession of her at sea, as a ship-of-war in the service of the French republic. He stated that under French practice, the admiral was fully authorised to take such a step without sending the prize first to France for adjudication according to process.[9] As a result of Laforey's challenge, Sir George Marriot, judge of the High Court of the Admiralty, cited the following from the Prize Act in declaring *Castor* to be a lawful prize: 'That if any ship or vessel re-taken, shall appear to have been, after the taking of his Majesty's enemies, by them set forth as a ship of war, the said ship or vessel shall not be restored to her former owners or proprietors, but shall in all cases, whether retaken by his Majesty's ships, or by any privateer, be adjudged a lawful prize for the benefit of the captors.'[10] *Castor* was returned to service and Laforey and his crew were awarded the full prize amount. The decision provided a significant precedent for subsequent similar cases.

Appointed to the fifth-rate frigate HMS *l'Aimable* (32) in the summer of 1795, Francis returned to the Caribbean, conveying his father to Antigua where he took up his post as Commander-in-Chief and Military Governor of the Leeward Islands Station. Francis remained in the Caribbean under his father, commanding the frigate *Beaulieu* for a short time early in 1796 before being placed in command of the third-rate HMS *Scipio* (64). He was very active during this time, supporting the capture of the Dutch Caribbean settlements of Demerara, Essiquibo, and Berbice. Sir John was relieved as commander-in-chief by Rear Admiral Sir Hugh

8   Wareham, *Star Captains*, pp.170-172.
9   Marshall, *Royal Naval Biography*, p.447.
10   Marshall, *Royal Naval Biography*, p.448.

Christian on 21 April 1796, the day Demerara surrendered. Soon afterward, he left for England. However, on 14 June 1796, two days out from England, he died of yellow fever, and was buried in Portsmouth on June 21. Francis succeeded to the baronetcy.

Upon returning from the Leeward Island Station in 1797, Laforey was appointed to the fifth-rate frigate HMS *Hydra* (38), and assigned to the Channel Station.[11] In company with the bomb vessel HMS *Vesuvius* and cutter HMS *Trial*, on 1 June 1798, off l'Havre, he gave chase to a French frigate, corvette, and cutter. The French frigate *Confiante* (36), with 300 men, ran on shore, and was protected from boarding by the gathering of troops on shore. However, *Confiante* was burned by a British boarding party the following morning; most of the crew escaped to shore. The French cutter likewise was driven on shore and destroyed while the corvette, *Le Vesuve* (20), escaped under the protection of a French land battery of two 24-pound guns. There were no British casualties.[12] Once again Laforey returned to the Leeward Islands Station, remaining there from 1799 to 1800. Upon his return to England he was appointed to the third-rate HMS *Powerful* (74), serving in the Baltic and Mediterranean, and then once more in the Caribbean until the Peace of Amiens was signed on 25 March 1802.

When the Peace of Amiens failed on 18 May 1803 and war resumed, Laforey took command of the third-rate HMS *Spartiate* (74). *Spartiate* was built in 1793 in Toulon, France. Large for her class, she nevertheless carried a reputation as a good sailor. She was captured at the Battle of the Nile on 1 and 2 August 1798, after battling with the British ships *Theseus*, *Vanguard* (Nelson's flagship), *Minotaur*, and *Audacious*, and taken into the Royal Navy.[13] Laforey and *Spartiate* were back in the West Indies in April 1805 as part of Rear Admiral Alexander Cochrane's squadron, returning to European waters following Nelson's pursuit of French Admiral Villeneuve and his combined fleet to the Caribbean.

On 21 October 1805 a British fleet of 27 ships-of-the-line, ranging in size from 64 to 100 guns each, was off Cape Trafalgar under the command of Vice Admiral Lord Nelson. The fleet was loosely formed into a weather and a lee column driving respectively to the centre and rear of the 33 ships-of-the-line of the French and Spanish combined fleet. The weather column formed up behind Nelson in HMS *Victory* (104), the lee column behind Vice Admiral Collingwood in the first-rate HMS *Royal Sovereign* (100). *Spartiate* was the last ship in Nelson's column, and due to the light winds prevailing during the battle, did not come into action until

11   Wareham, *Star Captains*, p.170.
12   Sylvanus Urban, *The Gentleman's Magazine and Historical Chronicle for the Year MDCCXCVIII, Vol. LXVIII, Part the Second,* London: John Nichols (1798).
13   Robert Holden Mackenzie, *The Trafalgar Roll* (London: Chatham Publishing, 2004), p.112.

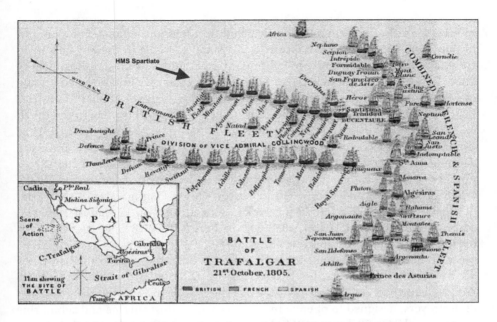

Map of the Battle of Trafalgar depicting position of HMS *Spartiate*. (Open source)

mid-afternoon. However, her position in the weather column proved fortuitous. *Spartiate* engaged *Formidable*, Admiral Pierre Dumanoir's flagship from the as-yet untouched French van, as it attempted to return to the aid of the centre and rear of the combined fleet. *Spartiate*, along with the third-rate HMS *Minotaur* (74), exchanged fire with five enemy ships-of-the-line as they passed, forcing the Spanish third-rate *Neptuno* (80), to surrender – the last surrender from the combined fleet. *Spartiate* survived the Battle of Trafalgar with three killed and 20 wounded, a relatively light butcher's bill. Her relatively good condition was invaluable during the severe storm that shook the British and French fleets after the British victory. She took the third-rate HMS *Tonnant* (80), in tow and kept her safe during the subsequent storm. Sir Francis Laforey was prominent during the funeral of Lord Nelson, carrying the standard in the first barge in the funeral procession from Greenwich.

In *Spartiate*, Sir Francis served under Rear Admiral Sir Richard Strachan before the port of Rochefort, France from 1807 – 1808, blockading Vice Admiral Allemand's five ships-of-the-line.[14] He then returned to the Mediterranean, serving under Vice Admiral Collingwood until promoted to rear admiral on 31

14   Mackenzie, *Trafalgar Roll*, p.113.

July 1810. During this time, he participated in numerous actions. For example, in June 1809 he aided in the capture of the island of Ischia in the Bay of Naples, commanding the landing of two light infantry battalions of the 81st Regiment of Foot (Loyal Lincoln Volunteers) and the Corsican Rangers under the command of Major General Robert MacFarlane and Brigadier General William Lumley.[15] Following his service in the Mediterranean, Laforey hoisted his flag in the third-rate HMS *Dragon* (74), and returned to the Caribbean he knew so well in 1811 as Commander-in-Chief of the Leeward Islands Station (his father's last command), commanding there until 1814. By the end of the War of 1812 he had captured a number of American merchantmen.[16] In 1815, Parliament decided to increase the Order of the Bath, and nominated Laforey a Knight Commander of the Order of the Bath (KCB). He achieved the rank of vice admiral on 12 August 1819, and admiral of the blue on 22 July, 1830. He died on 17 June 1835, at age 68, and is buried in St Nicholas' Churchyard, Brighton.[17]

Sir Francis Laforey did not marry and left no offspring, and so the baronetcy died with him. However, his legacy lived on through two world wars. HMS *Laforey*, launched at Glasgow in 1913, was the first of the Laforey class (L-class) of destroyers, designed to operate in home waters against surface and submarine enemy vessels. On 28 August 1914, she saw action at the first major battle between the Royal and German navies at the Battle of Heligoland Bight. On 23 January 1915, *Laforey* was at the Battle of Dogger Bank. The destroyer transferred to the Mediterranean Fleet in October 1915 and helped cover the evacuation of British and Empire forces from Gallipoli. Returning to the Harwich Force, she later served on the Dover Patrol. HMS *Laforey* was sunk by a British-laid mine in the English Channel off the coast of France on 23 March 1917.

The second HMS *Laforey* (G99) was a Second World War L-class destroyer of 1,935 tons launched in 1941. She participated in many important actions during the course of the war, including most of the Malta operations during 1941-42. She was present when HMS *Ark Royal* was torpedoed by German submarine U-81 and rendered assistance before the aircraft carrier went down. *Laforey* took part in Operation PEDESTAL, the convoy that saved Malta. She continued to serve throughout the Mediterranean, providing convoy escort as well as supporting the

---

15   Henry Bunbury, *A Narrative of Military Transactions in the Mediterranean, 1805-1810* (London: T&W Boon, 1891), p.168.
16   *Bulletin from the London Gazette of June 25, 1814, No. LVII* (1814) 'Admiralty Office, 21 June 1814. A Return of Vessels captured and detained by His Majesty's Ships and Vessels under the Command of Rear Admiral Sir Francis Laforey from Noon the 10th of January 1814 ... American Ship *Greyhound*, laden with provisions, captured by the *Elizabeth*, 13 January 1814, sent to St Christopher's ...'
17   Wareham, *Star Captains*, p.87.

Salerno and Anzio amphibious operations. This second HMS *Laforey* was sunk 30 March 1944 by U-233, the last ship sunk by the enemy action in the Mediterranean. Nevertheless, these two Royal Navy destroyers made for a fitting tribute to this legendary naval commander.

New England

9

The Brentons of Newport, Rhode Island[1]

Dr John B. Hattendorf

The extended Brenton family of Newport, Rhode Island; Newport Township, Nova Scotia, and Halifax, was a remarkable family of merchants and public servants, who produced seven North American-born naval officers, all who served in the Royal Navy in the late-eighteenth and early-nineteenth centuries:

Rear Admiral Jahleel Brenton (1729-1802)
Vice Admiral Sir Jahleel Brenton (1770-1844)
Captain Edward Pelham Brenton (1774-1839)
Lieutenant James Wallace Brenton (1778-99)
Purser John Brenton (1779-ca. 1834)
Vice Admiral John Brenton (1782-ca. 1859)
Lieutenant William Brenton (1783-1808)[2]

---

1   The author acknowledges with great appreciation the assistance of Henry L.P.Beckwith of North Kingston, Rhode Island, and Dr Evan Wilson of Oxford and Yale Universities.
2   There are others with the surname Brenton in the Royal Navy, but direct family connections with the North American branch of the family have not yet been fully researched and documented: John Brenton, appointed purser 21 Oct 1796; William Gagnon Brenton, purser 2 March 1810; Henry Brenton, purser 23 July 1827; Edward Brenton Stewart of Halifax, lieutenant 1814, married Francis Isabella Brenton 2 Aug 1830, commander 1844; Shovel Brenton Stokes, lieutenant 22 July 1830. Other known descendants with naval connections include: (1) A grandson of Vice Admiral John Brenton: Edward Pelham Brenton von Donop, captain 1855, retired 1870, rear admiral

The Arms and Crest granted 3 November 1812 to

JAHLEEL BRENTON

described as Esquire, a Post-Captain in His Majesty's Royal Navy, upon whom and his descendants His Majesty intended to confer the Dignity of Baronet; son and heir of Jahleel Brenton, Esquire, late a Rear Admiral of the Blue Squadron of His Majesty's Fleet, deceased, who was third son of Jahleel Brenton, late of Rhode Island in North America, deceased, by Frances, daughter of Samuel Cranstoun, Esquire, sometime Governor of that Colony. The Arms were also granted to the other descendants of his said late grandfather, Jahleel Brenton of Newport, Rhode Island, as was the Crest without the Crown. The grantee, Jahleel Brenton, was created a Baronet of even date with the grant of Arms and Crest, and was Knight Grand Cross of St. Ferdinand of the Two Sicilies (10 May 1810) and subsequently Knight Commander of the Bath (2 January 1815), and Vice Admiral of the White Squadron.

College of Arms   Thomas Woodcock, Norroy and Ulster.
London   Norroy and Ulster King of Arms

Brenton Coat of Arms. (Courtesy of Dr John Hattendorf)

The American eugenicist and biologist, Charles Benedict Davenport, wrote in 1919, that 'Thalassophilia is a family trait'[3] in the Brenton family. While scholars today are skeptical of his underlying claim 'that sea-lust is an inherited, racial

1873. (2) A grandson of Vice Admiral Jahleel Brenton and the son of his daughter Harriet and the Rev. Adolphus Carey, (see The Carey Family of Guernsey, *Carey Genealogy History* <http://www.careyroots.com/hd2.html> (accessed 5 April 2019)), Reginald O.B.C. Brenton, born 1848, lieutenant 1872, Royal Humane Society Medal second clasp 1875, commander 1885, superintendent for training Mexican Navy 1891, died 21 April 1922 and buried in Ometepec, Guerrero, Mexico. The Colegio Almirante Reginald Carey Brenton is a private secondary school named after him. On his role in Mexico, see also <http://www. careybrenton.edu.mx/index.php?option=com_content&view=article&id=18&Itemid=16> (This website no longer accessible on 5 April 2019).

3   Charles Benedict Davenport and Mary Theresa Scudder, *Naval Officers: Their Heredity and Development* (Washington DC: Carnegie Institution of Washington, 1919), p.49.

trait,[4] there is no doubt about the wide-spread and interrelated interests in the Navy within the Brenton family during this period.

The Brenton Family Comes to America

This American naval family first came to North America during the seventeenth century. William Brenton (ca. 1610-1674) came to America in 1633, sailing in the ship *Griffin* to Boston, Massachusetts, to join that Puritan colony as a merchant. Brenton carried with him a royal commission to be Surveyor of New England and he quickly came into public office, first as a selectman in Boston and Deputy for Boston to the General Court of Massachusetts, as well as serving on a number of committees.[5] Between 1636 and 1638, the Massachusetts Bay colony became deeply divided in the Antinomian controversy over the theological concepts of the 'covenant of grace' and the 'covenant of works.' This crisis led Massachusetts officials to banish the 'free grace' followers and forced them to move south, beyond the bounds of Massachusetts. In March 1638, they established a new settlement at Pocasset (renamed Portsmouth in 1639), at the northern tip of Aquidneck Island (from 1644, officially named Rhode Island) in Narragansett Bay. In August 1638, Brenton joined this group, even though Massachusetts had not banished nor disarmed him. Thus, he was able to retain his property and business interests in Boston and other parts of Massachusetts.

Eventually, Brenton became one of the largest landowners in Rhode Island and Massachusetts. Among the many positions he held during his 40 years of public service, he was elected president of the Rhode Island colony from 1660 to 1661. Then, between 1663 and 1666, he was the first deputy governor of the English Colony of Rhode Island and Providence Plantations under King Charles II's charter of 1663 and, from 1666 to 1667, was elected the second governor under that charter.[6] Married twice, William Brenton had 10 children, among whom he gave his eldest surviving son the name Jahleel (1655-1732);[7] the first of the Brentons to

---

4   Davenport and Scudder, *Naval Officers*, p.29.
5   Rhode Island Historical Society, MSS 306: Papers of Jahleel Brenton (1655-1732) includes three folders for his nephew, Jahleel Brenton (1691-1767).
6   This early family history is based on Robert Charles Anderson, *Immigrants to New England, 1620-1633*, Vol. 1, Great Migration Study Project (Boston, Massachusetts: New England Historic Genealogical Society, 1995), pp.218-224. This work, based on primary source documents, corrects older works such as John William Haley, *William Brenton of Hammersmith* (Providence, Rhode Island: Providence Institution for Savings, 1933); and Elizabeth C. Brenton, *A History of Brenton's Neck from 1638* (Newport, Rhode Island: John Sanborn, 1877).
7   Through Governor Brenton's daughter, Sarah (born c. 1670), who married Joseph Eliot, son of the Rev. Joseph Eliot, there are two American naval officer descendants seven

carry this Biblical name.[8] Between 1690[9] and 1699, he became widely known in the maritime affairs of New England, while serving as the Crown's Collector of Customs in Rhode Island, Massachusetts, and New Hampshire,[10] as well as Agent for Prizes.[11] In 1700, he became the agent for Rhode Island to the Board of Trade in London. Among his duties was the attempt to resolve the controversy over the border between Connecticut and Rhode Island.[12]

Jahleel did not marry, so the subsequent family members with the name descended through his brother, Governor William Brenton's second son, William Brenton (ca. 1657 - 1697). William Brenton's son, Jahleel Brenton (1691-1767), named for his uncle, became the second to bear the name. In 1715, he married Francis Cranston, eldest daughter of Samuel Cranston, governor of Rhode Island from 1698 to 1727, and granddaughter of John Cranston, who had been governor

generations later: Rear Admiral Andrew Hull Foote (1806-1863) and Commodore John Alfred Foote (1803-1891). See Chester F. Brenton, 'Descendants of William Brenton. Governor of Rhode Island.' Typescript (Spokane, Washington: C.F. Brenton, May 29, 1994), p.59. Copies are located at The Redwood Library and the Newport Historical Society, Newport, Rhode Island.

8   'Jahleel is the tenth son of Jacob and sixth of Leah', (Genesis 46:14). Jahleel is also one of the 66 who came to Goshen, and his brothers are Sered and Elon. The descendants of Jahleel formed their own sub-tribe: the ילאלחי, the Jahleelites (Numbers 26:26) *Abarim Publications Biblical Name Vault* <http://www.abarim-publications.com/Meaning/Jahleel. html> (accessed 4 April 2019). Also, 'ja'-le-el (yachle'el, "wait for God!")', *International Standard Bible Encyclopedia* (1915) <http://www.biblestudytools.com/dictionary/jahleel/> (accessed 4 April 2019).

9   'Entry Book: October 1690', pp.11-20, in *Calendar of Treasury Books, 1689-1692*, Vol. 9, in William A Shaw (ed.). (London: His Majesty's Stationary Office, 1931), pp.847-855. *British History Online* <http://www.british-history.ac.uk/cal-treasury-books/vol9/pp.847-855> (accessed 16 June 2016).

10   See among other sources, Mary Sarah Bilder, *The Transatlantic Constitution: Colonial Legal Culture and the Empire* (Cambridge, Massachusetts: Harvard University Press, 2004), p.58, pp.75-78; For his duties as customs collector, see references in Great Britain, Public Records Office *Calendar of Treasury Papers, 1697-1701* (London: Government Printing Office, 1871), p.91, p.326, p.435; Douglas R. Burgess, Jr., *The Politics of Piracy: Crime and Civil Disobedience in Colonial America.* (Lebanon, New Hampshire: University Press of New England, 2014), p.155, p.179, p.184; and some 45 entries in Cecil Headlam, 'Calendar of State Papers Colonial America and West Indies between 1690 and 1719', London: His Majesty's Stationary Office, *British History Online* <https://www.british-history.ac.uk/cal-state-papers/colonial/america-west-indies/vol5> (accessed 5 April 2019).

11   'Entry Book: April 1694', pp.16-20, *Calendar of Treasury Books, Volume 10, 1693-1696*, William A. Shaw (ed.), (London, 1935), pp.582-597. *British History Online* <http://www. british-history.ac.uk/cal-treasury-books/vol10/pp582-597> (accessed 16 June 2016).

12   See, for example, J. Brenton to Council of Trade, 17 Dec 1700, document 1018. 'America and West Indies: December 1700', pp.16-20, in Cecil Headlam (ed.), *Calendar of State Papers Colonial, America and West Indies, Vol. 18, 1700* (London, 1910), pp.744-759; *British History Online* <http://www.british-history.ac.uk/cal-state-papers/colonial/america-west-indies/vol18/> pp.744-759 (accessed 16 June 2016).

of the colony from 1678 to 1680. Jahleel and Francis raised 22 children. With the establishment of the Newport Artillery Company, he served, with the rank of captain, as its first commanding officer, 1741-1747.[13] Their eldest son, Jahleel (1729-1802), became a rear admiral in the Royal Navy, while two other sons, William Brenton (1750-1804) and James Brenton (1736-1806), married and provided them with six grandsons who joined the Royal Navy, while two of their granddaughters married their naval officer cousins.

Rear Admiral Jahleel Brenton (1729-1802)

Portrait of Rear Admiral Jahleel Brenton, 1729-1802. (Editors' Collection)

The son of Jahleel and Francis Cranston Brenton, the third Jahleel, was born in Newport, Rhode Island on 22 October 1729. The 23-year-old Jahleel passed his examination for lieutenant in the Royal Navy on 6 December 1752, having served five years and 11 months in warships and additional time in merchant ships. Three years later, in April 1757, he was promoted from passed midshipman to lieutenant. While still serving as a lieutenant, he married 22-year-old Henrietta Cowley in

13   Walter K. Schroder, *The Artillery Company of Newport: A Pictorial History* (Berwyn Heights, Maryland: Heritage Books, 2014), pp.1, 3, 98, 100. Jahleel Brenton's counting house from 1748 survives in Newport. See *Newport Restoration Foundation* <http://www.newportrestoration.org/property/39-washington-street/> (accessed 5 April 2019).

1765. In the spring of 1775, Brenton was at home on half-pay, but was acquainted with Captain James Wallace, RN, whom he apparently came to know when they served together as midshipmen. At this point, Wallace commanded the sixth-rate HM Frigate *Rose* (20), which had been in Rhode Island waters since 1774, attempting to enforce the Navigation Acts and to stop the flagrant smuggling that went on in Narragansett Bay. Wallace planned and executed operations to harass those rebels on the coasts of Narragansett Bay and southern New England.[14]

Brenton was one of nine 'Principal Inhabitants of Newport' who, on 1 May 1775, requested the protection of Wallace and *Rose*[15]. Coincidentally, 'He had many Whig friends who offered to see that he was appointed to the highest rank of naval service of Congress. These he declined, maintaining his staunchest loyalty to the Crown.'[16] On 31 October 1775, the Rhode Island General Assembly approved the seizure of Jahleel Brenton's property.[17] During this period of violence, Brenton fled for his personal safety to Boston, where he borrowed money from his attorney to take passage to London in order to apply in person to the Admiralty for an assignment to sea.[18]

In 1776, Brenton received his orders and was back on active duty in command of the fourth-rate HM Frigate *Pembroke* (44). He applied to the British Treasury for financial support for his destitute family and received a grant of £100 a year. But, it was discontinued in 1777. Promoted to master and commander on 23 August 1777 on taking command of *Tortoise,* a 26-gun store ship that had recently been purchased, Brenton remained in her in American waters until he sailed her back to England in early 1778.[19] After his return in her to American waters with supplies, the vessel foundered off Newfoundland in September 1779.[20] Soon thereafter in

---

14   On Wallace, see Kenneth Breen, 'Wallace, Sir James (1731–1803)', *Oxford Dictionary of National Biography*, Oxford University Press, 2004; online edition, Jan 2008 <http://www. oxforddnb.com/view/article/28536> (accessed 30 Dec 2016) 'Sir James Wallace (1731–1803)' doi:10.1093/ref:odnb/28536

15   William Bell Clark, (ed.), *Naval Documents of the American Revolution* (Naval History Division, Dept. of the US Navy, Washington, DC: Government Printing Office, 1964), Vol. 1, pp.255-256: Some of the Principal Inhabitants of Newport to Captain James Wallace, RN, 1 May 1775.

16   Brenton, 'Descendants of William Brenton', p.25.

17   John Russell Bartlett (ed.), *Records of the Colony of Rhode Island and Providence Plantations in New England.* Ten volumes (Providence, Rhode Island: A.C. Greene and Bros., State printers, 1856-1865), Vol. VIII, pp.376-77: Proceedings of the General Assembly, 31 October 1775.

18   Brenton, 'Descendants of William Brenton', p.25.

19   Clark (ed.), *Naval Documents of the American Revolution,* Vol. 11, p.36: Disposition of His Majesty's Ships and Vessels, 1 Jan 1778.

20   See Rif Winfield, *British Warships in the Age of Sail, 1714-1792* (Barnsley, South Yorkshire: Seaforth, 2008); J.J. Colledge and Ben Warlow, *Ships of the Royal Navy: The Complete*

December, 1779, Brenton took command of the fire ship HMS *Strombolo,* serving as a hulk at New York in 1780. Brenton remained near his family in New York until 23 May 1780, when he made arrangements to send his family to England, where they initially lived in Enfield, Middlesex.[21] Meanwhile back in Rhode Island, the General Assembly passed an act in July 1780 ordering Brenton's apprehension as a traitor, should he return to Rhode Island.[22]

On 29 September 1780, Brenton took a post in command of the armed ship HMS *Queen,* and soon moved on to the command of the sixth-rate HM Frigate *Termagant* (26).[23] By 1783, the 54-year-old Brenton, who had been in sea service for 37 years, applied for a naval pension and was granted £90 a year. In addition, he petitioned the commissioners for compensation for his losses in Rhode Island, which he estimated at £4,500. He was eventually awarded £646 for his loss.[24] In about 1784 or 85, he moved with his family to St Omer, France, where they lived until 1787. He settled fin Edinburgh, Scotland for the remainder of his life. In retirement, he was promoted to Rear Admiral of the Blue on 1 January 1801.[25] He died in Edinburgh at the age of 72 on 10 January 1802.

Vice Admiral Sir Jahleel Brenton, First Baronet (1770-1844)[26]

Sir Jahleel Brenton was the fourth to bear the name. The eldest of three sons, all of whom became naval officers, he was the third of the 10 children born to

      Record of all Fighting Ships of the Royal Navy from the 15th Century to the Present (Annapolis, Maryland: US Naval Institute Press, 2006).

21   Now Enfield Town in the London Borough of Enfield; it is located about 10 miles NNE of Charing Cross in central London.

22   Bartlett (ed.), *Records of the Colony of Rhode Island,* Vol. IX, p.139: 'An Act to prevent certain persons therein named … who have joined the enemy … from being admitted within this state'.

23   Henry Raikes (ed.), *Memoir of the Life of Vice-Admiral Sir Jahleel Brenton, K.C.B.* (London: Hatchard & Son, 1846), p.37.

24   Bartlett (ed.), *Records of the Colony of Rhode Island,* Vol. X, p.12; Howard W. Preston, 'Rhode Island and the Loyalists, Part II', *Rhode Island Historical Society Collections,* XXII:1 (June 1929), pp.9-11.

25   *The London Gazette,* 30-Dec to 3 Jan 1801, p.10.

26   There are number of sources available on the life of Sir Jahleel Brenton in addition to the detailed volume by the Rev. Henry Raikes, cited above. These include 'A Memoir', *The Spectator* (28 November 1846), pp.17-18, <http://tinyurl.com/ho317m>; 'Obituary', *The Gentleman's Magazine* , Vol. 176 (July 1844), pp.90-91, <.http://tinyurl.com/h3zfzuw>; Cataloguing record of a portrait at the National Maritime Museum, Greenwich, <http://collections.rmg.co.uk/collections/objects/42076.html>; baptismal record: <https://familysearch.org/ark:/61903/1:1:V2HJ-WQW> ; J. Ralfe, *The Naval Biography of Great Britain; Consisting of the Historical Memoirs of Those Officers of the British Navy who Distinguished Themselves during the Reign of his Majesty George III,* Vols. 1-4 (London:

Vice Admiral Sir Jahleel Brenton,
1st Baronet, KCB, 1770-1844.
(National Maritime Collection,
Greenwich, London, Caird
Collection)

Rear Admiral Jahleel and Henrietta Cowley Brenton. Born on 22 August 1770 at Newport, Rhode Island, his father first placed him at the age of seven on the muster roll of the store ship *Tortoise* that he commanded. His name appears from December 1777 through April 1779, listed as an able seaman and then as a clerk. He then served under his father in three successive ships: HMS *Strombolo*, 30 April 1779 to 6 April 1780; HMS *Queen*, 7 October 1780 to 23 September 1781, and HMS *Termagant*, 24 September 1781 to 17 May 1782. Brenton continued as an able seaman in the sixth-rate HM Frigate *Greenwich* (26), and the third-rate HMS *Belleisle* (64). His initial service in her lasted only a month and a half, after which he was enrolled in the Maritime School at Chelsea in 1783, where he studied

Whitmore & Fenn, 1828), Vol. IV, pp.292-306; John Marshall, *Royal Naval Biography* (London: Longman, 1824), Vol. III, pp.261-69; William R. O'Byrne, *A Naval Biographical Dictionary: Comprising the Life and Services of Every Living Officer in Her Majesty's Navy, from the Rank of Admiral of the Fleet to that of Lieutenant, Inclusive.* (London: J. Murray, printed by William Clowes and Sons, 1849), found under 'Brenton, John'. This essay has used all these sources and relied particularly on the most recent work: P.K. Crimmin, 'Brenton, Sir Jahleel, first baronet (1770-1844)', *Oxford Dictionary of National Biography* (Oxford: Oxford University Press, 2004); online edition, Jan 2008 http://oxforddnb.com/ view/article/3326 (accessed 27 Oct 2015).

navigation and seamanship.[27] On completion of that course in 1785, he joined his parents, who had moved to St Omer, France, and embarked on the study of the French language. In November 1787, he returned to duty in *Belleisle* for the next two years, with additional service in HM Sloop *Weazle* (14), and the third-rate HMS *Bellona* (74).

On 3 March 1790, he passed his examination for lieutenant and was certified as having more than six years at sea and being 21 years old.[28] In fact, he was only 19 years, six months, and nine days old. After passing his examination, Brenton saw very little opportunity for active service. He, like several other British naval officers and men—most notably Captain, later Admiral, Sir Sidney Smith – went to Sweden, where they hoped to see action in the Russo-Swedish War of 1788-1790. Obtaining an immediate commission as a lieutenant in the Swedish Navy,[29] Brenton was first assigned to *Konung Adolf Fredrik*, the flagship of Vice Admiral Karl Vilhelm Modée, where he was assigned the duty of introducing the British approach to naval discipline. Completing that duty, he was sent to the Swedish galley fleet, where he arrived very shortly after the Battles of Vyborg and Svensksund. The King of Sweden, Gustav III, expressed gratitude to the British officers for their assistance in the aftermath of those events. During this period, Brenton, through his recently acquired knowledge of French, was able to act as an effective liaison between the Swedish and British officers.[30]

After returning to Britain, Brenton was promoted through the patronage of Admiral Lord Hood. He was one of 160 lieutenants in the Royal Navy appointed on 22 November 1790. In order to determine their seniority, it was later determined that the eldest group of 15 took rank from 13 November and the youngest group from 22 November. Brenton's group of 15 took rank from 20 November.[31] Brenton was delighted with his orders as second lieutenant in the troop transport *Assurance,* ordered to sail for Halifax, Nova Scotia. It was, he wrote, 'a station of all others I should have chosen, having numerous friends and relations at that place; but particularly, from having formed an early attachment there.'[32] In 1790, the opportunity to visit in *Assurance* was dashed when he was arrested at Rochester,

27   H.T.A. Bosanquet, 'The Maritime School at Chelsea', *The Mariner's Mirror*, 7:11, (1921), pp.322-329.
28   TNA ADM 6/89/229: Passing Certificate for Jahleel Brenton, 3 March 1790.
29   Hjalmar Börjeson, *Biografiska anteckningar om Örlogsflottans Officerare 1700-1799*, edited by Karl Westin (Stockholm: Generalstabens litografiska anstalt, 1942), p.34.
30   Raikes (ed.), *Memoir*, pp.40-44.
31   Patrick Marioné, Jean-Marie Pâques, and N.A.M Rodger, *The Complete Navy List of the Napoleonic Wars, 1793-1815* (CD-Rom, Brussels, Belgium, SEEF, 2003) 'Brenton, Sir Jahleel (2)'.
32   Raikes (ed.), *Memoir*, p.44.

Kent, and imprisoned for a short time on a charge of impressing sailors within the city limits.

Forced to miss the ship's sailing, Brenton was reassigned as first lieutenant of *Speedy* on customs duties. In 1792, he took command of HM Brig *Trepassy* (12) operating in Newfoundland waters. His extended cold weather operations forced him on to sick leave in late 1795. On recovery, he was appointed as the first lieutenant in the store ship *Alliance*, sailing for the Mediterranean with supplies for the fleet. Just as the ship was about to leave, he received a private letter that he was to be appointed as first lieutenant of the fifth-rate HM Frigate *Diamond* (38), commanded by his friend Sir Sidney Smith. However, Jahleel's commanding officer would not allow him to be detached from the ship without a successor. The officer designated did not arrive in time and *Alliance* sailed with Jahleel still aboard.

On the ship's arrival in the Mediterranean, Jahleel's frustration in being unable to take up his assignment on a fighting frigate was made known to the commander-in-chief, Admiral Sir John Jervis. He sent for Jahleel and, on hearing his family's story, gave him priority over other officers as the son of a retired naval officer and ordered him to the third-rate HMS *Gibraltar* (80) as first lieutenant. This action marked the beginning of Jervis' interest in the Brenton brothers and their naval careers.[33] Jervis later credited Jahleel's service in *Gibraltar* as having a calming influence that helped to unify a faction-ridden wardroom. When the ship was sent home for repair after a gale and damage on the Pearl Rock,[34] Admiral John Jervis again took interest in the young Jahleel and ordered him on temporary duty to the second-rate HMS *Barfleur* (98), the flagship of Vice Admiral William Waldegrave. While in *Barfleur*, Brenton participated in the Battle of Cape St Vincent on 14 February 1797, following which he was appointed the ship's first lieutenant. Finding her a happy ship, he was, at first, reluctant to be ordered away to the flagship, the first-rate HMS *Ville de Paris* (110) in August 1798. A month later, he was compensated with the appointment to acting command of *Speedy*, in which he had served earlier. In 1799, while preparing to convoy Neapolitan merchant vessels carrying corn from Cagliari to Neapolitan ports, the young commander asked Lord Nelson what he should do if the Algerines attacked. 'Let them sink you,' Nelson replied, 'but do not let them touch the hair of the head of one of your convoy. Always fight and you are sure to be right.'[35]

---

33   Edward Pelham Brenton, *Life and Correspondence of John, Earl of St Vincent, G.C.B. Admiral of the Fleet, &c. &c. &c.*, Vol. 1 (London: Henry Colburn, 1838), pp.2-3.

34   Edward Pelham Brenton, *The Naval History of Great Britain, from the year MDCCLXXXIII to MDCCCXXII*, Vol. 2 (London: C. Rice, 1823-25), p.140.

35   Edward Pelham Brenton, *The Naval History of Great Britain, from the year MDCCLXXXIII to MDCCCXXXVI: A new and greatly improved edition*, Vol. 2 (London: H. Colburn, 1837),

Confirmed in this appointment in July 1799, he fought several successful actions against gunboats on the Spanish coast and in the Strait of Gibraltar, most notably on 6 November 1799, when *Speedy* was entering Gibraltar Bay, convoying two ships. She was attacked by 12 Spanish gunboats. In the fight that ensued, Brenton fought back the gunboats, and lost two men killed and one wounded. A few days after the action, Brenton was informed that during another action, his brother, Wallace, had been seriously wounded and was in the hospital at Port Mahon, Minorca. Jaheel's commander, Admiral Duckworth, immediately ordered *Speedy* to take dispatches to Minorca, allowing Jahleel to look into Wallace's condition. While Jahleel was sailing from Gibraltar to Minorca, Admiral Lord Nelson reported to the Admiralty that Jahleel had displayed 'uncommon skill and gallantry in saving the ship under his command and all his convoy.'[36] With such strong recommendations, the Admiralty promoted Jahleel to post-captain on 25 April 1800. Brenton then took temporary command of the third-rate HMS *Généreux* (74) that had been recently captured from the French in February 1800. Under Brenton's command, she got to sea and participated in the blockade of French-occupied Genoa.

In January 1801, Brenton was appointed to command the third-rate HMS *Cæsar* (80) as flag captain under Rear Admiral Sir James Saumarez. The ship was seriously damaged when the anchored French fleet repulsed the British attack at Algeciras, Spain on 6 July 1801. With repairs affected, Brenton returned his ship to action on 12 July in the successful defeat of the Franco-Spanish squadron in the second battle of Algeciras – the Battle of the Gut of Gibraltar.[37] After the event, Brenton drew a watercolour sketch of the departure of the fleet which was quickly published as an aquatint.[38] This is the first known published example of Jahleel Brenton's artwork. While serving in *Cæsar*, Brenton was deeply impressed by the influence that Chaplain Evan Halliday had on the ship's company in improving the conduct of seamen, as well as preventing punishment, and the crimes that produced disciplinary actions.[39] With the Peace of Amiens, Saumarez hauled down his flag and Brenton continued in command until 1802, when he returned

p.70.

36   Raikes (ed.), *Memoir*, pp.90-96; Sir Nicholas Harris Nicolas (ed.), *The Dispatches and Letters of Vice-Admiral Lord Viscount Nelson, with notes*, Vol. 4 (London: Chatham Publishing, 1998. Originally published by H. Colburn, 1845-46), pp.130-131: Nelson to Evan Nepean, Palermo, 7 Dec 1799.

37   Brenton, *Naval History*, Vol. 2, pp.489-490; Vol. 3, pp.37, 40-41.

38   'The British Squadron, consisting of five two deck'd ships, & two frigate, preparing to pursue the Combined Squadron, of France, & Spain, on the afternoon of the 12th of July 1801' by Hubert & Stadler (engraver), Harding, E. (publisher), 1802. Anne S. K. Brown Military Collection, Brown University, Providence, Rhode Island. GB-N 1801 gf-1.

39   Raikes, ed., *Memoir*, p.125; Richard Blake, *Religion in the British Navy, 1815-1879: Piety and Professionalism* (London: Boydell Press, 2014), pp.113-114.

Battle of the Gut of Gibraltar, 12 July 1801: Position of the English, Spanish and French Squadrons before the action. Stipples engraving by Wells after Owen, Published in the *Naval Chronicle*, Vol VI, by Bunney & Gold, London, 1801. (NHHC NH 66236)

to England to keep his long-awaited promise to marry Isabella Stewart, whom he had met in Halifax 22 years earlier.

With the Peace of Amiens breaking down, Britain began preparations for war, and the Admiralty appointed Brenton, in March 1803, to the command of the fifth-rate HM Frigate *Minerve* (38), to serve under Saumarez on the Channel Islands Station. He had been in command only a short time when a block fell and hit his head causing a brain concussion that put him ashore for recovery until June. Taking *Minerve* to sea in early July, Saumarez ordered Brenton to take station off Guernsey. On the evening of 2 July, after chasing a detachment of French gunboats in heavy fog close to the shore at Cherbourg, *Minerve* ran aground on part of Cherbourg's artificial breakwater. Under heavy fire from the forts and nearby French ships, Brenton responded vigorously by sending *Minerve*'s boats, with a boarding party, to cut out a larger ship from the harbour and use it to set an anchor in an attempt to get the ship off the breakwater. Continually under fire, *Minerve*'s men successfully refloated the ship momentarily, but with no wind, she grounded again on the falling tide. [40]

After sustaining enemy gunfire for 10 hours and having 11 men killed and 16 wounded, Brenton surrendered *Minerve*. With some glee, Napoleon personally

---

40   Brenton, *Naval History*, Vol. 3, pp.209-212.

announced the news. Brenton, with all his officers and men, were made prisoners of war and marched 400 some miles from Cherbourg to the French depôt for prisoners of war at the citadel in Verdun. There, Brenton remained with his officers and other senior prisoners of war, while his men were taken further down the Meuse River to Givet. Placed on parole, Brenton conducted himself honourably by remaining in the area and, at the same time, was able to initiate measures that improved conditions for British prisoners. Among the prisoners with Brenton at Verdun were two Anglican clergymen: Rev. Lancelot Charles Lee and Rev. William B. Wolfe. Brenton became a close friend of Lee, who accompanied him on visits to British prisoners of war in the area and ignited his initial interest in relieving the conditions of prisoners and promoting religion among them.[41] Somewhat later, Brenton encountered Wolfe, who had been detained earlier at Fontainebleau and had begun a prison ministry that he continued at Verdun.

After a proposed exchange of prisoners broke down in November 1804, Brenton was eventually granted permission for his family to join him. In April 1805, he was joined by his wife, sister, and eldest son – John Jervis Brenton (born 19 January 1803), whom he had named for Admiral Lord Jervis. Brenton was not in good health during this period, so he and his family were allowed to live in Tours, where his second child, Francis Isabella, was born in November 1805.

Meanwhile, the crew of *Minerve* was housed as prisoners of war in relatively harsh conditions. With his earlier positive experience with naval chaplains under Saumarez clearly in mind, Brenton worked to obtain Wolfe's appointment as chaplain to British prisoners of war in 1805, while, at the same time, leading Wolfe to organise a school of navigation for the British prisoners at Givet.[42] Wolfe's work there was not only impressive for the quality of its instruction in navigation, but it also served to create the crucible for a religious awakening among the British naval ratings at Givet, which eventually contributed to the wider turn to Christian piety among British seamen.[43]

At the same time, Brenton, himself, experienced a religious awakening. From his birth in Newport, he had practiced his religion in form, but he had only begun

41   Raikes (ed.), *Memoir*, p.184.
42   Mark J. Gabrielson, 'Enlightenment in the Darkness: The British Prisoner of War School of Navigation at Givet, France, 1805-1814', *The Northern Mariner*, XXV:1 & 2, (January-March 2015), pp.7-41. The only known student work from this school is the William Carter Navigation Journal, MS item 21, Naval Historical Collection, US Naval War College, Newport, Rhode Island; published online at <https://usnwcarchive.org/items/show/1113> See also, Mark J. Gabrielson, 'Enlightenment in the Darkness: The British Prisoner of War School of Navigation. Givet, France. 1805-1814', unpublished Master of Liberal Arts in Extension Studies (History), May 2014. Harvard University Library.
43   Richard Blake, *Evangelicals in the Royal Navy, 1775-1815: Blue Lights and Psalm Singers* (London: Boydell Press, 2008), pp.242-245.

to take religion seriously while serving under Saumarez in *Cæsar*. While a prisoner in France, he developed a deep Christian faith with evangelical convictions that marked the remainder of his career and life.[44]

In December 1806, Brenton was exchanged for Captain Louis-Antoine-Cyprien Infernet, the nephew of Marshal André Masséna who had fought bravely in command of the French *Intrépide* (74) and had been captured at Trafalgar. Soon after Breton's return to England, his third child, Lancelot Charles Lee was born on 18 February 1807 and named after Brenton's inspirational fellow prisoner. A court-martial honourably acquitted Brenton of the loss of *Minerve* and he was appointed to command of the newly-built fifth-rate HM Frigate *Spartan* (38). Brenton took her to the Mediterranean for duty under Admiral Lord Collingwood. In Collingwood's eyes, Brenton had lost *Minerve* due to his rash actions off Cherbourg and Brenton's first action in *Spartan* did little to assuage that opinion when his ship suffered heavy casualties after attacking an enemy polacre off Nice, France, in May 1807. Although a court of inquiry acquitted Brenton, Collingwood remained wary of him and assigned *Spartan* to the cruising station off Toulon for the remainder of 1807.

In 1808, Brenton redeemed his reputation with successful attacks on enemy shipping and French positions on the Spanish coast, followed by service in the eastern Mediterranean in 1809 as commodore of a four-ship squadron. During operations in the Adriatic, he conveyed British and Spanish ambassadors to Trieste, drove French ships from Pesaro in the Marche region, forced the surrender of the French garrisons at Lussin in Croatia, and in the Ionian Islands of Zante, Cephalonia, and Kythera.[45] In light of these successes, Brenton won over Collingwood, who wrote to Lord Mulgrave, the First Lord of the Admiralty; 'I cannot say too much to your lordship of the zeal and talent of Captain Brenton.'[46]

Another success followed on 2 May 1810, when Brenton, with *Spartan* and the sixth-rate HM Frigate *Success* (32), forced a large French frigate and three other Franco-Neapolitan warships to seek shelter behind the mole at Naples. On the next day, 3 May, the enemy ships sailed with a reinforcement of seven gunboats and 400 soldiers. The Franco-Neapolitan squadron met *Spartan* off the Amalfi coast at the entrance to the Bay of Naples, between the island of Capri and Sorrento. During a sharp and bloody action, *Spartan* caused severe damage to her opponents, but lost 10 men killed and 22 wounded. Grapeshot hit Brenton in the hip and the wound

---

44 Brenton, *Naval History*, Vol. 3, pp.217-228; Blake, *Evangelicals*, pp.184-185; Raikes (ed.), *Memoir*, pp.194-195.
45 *The London Gazette*, 2-5 December 1809, 1929-30: Jahleel Brenton's dispatch 13 October 1809.
46 Raikes (ed.), *Memoir*, p.365; Brenton, *Naval History*, Vol. 3, pp.339, 341-42, 355-356.

forced him to place Lieutenant George W. Willes in command.[47] In recognition of his achievement, he was appointed commander of the Adriatic Squadron. But, he was too ill with his wounds to accept the appointment. The heavily damaged ship and wounded captain returned to England in July 1810, where Brenton was placed on half-pay during a slow two-year period of recovery. While still in the Mediterranean, he was advised that King Ferdinand III of Sicily had conferred on him the honour of Commander of the Order of St Ferdinand on 10 May 1810.[48] Additionally, Lloyd's Patriotic Fund awarded him a 100-guinea sword.[49]

While ashore, Brenton faced hardships beyond recovery from his wounds. His agents had failed and lost all his property. A prize appeal was also lost and he was forced to return the proceeds previously awarded, placing him in debt by £3,000. Forced to give up his home in Bath and move to London lodgings, friends came to his rescue and paid the debt, while he was awarded a pension of £300 pounds for his wounds. Although only partially recovered in March 1812, Brenton accepted command of the third-rate HMS *Stirling Castle* (74) with the Channel Squadron. Expressing his devotion to the naval service, he wrote, 'My profession had been my delight from the very earliest period in my life at which I entered it, and no circumstance, however happy, had as yet possessed the power to tranquilise my mind ashore, whilst I could find myself capable of active service.'[50] On taking command, Brenton took his eldest son, Jervis, to sea with him, as *his* father had taken *him*.

Jervis's naval service was apparently short, as his father soon resigned his command due to his health. Then just nine years old, the boy had already shown interest and aptitude for the sea but died five years later on 27 August 1817 from scarlet fever before he could become a midshipman. On 3 November 1812, Brenton was made a baronet, followed by a grant of arms on 24 December. The arms showed a lion and three martlets with the stern of a warship in one quarter; surmounted by

---

47   *The London Gazette, 31 July to 4 August 1810*, pp.1133-1135: Jahleel Brenton's Dispatch of 3 May 1810 from Cerigo [Kythera].

48   Ralfe, *Naval Biography*, p.306. Brenton, *Naval History*, Vol. 3, pp.433-437; Raikes (ed.) *Memoir*, p.96, Letter from Marquis Circello to Rear Admiral Martin 10 May 1812 reporting that Brenton was awarded 'le croix de commandeur de l'Ordre'. P.K. Crimmin in the *ODNB* and others interpret this as being the grand cross of the order, rather than commander of the order.

49   The sword was sold at auction by Bonham's on 26 November 2008 for £84,000 in an antiques and amour sale. *Maine Antiques Digest* (January 2009), p.4-D. See also *Bonhams* <https://www.bonhams.com/auctions/15843/lot/409/> He also received a pair of flintlock dueling pistols that was sold at auction in 2010. See < https://www.bonhams.com/auctions/17944/lot/381/>

50   Raikes (ed.), *Memoir*, p.419; College of Arms, Grants XXVII, p.112.

a naval coronet labelled 'Spartan' and a swan.[51] The grant of arms was unusual in the very large number of people who were allowed to bear it through the provision that it was given to all the descendants of Brenton's grandfather, the second Jahleel Brenton (1691-1767), who had 22 children. However, only the direct descendants of *Spartan's* captain were allowed the naval crown with its label 'Spartan'.

At the end of 1813, Brenton was appointed commissioner of the dockyard at Port Mahon on Minorca. With the disestablishment of the Port Mahon Dockyard in 1815, he briefly commanded the 10-gun yacht *Dorset*, before going on to the Cape of Good Hope to be commissioner of the dockyard there. During this period, Brenton was involved with providing support for British forces at Saint Helena, where Napoleon was held prisoner. In addition, he worked to improve the wages and living conditions of the native civilian workers in the dockyard and he developed an interest in evangelising the indigenous peoples. In July 1817, Brenton's wife, Isabella, died after a long illness, and in August, his eldest son died at school in England. In late 1817, Brenton undertook a journey to the mouth of the Knysna River to develop a trade route to that farthest eastern edge of the Western Cape Province as a part of the initial effort to settle that region. He kept a journal of his journey and made a number of watercolours, five of which are known to have survived.[52]

After six years at the Cape, Brenton returned to England in January 1822 and, in April, was appointed Knight Commander of the Most Honourable Military Order of the Bath.[53] On 9 October of that same year, he married his first cousin, Harriet Mary Brenton (??? -1863), the daughter of Judge James Brenton of Halifax, Nova Scotia. For a short period, he was given command of the King's yacht, *Royal Charlotte*, and from November 1829 until the summer of 1830, he commanded the guard ship HMS *Donegal* at Sheerness. On 22 July 1830, he was promoted to Rear Admiral of the Blue and restored to the active list. In the following year, he was appointed Lieutenant Governor of Greenwich Hospital, in succession to Captain William Browell, with a salary of £800 a year.[54] While in that post, Brenton worked to improve the naval school and organised libraries for the Greenwich pensioners. He also published the first of his several books and pamphlets, *An Appeal to the British Nation on Behalf of Her Sailors*,[55] which represented the growing trend to

51   Raikes (ed.), *Memoir*, Chapter XVII, pp.491-611.
52   Frank R. Bradlow, 'Five New Pictures by Sir Jahleel Brenton (1770-1844) with special reference to one of the *Arniston* Memorial', *Quarterly Bulletin of the South African Library*, 24:2, (June 1970), pp.247-254.
53   *The Edinburgh Gazette*, 30 April 1822, p.1.
54   *The Edinburgh Gazette*, 12 August 1831, p.1.
55   Sir Jahleel Brenton, *An Appeal to the British Nation, on behalf of her Sailors* (London: J. Nisbet & Co., 1838).

consider seamen as people with moral responsibility.[56] This was followed the next year with *The Hope of the Navy, or the True Source of Discipline and Efficiency*,[57] in which he looked to religion as the true source of naval discipline and efficiency.[58]

For most of the last year of his active service, Brenton was Acting Governor of Greenwich Hospital,[59] until retiring on 1 July 1840. On retirement, he was promoted to Rear Admiral of the White, a rank that he had qualified for by seniority on the accession of Queen Victoria in 1837, but which was held in abeyance as incompatible with his appointment at Greenwich. He was promoted again on 10 January 1837 to Rear Admiral of the Red,[60] then on 1 July 1840 to Vice Admiral of the Blue,[61] and on 23 November 1841, having reached the seniority for Vice Admiral of the White. During his retirement years, he published two more works: a book, *A Memoir of Captain Edward Pelham Brenton*,[62] about his younger brother who had died in 1839, and a pamphlet, *Remarks on the Importance of the Coast Fisheries*,[63] in which he made an appeal to the public to reduce the sufferings of the poor through the fisheries, which would provide food as well as work.[64] On entering retirement, Brenton lived first at Casterton in Westmoreland, but his increasingly poor health forced him to move south, first to Elford House, near Litchfield, and then to 28 Lansdowne Place in Leamington Spa, where he died on 21 April 1844.[65]

After Brenton's death, the Reverend Henry Raikes published a memoir based on original documents in 1846, which his younger son, who succeeded as the second baronet, the Rev. Sir Lancelot Charles Lee Brenton, edited as a revised

---

56   Blake, *Religion in the Royal Navy*, p.28.
57   Sir Jahleel Brenton, *The Hope of the Navy, or, The true source of discipline and efficiency: as set forth in the articles of war provided for the government of the fleet of Great Britain: an address, etc.* (London: no publisher indicated, 1839).
58   Blake, *Religion in the Royal Navy*, p.70.
59   *Warder and Dublin Weekly Mail.* 28 September 1839, p.3.
60   *The London Gazette*, 10 January 1837, p.70.
61   *The London Gazette*, 3 July 1840, p.1570.
62   Vice-Admiral Sir Jahleel Brenton, *Memoir of Captain Edward Pelham Brenton, R.N., C.B., with Sketches of his Professional Life and Exertions in the Cause of Humanity as continued with the Children's Friends Society, &c., Observations upon his Naval History and Life of the Earl of St Vincent* (London: James Nisbet and Co., 1842).
63   Jahleel Brenton, *Remarks on the importance of our coast fisheries as the means of increasing the amount of food and employment for the labouring classes, and of maintaining a nursery for seamen* (London: James Nesbit and Co, 1843).
64   'The Importance of our Coast Fisheries', *Essex Standard*, 1 August 1843, p.4.
65   Newport Historical Society: Certified copy of Death Certificate of Sir Jahleel Brenton; Obituary, *Hampshire Telegraph*, 29 April 1844, p.4. British Library, Correspondence with Sir Robert. Peel 1844-45. Add MS 40543, ff. 292, 308: Letters of Harriet Brenton, widow of Vice Admiral Sir Jahleel Brenton, includes, f. 296: Vice Admiral Sir Jahleel Brenton, 1st Baronet: Statement of services of: 1844.

second edition of the book.[66] In addition, Admiral Brenton's daughter by his second marriage, Harriet Mary Cary, published *Evenings with Grandpa*[67], a book of children's stories in 1860 that were based on the tales that her father had told.

Reflecting on Sir Jahleel, Charles Davenport wrote 'There is evidently conservatism rather than radicalism; calmness under disappointment; capacity for enduring hardships; firmness and self-reliance …':

> His taste so refined, his manners so gentle, his kindness so constant, that much of what the world calls goodness seemed to grow in him spontaneously and cost him nothing. He was amiable without an effort, benevolent without reflection, and habitually thinking more of others than himself.[68]

Jahleel Brenton's second son, Lancelot, unlike his elder brother, Jervis, who had died young, did not carry on the naval tradition of his father and grandfather. The contrast between father and son was a stark one, but they did share a basic religiosity that the father had passed on to his son. The father had been a fighting man who saw no contradiction between his faith and his fighting, while the son was an Oxford graduate, clergyman, biblical scholar, and author of a book still in use in the late twentieth century,[69] as well as a pacifist who joined the Brethren.[70] Looking back on his youth, the son graphically described his upbringing:

> … from my birth upwards all my associations and impressions were in favour not only of the lawfulness but of the glory of war. All the senses of my childhood were crowded with memorials of the past, or tokens of the present connection of my family with the profession of arms. I was, so to speak, born and cradled in the midst of them. Epaulettes and cocked hats, the grapeshot that pierced my father's hipbone, the sword voted to him out of the Patriotic Fund … rich with blue steel and unwrought gold, my mother fainting at the news of my father's wounds – these are

66 L.C.L. Brenton (ed.), *Memoir of Vice-Admiral Sir Jahleel Brenton, Baronet, K.C.B.* (London: Longman, 1855).

67 Harriet M. Carey, *Evenings with Grandpapa, or, The Admiral on Shore: Naval Stories for Children* (London: Printed and published for the authoress by Dean & Son, 1860).

68 Quoted in Davenport, *Naval Officers*, p.49 from an as yet unidentified source.

69 L.C.L. Brenton, *The Septuagint with Apocrypha: Greek and English* (London: Samuel Bagster & Sons, Ltd, 1851); most recent edition: (Peabody, Massachusetts: Hendrickson Publishers, 1986).

70 Gareth Atkins, 'Christian Heroes, Providence, and Patriotism in Wartime Britain, 1793-1815', *The Historical Journal*, 58:2 (June 2015), pp.393-414, 412-413.

among the earliest visions of my infancy. The very playthings of our nursery were blocks, marlinspikes, or models of brigs and frigates with jacks and ensigns and appropriate rigging. War seemed the most normal condition of man, and peace a rare and vapid exception.[71]

While the son's recollection harboured a very personal reaction, it also reflected the characteristics that many others must also have felt during the long years when Britain was at war against France.

Captain Edward Pelham Brenton (1774-1839)

Edward Brenton was the middle of the three sons and the fifth child of Rear Admiral Jahleel Brenton and his wife Henrietta Cowley. He was four years younger than the future Sir Jahleel, and four years older than his little brother, James, known as Wallace to the family.[72] Edward's middle name, Pelham, was a family name on Edward's mother's side and one that carried much weight and social prestige in colonial New England. Herbert Pelham had been the first treasurer of Harvard College. He was from the same family line as Henry Pelham (1697-1754) and his elder brother, the Duke of Newcastle (1693-1768), successive Whig prime ministers of Great Britain, who held power in the years 1743-1754 and 1757-1762. Herbert Pelham's son, Edward (died 1730), was a member of the Harvard Class of 1673 and lived as a wealthy and cultured gentleman in Massachusetts. He had married Freelove Arnold, the daughter of Benedict Arnold (1615-1678), president and then governor of the English colony of Rhode Island and Providence Plantations for 11 years, alternating in that position with William Brenton (ca. 1610-1674). Thus, Edward's name reflects his heritage that united two of the most prominent families in the early history of colonial Rhode Island.[73]

Edward was born in Newport, Rhode Island, on 20 July 1774. According to his brother's memoir, Edward had begun his active naval service in May 1781, at the age of six, when he joined his father in *Queen*.[74] However, the Navy Office certified that his name had been borne as an able seaman on the muster books of his father's

---

71   L.C.L. Brenton (ed.), *Memoir of Vice-Admiral Sir Jahleel Brenton* quoted in Gareth Atkins, 'Christian Heroes, Providence, and Patriotism in Wartime Britain', p.412.
72   Biographical sketches of Edward Pelham Brenton appear in Marshall, *Royal Naval Biography*, Vol. IX, p.411; O'Byrne, *A Naval Biographical Dictionary*, Vol. 1, p.121n.
73   John L. Sibley, *Biographical Sketches of those who Attended Harvard College* (Cambridge, 1881), Vol. 2, pp.416-420. See also, Carl Bridenbaugh, *Peter Harrison: First American Architect* (Chapel Hill: University of North Carolina, 1949), pp.7, 9, 16-17, 23. Harrison, a sea captain and self-taught architect, was John Bannister's son-in-law and part of the extended Pelham family.
74   Jahleel Brenton, *A Memoir … of Edward*, p.2.

Portrait of Captain Edward Pelham Brenton, 1774-1839, London: Published by Henry Colburn 13 Great Marlborough Street 1837. (Courtesy of Dr John Hattendorf)

ship *Tortoise* as early as December 1777, when he was only three years old, and continued in *Dromedary, Tortoise* again, and *Strombolo* before joining *Queen* in October 1780. Remaining in her until September, 1781, he served in *Termagant* as a clerk for eight months in 1781-82, before going on to *Belleisle* in 1782-83. With the end of the American War, he left active service to attend school at Ware in Hertfordshire for two years, and then joined his father and family at St Omer in France, where he developed fluency in French.

In November 1788, he joined the third-rate HMS *Crown* (64), then fitting out at Chatham under Captain James Cornwallis, who was ordered as Commodore and Commander-in-Chief of the East Indies Station in 1788-92. Among Edward's papers, his brother found a detailed account of his first months in joining *Crown,* in which Edward remarked, 'Everything that Smollet says about the miseries of a man-of-war I found exactly and correctly true in 1788.'[75]

On his return from the East Indies, Edward was certified in June 1792, as having had more than eight years of sea service and being 21 years old, when he passed

75   Jahleel Brenton, *A Memoir … of Edward*, p.3, continuing the quotation in great detail to p.6.

his lieutenant's examination on 1 June 1792.[76] Although he was, in fact, only 18 at the time he passed, but he had turned 21 when he was actually promoted to lieutenant in 1795. In between the examination and his promotion, he was placed by a friend of his father, Vice Admiral Sir Philip Affleck, in the third-rate HMS *Bellona* (74), under Captain George Wilson. In 1794, he was transferred to Lord Howe's flagship, the first-rate HMS *Queen Charlotte* (100), where he was promoted to lieutenant, and then assigned successively to the sixth-rate frigates *Venus* (32) and *Phoenix* (36). He was serving in the third-rate HMS *Agamemnon* (64), as fourth lieutenant when the Nore Mutiny broke out in 1797.[77] He remained in her until he was appointed first lieutenant in HM Brig *Raven* (18). In February 1798, that vessel was wrecked near Cuxhaven at the mouth of the Elbe River. Boats from the town of Blankenese rescued the ship's officers and men, who were returned home to face a court martial.

After all were cleared of the charges, one of the members of the court-martial board, Captain John Bligh, offered Edward Pelham the opportunity to serve under him in the third-rate HMS *Agincourt* (64), flagship of Vice Admiral Lord Radstock, on the Newfoundland Station. Readily accepting, Edward was initially appointed sixth lieutenant. When Sir John Jervis had ordered Edward's brother Jahleel into *Barfleur* and then *Ville de Paris*, Jervis had enquired into the situation of his brothers, Wallace and Edward, saying 'I will do the best I can for the sons of officers.'[78] At that point, in 1801, Lord Jervis could do no better for Edward, but Radstock immediately moved him up from sixth to first lieutenant in *Agincourt*. After Jervis had been created Earl of St Vincent and then became first Lord of the Admiralty, Edward was ordered as first lieutenant under John Bligh in the third-rate HMS *Theseus* (74) in which he served in the West Indies. Following the Peace of Amiens in March 1802, St Vincent's influence led to Edward's promotion to command HM Sloop *Lark* (18). He was promoted to commander on 29 April, while taking his ship home to England from the West Indies to be paid off.[79]

While on half-pay, he married Margaretta Diana Cox, the daughter of Major General Thomas Cox, at St Marylebone Church, London, on 29 March 1803.[80]

---

76   TNA ADM 106/16/50: Edward Pelham Brenton's Passing Certificate.
77   For his account of the event, see Brenton, *Naval History*, Vol. 1, (1837) pp.222-223, 283.
78   Sir John Jervis quoted in Brenton, *Life and Correspondence of St Vincent*, Vol. 1, p.3.
79   Jahleel Brenton, *A Memoir. . . of Edward*, pp.11-13; J. K. Laughton, 'Brenton, Edward Pelham (1774–1839)', rev. Andrew Lambert, *Oxford Dictionary of National Biography* (Oxford: Oxford University Press, 2004), <http://www.oxforddnb.com/view/article/3325> (accessed 21 Dec 2016). Edward Pelham Brenton (1774–1839): doi:10.1093/ref:odnb/3325; Brenton, *Life and Correspondence of St Vincent*, Vol. 1, p.4.
80   'Marriages', *Naval Chronicle*, Vol. 9 (1803), p.339; *Family Search* https://family search.org/ark:/61903/1:1:V52H-C6Q. I am grateful to Dr John Houlding who provided the following information from his database on eighteenth century British Army officers: Thomas Cox:

With the renewal of the war in May 1803, Edward, again with St Vincent's favour, returned to sea duty in command of the 16-gun HMS *Merlin*, an old armed collier, in which he regularly cruised off the French coast near Cherbourg. On 10 December 1803, while off the island of Tatihou near La Hogue, he saw that the sixth-rate HM Frigate *Shannon* (36) had run aground during a gale, and was lying in danger under the island's gun batteries. During the night, he sent his boats in and burned the ship, preventing her capture by the enemy. Later, in 1804, he commanded *Merlin* during the bombardment of Le Havre in July and August.[81]

In January 1805, Edward was appointed to command the newly built brig-sloop HMS *Amaranthe* (18). In this ship, he first cruised in northern waters, capturing several prizes. In 1808, he was ordered to take her to the West Indies, where she served on the Leeward Islands Station. In one incident, he went ashore under a flag of truce to deliver letters to the governor of Martinique, the famous French admiral, Villaret de Joyeuse, who had commanded the French fleet in the Battle of the Glorious First of June in 1794. Later, on 13 December 1808, Edward and his men distinguished themselves during blockade operations off Martinique by destroying the 18-gun French brig *La Cigne*.[82] Following this action, Commodore George Cockburn placed Edward in temporary command as acting captain of the third-rate HMS *Pompée* (74). This promotion was confirmed by the Admiralty with a commission dating from the day that *La Cigne* had been captured, but Edward did not receive the official news until he returned to England in May 1809.[83]

Meanwhile, in his acting capacity in his new ship, *Pompée*, Edward carried the broad pennant of his friend and supporter, Commodore George Cockburn. With the British invasion of Martinique and the siege of Fort de France that began on 30 January 1809, under the overall command of Vice Admiral Sir Alexander Cochrane and Lieutenant General George Beckwith, George Cockburn had been appointed to act additionally as a major general with Edward Brenton, commanding a detachment of seamen in the batteries ashore. With 100 seamen and one of their own long 24-pound cannon, Brenton and his men participated in the five-day-long bombardment that began on 19 February and led to Admiral Villaret de Joyeuse's surrender of Martinique. Some 2,400 officers and men of the French garrison were embarked in the ships under Cockburn's command, with

Ens, 1st Ft Gds, 26.11.1753; Lt & Capt, 10.2.1758; Capt-Lt & Lt-Col, 5.2.1772; Capt & Lt-Col, 13.9.1772; Bvt Col, 19.2.79; 3rd Maj, 22.2.81; 2nd Maj, 18.3.1782; Maj-Gen, 20.11.1782; 1st Maj., 20.10.1784; died 12.3.1789; *The London Magazine ... Vol. XXXIII For the Year 1764*, p.599, lists under 'Promotions Civil and Military' for 17 Nov 1764, 'captains Cox and Blackwood made equerries to the Duke of Gloucester'.

81   Jahleel Brenton, *A Memoir... of Edward*, pp.14-15.
82   *The London Gazette*, 31 Jan-4 Feb 1809, pp.146-47: Dispatch of F.A. Collier, 14 Dec 1808.
83   Jahleel Brenton, *A Memoir... of Edward*, pp.29-30.

Cockburn now flying his flag in the third-rate HMS *Belleisle* (74), with Brenton in command. The prisoners of war were taken directly to France, in accordance with their terms of surrender, to obtain the release of an equal number of British prisoners of war held in France. When Brenton anchored in the bay of Morbihan to carry out this arrangement, French officials refused to release the British prisoners. So the embarked French prisoners were taken to Portsmouth, England, for continued incarceration.[84]

In July 1809, Edward took temporary command of the third-rate HMS *Donegal* (74) to deliver Richard, Marquis of Wellesley, to Cádiz, where he was to take up the post of British Ambassador to Spain, then governed during the Napoleonic occupation by the Supreme Central Junta at Seville. The ship's arrival coincided with the local celebration over the news that the ambassador's brother, General Sir Arthur Wellesley, had just won the Battle of Talavera on 27-28 July. Ambassador Wellesley was unsuccessful in his attempts to bring the Junta into cooperative measures with his brother, so in late November, *Donegal* returned the ambassador to England, where he soon became Foreign Secretary in Spencer Perceval's ministry. Edward relinquished his temporary command and was on half-pay until April 1810, when he briefly commanded the sixth-rate HM frigate *Cyane* (22) on convoy duty. On returning from convoy duty, he was surprised to learn that the First Lord of the Admiralty, Charles Philip Yorke, had nominated him to succeed his wounded brother, Jahleel, in command of the frigate *Spartan,* when the ship's battle damage had been repaired.[85] In appointing his brother, the First Lord wrote to Jahleel, 'I beg you will consider this a testimony of ... personal esteem and regard.'[86]

After *Spartan* was ready for sea, Edward initially commanded her on patrols off the coast of France until 25 July 1811, when he sailed for the North American Station to serve under Vice Admiral Sir Herbert Sawyer, and Vice Admiral John Borlase Warren, based at Halifax, Nova Scotia.[87] Between 16 July and 3 August 1812, he was credited with capturing nine American privateers in Nova Scotian waters.[88] The historian John Knox Laughton wrote of him that 'he met with no opportunity of distinguished service' in the War of 1812, but according to an obituary that appeared in a Rhode Island newspaper in 1839: 'It was repugnant to

84   Jahleel Brenton, *A Memoir... of Edward*, pp.24-29.
85   Jahleel Brenton, *A Memoir... of Edward*, pp.30-31.
86   Jahleel Brenton, *A Memoir... of Edward*, pp.30-31.; Charles Philip Yorke to Jahleel Brenton, 21 August 1810.
87   'Ships in Sea Pay, 1 July 1813', in William S. Dudley (ed.), *The Naval War of 1812: A Documentary History,* Vol. 2 (Washington, DC: Naval Historical Center, 1992), p.170.
88   *The London Gazette,* 19 Sept to 22 Sept 1812, pp.1907-1908.

his feelings to appear as a foe before his birth-place, and where some of his near kindred still resided, and he requested to be placed upon some other station.'[89]

Spartan remained on the North American Station for two years until the summer of 1813, when she returned home and was paid off in September. Edward remained on half-pay from 1813 until April 1815, when he was appointed to command the Trafalgar veteran, the first-rate HMS *Royal Sovereign* (100), then fitting out as the flagship for Rear Admiral Sir Benjamin Hallowell. He soon followed Hallowell into the third-rate HMS *Tonnant* (80), but resigned his command in November 1815, having no desire to serve in peacetime. While commanding *Tonnant*, Edward had the opportunity for a brief interview with Napoleon in French, when the deposed emperor was being transferred to the third-rate HMS *Northumberland* (74).[90]

From a very early age, Edward had developed a passion for naval history and had read widely in the available literature on the subject.[91] Shortly after Edward's retirement from active service, he began to think about how to realise his dream of becoming a naval historian, having already acquired a sound basis for such a project through his studying published works and in being prepared for the practical work involved. As he explained, 'I have been constantly in the habit of making memoranda of every public event which came under my notice and of taking sketches of any port in which I let go anchor.'[92] By 1819,[93] he was fully occupied in writing his five-volume *Naval History of Great Britain from the Year 1783 to 1822*, the first volume of which appeared in print in 1823 and was dedicated, with a frontispiece portrait of the Earl of St Vincent, 'as a mark of respect for his public service and of unfeigned gratitude for his parental kindness to the author.'[94] The volumes were illustrated with several engravings from his own sketches and those of his brother, Jahleel, as well as maps and portraits.

His motive in writing history was to inspire young people with the 'same ardour and zeal'[95] that he felt for the Royal Navy. Having been an experienced serving officer, he also wanted to communicate to the public an accurate understanding of the naval war, while at the same time presenting balanced professional judgements for his fellow naval officers that earned him the trust of his superiors. Only a very

89   'Obituary', *Rhode-Island Republican*, 12 June 1839, 3:34, p.3.
90   Brenton, *Naval History*, Vol. 5, p.220.
91   Brenton, *Naval History* (1837), Vol.1, p.vii. For Burchett, see Josiah Burchett. *A Complete History of the Most Remarkable Transactions at Sea* (1720), facsimile edition with an introduction by John B. Hattendorf. 'Maritime History Series', John B. Hattendorf, series editor. (Delmar, New York: Scholars' Facsimiles & Reprints for the John Carter Brown Library, 1995).
92   Brenton, *Naval History*, Vol. 1, p.v.
93   Brenton, *Naval History*, Vol. 5, p.iii, where he states it was the work of six years.
94   Brenton, *Naval History*, dedication page.
95   Jahleel Brenton, *A Memoir... of Edward*, p.222.

small portion of his correspondence survives, but it documents that in writing his history he had obtained permission from a number of key senior officers, such as Sir George Cockburn, James Saumarez, Exmouth, Sir Richard Keats, Lord Keith, Sir David Milne, and St Vincent. At the same time, many professional colleagues became subscribers to his work. Notable among them, the Duke of Clarence – the future King William IV – wrote to Brenton that he took '... great pleasure in subscribing to your highly useful work.'[96] His history clearly reflected his upbringing and family values with its devotion to the good of the naval service and, by its references, to the role of divine providence in naval affairs.[97]

As the volumes came out, one by one, Edward quickly discovered the dangers of writing contemporary history and the controversy it typically creates. In the preface to volume three, he ruefully remarked, 'He who writes the history of his own time must, if he does his duty, make himself enemies.'[98] In reply to his critics, Edward observed:

> I hope that the good sense and cool reflection of my opponents will convince them that I have had no other motive than the advantage of my profession, anxious above all things to do justice, I have invariably attended to kind and friendly communication, but the attacks in the daily press, I have by the advice of some of the best and bravest of my fellow officers treated with silent indifference.[99]

Brenton's work appeared nearly simultaneously with William James's five volumes on the same topic.[100] The two men came from quite different backgrounds and had different conceptions about how to write a naval history. Brenton was the trained naval professional and a Whig in his political leanings, while James was a Tory

---

96 Beinecke Library, Yale University. E.P.Brenton Correspondence. OSB Mss. 35, Box 1; folder 2, Sir George Cockburn to EPB, 6 Oct 1822; file 4: Saumarez to EPB, 30 Aug 1821; folder 5, Exmouth to EPB, 5 August 1819; File 8, Sir R. G. Keats to EPB, 25 Feb 1824; file 9, Keith to EPB, 9 Aug 1819; file 14, William, duke of Clarence to EPB, 28 June 1821.

97 Brenton, *Naval History* (1837), Vol. 1, p.xi.

98 Brenton, *Naval History,* Vol. 3, p.viii.

99 Brenton, *Naval History,* Vol. 5, p.i

100 William James, *The Naval History of Great Britain, from the declaration of war by France, in February 1793, to the accession of George IV in January 1820: with an account of the origin and progressive increase of the British Navy; illustrated from the commencement of the year 1793, by a series of tabular abstracts, contained in a separate quarto volume,* Five volumes (London: Printed for Baldwin, Cradock and Joy, 1822-1825). The 1837 edition appeared in six volumes.

THE

NAVAL HISTORY

OF

GREAT BRITAIN,

FROM THE YEAR

MDCCLXXXIII. TO MDCCCXXXVI.

BY

EDWARD PELHAM BRENTON,

CAPTAIN IN THE ROYAL NAVY.

A NEW AND GREATLY IMPROVED EDITION,

ILLUSTRATED WITH PORTRAITS, PLANS, ETC.

IN TWO VOLUMES.

VOL. I.

LONDON:

HENRY COLBURN, PUBLISHER,

13, GREAT MARLBOROUGH STREET.

1837.

Brenton's inside cover of his Naval History of Great Britain and Portrait of King William IV.
(Courtesy of Dr John Hattendorf)

who had studied law and had begun a career as a lawyer in the Vice-Admiralty Court of Jamaica.[101]

The two writers quickly became involved in a highly public debate over the merits of their respective works. Brenton took a comprehensive view to place the war into context, basing his work mainly on the dispatches of the major commanders that had been published in the *London Gazette* or had been provided directly to him, while providing a broad, succinct view of the naval actions. James

---

101 Holden Furber, 'How William James Came to be a Naval Historian', *American Historical Review*, 38:1 (October 1932), pp.74–85; Andrew Lambert, 'Introduction' to William James, *The Naval History of Great Britain* (London: Conway Maritime Press, 2002); William James, *A full and correct account of the chief naval occurrences of the late war between Great Britain and the United States of America: preceded by a cursory examination of the American accounts of their naval actions fought previous to that period* (London: Conway Maritime Press, 2002).

took a skeptical view of the reports of senior officers and focused on more detailed descriptions of naval actions, information from ships' logs, and testimony from individual officers.[102] Brenton felt that ships' logs were less likely to be accurate than the responsible officers' reports. There was another subtle aspect of their dispute. James had been held as a prisoner of war in the United States during the War of 1812 and held some resentment for Americans and was particularly critical of American accounts of their own naval actions. In contrast, the Loyalist Brenton, born in America, was careful to avoid showing any prejudice to the land where some members of his family still lived.

In this rivalry, Brenton's work was eventually overshadowed by James'. Although William James died in 1827, Captain Frederick Chamier (1796-1870),[103] later well-known as a naval novelist in the popular style of his fellow officer Captain Frederick Marryat,[104] took up James' work and issued a new and expanded six-volume edition in 1837, shortly after Brenton's second edition appeared.[105] Using it to have the last word in the debate, James' work went on to have seven editions, the latest reprinted as late as 2002 and carried Chamier's introduction that the eminent historian Professor Sir John Knox Laughton (1830-1915) described as having 'good-humouredly disposed of disparaging criticism of the original work' by Brenton.[106] Adding further damage to Brenton's reputation, Laughton remarked:

As an officer of rank, who had been actively employed during the period of his history, his opportunities of gaining information were almost unequalled, but he seems to have been incapable of sifting his evidence, and to have been guided more by prejudice than judgement. The plan of

102 Jahleel Brenton, *A Memoir … of Edward*, see pp.222-324 for a detailed 100-page defence of Edward's history.

103 John Knox Laughton, 'Chamier, Frederick (1796–1870)', Rev. Roger Morriss, *Oxford Dictionary of National Biography*, (Oxford: Oxford University Press, 2004) <http://www.oxforddnb.com/view/article/5090> (accessed 27 Dec 2016), Frederick Chamier (1796–1870) <doi:10.1093/ref:odnb/5090.>

104 J. K. Laughton, 'Marryat, Frederick (1792–1848)', rev. Andrew Lambert, *Oxford Dictionary of National Biography*, (Oxford: Oxford University Press, 2004); online edition, Sept 2016. <http://www.oxforddnb.com/view/article/18097> (accessed 27 Dec 2016); Frederick Marryat (1792–1848) <doi:10.1093/ref:odnb/18097>

105 James, *The Naval History of Great Britain … with an account of the origin and progressive increase of the British Navy and an account of the Burmese War and the battle of Navarino.* (London: R. Bentley, 1837); (London: Richard Bentley, 1847); (London: Richard Bentley, 1859); (London: Richard Bentley, 1860); (London: Richard Bentley & Son, 1886); (London: Macmillan, 1902); (London: Conway Maritime Press, 2002).

106 Laughton, 'Chamier, Frederick'.

his work is good, but the execution feeble, and its authority as to matter of fact is often slender.[107]

Despite having such a judgement passed on to later generations by such influential writers, Brenton's history contains useful insights from his own direct observations as well as information and viewpoints he obtained directly from participants. As Edward had protested, James used Brenton's work as a source for his own history.[108] In defending his brother's history, Jahleel pointed out that Edward had avoided personal attacks on individual officers, as he felt James had done. Edward's naval history 'is not without faults and errors, I freely admit.' Jahleel wrote:

> ... but my object has been to vindicate the writer from the charges made against him, of presumption in undertaking such a work, and of uncalled for harshness and severity in the execution of it ... My object has been to remove the false glare that has been thrown over some of the events recorded, which if suffered to remain, would only tend to throw suspicion over others and induce the rising generations to form an erroneous estimate of what is required to constitute a real triumph.[109]

The naval history had occupied the majority of Edward's time and effort between 1819 and the publication of its final volume in 1827. In the following years, he shifted his focus to assisting poor and disadvantaged youth, as his elder brother described:

> ... with the most invincible perseverance, during the remainder of his life. Not only to devising the means for improving the situation of the youthful poor, to promoting their temporal and eternal welfare, and making them good and useful servants of the state, but to ameliorate the conditions of the seafaring part of our population.[110]

In 1829, Edward had read in the newspapers the accounts of Ester Hibner, a tambour lace worker in London, who had held under a cruel tyranny the young girls apprenticed to her in St Pancras parish, and had murdered two of them.[111] This incident alerted him to the deplorable conditions of child labour in England.

107 Laughton, 'Brenton, Edward Pelham'.
108 Brenton *Naval History* (1837), Vol. 1, pp.xvii-xviii.
109 Jahleel Brenton, *A Memoir ... of Edward*, pp.323-24.
110 Jahleel Brenton, *A Memoir ... of Edward*, p.38.
111 Jahleel Brenton, *A Memoir ... of Edward*, pp.47-48, dates this to '1827, or thereabouts'. A
     search of the newspapers shows that it was 1829. See, for example, 'Horrible Cruelty to

Joining with a group of six other like-minded men, Edward was a key figure in establishing in 1830 the Society for the Suppression of Juvenile Vagrancy. He authored the first public statement of the society's aims, explaining its purpose in 'training the poor and destitute or partially depraved children, to such habits as would fit them for useful service in this country.'[112]

The plan was first implemented at West Ham Abbey, near Bow, Essex, in 1830 with 20 boys of 'forlorn and neglected condition.'[113] In 1833, it was moved to Hackney Wick and was initially renamed the Brenton Juvenile Asylum, and soon after, The Children's Friend Society. In 1834, Princess Victoria, the future queen, and her mother, the Duchess of Kent, became the patronesses of the society with an asylum for female children established at Chiswick, named the Royal Victoria Asylum.

Some years earlier, from 1821 to 1828, Sir Robert Wilmot-Horton had been Under Secretary of State for War and the Colonies and advocated resettling the poor in the British colonies. Initially, Brenton opposed such plans,[114] but the Society soon took them up and resettled several hundred poor English and Irish children in the Cape Colony in South Africa, the Swan River colony in Australia, as well as in New Brunswick and Upper Canada. Although such plans were well-intentioned – envisaging open land, good accommodation, and remunerative employment for those children who were sent to the colonies – the intentions rarely, if ever, materialised, and have earned the condemnation of later generations.[115]

Edward Brenton returned to his historical studies with 'a new and greatly improved edition' of his naval history in two large octavo volumes that extended the original work another fourteen years from 1822 up to 1836. He dedicated this edition to King William IV, 'whose name stands enrolled in every rank from that

Parish Apprentice's and Murder', Bell's Life in London and Sporting Chronicle, 22 Feb 1829, p.1.

112 Edward Pelham Brenton, Statement of the views and reports of the Society for the Suppression of Juvenile Vagrancy: upon the plan that has proved so successful in Holland, by providing agricultural and horticultural employment for the destitute children of the metropolis (No place or publisher, 1830).

113 Quoted in Jahleel Brenton, A Memoir … of Edward, p.51, from Edward P.Brenton, The Bible and the Spade, or Captain Brenton's Account of the Children's Friend Society, etc. (London: J. Nisbet & Co., 1837) or Brenton, Continuation of 'The Bible and the Spade', or, the History of Fanny Forsher, a moral tale, etc. (London: J. Nisbet, 1837). In addition, Jahleel's memoir contains a long and detailed description of the Society on pp.44-221.

114 Edward Pelham Brenton, A letter to the Rt. Hon. R.W. Horton: shewing the impolicy, inefficacy and ruinous consequences of emigration and the advantages of home colonies (London: C. Rice, 1830).

115 See for example, Ester Inglis-Arkall, 'The Dark and Twisted History of the Children's Friend Society', Gizmodo <http://io9.gizmodo.com/the-dark-and-twisted-history-of-the-childrens-friend-so-1677705809> (accessed 17 April 2019)

of Midshipman to Lord Admiral' and 'is the better able to appreciate the laborious task I have undertaken.'[116] In his preface to the lengthy new edition, he commented on a number of points that reviewers had made on the first edition. Among them, he replies to a 'kind Reviewer' who had apparently taken issue with his description of American independence as being the result of a rebellion. In ending his retort, he wrote:

> I wish the Americans every happiness as a nation. I cannot forget that I was born among them and have forgiven their unkind treatment of my family when I was an infant. I will add one word of friendly admonition to them: as they fought and gained their own liberty, let them 'do as they would be done by.' Let them recollect their slave population; let them instruct and then emancipate them; let them look to their parent country for a noble though recent example; and let them remember that the neglect of this and other similar warnings may be the cause of deluging their now happy land in blood: injustice ever brings its punishment along with it.[117]

Continuing with his reference to the United States, Brenton wrote:

> Should England and America unhappily be ever at war, this most vulnerable point may prove the cause of interminable discord. Let us hope that such a contingency will never happen, and that the present bond of peace between us and the United States may remain forever unbroken.[118]

He also included in this edition a five-page 'Reply to Some of the Statements in Mr James's History,' in which he lamented the attacks that James had initiated and Chamier had continued in the recent second edition of James's work, pointing out James' use of Brenton's own words as well as a number of inaccuracies.[119] Pointing out in one instance how James had distorted his words, Brenton wrote 'This is one of many errors arising from want of local knowledge so common to the class of writers who consider that acquaintance with the subject is a very unimportant part of their business.'[120]

The following year, 1838, Brenton published his two-volume *Life and Correspondence of John, Earl St Vincent*, the first major biographical work to

---

116 Edward Pelham Brenton, *Naval History* (1837).
117 Brenton, *Naval History* (1837), Vol. 1, p.x.
118 Brenton, *Naval History* (1837), Vol. 1, pp.x-xi.
119 Brenton, *Naval History* (1837), Vol. 1, pp.xvii-xxii.
120 Brenton, *Naval History* (1837), Vol. 1, pp.xvii.

appear on that officer. [121] Edward dedicated the two-volume work to the second Earl of Minto, who was then serving as one of St Vincent's later successors as First Lord of the Admiralty. Brenton had already indicated, by his dedication of the first edition of his *Naval History*, that St Vincent had played an important role in providing him with documents and personal insights for use in his history. In this new work, Brenton explained the wider range of St Vincent's friendship and patronage to him and to his brothers, Jahleel and Wallace, as well as the personal friendship that his eldest sister, Francis, had with Lady St Vincent and the family. Lord St Vincent allowed Francis to transcribe St Vincent's papers as part of her brother's historical research. At the time of St Vincent's death in 1823, Francis was staying at Rochetts, St Vincent's home near Brentwood, Essex. [122]

In Queen Victoria's coronation honours, Edward Brenton was appointed Companion of the Most Honourable Military Order of the Bath on 19 July 1838.[123] He died at his home at 18 York Street, Gloucester Place, London on 6 April 1839, at the age of 64.[124] A hundred boys from the Children's Friend Society attended his funeral at St Marylebone Church, London, where he was buried. The Society continued until about 1842, when it was disestablished for lack of funds. A monument to him is still to be seen in Marylebone Parish Church.[125]

Lieutenant James Wallace Brenton (1778-1799)

The sixth child and the youngest of the three naval officer sons of Rear Admiral Jahleel Brenton (1729-1802), Wallace Brenton was born at Newport, Rhode Island, in 1778 and christened at Trinity Church, Newport, on 5 November 1778, with his father's long-time friend, Captain (later Admiral of the Blue Sir) James Wallace, RN, as his godfather, for whom he was named.[126] At that time, Captain Wallace commanded the fourth-rate, two-deck HMS *Experiment* (54), and had been in the area during the summer of 1778 to oppose the French fleet under d'Estaing that

121 Brenton, *Life and Correspondence of St Vincent*.
122 Brenton, *Life and Correspondence of St Vincent*, Vol. 1, pp.1-5; Vol. 2, pp.363-367, 374. Edward persistently refers to her only as his "eldest sister:" her identity as Francis Brenton is found in Brenton, 'Descendants of William Brenton', p.26.
123 *Supplement to The London Gazette*, 20 July 1838, p.1660.
124 Newport Historical Society: Certified copy of Death Certificate of Edward Pelham Brenton.
125 A photograph and description of the monument to Edward Brenton may be found at *The Second Website of Bob Speel* <http://www.speel.me.uk/chlondon/chm/marylebonenewch/marylebonebrenton.jpg> (accessed 9 May 2019)
126 'Rhode Island Births and Christenings, 1600-1914', database, *Family Search*. The records of Trinity Church at the Newport Historical Society do not list godparents, but this fact is confirmed in Brenton, *Life and Correspondence of St Vincent*, Vol. 1, p. 3.

threatened the British position at Newport. The infant Wallace Brenton remained in Newport with his family until they were evacuated to New York with British forces in 1779, and later to England.

As Wallace's father had done for his elder brothers, Jahleel and Edward, Wallace's name was also listed on the muster of the ships that his father commanded. The youngest of all three at the time of his enrolment in the navy, Wallace's name was entered on 20 April 1779, when he was just six months old, and continued for just over a year in *Strombolo*'s muster book as an ordinary seaman.[127] When his father transferred to command the armed ship *Queen* in April 1780, he listed Wallace as 'Captain's servant' as he continued to do in *Termagant* until 16 May 1782, when he left active service to retire in France. Wallace's name does not appear again in the muster books for a decade, until July 1792, when he is enrolled for a month as a supernumerary in *Bonito,* and from September of that year for another 13 months he is listed as 'lieutenant's servant' in *Trepassy,* the brig commanded by his elder brother, Jahleel. In April 1794, Wallace's godfather, Rear Admiral Sir James Wallace, was appointed Commander-in-Chief of the Newfoundland Station with his flag in the fourth-rate HMS *Romney (50).* From the first of June 1795 until April 1797, Wallace is listed in *Romney*'s muster book as an able-bodied seaman, then as a midshipman, and finally as a mate. In April 1797, the Earl of St Vincent had taken a personal interest in his brother Jahleel's assignments and ordered him to the *Ville de Paris,* where Wallace was soon listed in the muster book from 1 June 1795 until 20 January 1798.[128]

Wallace was certainly physically present in both *Romney* and *Ville de Paris,* as his brother Edward mentions him serving with his godfather and he produced journals from those two ships for his lieutenant's examination.[129] Wallace passed his lieutenant's examination on 20 January 1798, when he was 19, and, through the favour of St Vincent, was promoted the next day and ordered as a lieutenant to HM Sloop *Petterel* (18), commanded by Commander Francis W. Austen, the brother of the author Jane Austen. In *Petterel,* Wallace participated in a number of successful actions that resulted in prizes taken.[130] While off Barcelona, Austen ordered Wallace to take the ship's boats to capture a Spanish privateer that *Petterel* had run ashore. In the action that followed, Wallace was gravely wounded and taken to the hospital at Port Mahon, Minorca. His brother Jahleel, arriving a week later, wrote to his father, 'Poor Wallace is no more; he died of his wounds the 15th

---

127 TNA ADM 6/96/6: James Wallace Brenton's Passing Certificate.
128 TNA ADM 6/96/6: James Wallace Brenton's Passing Certificate.
129 TNA ADM 6/96/6: James Wallace Brenton's Passing Certificate; Brenton, *Life and Correspondence of St Vincent,* Vol. 1, p.3.
130 Brenton, *Life and Correspondence of St Vincent,* Vol. 1, p3n; Brenton, *Naval History* Vol. 3, pp.5-6.

of last month [November]. He died as he lived. A hero; and a pattern to every young man both in public and private life, universally regretted and esteemed.' Jahleel noted that Lieutenant W. Pemberton and his wife 'took unwearied care of the poor fellow during his illness.' [131]

When Nelson wrote to praise Jahleel's action in *Speedy* to the Admiralty, he added to his letter; 'if the merits of a brother may be allowed to have any weight. I have the sorrow to tell you, that he lost his life, then [lieutenant] of the *Petterel* attempting, with great bravery, to bring off a vessel that the Sloop had run on shore.'[132]

Conclusion

The extended Brenton family represents an interesting example of a socially prominent family from colonial Rhode Island that served well as Loyalists during and following American Independence and in the years beyond. Their service in the Royal Navy between the mid-eighteenth century and the end of the Napoleonic Wars illuminates how family dynamics forged naval careers within a family and the manner in which patronage from a family member who is a commanding officer could be used within a family to list their children on the muster books, providing them seniority for a future career, as Rear Admiral Jahleel Brenton did for his three sons, as well as to help promote their later careers as young lieutenants, as his son, Vice Admiral Sir Jahleel Brenton, did with his brothers and cousin.

Another feature of the Brenton family's experience was the way in which they moved from one patron to another. The elder Jahleel started out with the patronage of Sir James Wallace and this was passed on to Jahleel's third son and Wallace's namesake. The younger Jahleel gained, through his demonstrated professional competence, the attention and, then, the patronage of Admiral Lord St Vincent. St Vincent's predilection for encouraging the sons of serving officers over the sons of the landed aristocracy is clearly demonstrated in the way in which St Vincent's patronage extended by the younger Jahleel to his brothers, Edward and Wallace, as well as a connection with their elder sister, Francis. After St Vincent left the scene, Sir James Saumarez becomes an influential figure for the younger Jahleel as well as for his cousin, John.

For two centuries, from the time of William Brenton's first arrival in America in the 1640s to the civic work of Sir Jahleel and Edward Brenton in the 1830s and

---

131   Raikes, *Memoir,* pp.94-95. A death notice appeared in 'Marriages, Births, Deaths', *The Scots Magazine or General Repository of Literature, History, and Politics for the Year MDCCC* (January 1800), p.71.

132   Nicolas (ed.), *The Dispatches of Nelson,* Vol. 4, pp.130-131: Nelson to Evan Nepean, Palermo, 7 Dec 1799.

1840s, there are two recurring themes across the generations: devotion to public service, both in terms of holding government positions and later in charitable activities, and a religious faith grounded in Protestant values that were initially Presbyterian, but were carried on into the family's Anglicanism. To some observers today, the intermarriage of the two vice admirals in the family, the younger Jahleel and John Brenton, with their first cousins, Harriet and Henrietta, might seem to be contradictory to such values. The practice, however, was not banned in the Bible, but the Roman Catholic Church had banned it as early as the sixth century. In the United States, a number of states banned it in the mid-nineteenth century, but such bans were not in place in British colonial America nor by the Church of England.[133] Perhaps, for the readers of this volume, one of the most remarkable features of all among these American-born naval officers is that such a family of naval professionals could produce a naval historian among them at a time when such individuals were among the rarest of *rarae aves*.

133 'A Table of Kindred and Affinity, wherein whosoever are related are forbidden in Scripture and our Law [in the Church of England] to Marry', *The Book of Common Prayer* (1662) <https://www.eskimo.com/~lhowell/bcp1662/misc/kindred_1662.html> (accessed 17 April 2019). Special thanks to the Rev. Alan Neale, Trinity Church, Newport for this citation.

10

Able Seaman Philip Brimblecom (1786-1824) – Marblehead, Massachusetts

Matthew Brenckle

The story of Philip Brimblecom represents all the tensions and dangers of the early nineteenth-century Atlantic world. Born in Marblehead, Massachusetts in 1786, Brimblecom launched his career like many other young men in town, by going to sea in search of cod. In 1809, he gave up the hook and line and shipped on board his uncle's schooner, the *Springbird*, for a voyage to Spain with a cargo of salt fish.[1] As they approached San Sebastian, the *Springbird* fell in with two French privateers and was carried into St Jean-de-Luz, France. The French authorities impounded Brimblecom's vessel because it carried a cargo destined for a port under the control of the British or their allies. Brimblecom stayed by his uncle's side until March 1810, but as there was 'no prospect of the Schooner's being cleared for a long time,' he signed on board a French merchant ship bound for the Isle of France in the Indian Ocean.[2] Four days out, a British frigate took the ship and Brimblecom found himself a prisoner of the Royal Navy. He was sent to a prison ship in Plymouth, England and later transferred to the infamous Mill Prison there.[3]

---

1 National Archives, Washington, DC, Philip Brimblecom pension application, War of 1812 Pension files, File No. 201, RG 15.

2 The *Springbird*'s captain, Nicholas Tucker, stayed with his vessel and eventually negotiated her release. He was allowed half the net proceeds of his cargo and was permitted to buy brandy and wine for the return voyage. He sailed for Marblehead on 29 July 1810 and arrived home at the beginning of September. *Anti-Monarchist and Republican Watchman*, Northampton, Massachusetts, 19 September 1810.

3 National Archives, Washington, DC, Letters Received by the Department of State Regarding Impressed Seamen, 1794-1815, RG 59. Hannah Brimblecom to James Monroe,

In December 1810, the young sailor managed to send a letter describing his ordeal to his mother, Hannah, back in Marblehead. Because the United States was not at war with England, American citizens should not have been held as prisoners of war. Hannah sent Philip's protection certificate (which was a sort of passport and birth certificate in one) and his baptismal record to the American consul in London to prove her son was, in fact, an American citizen. The consul responded that the British considered Brimblecom a prisoner of war because he had been captured while serving on a French 'privateer.'[4] Finding this response unacceptable, in March 1812 Mrs. Brimblecom wrote to Secretary of State James Monroe to request his help. While the diplomatic wheels slowly turned, the British took Brimblecom from prison and, according to him, forced him to serve aboard HM Sloop *Martin* (18). [5] It is possible, however, that he volunteered to escape the horrible conditions in the British prison. Not willing to wait for a bureaucratic resolution to his ordeal, he made his escape by deserting on 4 March 1812, and found a berth on board a ship bound for Newburyport, Massachusetts.

Bad luck continued to plague Brimblecom, and during the passage home his new ship wrecked on the Orkney Islands. Brimblecom and his shipmates travelled from those bleak islands to Scotland, where he shipped on board an American brig bound for New York. The vessel sailed for home on 2 July 1812, her crew unaware that the United States had declared war on Great Britain on 18 June. On 9 August, the ship fell in with HM Sloop *Avenger* (18), off the American coast and was captured.[6] The British took him to Newfoundland, whence he was sent home in a prisoner exchange in September 1812.[7] At age 26, Brimblecom had experienced enough misfortune to last most men several lifetimes. His next step made sense for someone who must have seethed with a desire for vengeance. On 25 September 1812, three days after arriving home, he enlisted as an able seaman on board the frigate *Constitution*. The ship had just returned victorious from an

2 March 1812.

4   National Archives, Washington, DC, Letters Received, RG 59, American consulate to Hannah Brimblecom, 23 December 1811.

5   HMS *Martin* was an 18-gun sloop-of-war commanded by John Evans. David Steel, *Steel's Original and Correct List of the Royal Navy and Hon. East-India Company Shipping, January-June 1813* (London: Steel's Navigation Warehouse, 1813). Additionally, Martin was Bermuda-built. She wrecked off the west coast of Ireland on 8 December 1817. J.J. Colledge and Ben Warlow, *Ships of the Royal Navy: The Complete Record of all Fighting Ships of the Royal Navy from the 15th Century to the Present* (London: Chatham Publishing, 2006), p.217.

6   Brimblecom was very lucky, because the converted collier, HMS *Avenger*, was wrecked off St John's, Newfoundland on 8 October 1812. Colledge and Warlow, *Ships of the Royal Navy*, p.26.

7   National Archives, Washington, DC, Brimblecom pension application.

encounter with the fifth-rate frigate HMS *Guerriere* (38), off the coast of Nova Scotia, and her new captain, William Bainbridge, had no trouble recruiting men to serve on the lucky vessel.

USS *Constitution* vs HMS *Java*, 29 December 1812. (NHHC NH 118645)

Constitution's far-famed luck did not extend to Seaman Brimblecom. As the ship and her crew sailed south during October and November, the sailors frequently 'exercised at the great guns,' learning to perform their duties with speed and accuracy. According to the ship's 'quarter bill,' Brimblecom served as the first loader to gun number one on the gun deck. He did his duty there on 29 December 1812, when *Constitution* encountered the fifth-rate frigate HMS *Java* (38) off the Brazilian coast. It was a dangerous position and this was the ship's most ferocious battle of the war. To load the gun by ramming the powder, ball, and wad, the loader exposed his body in the open gunport. In the midst of the action, as Brimblecom bent to load the gun, a British cannonball shattered his arm below the elbow. Surgeon Amos Evans amputated the limb, and although the stump quickly healed, the young sailor remained in constant pain.[8]

With only one arm, Brimblecom could not work as a sailor, the only work he had ever known. Twice he wrote to the Navy Department seeking employment and for an increase in his six dollars per month pension, which he and his mother relied upon. 'Some of the rest that was wounded with me has had an addition to their pension money,' he asserted. [9] With the help of Captain Isaac Hull, Brimblecom found work at the Charlestown Navy Yard in 1816 and at the Portsmouth Navy Yard the following year. By 1820 he was unable 'to do anything for a living,' and, since he had 'no friends on earth,' he asked the government to take his request 'into consideration and look after a poor distressed crippled sailor,' who 'for 22 long months ... [has] never seen a well day.' His file contains no evidence of a reply, but it would have come too late to do much good. Philip Brimblecom died of a fever on 1 February 1824 in Marblehead. He was only 37 years old.[10] Ultimately, Brimblecom's story serves as a powerful reminder of the harsh realities that many lower deck personnel faced in multiple navies during the Napoleonic Age.

8   William L. Clements Library, University of Michigan, Medical day book of Surgeon Amos A. Evans, USS *Constitution, 28* August 1812 to 5 March 1813.
9   National Archives, Washington, DC, Brimblecom pension application.
10   'Massachusetts, Town and Vital Records, 1620-1988', *Ancestry.com*, Provo, Utah <https// www.ancestry.com>

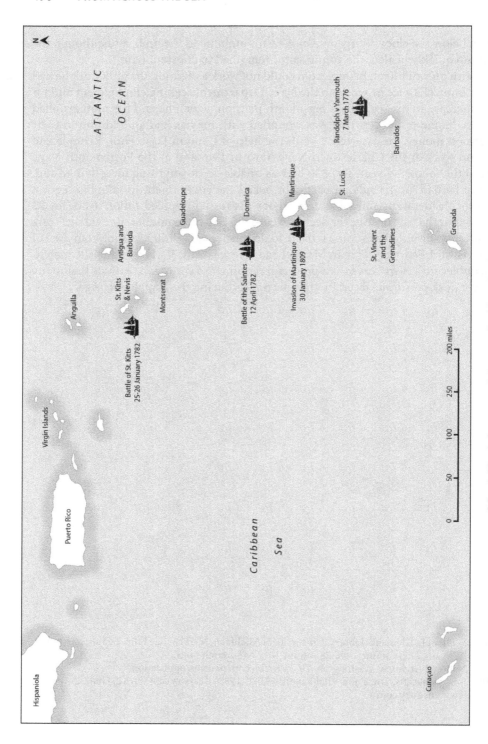

Map 3. North Americans fighting in Caribbean battles.

11

Admiral Sir Isaac Coffin, 1st Baronet, GCH (1759-1839) – Boston Massachusetts

Andrew Zellers-Frederick

In 1759, Boston was the capital of His Majesty's Colony of Massachusetts, which was firmly involved in America's French and Indian War or, as the struggle was known in Europe, the Seven Years War. The city was the third largest within the American Colonies, behind Philadelphia and New York City. It was at this time that Isaac Coffin was born on 16 May 1759 to a prominent Bostonian Family that served the interests of the British Crown. His father, Nathaniel Coffin, the first generation of the family born in America, held a high civil service position as the official paymaster or cashier of the Customs Office of Boston. By 1774, he was appointed addresser, an individual who possessed skill and grace in dealing with people and situations. Nathaniel and his family developed strong personal and professional ties with Lieutenant Governor Thomas Hutchinson, senior officers of the Royal Navy, and Governor Thomas Gage, who was commander-in-chief of all British forces in North America. The Coffin family evolved into a leading and powerful Loyalist family, steadfast to the core to the monarchy, and completely dependent on the ebb-and-flow of colonial royal authority as Massachusetts fractured into two groups with radically different political beliefs.[1]

The influence of Boston, surrounded by all aspects of water and its international maritime trade, obviously nurtured Isaac's desire to serve in the Royal Navy, the largest naval force in the world and the defender of the British Empire. At the age of 14, Isaac entered the service through the patronage and support of a close

---

1   Lorenzo Sabin, *The American Loyalists* or *Biographical Sketches of Adherents to the British Crown in The War of the Revolution* (Boston, Massachusetts: Charles C. Little & James Brown, 1848), pp.18-22.

Portrait of Admiral Sir Isaac Coffin, 1st Baronet, GCH (1759-1839) who remained closely connected with his New England roots. (Open source)

family friend, Rear Admiral John Montagu, Commander-in-Chief of the Royal Navy's North America Station (1771-74). Coffin's first assignment was aboard HM Brig *Gaspee* (6).[2] His training was entrusted to the ship's commander, Lieutenant William Hunter, who had great praise for his dedicated midshipman:

> Of all the young men I ever had a care of, none answered my expectations equal to Isaac Coffin. He pleased me so much that I took all the pains in my power to make him a good seaman; and I succeeded to the height of my wishes; for never did I know a young man to acquire so much nautical knowledge in so short a time.[3]

---

2   The *Gaspee* was named for the customs service schooner *Gaspee* which was attacked and burned by a mob off Rhode Island earlier in 1773.
3   Thomas C. Amory, *The Life of Admiral Sir Isaac Coffin, Baronet* (Boston, Massachusetts: Cupples, Upham and Company, 1886), p.36.

In October 1773, Midshipman Coffin reported aboard HM Sloop *Kingfisher* (14) commanded by Captain George Montagu, the son of his first major patron. Coffin then followed his commander aboard his new command, the sixth-rate frigate HMS *Fowey* (24). Both vessels soon became tangled in the collapse of British government in Virginia. The Royal Governor John Murray, the Earl of Dunmore, did much to cause the rebellion when he ordered the Royal Marines to seize the colonial supply of gunpowder from the magazine stored in the capital of Williamsburg. Dunmore had expected this 'display of force to overawe' what he considered to be a relatively few disorganised rabble-rousers, and to 'soothe' the rapidly growing opposition to British rule.[4] Although a military showdown was narrowly avoided, it was clear that the governor's rule in the name of King George III was finished.

From aboard the *Fowey*, anchored off the nearby port of Yorktown, Midshipman Coffin had a front-row seat to these momentous historical events in Virginia. Dunmore ordered Montagu to send 40 marines (nicknamed 'boiled crabs' by the *Virginia Gazette*) and sailors from *Fowey* to fortify his dwindling area of royal control. Captain Montagu brusquely warned that he would bombard Yorktown if there was further patriot interference with the royal governor.[5] Dunmore had already wisely placed Lady Dunmore and her children on *Fowey* for their safety.

Captain Montagu managed to get himself into trouble with his new superior, Admiral Thomas Graves. He allowed Dunmore to persuade him to order HM Schooner *Magdalen* to sail his family to Great Britain under the guise that the schooner was sending urgent dispatches to the British government. This action countermanded Grave's order to position the schooner in the Delaware Bay. Admiral Graves was not at all impressed by Montagu's claim that the dispatches were urgent and threatened Montagu with court-martial.[6] It is apparent that Coffin's benefactor's family prevented the court martial from occurring. In the meantime, the *Fowey* enabled many of Virginia's other royal officials to escape the deteriorating Virginia situation. Coffin would have also intermingled with other British colonial officials when Maryland's popular royal governor, William Eden, and his entourage were given safe conduct to depart the colony from Annapolis aboard the *Fowey*.

If Coffin's political views on the need to serve the British Crown were not already decided in his mind, they were now certainly hardened as he surely realised that members of his own family in Boston could suffer a similar fate. The British garrison

---

4   John E. Selby, *The Revolution in Virginia, 1775-1783* (Williamsburg, Virginia: Colonial Williamsburg Foundation, 1988), p.2.
5   Selby, *Revolution in Virginia*, pp.4-5.
6   Selby, *Revolution in Virginia*, p.46.

was evacuated in March 1776, taking with them Loyalist families. Coffin's patron, Admiral Montagu, commanded the evacuation. Following his service aboard *Fowey*, Coffin was assigned to the former merchantman, HM Schooner *Diligent* (6), under the command of Lieutenant Edmund Dod. Dod's main mission was for *Diligent* to escort British convoys in the vicinity of Halifax. It was on *Diligent* that Coffin was informed that he would be promoted to lieutenant.

Before Coffin could assume his new rank, he was transferred to the fourth-rate HMS *Romney* (50) which often served as the flagship for the Commander-in-Chief of the Newfoundland Station. In June 1778, he was transferred to the third-rate HMS *Europe* (64), formerly the French *Europa*. Once more, this posting did not last long as Coffin's long-awaited lieutenancy became official in October of 1778. He was then posted to the cutter *Placentia* assigned to Halifax under Admiral Montagu. This posting was quickly followed by his assuming command of the armed vessel *Pinson* on which he survived her shipwreck off the coast of Labrador later that year.

With the loss of *Pinson*, Coffin sailed to England and volunteered his services to Captain Thomas Pasley who was in command of the new sixth-rate frigate HMS *Sibyl* (28) commissioned in 1779 in England.[7] It appears that Coffin's experience was such that he became a sort of seafaring 'fireman' as he filled officer vacancies needed by the Royal Navy. With the launching of the new fourth-rate HMS *Adamant* (50) under the command of Captain Gideon Johnson in January 1780[8], Coffin was assigned as the ship's second lieutenant. There he helped to supervise the final stages of her fitting out. Coffin was instrumental in successfully sailing the warship, using jury-rigged masts, from Liverpool to Plymouth, so that his ship could complete her fitting-out. By August, *Adamant* had sailed for New York where she was urgently needed to escort British convoys that were frequently attacked by American privateers and ships of the Continental Navy.[9] It was not long until Coffin was transferred to the second-rate HMS *London* (98), the flagship of Rear Admiral Graves, the second in command of the North American Station. He quickly moved to the third-rate HMS *Royal Oak* (74), flagship of Vice Admiral Marriott Arbuthnot, Commander-in-Chief of the North American Station. He was the Admiral's signal lieutenant. For such a young officer, this responsibility again demonstrated his advanced abilities.

The Battle of Cape Henry was part of the large-scale naval chess match that would conclude with the American/French victory at Yorktown approximately

---

7   J.J. Colledge & Ben Warlow, *Ships of the Royal Navy: The Complete Record of all Fighting Ships of the Royal Navy from the 15th Century to the Present* (London: Chatham Publishing, 2006), p.320.
8   Colledge & Warlow, *Ships of the Royal Navy*, p.4.
9   Selby, *Revolution in Virginia, 1775-1783*, p.37.

seven months later. Seven French ships-of-the-line, which had escorted the 6,000 troops of the Comte Jean Baptiste de Rochambeau to the shores of Rhode Island, were a constant source of trepidation for Admiral Arbuthnot. The 70-year-old Admiral was not a well man; he experienced blindness in one eye and was prone to fainting spells that debilitated him for days at a time. He was in New York waiting for permission from the Admiralty to resign his command and return home to England. As part of the naval chess match, the French tricked Arbuthnot's second in command, Rear Admiral Thomas Graves, into believing they had weighed anchor in Newport and were sailing to Virginia to interfere with the raids of the British forces under General Benedict Arnold. While the French merely feigned their movements and returned to the safety of their Rhode Island anchorage, the British continued to sail on an intercept course into a violent storm. Three of the British ships suffered heavy storm damage; the third-rate HMS *America* (64) was blown hundreds of miles off course; the third-rate HMS *Bedford* (74) was dismasted, and the third-rate HMS *Culloden* (74) was wrecked on Long Island on 24 January 1781.[10]

Infirm at 70, Arbuthnot was still a dutiful and skilled seaman. Learning of *Culloden's* wrecking, he hoisted himself out of his sick bed and personally supervised the multi-week tasks of removing the masts, yards, and rigging from the smashed third-rate and reinstalling them on the *Bedford*. Arbuthnot appeared in contemporary accounts as 'a coarse, blustering, foul-mouthed-bully' and in history as an example of the extremity to which the maladministration of Lord Sandwich had reduced the Royal Navy, but clearly, on urgent occasions, the elderly Admiral's actions undoubtedly did much to inspire and invigorate young officers such as Coffin.[11] On 8 March 1781, the French squadron finally sailed from Newport to support the Marquis de Lafayette's expedition against Arnold's forces in Virginia. Admiral Arbuthnot detected this movement and, as quickly as possible, assembled his own forces and sailed on the 10th. On board the Admiral's flagship, the third-rate, HMS *Royal Oak* (74), Coffin was a direct observer as the British fleet surmounted their handicap of 36 hours and caught the French fleet off the capes of the Chesapeake. In his book, *The Major Operations of the Navies in the War of American Independence*, Alfred Thayer Mahan summarised the action:

> In this encounter, both sides had eight ships of the line, besides smaller craft. The advantage in force was distinctly with the British, who had one three-decked ship, three 74's, three 64's, and a 50; while the French had

---

10   Colledge and Warlow, *Ships of the Royal Navy*, p.85.
11   Mark M. Boatner III, *Encyclopaedia of the American Revolution* (Mechanicsburg, Pennsylvania: Stackpole Books, 1994), p.23.

one 84, two 74's, four 64's, and the late British Romulus, 44. Because of this superiority, probably, the action was considered particularly discreditable by contemporaries; the more so because several vessels did not engage closely, – a fault laid to the British admiral's failure to make the signal for close action, hauling down that for the line. This criticism is interesting, for it indicates how men's minds were changing; and it shows also that Arbuthnot had not changed, but still lived in the middle of the century. The French commodore displayed very considerable tactical skill; his squadron was handled neatly, quickly, and with precision. With inferior force he carried off a decided advantage by sheer intelligence and good management. Unluckily, he failed in resolution to pursue his advantage. He probably could have controlled the Chesapeake had he persisted.[12]

As the Admiral's signal lieutenant, Coffin had the responsibility to inform Arbuthnot or his flag captain that the signal, 'engage the enemy more closely,' should be raised whilst lowering 'form a single line.' However, this miscue did not affect his career, as this engagement did achieve a short-lived victory for the British, forcing the French to return to Newport for repairs.[13]

As the Virginia campaign was ultimately to end in defeat for the British on both the land at Yorktown and on the sea at the Battle of the Capes on 5 September 1781, it was not Coffin's destiny to play a role. After the first Battle of Cape Henry, the *Royal Oak* sailed to New York where she ran aground while passing from the North to the East River. The ship sailed to Halifax for major repairs after which she returned to New York, while Arbuthnot returned to Britain into naval obscurity. As Graves succeeded Arbuthnot, Coffin received the news every young naval officer waited to hear; he was promoted on 3 July 1781 to master and commander and given command of HM Sloop *Avenger* (8), the former fireship *Lucifer,* initially stationed in New York's North River.[14] After six months, he exchanged commands with Alexander Cochrane and assumed command of HM Sloop *Pacahunter* (14). While his new command was anchored in St John's, Nova Scotia, a great fire erupted in the Canadian port town. Coffin and his crew assisted with the

12   Alfred T. Mahan, *The Major Operations of the Navies in the War of American Independence* (London: Sampson Low, Marston & Company 1913), pp.173-174.

13   Richard L. Blanco (ed.), *The American Revolution 1776-1783: An Encyclopaedia*, Vol. I (New York: Garland Publishing, 1993), pp.253-256; Brian Tunstall, *Naval Warfare in the Age of Sail: The Evolution of Fighting Tactics 1650-1815* (Edison, New Jersey: Wellfleet Press, 2001), pp.168-169.

14   Colledge and Warlow, *Ships of the Royal Navy*, p.208.

firefighting efforts; a service that earned him the official thanks and praise of the House of Assembly.

Coffin's service aboard the *Pacahunter* repeated his vocational pattern. When the opportunity arose to serve on Rear Admiral Samuel Hood's flagship, the second-rate HMS *Barfleur* (90), Coffin and his entire crew volunteered to do so. There was a strong personal connection between Hood and Coffin, as Hood knew Coffin and his family well. It required little solicitation on Hood's part to persuade Coffin and his crew to volunteer to serve on his flagship.[15] The Admiral learned that the French admiral, the Comte Francois Joseph Paul de Grasse, the victor of the Battle of the Capes, was sailing his fleet to the island of St Kitts. This news only added to the crisis facing Britain's global empire. Gibraltar was under a desperate siege; the island of Menorca was about to surrender; the French were victorious in the Indian Ocean; the remaining American colonies appeared lost; Spain had captured West Florida, and the Dutch had entered the war. In the West Indies, the situation was equally desperate with the French seizing the island of Tobago, and Jamaica appeared particularly vulnerable to French designs. Compounding the situation, British maritime and military resources were spread thin with the plethora of worldwide commitments.

Britain hoped for a needed victory to restore morale and faith in their government. King George III expressed his strong opinion on the Caribbean that, 'Our Islands must be defended even at the risk of an invasion of this island ... If we lose our Sugar Islands, it will be impossible to raise money to continue the War.'[16] On 11 January 1782, British Brigadier General Thomas Fraser's small St Kitts garrison of only 600 regulars and militia found themselves opposing the Marquis de Boulle with more than 10 times their number. Coffin was aboard Hood's flagship, the second-rate HMS *Barfleur* (98). Hood decided to attack the de Grasse's fleet's island anchorage and relieve the vastly outnumbered garrison. Although his forces were also inferior to de Grasse by 29 to 22, Coffin witnessed how skillfully Hood manoeuvred his fleet to defeat de Grasse. Hood lured de Grasse's fleet from St Kitts and then occupied the same anchorage the French had left. Maintaining his position through the middle of February, Hood had repulsed de Grasse's fleet, which suffered considerable damage in its effort to dislodge Hood. Although Hood succeeded in landing a small number of reinforcements to assist the besieged garrison, it fell to the French on 12 February. This gave the French possession of St Kitts. However, it was now the French who were the ones to be besieged and isolated from de Grasse's fleet.

15   Amory, *Life of Admiral Sir Isaac Coffin*, p.38.
16   'Letter from George III to Lord Sandwich' in G.R. Barnes & J.H. Owens (eds.) *Private Papers of John, Earl of Sandwich*, Vol. III (London: Navy Records Office, 1933), p.201.

Coffin saw action at The Battle of Frigate Bay, St Kitts, 24-25 January 1782. Painting by Nicholas Pocock. (Open source)

These British naval operations in the Caribbean, in which Coffin undoubtedly played his part, constitute a major historical era in the annals of the Royal Navy. Hood's actions became legendary by compelling a superior enemy to quit their anchorage and defeating them at every turn. Cutting the French off from their land forces was a tactic that reflects Hood's genius. His actions demonstrated bravery and knowledge of naval manoeuvres, drawing on the precision skills of his officers and the crews they led. Naval historians believe that Nelson's excellent relations with his officers evolved from his studies of Hood's actions in the various Caribbean engagements. Hood kept an exceptional rapport with his officers to an extent that they could anticipate his actions and signal flags were not always required.[17] On 14 February, Hood slipped away to join Admiral George Rodney who had returned with his forces from Britain. The British now had the superior naval numbers they required to protect and recapture their West Indies colonies.[18]

The Caribbean continued its high stakes competitive role as the British and the French forces, the latter now joined by the Spanish fleet, manoeuvred for what would amount to the final major naval engagement of the American War

17   Blanco, *The American Revolution*, p.772.
18   Peter Trew, *Rodney and the Breaking of the Line* (Barnsley, South Yorkshire: Pen & Sword Military, 2006), pp.136-137; Tunstall, *Naval Warfare in the Age of Sail*, pp.177-179.

for Independence. The British were determined to defend their prized colony of Jamaica which was in the cross-hairs of the French forces. With Admiral Rodney in overall command, this battle would be a rematch for Hood and de Grasse. For a young lieutenant, the sight of 36 British ships-of-the-line, with escorting frigates and other supporting vessels, must have been an extraordinary sight. Coffin certainly would have been fascinated as the British fleet closed on 8 April with de Grasse's 35 ships-of-the-line accompanied by six frigates and 150 unarmed ships with the supplies required for their Jamaican invasion.

The ensuing epic, multi-day Battle of the Saintes broke French naval power in the Caribbean. Coffin was present as de Grasse struck the colours on his powerful flagship (after receiving more casualties on the *Ville de Paris* than the entire British fleet) following a solid pounding by Hood's division. It is certain that Coffin also witnessed the momentous moment when a French naval commander-in-chief was captured for the first time in the annals of British naval history. The victory had a human side that would have moved any officer such as Coffin. As the captured French ships were inspected by Hood's officers, they not only discovered the vast carnage, but also the inconceivable filth and squalor typical of the enemy's navy.[19] Unlike British ships in which Coffin served, the French vessels were sealed by hatches rather than gratings, with their scuppers never opened to permit the accumulated waste to flow into the sea. Certainly these experiences made an impression on Coffin concerning the treatment of those on the lower deck.[20]

Following this epic British naval victory, Coffin's contributions to the battle and his bravery and talents were amply rewarded by Admiral, now 1st Viscount Hood, supported by Admiral, now Lord Rodney. On 13 June 1782, at the age of only 22, Captain Coffin was awarded the command of the third-rate HMS *Shrewsbury* (74). Before assuming command, Coffin was in Antigua where his courage and tenacity were again called on as if to demonstrate that this young officer was worthy of commanding a major warship. A fire erupted in the town of St Johns and the community was in danger of being totally consumed by the conflagration. As he had demonstrated in the Canadian St Johns incident, Coffin led a collection of sailors in stemming the progress of the flames at the risk of his own life. As he had previously received recognition in Canada for his bravery, he was honoured with an official address of thanks from the island's parliament.[21]

19   Bob Rupert, 'Who Really "Crossed the T" in the Battle of the Saintes?' *Journal of the American Revolution* (Yardley, Pennsylvania: Westholme Publishing, 2015), p.312.
20   Sam Willis, *The Struggle for Sea Power: A Naval History of American Independence* (London: Atlantic Books, 2015), p.465; Tunstall, *Naval Warfare in the Age of Sail*, pp.179-182.
21   Amory, *Life of Admiral Sir Isaac Coffin*, p.41.

Consequently, many in the Royal Navy considered Coffin a valuable asset as demonstrated by a meteoric career that emphasized his tremendous energy, aptitude, and gallantry that earned him prestige and many promotions. These talents also exposed him as an attraction for jealous disputes and misunderstandings. Within only a few weeks of accepting his command of the *Shrewsbury*, he rejected instructions to add three ill-equipped midshipmen to his crew as new lieutenants, despite the orders of Admiral Lord Rodney. He eventually acceded to the Admiral's order; however, Coffin was subsequently brought before a naval court martial on 29 July 1782 on charges of disobedience and contempt. He was ultimately acquitted, but now he had acquired some powerful enemies. In 1783, he was appointed to command the sixth-rate frigate *HMS Hydra* (24). But, with war's end, she paid off and Coffin found himself unemployed and on half-pay.

After a prolonged visit to France, he returned to service in May 1786 to command the sixth-rate frigate HMS *Thisbe* (28). His initial orders were to convey General Sir Guy Carlton along with his family to Carlton's new post as Governor-in-Chief in Quebec. Upon *Thisbe's* arrival on 10 October, Coffin departed for a better winter anchorage in Halifax. The next year, while conducting naval operations in the Gulf of St Lawrence, Coffin took a keen interest in the Madelaine Islands. Because he was an ardent American Loyalist who was deprived of patrimony due to the outcome of the recent war, the Crown would grant him these islands for good service in 1798.

While at Halifax station, Coffin entered four boys, including two of Lord Dorchester's sons, onto the *Thisbe's* muster as captain's servants. The boys actually never served on the ship and the suspicion is they were still at school. The practice was theoretically prohibited, but it was widespread throughout the Royal Navy with many officers beginning their service while living ashore and serving at sea in name only. Coffin's enemies now gathered against him and charges were made accusing him of knowingly falsifying the ship's muster. He was subsequently court martialed and was found guilty. Such a breach of naval regulations normally required the defendant to be dismissed from the service. However, because of the malevolent character of the charge, and the fact the practice was widespread, the court only relieved him of command of the *Thisbe*.

Upon Coffin's return to Britain, Admiral Richard Howe, the First Lord of the Admiralty, insisted that the full punishment required by the 31st Article of War be enforced with Coffin fully dismissed from the Royal Navy. Howe's orders were dutifully carried out, but Coffin bravely lodged an appeal against the judgement. While the judges of the Admiralty deliberated for several years, Coffin searched for a post with the Danish, Swedish, and Russian navies. By 1790, Howe's decision to override the original court-martial's judgment was pronounced illegal, and Coffin was restored to his rank along with the payment of his missed earnings. It should be noted that because of Coffin's persistence in appealing Howe's interference, a legal precedent was established to limit the Admiralty's intrusion in verdicts decreed by courts-martial.

In 1791, Coffin, now commanding the sixth-rate frigate HMS *Alligator* (20), transported Guy Carlton, now Lord Dorchester, back to Britain from Canada. With his return to Britain, Coffin was again placed on half-pay until war erupted again in 1793 during which he was given command of the fifth-rate frigate HMS *Melampus* (36).[22] However, within a year, Coffin was injured, compounding a previous hernia injury that he received when he heroically jumped overboard to save the life of one of his seamen. This new injury was so debilitating that Coffin was never again medically fit for sea duty. For months Coffin was virtually crippled, but as a relatively young man, he managed to partially recover. In 1795, he was appointed as the regulating captain at Leith, Scotland. He would later become the Naval Civil Commissioner at Corsica until the French forced the British evacuation in 1796.

Sailing from Corsica, Coffin's new assignments took him to Elba, Lisbon, Halifax, and finally to Sheerness. As commandant of its naval yard, Coffin recognised that its officials were overwhelmingly corrupt. With support from the First Sea Lord, Admiral the Earl of St Vincent, he zealously enforced the naval regulations to end the corruption. This earned him a promotion to the rank of rear admiral on 23 April 1804. His forthright reputation as an effective, efficient, and enthusiastic officer finally merited him the title of 'Baronet of the Madelaine Islands in the Gulph [sic] of St Lawrence.' His rank advancements (albeit now on land) included a promotion to admiral-superintendent of the Portsmouth Dockyard followed by vice admiral when he decided to retire on 28 April 1808.

Retired at 52, Coffin married the heiress Elizabeth Browne (he briefly changed his name for two years to Coffin-Greenly) and started a family. He became a full admiral on 4 June 1814 and entered politics as an elected Member of Parliament for Ilchester in 1818, holding the seat until 1828. Other honours were bestowed upon him. In 1832, he was made a Knight Grand Cross of the Royal Guelphic Order. As a friend of the Duke of Clarence (later King William IV), he was placed on the King's 1832 private list for peerage. Unfortunately, Coffin's life turned full circle as several government ministers opposed his ennoblement because of his American roots. His rejection was not unusual; many American Loyalists who had both upheld the royal cause and who served the Crown militarily were treated badly.[23] It also appears that Coffin still considered himself more American than

22   Rif Winfield, *British Warships in the Age of Sail 1793-1817* (London: Chatham Press, 2005), p.223.
23   North Callahan, *Flight from the Republic: The Tories of the American Revolution* (New York: Bobs-Merrill Co., 1967), p.110.

ever. But despite his trying, he and other Loyalists could never fully consider themselves to be English.[24]

However, as a descendant of the Coffins who had originally settled on Nantucket, the Admiral still wished to give something back to his homeland and island, which was still populated with many of his kinsmen. As he had no heirs, Coffin wanted his name to be remembered. There were suggestions of a monument, a church and even a training ship, but the proposal that persuaded him was to create a school for his relatives. He decided to establish a school on the island; one based upon the Lancasterian School model. Known as the Coffin School, it was founded in 1827, 'for the purpose of promoting decency, good order and morality, and for giving a good English education to youth who are descendants of the late Tristram Coffin …' In keeping with his principles, instead of making the school free, the Admiral decided a small fee should be charged because he felt that free things were treated as having little value. One of the Admiral's greatest wishes was that the male students receive nautical training. In keeping with his desire, the brig *Clio* was purchased to serve as a training ship.[25] On 23 July 1839, Sir Isaac Coffin died at the age of 80 and was buried in Cheltenham, Gloucestershire. With no sons to carry his name, his baronetcy expired.

24   Callahan, *Flight from the Republic*, p.90.
25   Jascin Leonardo Finger, 'Do You Know This Building? The Admiral Sir Isaac Coffin Lancastrian School, Part One', *Nantucket Chronicle*, February 2, 2016 <https://www.nantucketchronicle.com/nation-Nantucket/2016/do-you-know-this-building-admiral-site-isaac-coffin-lancasterian-school-part> (accessed 14 September 2016)

12

Rear Admiral Francis Holmes Coffin (1768-1842) – Boston, Massachusetts

Dr Samantha A. Cavell

Born in Portsmouth, New Hampshire on 12 July 1768,[1] Francis Holmes Coffin was the son of John Coffin, a Nantucket merchant, distiller, and Loyalist who fled Boston for Quebec, Canada with his family in 1775. John fought nobly at the Siege of Quebec on 31 December of that year and was officially praised for his role in thwarting the attack by American Patriot forces under Major General Richard Montgomery and Colonel Benedict Arnold, the first major defeat for the revolutionary cause in North America.

Francis' Loyalist pedigree and the patronage of his cousin, Commander Isaac Coffin RN, who was then serving under Admiral Hood in the West Indies, helped him enter the Royal Navy as a captain's servant aboard the fifth-rate frigate HMS *Daedalus* (32), on 26 April 1782. He subsequently served as a midshipman and master's mate aboard the sixth-rate HMS *Thisbe* (28), then under the command of Isaac Coffin, and the sixth-rate frigate HMS *Dido* (28), on the Halifax Station. Undoubtedly, Francis was therefore present for Captain Coffin's disgrace. A 1788 court martial aboard *Dido*, in Halifax, found him guilty of false muster, having entered the names of four boys on the ship's books, two of whom were sons of Lord Dorchester, while they were still away at school. In practice, captains engaged in the false muster of captains' servants and first-class volunteers on a regular basis.[2]

---

1   Date according to the baptismal certificate attached to Coffin's application for the examination for lieutenant. The National Archives, Kew, London (TNA) ADM 45/15/518, ff. 44-45.
2   S.A. Cavell, *Midshipmen and Quarterdeck Boys in the British Navy, 1771-1831* (London: Boydell Press, 2012), p.54.

Isaac Coffin, however, had made enemies during his time on the West Indies Station; Rodney among them, and the charges were likely related to these earlier incidents.[3] Isaac Coffin was ultimately dismissed from the *Thisbe*, but not from the service, and, with the onset of the French Wars,[4] his service in the navy progressed despite the controversy. Francis Coffin, like many of his colleagues, benefitted from the Spanish armament and the threat of war over Nootka Sound in 1790. A shortage of lieutenants presented the Admiralty with a potentially crippling problem, a situation that only helped Coffin's chances of passing the examination for lieutenant for which he sat in December 1790. He received a commission on 13 July 1791.

In 1795, Coffin was part of Rear Admiral George Elphinstone's (later Lord Keith) campaign to seize the Cape of Good Hope from the Dutch, after their alliance with France in the previous year. Serving first in the sloop-of-war HMS *Rattlesnake* (16), Coffin distinguished himself in an action with Captain Thomas Masterman Hardy in which the British squadron faced heavy fire from Dutch forces and overcame their position at Cape Town in August. Major General Sir James Craig, commanding British forces at Cape Town, related that: 'Captain Hardy and Lieutenant Coffin crossed the water with the seamen and marines under their command, received the enemy's fire without returning a shot, and manoeuvred with a regularity that would not have discredited veteran troops.'[5] Coffin's success saw him appointed to Elphinstone's flagship, the third-rate HMS *Monarch* (74), from which he participated in the reduction of the Dutch squadron at Saldanha Bay in August 1796. He also served as Elphinstone's courier in correspondence with the Dutch Rear Admiral Lucas after his capitulation. Coffin's role in the negotiations spoke to Elphinstone's faith in his ability to conduct himself with tact and discretion.

As a reward for his efforts at the Cape, Coffin was given command of the sixth-rate frigate HMS *Sphinx* (20). He then played an active role in the capture of the French settlement at Foul Point, Madagascar in December 1796. He was promoted to commander on 23 August 1797 and although his subsequent appointments are difficult to trace, he appears next in the list of officers promoted to post-captain

---

3   Coffin, Sir Isaac (1759-1839), *Oxford Dictionary of National Biography* (Oxford 1893), p.216.
4   The case against Isaac Coffin continued when Lord Howe challenged the leniency of the court martial and demanded that he be dismissed from the service forever. A subsequent court found Howe's overturning of the original sentence to be unlawful and reinstated Coffin to his previous rank. John Delafons, *Treatise on Naval Courts Martial 1805* (Cambridge, Massachusetts: Gale, 2012), pp.22-27.
5   Quoted in John Marshall, *Royal Naval Biography* (London: Longman, Hurst, Rees, Orme & Brown, 1823), pp.586-587.

on 29 April 1802.[6] Coffin's was one of a mass distribution of promotions on this date, which came just one month after the signing of the Peace at Amiens. It was a common practice in the Royal Navy to 'promote out' at the end of a war, which meant unemployment for the vast majority of naval officers.[7] Such a promotion would entitle the officer to more generous half-pay as a reward for service. Fortunately for Coffin, and thousands like him, the peace was short-lived and hostilities recommenced with Napoleonic France in May 1803.

Coffin appears to have languished, however, in the competition for appointments. A glut of lieutenants, commanders, and post-captains was met with a limited number of ships and positions to command them. In 1804, he led a division of the Sea Fencibles, a militia-like organisation of boatmen and fishermen organised by locality for the defence of the British coastline. Renewed threats of a French invasion saw the Fencibles joined with the Impress Service to ensure manpower on board Britain's warships and along her vulnerable shores. For a new post-captain, appointment to the Fencibles was likely a disappointment. This land-based, inglorious job, which many naval and civic commentators dismissed as a useless folly, was understandably unpopular with ambitious officers who saw it as a dead-end in their career progress.[8] Coffin, it seems, was confined to the Fencibles for several years, serving in England and on the Irish Coast at Tralee.[9] In a remarkable stroke of luck, Coffin found his way back to sea in 1811 in command of the crack fifth-rate frigate HMS *Arethusa* (38). Frederick Chamier recalled life as a young midshipman aboard *Arethusa* on her mission to defeat slavers off the coast of Sierra Leone, and related tales of violent storms and a grounding that almost sank the ship. Chamier's youthful impressions of his captain, however, left much to be desired.[10] In November, Coffin sailed *Arethusa* to Jamaica and served under the command of Admiral Stirling, where he was active during the first year of the War of 1812. In 1813 he returned to England and *Arethusa* was broken up at Sheerness the following year.

Coffin failed to obtain another command or another appointment on land or at sea and spent the rest of his career on half-pay. A clue to his modest success is suggested by Chamier, when he wrote of Coffin's grounding of *Arethusa*:

6   Marshall, *Royal Naval Biography*, p.587.
7   Cavell, *Midshipmen*, p.222; Michael Lewis, *The Navy in Transition: A Social History 1814-1864* (London: Hodder & Stoughton, 1965), pp.67-68.
8   James Davey, *In Nelson's Wake: The Navy and the Napoleonic Wars* (Greenwich: National Maritime Museum, 2015), pp.48-49, 168-170.
9   Obituary in the *Gentleman's Magazine*, Vol. 18 (London, 1842), p.443.
10   Frederick Chamier, *Life of a Sailor, Seafarers' Voices*, Vol. V, edited by Vincent McInerney (Annapolis, Maryland: US Naval Institute Press, 2011), pp.78-94.

The captain called out loudly, 'Let go the anchor,' an order instantly countermanded by the first lieutenant, who wisely remarked that should we anchor on the shoal, the land wind would swing us on the rock. The rudder being useless, the sails were now worked as the first lieutenant directed, the captain, like a good boy, repeating the first lieutenant's orders until the ship was afloat.[11]

Chamier was writing for dramatic effect, although Coffin's limited career progress tends to reinforce the impression that he was a sailor without significant talent. It is also possible that his connections to the always-controversial Sir Isaac Coffin (a rear admiral and superintendent of the Portsmouth Dockyard from 1804 until his retirement in 1808) hampered his employment ambitions as much as they helped. A letter written from Dover in 1838 suggests however, that Coffin's talents may have lain in marine engineering rather than on the quarterdeck. The letter, addressed to 'Lt. B. Worthington RN,' offered insight and a technical critique of the young officer's plans for a breakwater at Dover Harbour and demonstrated a keen understanding of the defensive needs and hydrographical challenges facing the project.[12]

Francis Coffin eventually achieved the rank of Rear Admiral of the Blue (Retired) on 10 January 1837 and Rear Admiral of the White (Retired) in August 1840. He died on 10 April 1842, aged 74, at Dover. It appears that a substantial portion of Coffin's pay was still owing at the time of his death. His daughter, Ann Marie Fletcher, later filed a petition to the Admiralty to collect the unpaid portion.[13] His son, Isaac Campbell Coffin, was baptised 21 August 1801 and went on to become a major general in the Indian army and was knighted (Knight Commander Star of India) in 1866.

11   Chamier, *Life of a Sailor*, p.84.
12   B. Worthington, *Proposed Plan for Improving Dover Harbour* (Charleston, South Carolina: Nabu Press 2010 reprint of 1838 edition), pp.165-66.
13   TNA ADM 45/15/518, ff. 44.

13

Captain John Loring (ca. 1760–1808) – Boston, Massachusetts

Dr Sean M. Heuvel

Several native-born sons of what is now the greater Boston, Massachusetts area found their way into the Royal Navy – serving on both the lower deck and quarterdeck – and made significant contributions in the fight against Revolutionary France as well as Napoleon. One of the more legendary sons of Boston who enjoyed a distinguished – albeit too short – career in the Royal Navy was Captain John Loring. Born into a prominent Loyalist family, Loring rose quickly from a penniless exile following the American Revolution to become one of the Royal Navy's most daring and respected post-captains. Had illness not conspired to prematurely end his sea-faring career, he would have likely gone on to achieve flag rank, accolades from the Crown, and possibly more. Until now, relatively little has been written about Loring, who has been somewhat overshadowed in the history books by some of his better-known relatives. This brief biographical sketch is therefore intended to re-introduce Loring to modern readers and renew interest in his many achievements and contributions to the Nelson-era Royal Navy.

Loring was born in approximately 1760 in the community of Jamaica Plain, now part of Boston.[1] At the time, Loring's father, Commodore Joshua Loring, was away commanding the Royal Navy's Great Lakes fleet during the French and Indian

---

1   Eva Phillips Boyd, 'Commodore Joshua Loring: Jamaica Plain by Way of London', *Old-Time New England Magazine* (April-June 1959) <http://www.jphs.org/people/2005/4/14/commodore-joshua-loring-jamaica-plain-by-way-of-london.html> (accessed 2 January 2017); Loring's exact birthdate has not yet been determined. Some sources claim he was born in 1760 while others list his birth as taking place in 1759 or 1761; Loring was born with a twin named Thomas, but Thomas died in 1768 at approximately the age of seven.

Captain John Loring, 1760-1808. (Courtesy Museum of the Shenandoah Valley, Julian Wood Glass Jr. Collection)

War.[2] However, on 23 August 1760, Commodore Loring (then commanding the British snow *Onondoga*) was seriously wounded by cannon fire near Fort Levis during the Battle of the Thousand Islands, bringing about a swift end to his naval career.[3] Following the battle, Commodore Loring joined his wife, Mary Curtis Loring,[4] and family in an affluent retirement in their newly-built home in Jamaica Plain, now known as the Loring-Greenough House. Their children included Hannah, Joshua ('the Younger'), twins Joseph Royal and Benjamin, Mary, and John (the subject of this piece).[5] As a child, young John Loring would have

---

2   James Henry Stark, *The Loyalists of Massachusetts and the other side of the American Revolution* (Salem, Massachusetts: Salem Press, 1910), p.424.
3   Thomas Mante, *History of the Late War in North America* (London: W. Strahan and T. Cadell, 1772), pp.301-307; a cannon shot tore the calf of Commodore Loring's right leg. According to Thomas Mante, the fact Loring survived the severe wound was remarkable.
4   Mary Curtis Loring (1720-1789) is my second cousin, nine times removed.
5   Boyd, 'Commodore Joshua Loring', pp.5-6.

been immersed in affluence and privilege, belonging to one of colonial Boston's most prominent families. However, all of that abruptly changed with the onset of the American Revolution, which brought about the Loring family's downfall in America. Following considerable debate and anguish, Commodore Loring re-affirmed his allegiance to the Crown in August 1774, forcing him to flee to British Army protection in inner Boston to escape his angry Patriot neighbours.[6] Further, Commodore Loring's Loyalist leanings enraged his wife's Curtis relatives, who were also predominantly Patriot.[7]   Consequently, the Lorings lost their home, along with much of their wealth, and ultimately fled to England, where Commodore Loring and his wife later died in exile.

Meantime, young John Loring followed his father into allegiance with the British Crown. Around 1774, he joined the Royal Navy as a midshipman and immediately saw service, likely aboard the sixth-rate HMS *Scarborough* (22), which was at the time patrolling the Portsmouth, New Hampshire harbour.[8] By April 1776, Loring was serving as a member of the prize crew aboard the merchant schooner *Valent*, which had been captured from the Patriots earlier in the year by *Scarborough*.[9] Under the command of Royal Navy Master Edward Marsh, *Valent's* mission was to bring food to the besieged British troops in Boston.[10] However, Marsh and his men were unaware that the British Army had finished evacuating Boston on 17 March 1776. Thus, unable to dock in that city, they were forced to put into Martha's Vineyard, where they were subsequently captured by Patriot militiamen.[11] Loring and his colleagues were processed in Boston and then ordered to be imprisoned in Concord by order of the Massachusetts Council.[12]

Although the Loring family had fallen from favour in Patriot-leaning Boston, young John Loring still had enough clout to avoid doing hard time in prison. He quickly reached out to his uncle, prominent Boston merchant and Patriot Obediah

---

6   Catherine P. Curtis, *The Curtis Family* (Boston, Massachusetts: New England Historic Genealogical Society, 1876), p.8; the author was a grandniece of Commodore Loring's wife, Mary Curtis Loring; E. Alfred Jones, *The Loyalists of Massachusetts: Their Memorials, Petitions, and Claims* (Baltimore, Maryland: Genealogical Publishing Company, 1969), p.199.

7   Boyd, 'Commodore Joshua Loring', p.6.

8   Stark, *The Loyalists of Massachusetts*, p.425; J.L. Bell, 'John Loring, Midshipman', *Boston 1775* (blog), 3 December 2008 <http://boston1775.blogspot.com/2008/12/john-loring-midshipman.html>

9   J.L. Bell, 'John Loring, Prisoner of War', *Boston 1775* (blog), 4 December 2008 <http://boston1775.blogspot.com/2008/12/john-loring-prisoner-of-war.html>

10   Bell, 'John Loring, Prisoner of War'.

11   Bell, 'John Loring, Prisoner of War'.

12   J.L. Bell, 'The Ransom of John Loring'. *Boston 1775* (blog), 5 December 2008 <http://boston1775.blogspot.com/2008/12/ransom-of-john-loring.html>

Curtis, to intercede on his behalf.[13] Curtis then persuaded the local authorities to release Loring from jail and move him to his father-in-law Joseph Buckminster's farm in Framingham to await a prisoner exchange.[14] Widely respected throughout the region, Buckminster had served over the course of his long career as a militia colonel, town clerk, and colonial legislator.[15] Curtis therefore assumed that Loring would not get into too much trouble under the protection of such an influential Patriot leader. However, Loring proved to be a quite unruly guest, treating Buckminster with insolence while also harassing Buckminster's fellow Patriot neighbours.[16] Consequently, Buckminster was soon in danger of having his home demolished by enraged local citizens for harbouring the young Tory.[17] Fortunately, Loring was exchanged in late 1776 for an unknown prisoner held by the British and returned to England shortly thereafter.[18]

Relatively little is known about Loring's life and Royal Navy service through the late 1770s and 1780s, but he was reportedly promoted to lieutenant on 3 December 1779.[19] Existing evidence then suggests that Loring was on half-pay for a period of time in the 1780s.[20] During those years, Loring's mother and brothers were actively engaged in securing compensation from the British government for the immense financial losses they suffered during the American Revolution. They were partially successful, securing £3,356 from their original claim of £4,815.[21] However, the family remained largely in dire financial straits and Loring was largely left to his own devices to support himself. This was likely challenging during the Royal Navy's lull period following the American Revolution, which forced many officers to languish on half-pay.

While the pace of Loring's naval career certainly slowed in the 1780s, it picked up dramatically with the French Revolution's onset in 1789. In January 1793, he was appointed to command the fireship HMS *Conflagration* and also promoted to commander in May of that year.[22] Loring commenced sailing *Conflagration* into

13   Bell, 'The Ransom of John Loring'; Stark, *The Loyalists of Massachusetts*, p.425.
14   Bell, 'The Ransom of John Loring'; Stark, *The Loyalists of Massachusetts*, p.425.
15   Bell, 'The Ransom of John Loring'.
16   Bell, 'The Ransom of John Loring'.
17   Stark, *The Loyalists of Massachusetts*, p.425.
18   Stark, *The Loyalists of Massachusetts*, p.425.
19   'John Loring (Royal Navy officer, died 1808),' *Wikipedia*, <https://en.wikipedia.org/w/index.php?title=John_Loring_(Royal_Navy_officer,_died_1808)&oldid=7215637> (accessed May 22, 2016); this is the only source that provides a specific date for Loring's promotion to lieutenant, so more research would be necessary for confirmation.
20   Stark, *The Loyalists of Massachusetts*, p.199.
21   Stark, *The Loyalists of Massachusetts*, p.199. Mary Curtis Loring died in 1789.
22   Rif Winfield, *British Warships in the Age of Sail 1793-1817: Design, Construction, Careers and Fates* (Barnsley, South Yorkshire: Seaforth Publishing, 2008), p.369

the Mediterranean on 22 May 1793 and served as part of Lord Hood's fleet during the occupation and siege of Toulon. *Conflagration* was under repair there when the city was evacuated and subsequently burnt on Hood's orders on 18 December 1793 to avoid falling into French hands.[23] Loring then returned to England and was given command of the sloop HMS *Hazard* (16), where he served from April 1794 to 1795.[24] Shortly thereafter, Loring was appointed acting captain of the third-rate HMS *Bellerophon* (74), which was then serving off Ushant in the Brest blockade.[25] He was later superseded by Captain Henry d'Esterre Darby on 11 September 1796 and promoted to post-captain sometime during that period.[26]

In Loring's first independent command as a post-captain, he was assigned to the newly commissioned fifth-rate HMS *Proselyte* (32), which had recently been surrendered to the Royal Navy by a mutinous Dutch crew.[27] Assigned to prepare *Proselyte* for Royal Navy service, Loring took her out to Jamaica in February 1797 and saw action against local privateers. He also captured the French privateer schooner *Liberté* (6) later that year.[28] Around 1798, Loring assumed command of the third-rate HMS *Carnatic* (74), then stationed in Jamaica, and held the post until 1800.[29] In this capacity, Loring was at the centre of an international incident on 16 November 1798 when he overtook the sixth-rate frigate USS *Baltimore* (20) and removed several of its sailors under the pretense that they were Englishmen.[30] *Baltimore's* commanding officer, Captain Isaac Phillips was later dismissed from US Navy service on the grounds that he should have resisted instead of surrendering the ship so quickly.[31] According to one historian, 'this conduct of Captain Loring was characteristic of his family, who seem to have been very bitter against their countrymen.'[32] Following the incident with USS *Baltimore*, Loring commanded briefly the third-rate HMS *Hannibal* (74) and the second-rate HMS *Prince* (98)

23   Winfield, *British Warships*, p.369
24   Winfield, *British Warships*, p.235.
25   Peter Goodwin, *The Ships of Trafalgar: The British, French and Spanish Fleets, 21 October 1805* (London: Conway Maritime Press, 2005), p.67; *Bellerophon's* nominal commander, Captain James Cranstoun, 8th Lord Cranstoun, had been appointed Governor of Grenada and left the ship to prepare for his new post.
26   Goodwin, *The Ships of Trafalgar*, p.67.
27   *Proselyte* was formerly known as the 36-gun Dutch frigate *Jason* built in 1770 in Rotterdam.
28   Winfield, *British Warships*, p.197.
29   Winfield, *British Warships*, p.53.
30   Samuel C. Clarke, *Records of Some of the Descendants of William Curtis, Roxbury, 1632* (Boston, Massachusetts: David Clapp & Son, 1869), p.9.
31   Clark, *Records of Some of the Descendants*, p.9. However, others argued that Captain Phillips could have done little to resist the British naval force of which Loring was part, which included three 74-gun ships and two frigates.
32   Clark, *Records of Some of the Descendants*, p.9.

before returning to the ship to which he is most associated, the *Bellerophon*, on 25 November 1801.[33] At the time, *Bellerophon* was serving with the Channel Fleet, but was given new orders in early 1802 to join then-Rear Admiral John Duckworth's squadron in the West Indies.[34] However, by the time of her arrival on 27 March 1802, the Treaty of Amiens had been signed and Great Britain and France were at peace. Thus, *Bellerophon* spent the next year and a half patrolling the Jamaica Passage and escorting merchant convoys between Jamaica and Halifax.[35]

With the outbreak of the Napoleonic Wars in May 1803, Loring and his crew on *Bellerophon* were quickly returned to a wartime footing in the West Indies. Loring was appointed commodore of the British squadron and assigned to mount an offensive against French shipping during the Blockade of St Domingue, where Royal Navy ships blockaded the French-held ports of Cap Français and Môle-Saint Nicolas on the northern coast of modern-day Haiti.[36] Another objective of this campaign was for the Royal Navy to support native rebel forces under Jean-Jacques Dessalines (later Emperor Jacques I of Haiti), in revolt against the French, who were laying siege to the French military's garrisons there.[37] A highlight of Loring's command during this period was his capture of the French *Téméraire* class ship-of-the-line *Duquesne* (74), along with several French frigates, as they attempted to escape the siege and return to France.[38] In November 1803, Loring was also privileged to accept surrender of the French garrison's commander, General Rochambeau, who had requested the evacuation of his forces from the Haitian rebel siege.[39] Observing the beleaguered French forces, Loring noted that 'such a set of blood-thirsty looking devils my eyes [have] never beheld.'[40] The French were ultimately allowed to evacuate on three of their frigates and were escorted back to Jamaica by Loring's squadron.[41]

---

33   Winfield, *British Warships*, p.24.
34   Goodwin, *The Ships of Trafalgar*, p.68.
35   David Cordingly, *The Billy Ruffian: The Bellerophon and the Downfall of Napoleon: The Biography of a Ship of the Line, 1782-1836* (London: Bloomsbury Publishing, 2004), p.163.
36   'Blockade of Saint-Domingue', *Wikipedia* <https://en.wikipedia.org/w/index. php?title=Blockade_of_Saint-Domingue&oldid=755060401> (accessed 16 December 2016).
37   *Wikipedia*, 'Blockade of Saint Dominique'.
38   J. Aiken, *The Athenaeum Magazine of Literary and Miscellaneous Information*, January to June 1809, Vol. V (London: J. McCreery, 1809), p.177.
39   *Wikipedia*, 'Blockade of Saint-Domingue'; Donatien-Marie-Joseph de Vimeur, vicomte de Rochambeau (1755-1813) was the son of Jean-Baptiste Donatien de Vimeur, comte de Rochambeau (1725-1807) of American Revolutionary War fame.
40   John Loring to Hector Macneal, 29 April 1804, Loring Family Papers, Massachusetts Historical Society.
41   Goodwin, *The Ships of Trafalgar*, p.68; Winfield, *British Warships*, p.51.

Loring's successful command in Haiti proved to be the high point of his illustrious Royal Navy career, as illness later conspired to end his sea-going service, following a period of relative inactivity aboard *Bellerophon*. In February 1804, a severe malaria outbreak struck the ship, causing 212 members of her crew to become seriously ill – of which 57 ultimately passed away.[42] Meanwhile, *Bellerophon* was engaged in uneventful convoy and patrol duty for most of the spring and summer of that year.[43] A far cry from his earlier combat commands, the resulting boredom and frustration from this assignment appeared to wear heavily on Loring. As he phrased it in a letter to his wife's uncle, 'I am now on my return from a twelve weeks cruise and taken nothing – indeed there is nothing to take …'[44] Apart from this boredom, Loring was also showing signs of wanting to return home to England after serving so many years at sea.[45] Nevertheless, Loring was pleased with his tenure in the Caribbean overall, noting that 'as matters have turned out it has been a fortunate thing for me that I came out to this horrid climate, [as] I shall expect to realise about £6,000 sterling [in prize money] - four thousand of which is already gone home and in the funds.'[46]

It is highly likely that Loring's health was also adversely impacted by the earlier malaria outbreak, as an undisclosed illness forced him to abruptly conclude his sea-going service after *Bellerophon* returned to England in August 1804. Following a short tenure commanding the Plymouth guardship, the first-rate 112-gun HMS *Salvador del Mundo*, he was assigned command of the Sea Fencibles covering the district between Emsworth and Calshot in June 1807.[47] The fact that such a distinguished and experienced officer would be so quickly relegated to commanding Sea Fencibles further suggests that his health was rapidly deteriorating. Loring passed away the following year on 9 November 1808 in Fareham at the age of 48 and left behind his wife, Mary Macneal Loring of Argyleshire, Scotland, along with three children.[48] Described as a 'most able, brave, and experienced officer,' one period source maintained that Loring would have been destined for even greater distinction and seniority in the Royal Navy had he lived longer.[49]

---

42 Goodwin, *The Ships of Trafalgar*, p.68; Winfield, *British Warships*, p.51; Cordingly, *The Billy Ruffian*, p.166.
43 Loring to Macneal, 29 April 1804, Loring Family Papers, Massachusetts Historical Society.
44 Loring to Macneal.
45 Loring to Macneal.
46 Loring to Macneal.
47 Winfield, *British Warships*, p.16; Aiken, *The Athenaeum Magazine*, p.177.
48 Aiken, *The Athenaeum Magazine*, p.177; Stark, *The Loyalists of Massachusetts*, p.426; Both of Loring's sons followed him into Royal Navy service. His eldest son John Loring died of yellow fever in Bermuda as a midshipman aboard the Apollo-class frigate, HMS *Euryalus* (36) in 1820. His other son, Hector, reached the rank of commander in the Royal Navy.
49 Aiken, *The Athenaeum Magazine*, p.177.

14

Admiral Sir John Wentworth Loring, KCB, KCH (1775-1852) – Boston, Massachusetts

Dr Sean M. Heuvel

One of the more intriguing yet largely unknown North Americans who served in Nelson's Navy was Admiral Sir John Wentworth Loring, the scion of a distinguished Massachusetts family who devoted over four decades of his life to the Royal Navy. This Boston-area native began his career as a destitute, Loyalist exile, but ended it as an affluent and respected Royal Navy senior officer. Moreover, Loring excelled in both operational and administrative commands, earning admiration from his peers and knighthoods from King William IV and Queen Victoria. Despite these achievements, modern historians have not really examined Loring in any great depth. He has been mentioned only as a minor reference in published works about his parents, Joshua Loring Jr. and Elizabeth Lloyd 'Betsey' Loring, or other close relatives. What follows here is a brief biographical sketch that provides a closer, more detailed, look at this compelling Royal Navy officer.

Loring was born on 13 October 1775 to one of the most powerful and influential families in Massachusetts.[1] His grandfather, Joshua Loring Sr., had risen from obscure origins as a Boston tanner's apprentice to become a wealthy Royal Navy officer.[2] As a commodore, Joshua Loring Sr. later commanded Royal Navy forces on the Great Lakes during the French and Indian War, working closely

---

1 Loring was named after his father's good friend, Sir John Wentworth (1737-1820) who served as governor of New Hampshire from 1767 to 1775 and as lieutenant governor of Nova Scotia 1792-1808.
2 W. A. B. Douglas, 'Loring, Joshua', in *Dictionary of Canadian Biography*, Vol. 4, University of Toronto/Université Laval <2003–http://www.biographi.ca/en/bio/loring_joshua_4E.html> (accessed 6 January 2014)

Admiral Sir John Wentworth Loring, KCB KCH (1775-1852) with his wife, Lady Anna Patton Loring. (Courtesy of Chris Farey)

with Lord Amherst.[3] Commodore Loring went on to become a prominent Boston-area Loyalist before being forced into exile at the dawn of the American Revolution.[4] Loring's father, Joshua Loring Jr., was also a prominent figure in pre-Revolutionary Boston. A former British Army officer, Joshua Loring Jr. held a variety of government posts, such as surveyor of the King's woods and sheriff of Suffolk County, before serving as the controversial Commissary General of Prisoners during the Revolution.[5] In that capacity, some contemporaries claimed that he profited from the misery of Patriot prisoners, allegedly pocketing much of

3   James Henry Stark, *The Loyalists of Massachusetts and the other side of the American Revolution* (Salem, Massachusetts: Salem Press, 1910), p.424.
4   It is through Commodore Loring's wife, Mary Curtis Loring – my second cousin, nine times removed – that I am related to Admiral Sir John Wentworth Loring.
5   John R. Alden, *A History of the American Revolution* (New York: Knopf, 1969), p.503.

the money intended for their care. However, others argued that he did the best job he could under the circumstances.[6] Due to a lack of non-biased primary source materials, the truth is difficult to determine.

Loring's mother, Elizabeth Lloyd "Betsey" Loring, was even more controversial than his father. A New York native known for her alluring beauty, she was rumoured, during the Revolution, to have been a lover of her husband's old friend, General Sir William Howe.[7] In fact, some claimed that Joshua Loring Jr. was given the lucrative post of commissary of prisoners by Howe as a reward for his compliance with the relationship.[8] Although Sir William Howe and Betsey Loring were frequently seen in each other's company through much of 1776 and 1777, it is difficult to say for certain if there was an actual affair, as the rumours about it were spread primarily by Patriot propagandists and disaffected Loyalists.

What is certain is that in fall 1775, the Lorings were forced to flee to British-occupied Boston for protection. In the midst of the chaos, an infant John Wentworth Loring was separated from his parents and taken into custody by Patriot forces before the Loring home was burned to the ground.[9] Existing family accounts shed light on how Loring was later retrieved. According to Betsey Loring, friends helped her to cross enemy lines in disguise to covertly check on her son.[10] Following that initial encounter, Betsey Loring's daughter, Eliza Loring, wrote that her brother was recovered shortly thereafter through an arrangement between Generals Gage and Washington.[11]

Following the loss of all of their property, the Lorings fled to Berkshire, England around 1778 as exiles. After years of vainly applying for government pensions to compensate for some of his lost fortune, Joshua Loring Jr. passed away in 1789, leaving Betsey Loring to raise their young family alone.[12] Short of money, she still managed to move to Reading to enrol her eldest son, John Wentworth Loring, in the grammar school there. At the same time, his name was entered on the books of the fourth-rate HMS *Salisbury* (50), which was then stationed in Newfoundland. He was listed as a servant to his uncle, Captain John Loring, who is also profiled in this book. Later in 1789, the young Loring became a midshipman aboard *Salisbury*, serving under a succession of captains including the legendary Sir Edward Pellew

6   Alden, *History of the American Revolution*, p.504.
7   As a young British Army officer, Joshua Loring Jr. had served under Sir William Howe in the early 1760s.
8   Alden, *History of the American Revolution*, p.504.
9   Loring had a twin brother named Joshua, who was also taken into custody by Patriot forces. However, he died shortly thereafter.
10   Elizabeth Lloyd Loring, 'Family History', undated. Loring family papers, private collection.
11   Loring, 'Family History'.
12   The Lorings had five children – one daughter and four sons. Admiral Sir John Wentworth Loring was the eldest son.

(later Lord Exmouth).[13] Knowing that his mother was in dire financial straits struggling to maintain and educate his siblings, Loring endeavoured to live on his own pay. He did this by going to mess on ship with the warrant officers instead of more senior officers; an unusual step for someone of his societal station during this time.[14] Over the next few years, he served on a succession of HM ships, including the third-rate *Alcide* (74), the fourth-rate *Romney* (50) and the Dutch-built and former Dutch privateer sloop-of-war *Orestes* (18).

By the dawn of the French Revolution, Loring had received orders to the first-rate HMS *Victory* (104) in the Mediterranean. Serving on-shore as a volunteer in 1793, he was severely wounded in the leg during the Siege of Toulon. Despite being on crutches, Loring was determined to serve and rejoined *Victory* shortly thereafter. During the Siege of Bastia, he was entrusted with the command of a small gunboat that constantly passed and re-passed under the stern of *Victory* during its daily operations. At the time, *Victory* was Admiral Lord Samuel Hood's flagship. He often watched Loring through his cabin windows, admiring the determination of the young officer on crutches. Loring was therefore promoted to lieutenant in 1794.[15]

By this time, Loring came under the patronage of then-Vice Admiral Sir Hyde Parker, who assigned the young lieutenant to a succession of his flagships, including the second-rate HMS *St George* (98), the first-rate HMS *Britannia* (100), and the second-rate HMS *Queen* (98). In 1795, Loring was also involved in Admiral William Hotham's actions of 14 March (the Battle of Genoa) and 13 July (the Battle of Hyères Islands).[16] Following his patron Admiral Parker to the West Indies, Loring was actively employed on that station. As acting commander of HM Sloop-of-War *Rattler* (16) in 1798, he was involved in supervising the evacuation of the Cayemites Islands off the southwest coast of modern-day Haiti. Following his promotion to commander in 1799, he captured eight privateers and 27 merchant vessels with HM Sloop-of-War *Lark* (18).[17] Accumulating a small fortune in prize money, Loring sent home nearly £5,000 to subsidise the education of his brothers.[18] After leading the *Lark* successfully through a tremendous hurricane in 1801, Lord Hugh Seymour appointed Loring acting captain of the fourth-rate HMS

13   *The Services of the Late Admiral Sir John Wentworth Loring, K.C.B., K.C.H., in the two French Wars from 1789 to 1816, etc.* (Bournemouth: Francis Nash, 1880), p.7.
14   *The Services of the Late Admiral Sir John Wentworth Loring*, p.8. Officers usually had to pay for their own food and provisions while the Royal Navy provided for warrant officers and those on the lower deck.
15   *The Services of the Late Admiral Sir John Wentworth Loring*, p.9.
16   Sylvanus Urban, *The Gentleman's Magazine*, Vol. 38 (London: John Bowyer Nichols and Son, 1852), pp.312-313.
17   Urban, *Gentleman's Magazine*, pp.321-313.
18   Loring, 'Family History'.

Abergavenny (54), and the fifth-rate frigate HMS *Syren* (32) shortly thereafter. A year later, Loring's intrepidity in quelling a mutiny aboard the latter ship prompted the Lords of the Admiralty to confirm him to post-rank. Further, in recognition of his service, Loring's promotion was antedated to 28 April 1802, the day before a general promotion that had taken place in recognition of the Peace of Amiens.[19]

The promotion to post-captain brought Loring's service in the West Indies to a close. It had been a lucrative chapter in his career both professionally and financially, as he had obtained rapid promotion along with roughly £25,000 in prize money. Nevertheless, on 14 September 1803, he was appointed to the third-rate HMS *Utrecht* (74), which was stationed in the Downs. It was also flagship to a succession of admirals during this period, to include Robert Montagu, Philip Patton, and John Holloway. For Loring, the association with Admiral Patton was most beneficial; as he went on to marry one of the Admiral's daughters (Anna) in 1804. Following the wedding, Loring was permitted a few months on shore. It was the first time he had enjoyed any length of time on land since joining the Royal Navy as a midshipman in 1789.[20]

Following his leave and a couple of temporary assignments, Loring was appointed to the ship that would solidify his reputation as one of the Royal Navy's top frigate captains. On 13 November 1805, he was posted to the fifth-rate frigate HMS *Niobe* (40), assigned to Lord St Vincent's fleet that was operating off the coast of Spain before being transferred for duty on the North Sea. While on an independent cruise in March 1806, Loring achieved great acclaim for his silent capture of the French corvette *Nearque* near the Isle of Groix.[21] *Nearque* had been in the rear of a squadron of three French frigates (*Revanche*, *Guerrier*, and *Syrene*) heading toward the coast of Greenland.[22] Loring and his crew managed to catch up with *Nearque* and take her in a nighttime assault with only minimal small arms fire and no casualties.[23] Assuming that *Niobe* was part of a much larger British squadron, the French frigates decided not to engage, and *Nearque* was carried off as a prize to Lord St Vincent's fleet.[24] Over the next few years, Loring also captured two French privateers and successfully prevented two French frigates from leaving port.[25] Along with his active involvement in combat operations, Loring took time

19 Urban, *Gentleman's Magazine*, p.313; *The Services of the Late Admiral Sir John Wentworth Loring*, p.15.
20 *The Services of the Late Admiral Sir John Wentworth Loring*, p.19.
21 *The Services of the Late Admiral Sir John Wentworth Loring*, p.22. Groix is an island in the Brittany region of northwestern France.
22 *The Services of the Late Admiral Sir John Wentworth Loring*, p.22.
23 *The Services of the Late Admiral Sir John Wentworth Loring*, p.22.
24 *The Services of the Late Admiral Sir John Wentworth Loring*, p.22.
25 Urban, *The Gentleman's Magazine*, p.313; *The Services of the Late Admiral Sir John Wentworth Loring*, p.26. Loring was also involved in the later destruction of both vessels in

on *Niobe* to perfect his skills in taking soundings. He subsequently developed a reputation as the best Royal Navy pilot on the North Sea.[26]

However, Loring's success on the *Niobe* came at a cost to his health. Constant exposure to all types of weather on deck, combined with constant stress and a refusal to rest, caused him to develop pneumonia. Loring was forced to take a leave of absence from his ship. It took six months under a London physician's care for him to resume his duties. However, complete recovery was not possible and his health remained impaired for the rest of his life.[27] After paying off *Niobe* in 1813, Loring served as flag-captain for Admiral Sir William Young on the second-rate HMS *Impregnable* (98), engaging mostly in blockade duty on the North Sea. Loring remained on *Impregnable* until 1815, when he was made a Companion of the Bath (C.B.) for his services in the war.[28]

Following a short post-war stint in 1816 as superintendent of the Ordinary at Sheerness, Loring faced the possibility of spending the rest of his career on half-pay as a semi-retired post-captain. However, a chance occurrence facilitated a new phase in his Royal Navy service. In fall 1819, a family illness prompted Loring to visit the seaside resort of Southsea in Portsmouth in order to consult with a well-known physician there. While Loring was in the area, the incoming lieutenant governor of the Royal Naval College at Portsmouth Dockyard died unexpectedly.[29] Loring heard of the vacancy shortly thereafter and immediately travelled to London in order to lay his application before the Admiralty. Since he possessed a distinguished service record and enjoyed support among many influential Royal Navy senior officers, Loring was appointed Lieutenant Governor of the Royal Naval College on 4 November 1819.[30]

As lieutenant governor, Loring oversaw the day-to-day operations of the College, supervising its faculty and staff. Since the College's governor was the First Lord of the Admiralty, he worked closely with a succession of influential political leaders who held that post.[31] One of them was the Duke of Clarence, an active supporter of the College before his reign as King William IV.[32] These connections, coupled with his legendary war record, prompted cadets to approach Loring with a combination

spring 1811.

26   *The Services of the Late Admiral Sir John Wentworth Loring*, p.30.

27   *The Services of the Late Admiral Sir John Wentworth Loring*, p.30; Dr J.E.B. Stuart V, personal correspondence, 11 November 2013.

28   *The Services of the Late Admiral Sir John Wentworth Loring*, pp.31-32.

29   The Royal Naval College at Portsmouth was founded in 1729 and closed in 1837.

30   *The Services of the Late Admiral Sir John Wentworth Loring*, p.34.

31   *The United Service Journal and Naval and Military Magazine*, Part II (London: Samuel Bentley, 1829), p.467.

32   *A Memoir of the Life and Works of William Wyon, Esq., A.R.A., Chief Engraver of the Royal Mint* (London: W. Nicol, 1837), p.163. The then-Duke of Clarence served as governor of

of reverence and awe. In his memoirs, Admiral Sir Henry Keppel reflected on his first encounter with Loring, as a young cadet in 1822, after seeing ships-of-the-line for the first time. Keppel described him as 'a warrior in uniform, as imposing to me as the leviathans I had just seen.'[33]

A highlight of Loring's tenure occurred when he received a diamond ring from the Empress Consort of Russia, Elizabeth Alexeievna (wife of Czar Alexander I) in recognition of his work with one of her young protégés.[34] The student went on to complete his education at the Royal Naval College and serve aboard a British frigate. This Russian was just one of the many cadets Loring mentored who served successfully. Loring continued as Lieutenant Governor of the Royal Naval College until his promotion to rear admiral in January 1837. In recognition of his former colleague's successful tenure, King William IV appointed Loring to the Royal Guelphic Order at the rank of knight commander (Knight Commander of the most Honorable Order of the Bath) in April 1837.[35] The following month, the King also conferred knighthood upon Loring, as a knight bachelor, at a ceremony at St James' Palace.[36] It was one of the last such appointments before the King's death a few weeks later.

Following Loring's retirement from active service in spring 1837, he and his family divided their time between a home in Southampton and his estate in Ryde, Isle of Wight. In July 1840, Loring was made a Knight Commander of the Bath (Knight Commander Order of the Bath) by Queen Victoria at a ceremony in Buckingham Palace.[37] This recognition was part of a larger effort by Her Majesty to honour senior Royal Navy officers as Loring who were distinguished veterans

the Royal Naval College at Portsmouth from 1827 to 1828 in his capacity as Lord High Admiral of the United Kingdom.

33   The Hon. Sir Henry Keppel, *A Sailor's Life Under Four Sovereigns* (London: Macmillan, 1899), p.16.

34   John Marshall, *Royal Naval Biography; or Memoirs of the Services of all the Flag Officers, Superannuated Rear-Admirals, Retired-Captains, Post-Captains, and Commanders*, Vol. II, Part II (London: Longman, Hurst, Rees, Orme, Brown, and Green, 1825), p.549. This source did not identify the specific Russian empress who awarded Loring the diamond ring. However, considering the date of publication, it was most likely Elizabeth Alexeievna, wife of Czar Alexander I of Russia, who reigned during 1801-25.

35   The Royal Guelphic (or Hanoverian) Order is a Hanoverian order of chivalry instituted by the Prince Regent in 1815. King William IV often used it to reward old navy friends and associates such as Loring. The Royal Guelphic Order has not been conferred by the British Crown since 1837, when the personal union of the United Kingdom and Hanover ended following King William IV's death.

36   *The London Gazette*, 5 May 1837. Since the Royal Guelphic Order was technically a foreign order, King William IV usually conferred simultaneous knighthood (as knight bachelor) on honorees, thus allowing them to use the accolade, 'Sir', in British society.

37   *The Nautical Magazine and Naval Chronicle for 1840: A Journal of Papers on Subjects Connected with Maritime Affairs* (London: Simpkin, Marshall & Company, 1841), p.604.

of the wars with France. A few years later, Loring was awarded the Naval General Service Medal 1793-1840 with one clasp, *14 March 1795*. He was also honoured during this period with a succession of promotions, culminating in advancement to Admiral of the Blue on 8 July 1851.[38]

In his late seventies and in failing health, Loring passed away on 29 July 1852, at his estate in Ryde. He was buried at Pear Tree Church in Southampton, leaving behind a widow, three daughters, and three sons.[39] One of his sons, Sir William Loring, continued the family's maritime tradition by pursuing a career in the Royal Navy. Following distinguished service in the Crimean War, Sir William went on to become a full admiral, like his father. He also served as a naval aide-de-camp to Queen Victoria.[40] While talent fuelled much of Sir William's success, his father's legendary reputation and legacy were also key factors. Despite his colonial roots and humble upbringing, Admiral Sir John Wentworth Loring enjoyed a noteworthy career in the Royal Navy. His achievements were later recognised during World War II, when the American-built, British Captain class frigate, HMS *Loring* (K565), was named in his honour. In active employment for 44 years and on half-pay for only four, Admiral Loring added a remarkable chapter to his family's legacy of public service and leadership.[41]

38   *The London Gazette*, 11 July 1851.
39   Marshall, *Royal Naval Biography*, p.549. The lettering on many of the older tombstones in Pear Tree Church cemetery has worn off, so the exact location of Loring's grave within the cemetery is currently unknown.
40   *The Services of the Late Admiral Sir William Loring, K.C.B.* (Woolwich: Royal Artillery Institution, 1900), pp.8-22, 27.
41   Another one of Loring's distinguished naval relatives was Admiral of the Fleet John Rushworth Jellicoe, 1st Earl Jellicoe, GCB, OM, GCVO, SGM (1859-1935), who commanded the Grand Fleet at the Battle of Jutland in May 1916. Jellicoe was Loring's grandnephew by marriage.

Canada and West Indies

15

Captain William Carleton (1789-1874) – New Brunswick

Dr John R. Satterfield

Nelson and HMS *Victory* are so closely associated with the naval engagement at Trafalgar that we may forget 32 other Royal Navy vessels were present for the battle, including 26 ships-of-the- line that actively participated in the fighting. *Victory* lost 57 crewmen killed in the battle, more than any other British ship, and more than 100 wounded while trading blows with the French 74-gun *Redoubtable*.[1]

Other British ships suffered mightily, however – none more so than the third-rate ship-of-the-line, HMS *Colossus* (74), under the command of Captain James Nicoll Morris. *Colossus* was new, launched in April 1803, fast and powerful, with 30 24-pound cannon instead of standard 18-pounders on her upper gun deck. Nelson regarded her highly, thanks in great part to Morris's discipline and administrative skills. The ship attacked the French and Spanish line of battle from the middle of Vice Admiral Collingwood's lee column, taking fire from the enemy until she reached the rear of the enemy line. She engaged the French *Swiftsure* (74), a third-rate captured from the British, on the latter's starboard. At the climax of their gun duel, with smoke enveloping the ships, the heavy French *Argonaute* (74) slammed into *Colossus*, tangling yardarms and pushing the British vessel into *Swiftsure*. The three vessels exchanged carronade fire, sweeping the decks with lead, to prevent boarding. After drifting apart, *Colossus* attacked and dismasted another French

---

1   Peter Goodwin, *Ships of Trafalgar: The British, French and Spanish Fleets, October 1805* (Annapolis, Maryland: US Naval Institute Press, 2005).

74, the *Bahama*. *Colossus* lost 40 crewmen killed, among them the ship's master, and 160 wounded, including her captain and 14 other officers, fully 35 percent of those on board, the highest British numerical and proportional casualty tally in the battle.[2]

Trafalgar was a remarkably violent episode in the early naval service of one the youngest *Colossus* crew members, Midshipman William Carleton (1789 – 1874). Carleton was just 15, having entered the Royal Navy as a first-class volunteer at age 14 on April 21, 1804.[3] According to O'Byrne's *Naval Biographical Dictionary*, published in 1849, Carleton's first ship was the HMS *Leopard* (50), a fourth-rate Portland class frigate, launched in 1790. The entry misidentified *Leopard*'s commander at the time as Captain Morris. She was, instead, under the command of Captain (later Admiral of the Fleet) Francis William Austen, Jane Austen's older brother, from May 1804, deploying from Chatham that month where she had been in repair. *Leopard* served as the flagship of Rear Admiral Sir Thomas Louis and participated in the blockade of Boulogne for the rest of the year to prevent a French invasion of England.[4] Admiral Louis joined the Mediterranean Fleet off Cadiz in early 1805, shifting his flag to the HMS *Canopus* (84) with Captain Austen. Midshipman Carleton (misspelled Carlton in the *Colossus* muster and pay book) probably joined *Colossus* under Captain Morris at this time. A copy of the ship's muster and pay book is not readily available, and the sketchy record with his misspelled surname shows his birthplace only as America.[5]

In fact, Carleton was from a particularly distinguished military family associated with Canada, where he was born. His father, Thomas Carleton, was a British Army officer who served in Canada during the American Revolution. Colonel Carleton was the younger brother of General Sir Guy Carleton, Lord Dorchester, Governor General of Quebec from 1768 until 1778. The Carleton brothers were active in Canada's defense during the American Revolution, and Sir Guy later served as commander-in-chief of British forces in America after the British defeat at Yorktown until the war's end in 1783. Thomas returned

2   Goodwin, *Ships of Trafalgar*. Rif Winfield and David Lyon, *The Sail and Steam Navy List: All the Ships of the Royal Navy 1815 – 1889* (London: Chatham Publishing 2004), p.40.
3   Bruno Pappalardo, 'Trafalgar Ancestors', *Nelson, Trafalgar, and Those Who Served*, The National Archives, Kew, London (TNA) <http://www. nationalarchives.gov.uk/aboutapps/trafalgarancestors/> (accessed 17 June 2016).
4   William R. O'Byrne, *A Naval Biographical Dictionary: Consisting of the Life and Services of Every Living Officer in Her Majesty's Navy, From the Rank of Admiral of the Fleet to that of Lieutenant, Inclusive* (London: John Murray, 1849), pp.168-169; Winfield and Lyon, *The Sail and Steam Navy List*, p.107; T.A. Heathcote, *The British Admirals of the Fleet 1734-1995: A Biographical Dictionary* (Barnsley, Yorkshire, UK: Pen & Sword Books, 2002), pp.17-19.
5   Heathcote, *British Admirals*; 'Trafalgar Ancestors', pp.17-19.

from England to Canada as the lieutenant governor of the new province of New Brunswick after its partition from Nova Scotia in 1784. Appointed on Sir Guy's recommendation, he helped to relocate British loyalists from the United States to Canada after the Revolution. Carleton's career as a Canadian administrator was contentious at best. He was an authoritarian military officer with a prickly personality. He developed a long list of political opponents who undercut much of his governing authority. He requested a leave of absence in 1803, sailing to England and the family estate near Basingstoke with his wife, teenage son William and two daughters. Although he retained his office, he never returned to Canada and governed *in absentia* until his death in 1817.[6]

William entered naval service just months after arriving in England. He remained active in his career and remained so for nearly a decade after Trafalgar. According to O'Byrne, in January 1806, he joined the fifth-rate frigate HMS *Amazon* (38) as master's mate under the command of Captain (later Admiral of the Fleet) William Parker. *Amazon* was a fifth-rate frigate launched in 1799. In 1801, she was commanded by Captain Edward Riou, who was famously cut in half by Danish cannon shot at the Battle of Copenhagen.[7]

By March 1806, the frigate sailed in advance of an Atlantic squadron under the flag of Rear Admiral Sir John Borlase Warren. From his flagship HMS *London* (90), Warren commanded seven ships-of-the-line and several frigates assigned to destroy French commerce raiders. Purely by chance, the squadron crossed paths with the French ship-of-the-line *Marengo* (80), and the French frigate *Belle Poule* (40). Warren gave chase, engaging and defeating the *Marengo*, and *Amazon* caught up with and captured *Belle Poule*. The battle was costly. *Amazon* recorded that Richard Seymour, her first lieutenant, a Royal Marine second lieutenant and two others were killed, and six other crewmen were wounded. Lieutenant (later Admiral) Philip Westphal, younger brother of George Westphal, a midshipman wounded on HMS *Victory* at Trafalgar, took charge of the prize, with assistance from Master's Mate Carleton. In 1849, Carleton and other crewmen still living were recognised belatedly for the victory, receiving the General Service Medal with clasp. Later on the same voyage, Carleton assisted Westphal twice more, serving in the ship's boats under Westphal's command, which cut out and captured a West

6   'Thomas Carleton', *Dictionary of Canadian Biography Volume V (1801-1820)* (Toronto: University of Toronto/Université Laval, 2003-16) <http://www.biographi.ca/en/bio/carleton_thomas_5E.html> (accessed on 16 June 2016)

7   O'Byrne, *A Naval Biographical Dictionary*, pp.168-169; Winfield and Lyon, *The Sail and Steam Navy*, p.107.

Indiaman under the French flag near La Palma in the Canary Islands, and again during an attack on a convoy near the Brittany coast.[8]

Carleton, by now a seasoned mariner, passed his lieutenant's examination and was promoted on 1 July 1810. He was not yet 21 years old. He served in HMS *Temeraire* (98), the second-rate and Trafalgar veteran, under the flag of Rear Admiral Francis Pickmore in the Mediterranean. In the spring of 1812, Carleton joined HMS *Union* (98), a new second-rate stationed in Plymouth and commanded by Captain Samuel Hood Linzee. The Lieutenant's next assignments were HMS *Tremendous* (74), a third-rate rebuilt in 1810 that voyaged to the Mediterranean, and HMS *Royal George* (100), again under the flag of Admiral Pickmore.[9]

With peace at hand, the Royal Navy and many of its ships stood down. Carleton came home to England in July 1814 and was paid off. He would not resume active service for a decade, when on January 6, 1824, he was appointed first lieutenant of *Jupiter* (50), a fourth-rate that by then was no longer considered a ship-of-the-line. Under Captain David Dunn, the ship sailed for Halifax, Nova Scotia, and remained there for two years as the flagship for Admiral Willoughby Thomas Lake, Commander-in-Chief of the North American and West Indies Station. Halifax served as the station's summer base, since the command had moved its headquarters to Bermuda in 1819; better to counter any potential threat from the United States. Carleton's tenure was probably a pleasant one, affording him a chance to visit his birth place and meet old friends and acquaintances once again.[10]

William Carleton's last voyage as an active naval officer took him home to England as acting commander of HMS *Rifleman* (18), a Cruizer class brig-sloop. *Rifleman* was his first and only command and earned him a promotion to commander on December 2, 1826. He was 37- years-old, and his Royal Navy career effectively came to an end.[11]

Carleton's story did not end, however, for many years. In 1832, he married Rosamond Orde, daughter of the late Lieutenant General Leonard Shafto Orde, part of a family with roots in Northumberland stretching to the early seventeenth century. Carleton would continue serving at half-pay on the reserve list and receive

8   Joseph Allen, *The New Navy List and General Record of The Services of Officers of the Royal Navy and the Royal Marines* (London: Parker, Furnival & Parker, January 1851), p.93; William Laird Clowes, *The Royal Navy, A History from the Earliest Times to 1900: Vol. V* (London: Chatham, 1997); Richard Woodman, *The Sea Warriors* (London: Constable Publishers, 2001).

9   Allen, *The New Navy List*, p.93; O'Byrne, *A Naval Biographical Dictionary*, pp.168-169.; Winfield, and Lyon, *The Sail and Steam Navy List*, p.107.

10 O'Byrne, *A Naval Biographical Dictionary*, pp.168-169; 'Royal Naval Dockyards', *Royal Museums Greenwich* (Greenwich) <http://www.rmg.co.uk/discover/researchers/research-guides/research-guide-b5-royal-naval-dockyards> (accessed 20 June 2016).

11 O'Byrne, *A Naval Biographical Dictionary*, pp.168-169.

a ceremonial promotion to captain on 1 April 1856, when he moved to the retired list.[12] He lived at his family estate until his death in 1874, nearly seven decades after Trafalgar, and was buried in the cemetery of a nearby parish church, near his father and uncle.[13]

It is interesting to note that Britain would engage in no less than 20 wars from the end of the Napoleonic era until Carleton's death, most of them relatively small colonial land campaigns not involving the Royal Navy. These conflicts stretched from North America to India to Africa and Asia, reflecting the extent – and burden – of the British Empire. After Carleton's death, these wars grew larger and more costly, ultimately leading, after another seven decades, to the Empire's dissolution.[14]

William Carleton was certainly one of the longest surviving British veterans of Trafalgar. Only one other, Admiral Sir George Westphal, older brother of Carleton's shipmate Philip, seems to have lived longer, and not by much. Westphal died on 12 January 1876, aged 89. He was considered the last of the Royal Navy's Trafalgar participants.[15] Other remnants of Trafalgar would remain even longer. The last known battle survivor was a Spanish sailor, Pedro Antonio Martinez Zia. Born in 1789, the same year as Carleton, he died on 1 February 1898, aged 109, in Dallas, Texas![16]

Today, a long-standing English joke is that all 69 million citizens of the British Isles and Ireland claim a Trafalgar ancestor. Even after more than 210 years, that is quite a reproductive feat for the crews of the 33 Royal Navy vessels present for the engagement, numbering almost 18,500 men (and a handful of women), of whom about 430 died in action.[17] The substantial number of participants in the battle represented about 17 percent of the Royal Navy's 110,000 personnel in 1805, a tiny part of the more than 16 million citizens of the United Kingdom at that time. Many of these seamen would contribute measurably to the Navy's development

12   O'Byrne, *A Naval Biographical Dictionary*, pp.168-169.
13   O'Byrne, *A Naval Biographical Dictionary*, pp.168-169.
14   Stuart Laycock, *All the Countries We've Ever Invaded: And the Few We Never Got Round To* (Charleston, South Carolina: History Press, 2012).
15   John Marshall, *Royal Naval Biography; or, Memoires of the Services of All the Flag officers, Superannuated Rear-Admirals, Retired-Captains, Post-Captains, and Commanders, Volume III Part II* (London: Longman, Rees, Orme, Brown and Green, 1832), pp.185-200, <http://www.elklanding.org/research/westphal.pdf> (accessed 19 June 2018); O'Byrne, *A Naval Biographical Dictionary*, pp.168–169; Winfield and Lyon, *The Sail and Steam Navy List*, p.107.
16   'Pedro Antonio Zia Martinez', *Guerres de 1792 – 1815: Quelques uns des derniers soldats de la Republique et de l'Empire* <http://derniersveterans.free.fr/napoleon1.html> (accessed 16 June 2016)
17   'Battle of Trafalgar', *Nelson, Trafalgar, and Those Who Served*, TNA <http://www.nationalarchives.gov.uk/nelson/gallery7/trafalgar.htm> (accessed 17 June 2016).

or at least witness extraordinary change in the decades following Trafalgar.[18] The longest-lived survivors, including William Carleton, must have been astonished to see or read about so much global change, incomprehensible in its breadth and complexity. Carleton's life, despite the inevitable personal and professional disappointments he must have experienced, seems miraculous indeed.

18   'Trafalgar Ancestors', pp.17-19.

16

Admiral of the Fleet James, First Baron Gambier, GCB (1756-1832) – Bahamas

Dr John B. Hattendorf

Admiral Lord Gambier (1756-1832) is a controversial figure in British naval history. Many historians have tended to assume the worst about him, enjoying a verbal jibe at 'Dismal Jemmy' without careful consideration.[1] Lord Cochrane's bumptious and vindictive criticism over the operations at Basque Roads in 1809 was the most effective and most widely known attack on his reputation.[2] Tied to it is a tendency to ridicule Gambier as one of the most widely known of the so-called 'Blue Lights' – those naval officers who promoted evangelical Anglicanism as a matter of key value for one's own sake as well as something of professional value within the naval service. These one-sided assumptions and attacks by some of Gambier's contemporaries have been followed by many historians and need to be corrected so that Gambier may be seen in a more balanced manner for what he was. As the historian Richard Blake observed in 2008:

> Nowadays we have come to be more critical of Cochrane's veracity at various points in his self-advertising and self-justifying autobiography and are now less ready to accept his own evaluation. Gambier deserves his day in court – once again.[3]

---

1 See, for example, Sam Willis, *In the Hour of Victory: The Royal Navy at War in the Age of Nelson* (New York and London: W.W. Norton, 2013), p.175.
2 Thomas, Admiral the Earl of Dundonald, *The Autobiography of a Seaman* (London: Richard Bentley, 1860), Vol. 2, passim, but especially chapters 26-28.
3 Richard Blake, *Evangelicals in the Royal Navy, 1775-1815: Blue Lights & Psalm Singers* (Woodbridge: Boydell Press, 2008), p.221.

Admiral of the Fleet James, First Baron Gambier. (NMM)

Evaluating Gambier is not easy, as he left no collection of personal papers or diaries. There was much more to Gambier's naval career than Cochrane's criticism, and there is a positive side to his religious beliefs and philanthropy which should not be discounted in taking the measure of the man.

Historians have often overlooked that Gambier had fought successfully during the American War for Independence; he had been a prisoner for a short period. He served as Commander-in-Chief and Governor of Newfoundland, 1802-04, and was one of the Lords Commissioners of the Admiralty, 1795-1801, 1804-06, and 1807-08. Gambier led the attack on Copenhagen in 1807, seizing the entire Danish Navy to prevent it coming under Napoleon's control. He was the senior British negotiator at the Treaty of Ghent that ended the War of 1812. After his retirement, Gambier became the first president of the Church Missionary Society. In his honour, Gambier became a geographical place name: the Gambier Islands at the entrance to Spencer Gulf in South Australia; Mount Gambier, a dormant volcano and a city on its slopes in South Australia; the Gambier Islands in modern-day French Polynesia; Gambier Island in Howe Sound, near Vancouver, British Columbia, Canada; Point Gambier, Gambier Island, and Gambier Bay at the southeast tip of Admiralty Island in Alaska; and the village of Gambier, Ohio, in the United States, the seat of Kenyon College, for which Admiral Gambier played a key role in its founding.[4]

James Gambier was born on 13 October 1756 on New Providence Island in the Bahamas, while his father, John Gambier, was serving as lieutenant governor of the colony. James Gambier's mother, Deborah, died in 1766, when the boy was only 10 years old. At some earlier point, however, John and Deborah had sent infant James home to England, along with his elder brother and two sisters, to be raised by his father's sister, Margaret Gambier.[5] In 1761, she had married Captain Charles Middleton, having first made his acquaintance through her uncle and his first commanding officer, Captain Samuel Mead. As a Scot, Charles Middleton had been brought up as a Presbyterian. According to one speculative account, the two first met as early as 1747, when Middleton was a lieutenant and just 20 years old. Margaret slowly began to interest Middleton in her growing evangelical religious beliefs. Very likely, the two heard one of the most famous preachers of the mid-eighteenth century, the Reverend George Whitefield. A renowned open-air preacher, he became a founder of Methodism and had led the way for the 'First Great Awakening' of the 1730s and 1740s in colonial North America.[6] Margaret's father, the elder John Gambier and his wife Mary Mead Gambier were said to have thought Middleton an inappropriate match. Margaret broke with her parents over both her religion preference and her choice of a future husband, leading her

---

4   General biographical sketches on Gambier's life are, in chronological order, as follows: John Marshall, *Royal Naval Biography*, Vol. 1 (London: Longman, Hurst, Reese, Orme and Brown, 1823), pp.74-86; James Ralfe, *The Naval Biography of Great Britain*, Vol. 2 (London: Whitmore & Fenn, 1828), pp.82-90; John Knox Laughton, 'Gambier, James, Baron Gambier,' *Oxford Dictionary of National Biography* (Oxford: Oxford University Press, 1889); T.A. Heathcote, *The British Admirals of the Fleet. 1734-1995: A Biographical Dictionary* (Barnsley, South Yorkshire: Pen and Sword Books, 2002), pp.94-96; Lee Bienkowski, *Admirals in the Age of Nelson* (Annapolis, Maryland: US Naval Institute Press, 2003), pp.152-169; Frederic F. Thompson, 'Gambier, James, 1st Baron Gambier,' in *Dictionary of Canadian Biography*, Vol. 6, University of Toronto/Université Laval, 2003 <http://www.biographi.ca/en/bio/gambier_james_6E.html> (accessed 25 February 2017); Richard C. Blake, 'Gambier, Baron James (1756-1833),' *Oxford Dictionary of National Biography* (Oxford University Press, 2004); online edition, Jan 2008 <http://oxforddnb.com/view/article/10321> (accessed 2 Nov 2015); Nicholas Tracy, *Who's Who in Nelson's Navy: 200 Naval Heroes* (London: Chatham Publishing, 2006), pp.148-150, and the website More than Nelson <http://morethannelson.com/officer/lord-james-gambier/>

5   Georgina, Lady Chatterton (ed.), *Memorials, Personal and Historical of Admiral Lord Gambier, G.C.B.* Second edition, Vol. 1 (London: Hurst and Blackett, 1861), pp.1-15.

6   Blake, *Evangelicals*, pp.38-39.

to move to Teston to live with a school friend with similar religious views, the wealthy Elizabeth Bouverie.

Following the marriage of Charles and Margaret Middleton in 1761, Charles returned to sea duty in command of fifth-rate HM frigate *Adventure* (32) until 1763. From that point, until the beginning of the War for American Independence in 1775, Middleton declined peacetime naval appointments and was on half-pay. He managed the farm lands owned by Bouverie and lived in the manor house, later to be known as Barham Court. Using the funds that he accumulated from prize money, he invested in East India Company stock to supplement his half-pay and support his lifestyle ashore.

That period was an important one for the Middletons – and by extension to James Gambier – as the Middleton's developed further their evangelical leanings and social life among a growing group of like-minded people; most notably William Wilberforce and his group interested in the abolition of the slave trade that included Granville Sharp and Thomas Clarkson, who often met at Barham Court. Further, the Middletons were among the Clapham Sect, the influential and wealthy group of evangelicals led by The Rev. John Venn, the rector of Clapham Parish Church and founder of the Church Missionary Society.[7] As the historian Richard Blake has explained: 'Charles and Margret shared a world-view where Christianity was central and its implications clear – evangelism, abolition of slavery, and the moral reformation of society – and where high office gave singular opportunities for these goals to be attempted.'[8] It is not certain exactly how long young James Gambier lived with the Middletons as a child or when, precisely, he left their home to go into naval service. Nevertheless, the Middletons' religious life, values, principles of self-discipline, and connections certainly became major elements of his life as an adult and were the key elements of his naval service.

Captain James Gambier carried the name of his nephew James on the muster books of his third-rate HMS *Yarmouth* (64) at Chatham, between 1766 until 1770. The boy is listed successively from 1767, when he was just 11 years old, as being a captain's servant, midshipman, and able seaman for a total of two years, 11

---

7   John Knox Laughton (ed.), *Letters and Papers of Charles, Lord Barham, Admiral of the Red, Publications of the Navy Records Society,* Vol. 32 (London: Navy Records Society, 1907), Vol.1, pp.xxi-xxiv; Gareth Atkins, 'Religion, Politics, and Patronage in the late Hanoverian Navy, c. 1780-c.1820', *Historical Research,* 88:240 (May 2015), pp.272-290; Roger Morriss, 'Charles Middleton, Lord Barham, 1726-1813' in Peter LeFevre and Richard Harding (eds.), *The Precursors of Nelson: British Admirals of the 18th Century* (London: Chatham, 1998), pp.301-323; John E. Talbot, *The Pen and Ink Sailor: Charles Middleton and the King's Navy, 1778-1813* (London: Frank Cass, 1998); Blake, *Evangelicals,* pp.37-43.

8   Blake, *Evangelicals,* p.41. Venn was also related to the Gambier family by marriage; his aunt, Mary Venn, had married William James Gambier, a first cousin to Lieutenant Governor John Gambier and the Rear Admiral James Gambier.

months, four weeks, and 13 days.[9] James would have been about 14 years old at the time that his uncle left *Yarmouth* and took command of the North American Station for 10 months in 1770-71. At that point, the muster book of the fourth-rate HM Frigate *Salisbury* (50) carried the boy as a midshipman for one year, nine months and three weeks. In 1772, the 16-year-old James Gambier was assigned as able seaman and then midshipman in the fifth-rate HM Frigate *Chatham* (50), the flagship of Rear Admiral William Parry, commanding the Leeward Island Station. After some three months aboard, Gambier was appointed to HM Sloop *Spy* (10), in which he served in the West Indies for five months as master's mate and three and a half more months as a midshipman. Gambier returned to *Chatham* for two months as an able seaman, then served as a midshipman for a year, before sitting for his lieutenant's examination at the Navy Office, St Mary-le-Strand, Westminster, on 28 September 1774. He produced journals that he had kept in *Chatham* and *Spy* as well as certificates from all his commanding officers, including his uncle.[10] Although he produced a certificate that he was 'more than 20 years of age,' he was two weeks short of his 18th birthday. Although he passed, he was not promoted to lieutenant until two and a half years later, 12 February 1777, just five months after he had passed his 20th birthday.[11]

Following his examination in 1777, Gambier served in the third-rate HMS *Royal Oak* (74), the guard-ship at Spithead. Shortly after that posting, he transferred to the fifth-rate HM Frigate *Portland* (50), and returned to the West Indies, on the Leeward Islands Station. While serving in the West Indies, Gambier was appointed an acting lieutenant in HM Sloop *Shark* (16), and later in the sixth-rate HM Frigate *Hind* (24). While in *Hind*, Gambier's promotion to lieutenant took effect on 12 February 1777. He returned to England in August 1777 and served briefly in the third-rate HMS *Sultan* (74), before he was assigned to his uncle's flagship as the second in command on the North American Station, the third-rate HMS *Ardent* (64). Through his uncle's patronage, the 21-year-old James Gambier was promoted to Master and Commander on 9 March 1778, just 13 months after he became a lieutenant, and took command of the 8-gun bomb ketch *Thunder*,

---

9   TNA ADM 107/6/314: James Gambier's Passing Certificate as a Lieutenant, 28 September 1774.
10   TNA ADM 107/6/314: James Gambier's Passing Certificate as a Lieutenant, 28 September 1774. On the typical length of time between passing and promotion, see Evan Wilson, *A Social History of British Naval Officers, 1775-1815* (London; Boydell Press, 2017), p.35. While not within the 58 percent commissioned within a year of his examination, Gambier was within the three-year period during which 80 percent were promoted.
11   J M Collinge (ed.), 'Principal Officers and Commissioners', in *Office Holders in Modern Britain: Volume 7, Navy Board Officials 1660-1832* (London, 1978), pp.18-25; *British History Online* <http://www.british-history.ac.uk/office-holders/vol7/> (accessed 20 March 2017).

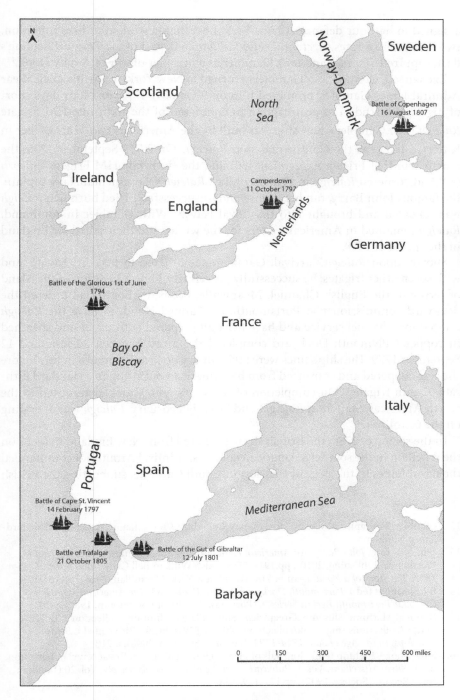

Map 4. North Americans fighting in Royal Navy European battles.

assigned to harbour defence at New York. Less than a week after his promotion, two French third-rates, *Hector* (74) and *Valliant* (64), part of the Comte d'Estaing's fleet, captured *Thunder* and took Gambier as a prisoner of war off Sandy Hook.[12]

Exchanged, Commander Gambier returned to New York, where his uncle, Rear Admiral James Gambier, promoted him on 9 October 1778, just four days short of his 22nd birthday, to post-captain in command of the sixth-rate HM Frigate *Raleigh* (32). Gambier's new ship was built by the Americans two-years earlier in Kittery, Maine, as the Continental ship *Raleigh*. On 27-28 September 1778, the fourth-rate HM Frigate *Experiment* (50) and the sixth-rate HM Frigate *Unicorn* (20) had cornered *Raleigh* in Penobscot Bay. *Raleigh*'s Continental Navy captain, the famous John Barry, ran her ashore and unsuccessfully tried burn her. *Raleigh* was refloated and brought into the Royal Navy.[13] With Gambier in command, *Raleigh* remained in American waters for the winter and then sailed for England in the spring of 1779.

Shortly upon *Raleigh*'s arrival, Gambier was ordered to take his frigate, and with seven other frigates, he successfully prevented a French invasion of the island of Jersey in the English Channel. Meanwhile, the Navy Board had ordered the dockyard commissioner at Portsmouth, Sir Samuel Hood, to have the *Raleigh* refitted for Channel service and have her hull prepared with paper and sheathed in copper.[14] Plymouth Dockyard completed this work between 24 June and 12 September 1779. The ship's lines were taken in dry dock at Plymouth in July before she was coppered and converted from her American outfitting to a standard fifth-rate 32-gun frigate.[15] On completion of the ship's refit, Gambier returned to the North American Station in *Raleigh,* and by early February, *Raleigh* was operating off the Carolinas.[16]

In the spring of 1780, the British strategy shifted from New England to focus on the rebellion in the southern American colonies. Admiral Arbuthnot commanded the naval forces in the siege of Charleston, South Carolina, supporting the British

---

12 Gambier Biography at website *More than Nelson* <http://morethannelson.com/officer/lord-james-gambier/>

13 Tim McGrath, *John Barry: An American Hero in the Age of Sail* (Yardley, Pennsylvania: Westholme Publishing, 2010), pp.191-257; see also William Bell Clark, *John Barry, 1745-1803: The Story of a Naval Hero in Two Wars* (New York: Macmillan, 1938), pp.164-171.

14 R.J.B. Knight (ed.), *Portsmouth Dockyard Papers, 1774-1783: The American War: A Calendar Portsmouth Record Series*, 6 (Portsmouth: City of Portsmouth, 1987), p.20.

15 National Maritime Museum, Greenwich, 'Ships' Plans', Admiralty Collection ZAZ3127, <http://collections.rmg.co.uk/collections/objects/82918.html> Rif Winfield, *British Warships, in the Age of Sail, 1714-1792* (Barnsley: Seaforth, 2008), p.218

16 John Knox Laughton (ed.), 'Journals of Henry Duncan, Captain, Royal Navy' in Laughton, (ed.), *Naval Miscellany, Vol. 1, Publications of the Navy Records Society*, Vol. 20 (London: Navy Records Society, 1902), pp.177-179, 186.

Army under generals Sir Henry Clinton and Lord Cornwallis. Arbuthnot's squadron had left New York, escorting Clinton's troops, where they disembarked near Charleston. On 20 March, the squadron, which included Gambier's *Raleigh*, crossed the bar at the entrance to Charleston Harbour and captured one French and eight American warships. As the British land forces crossed the Ashley River and set up their batteries against the city, Arbuthnot led eight ships, including *Raleigh*, through heavy American gunfire to anchor under James Island. With his further advance into the Cooper River blocked by sunken ships and gun emplacements on Sullivan's Island and Mount Pleasant, Arbuthnot ordered 500 seamen and marines from the ships in the squadron to land. On the morning of 29 March, captains Charles Hudson, John Orde, and James Gambier landed with this force and moved to capture the American positions on Mount Pleasant.

Learning that the Americans were abandoning their redoubt at Lampres Point, overlooking the Cooper River, they moved ahead and seized it before the enemy could remove their guns, ammunition, and supplies.[17] In the next stage of the operation, Arbuthnot decided to attack the weak western and northwestern side of Fort Moultrie. During the night of 4 April, Hudson and Gambier, with Commander John Knowles of the Transport Service, took 200 sailors and marines in boats and passed unobserved under the guns of Fort Moultrie to capture a redoubt on the east end of Sullivan's Island. While Captain Orde prepared to move 200 men from Mount Pleasant and the Arbuthnot's squadron waited only for the tide to come closer to begin the bombardment, Captain Hudson called for the fort to surrender, which it did on 6 April. The city surrendered four days later. In his dispatch to the Admiralty, Arbuthnot gave his highest praise to Sir Andrew Hammond. The admiral then noted: 'Captains Hudson, Orde, Gambier, Elphinston[e], and Evans have distinguished themselves particularly on shore; and the officers and seamen with them on this occasion, have observed the most perfect discipline.'[18]

On 23 October 1780, *Raleigh*, in company with the third-rate HMS *Intrepid* (64), captured the 10-gun Pennsylvania privateer *Greyhound*.[19] In December 1781, *Raleigh* captured the 20-gun American privateer *General Mifflin* with two prizes off Charleston, South Carolina, bound for Cork, Ireland. At the same time, *Raleigh* prevented *General Mifflin* from taking as a prize the ship *Roman Emperor*

17   W.G. Perrin (ed.), *The Keith Papers: Selections from the Letters and Papers of Admiral Viscount Keith, Publications of the Navy Records Society*, Vol. 62 (London: Navy Records Society, 1927), p.169: Arbuthnot to Elphinstone, 18 April 1780.

18   *Bath Chronicle*, 22 June 1780, p.1: Vice Admiral M. Arbuthnot to Admiralty Secretary Philip Stephens, 14 May 1780.

19   *The London Gazette*, Issue 12331 (14 September 1782), p.2; See also the website *American War of Independence at Sea* <http://www.awiatsea.com/Privateers/G/Greyhound%20 Pennsylvania%20Schooner%20[Kemp].html> (accessed 22 May 2019).

and convoyed her safely into Charleston.[20] Gambier brought *Raleigh* back to Portsmouth in May 1782, where the crew was paid off and the ship placed on sale, 13 February 1783. A buyer purchased her at auction for £550 on 16 May.[21] With the end of the war in sight, Gambier apparently made no effort to find an assignment, although with his uncle Charles Middleton at the Navy Board, it would have seemed entirely possible for him to do so. On Gambier's departure from active service in 1782 to go on half-pay as a captain at only 26 years of age, he had shown himself to be a capable officer. In command of a frigate, he had been successful in combat, both afloat and ashore.

Very little is known about Gambier's activities during the decade between leaving *Raleigh* in late 1782 until he took command of the third-rate HMS *Defence* (74) in April 1793. Among the scarce facts available, he married Louisa Matthew in July 1788, the second daughter of Daniel Matthew of Felix Hall, Kelvedon, Essex, who in 1770 had served as High Sheriff of Essex.[22] Two years earlier in 1786, Daniel Mathew's eldest daughter, Jane, had married Sir Samuel Gambier, James's elder brother, who was Secretary, then a Commissioner of the Navy Board, between 1795 and 1813. Soon after France declared war against Britain and the Netherlands in 1793, the Admiralty called the 37-year-old Gambier to command the *Defence* in the Channel Fleet under Admiral Lord Howe. William Henry Dillon, who had served as a midshipman under Gambier in 1793-94, left a detailed memoir of those years as part of the reminiscences that he wrote in 1820. On first reporting to Gambier in September 1793, Dillon remembered him as 'rather tall, good looking, light limbed, and of a very genteel appearance.'[23] Gambier's acquaintance, William Wilberforce, the leader in the movement to abolish the slave trade, had recommended Dillon to Gambier, as had Dillon's most recent commanding officer. In his first interview, Gambier told him in a revealing statement, 'Mind the prospects before you. I was a captain in nine years from my entering the Navy. Keep up your spirits, and, if you attend to your duty, you will find a friend in me.'[24] This statement confirms that since Gambier became a post-captain in October 1778, he actually went to sea for the first time in 1769, rather than in 1766, as the muster books had recorded. At

---

20   'Postscript', *Northampton Mercury,* 29 January 1782, p.3, reprinted report from *Rivington's Royal Gazette,* New York, 30 December 1781.

21   *The London Gazette,* issue 12409, (26 January 1783), p.2; Winfield, *British Warships, 1714-1792,* p.20.

22   Felix Hall was reduced in size in the 1930s and gutted by fire. What survives in 2017 is only the partial shell of the burned-out structure.

23   Sir William Henry Dillon, KCH, Vice Admiral of the Red, *A Narrative of my Professional Adventures, (1790-1839),* Michael A. Lewis ed., *Publications of the Navy Records Society,* Vol. 93 (London: Navy Records Society, 1953), p.95.

24   Dillon, *Narrative,* p.95.

the same time, the remark reveals Gambier's attitude that patronage needed to be matched by performance for a successful career.

Dillon's words clearly show himself as a conceited and very demanding young man, who found his rigid views correct against most others being in the wrong. Tending to favour hard discipline, he had little sympathy with Gambier's attempts to inculcate religion or to introduce a lighter and more innovative approach to leadership. At one point, he ridiculed Gambier's views. On 18 November 1793, in rough seas and high winds, Howe's fleet sighted a French squadron at dawn and Howe ordered his fleet to engage the enemy. In the van, *Defence* was ready for action, when suddenly the ship's fore topmast was carried away, taking the main topmast with it:

> Here was a transition from a hope of glory to the keenest feelings of disappointment. Capt. Gambier, who had reckoned upon distinguishing himself that day, was so completely cast down that he could not refrain from saying 'D—n it all. We have lost the glory of the day!' Everyone who heard him could not help remarking that he had broken his own orders by swearing.[25]

On another occasion, Gambier upbraided Dillon for not attending prayers, telling him: 'You are a refractory young gentleman. I see how it is. You rely on your influential connections.'[26] In an attempt to justify himself, Dillon showed his annoyance with Gambier and blurted out. 'Since you will not, Sir, do me the justice to give credit to the sincerity of intentions, I hope I may be allowed to say that I did not come to sea to learn my prayers.'[27] Gambier never again required his presence at prayers, but Dillon was surprised and offended when Gambier declined Dillon's offer, without any hesitation, to accompany him to his next command.[28] These anecdotes provide rare insight into Gambier's temperament and personality, but they do not warrant the conclusion that Michael Lewis drew from them about 'that unique officer James Gambier – "Preaching Jemmy" – whose running of a capital ship in wartime is an almost unbelievable tragic-comedy.'[29] Dillon, however, was perceptive and self-serving enough to see that Gambier, 'by his gallant conduct in [command of *Defence* during the battle of] the First of June established a reputation that led one to expect that he would rise to a prominent station in the

25   Dillon, *Narrative*, p.100.
26   Dillon, *Narrative*, p.110.
27   Dillon, *Narrative*, p.100.
28   Dillon, *Narrative*, pp.163-164.
29   Dillon, *Narrative*, p.xxxii.

profession. It was, therefore, desirable to be on good terms with him.'[30] In the end, Dillon changed his attitude, and Gambier forgave the midshipman his youthful indiscretions and allowed Dillon not only to follow him to his next command but provided him patronage for many years to come.

In the Battle of the Glorious First of June 1794, Gambier earned both a reputation as a fighting captain and the approval of Lord Howe. The battle was the first of the major engagements of the war and, despite its name, was a series of three major actions with the French fleet fought over a five-day period beginning on 28 May and culminating on the first of June.[31] In the culminating battle with the French fleet under Villaret de Joyeuse, Lord Howe wanted to implement an innovative tactical plan. The two opposing fleets gradually closed with each other on nearly parallel courses in a line ahead. Instead of having each ship in the battle line continuing to follow the others in the line, Howe wanted each ship, on his signal, to turn individually toward the French line. Then, each ship was to run down wind and pass through the French line, firing at the bows and sterns of the French ships as they passed through, then turning to engage one of the ships on the leeward side, to prevent the French from escaping. When Howe in his flagship, *Queen Charlotte*, executed the plan and turned toward the French fleet, only a few of his ships followed, either ignoring or not seeing the signal.

Gambier, commanding *Defence* as the seventh ship of the British van, was the first and, for a time, the only ship to follow Howe's order. Passing through the French line between its sixth and seventh vessels, he raked both and manoeuvred into the planned position on the leeward side. *Marlborough* soon followed the example set by Gambier in *Defence,* but the failure of so many other commanding officers to carry out Howe's plan left Gambier and his ship in a perilous situation. Dismasted, *Defence* continued to fire her guns. In action, she had 18 of her ship's company killed and 39 wounded. As she was severely damaged, another ship towed her back to England.[32] Gambier exemplified Howe's desires. Midshipman Dillon heard that Lord Howe had remarked, 'If every ship of the Fleet had followed Captain Gambier's example, the result of this action would have been very different.'[33]

30   Dillon, *Narrative*, p.164.
31   For a detailed description of the battle, with transcriptions of the dispatches, see Willis, *In the Hour of Victory,* Chapter 1; See also, Michael Duffy and Roger Morriss (eds.), *The Glorious First of June: A Naval Battle and its Aftermath* (Exeter: Exeter University Press, 2001); Sam Willis, *The Glorious First of June: Fleet Battle in the Reign of Terror* (London: Quercus, 2011).
32   Willis, *In The Hour of Victory,* pp.74-75.
33   Dillon, *Narrative*, p.135.

In the aftermath of the battle, the first British fleet victory in this war against France, the King personally came to Portsmouth to congratulate Howe and to distribute the honours and distinctions. These awards produced considerable dissension and complaint among the officers who received that recognition. Gambier received the Naval Gold Medal and was made a Colonel of Marines for his services, and Dillon believed that Gambier had been offered a knighthood but had declined it.[34] The action was certainly a highlight and turning point of Gambier's service. Widely known and admired, the artist James Stow engraved the first publicly circulated image of Gambier in 1808 in a print that commemorated the battle and the key captains serving with Howe.[35] As a memento of the battle, Gambier commissioned the artist Nicholas Pocock to paint the scene in which *Defence* is shown dismasted and surrounded by enemy ships.[36] Completed in 1811, Gambier bequeathed the work in his will to the Greenwich Hospital Collection and it has since become a much-admired painting.[37]

On 30 August 1794, Gambier received orders to leave *Defence* and to take command of the second-rate HMS *Prince of Wales* (98), then fitting out at Chatham.[38] Gambier stayed only six months in this command. Through Howe's influence, the 38-year-old captain became one of the Lords Commissioners of the Admiralty on 7 March 1795. Exactly one year after the battle, on 1 June 1795, Gambier was promoted two steps at once, to Rear Admiral of the Blue and Rear Admiral of the White. He remained at the Admiralty Board until 19 February 1801, serving as Senior Naval Lord from 10 September 1798 to 1801. During this same period, he was promoted, moving up two steps as Rear Admiral of the Red and Vice Admiral of the Blue on 14 February 1799, and then, on 1 January 1801, to Vice Admiral of the White.[39]

---

34   Dillon, *Narrative*, p.153.
35   British Museum. Print Collection. 1875, 0814.752: 'Commemoration of the Victory of June 1st MDCCXCIV', lettered with the title, and the names of the admirals and captains (Including Captain James Gambier) around the individual medallions; lettered below the image 'R. Smirke, R.A. Delt. The Figures Engraved by R. Bartolozzi, R.A. Pub. by R. Bowyer, 1803 Historic Gallery, Pall Mall Landscape & Water Engd. by Landseer Portraits of the Admls. Engd. by Ryder. Portraits of the Capts. Engd. by Stow.'
36   National Maritime Museum (NMM) BHC0474: Nicholas Pocock, 'The "Defence" at the Battle of the First of June 1794'.
37   NMM PAD8791: 'The Battle of the Glorious First of June 1794; The "Defence" under tow by a frigate.'
38   Dillon, *Narrative*, pp.163-166, 178, 185.
39   Patrick Marioné, The Complete Navy List of the Napoleonic Wars, 1793 - 1815 (CD-Rom, Belgium: SEEF, 2003); J.C. Sainty, Admiralty Officials, 1660-1870 (London: Athlone Press [for] the University of London, Institute of Historical Research, 1975); With special thanks to Roger Knight for the latter reference.

As an Admiralty commissioner, Gambier became fully immersed in the complex business of managing the fleet, but in addition to these duties, he undertook two major tasks: designing an experimental frigate and revising the signal book. As an experiment, Gambier developed a frigate to be built of fir, rather than oak.[40] The fifth-rate HM Frigate *Triton* (32) was constructed at Deptford and later became famous as one of four frigates that captured two Spanish galleons laden with silver in the Bay of Biscay in 1799.[41] To mark the success of his project, Gambier commissioned Nicholas Pocock to paint a portrait of *Triton*, showing her from three aspects in a fresh breeze. The main detailed view shows her hove-to with backed foresails, while the other two views show the ship in the distance.[42] Also,

Gambier's design, HMS *Triton*. (NMM)

40   Winfield, *British Warships, 1714-1792*, p.203.
41   William M. James, *Naval History of Great Britain During the French Revolution and Napoleonic Wars: 1797-1799,* Vol. 2, with a new introduction by Andrew Lambert (London: 1837; Conway, 2002), pp.357-58; Edward Brenton, *Naval History of Great Britain from 1793 to 1836*, Vol. 1 (London: Henry Colburn, 1837), p.439.
42   National Maritime Museum, Greenwich, Oil Paintings. BHC 3675: 'The Frigate Triton,' by Nicholas Pocock, 1796 <http://collections.rmg.co.uk/collections/objects/15148.html> (accessed 22 May 2019). The National Maritime Museum also holds a 1796 Admiralty model of Triton.

Gambier heavily influenced Sir William Rule's design of the third-rate HMS *Plantagenet* (74).[43]

Gambier's second task, the revision of the fleet signal book, was a critical task that filled a long-standing need. Over the years, numerous changes had been suggested and had been instituted by various fleet commanders, but they were not consolidated into a single authoritative document. The Battle of the First of June had demonstrated some of the signalling difficulties that the fleet faced. Admiral Lord Howe had been an innovator in this area and his ideas were widely accepted, but with his retirement, Gambier, as one who fully understood Howe's thinking on signalling, was in a position to undertake the revision as Senior Naval Lord.[44] The new signal books were approved and issued on 13 May 1799. The new version consolidated many ideas that had been current in the fleet and rationalized the approach by creating two books, one for day and one for night, which contained both the signals and the instructions placed together for the first time. Also, the books provided an authoritative list of the 700 some warships in the Royal Navy, each with a standard identifying number, with blank lines for the addition of new ships joining the fleet. Thus, it was Gambier's signal book that the fleet used at Trafalgar.[45]

On leaving the Admiralty in February 1801, Gambier became third in command of the Channel Fleet under Admiral William Cornwallis and flew his flag in the second-rate HMS *Neptune* (98). Soon after, the Peace of Amiens was signed in March 1802, creating a 14-month period of uneasy peace with France, the Admiralty ordered Gambier to take up the position of Commander-in-Chief and Governor of Newfoundland. In the eyes of officials in London, Newfoundland was not a colonial settlement, but rather an important cod fishery that needed the Royal Navy's protection. In the century between 1729 and 1825, naval officers served in the dual position of commander-in-chief of the warships on that station and governor of the colony. During the second decade of the eighteenth century, these officers were usually naval captains, but from the American War for Independence through the Napoleonic Wars, vice admirals usually held the post. In their dual civil-military role, the naval officers were primarily concerned with the protection of the fisheries and their support bases ashore in wartime.

43 Winfield, *British Warships, 1714-1792*, p.65.
44 Chatterton, *Memorials . . . of Lord Gambier*, Vol. 1, pp.341-344: Rear Admiral Hugh Seymour to Rear Admiral Gambier, 15 July 1798.
45 Brian Tunstall, *Naval Warfare in the Age of Sail: The Evolution of Fighting Tactics 1650-1815*, Nicholas Tracy ed. (London: Chatham, 1990), pp.227-229; Julian S. Corbett (ed.), *Signals and Instructions, 1776-1794, with addenda to volume XXIX, Publications of the Navy Records Society*, Vol. 35 (London: Navy Records Society, 1908), pp.78-79.

With the collapse of the peace in June 1803 toward the end of his term, Gambier turned his attention to defence. At that point, the local military commander was authorised to raise a thousand men, but with the garrison numbering only 63 men, this alone proved a formidable task, even before considering the problems of training and equipping the force. On 23 April 1804, Gambier was promoted to Vice Admiral of the Red and, with William Pitt's return to power as Prime Minister on 10 May 1804, Gambier was recalled from Newfoundland to resume his seat as Senior Naval Lord among the Commissioners of the Admiralty. From the formation of the new Admiralty Board on 15 May 1804, Lord Melville became the First Lord of the Admiralty and remained in that post until May 1805, when Gambier's uncle, Sir Charles Middleton, succeeded to that position with his new title, Baron Barham of Barham Court and Teston. Gambier remained with Barham at the Admiralty until 10 February 1806, following Pitt's death on 23 January 1806 and the formation of the Ministry of All the Talents (a coalition government) under Lord Grenville on 10 February. While on the Admiralty Board, Gambier was promoted to Admiral of the Blue on 9 November 1805.

During this period, Barham, Gambier, and the other Admiralty commissioners managed successfully the complex series of strategic and operational manoeuvres that led up to and beyond the Trafalgar campaign.[46] On coming to the Admiralty as Senior Naval Lord in 1804, Gambier had begun a project to revise the *Regulations and Instructions Relating to His Majesty's Service at Sea*. Long overdue, the Admiralty had last issued the *Regulations and Instructions* in 1731.[47] During the intervening 75 years, a range of conflicting and inconsistent practices had come into use that needed regularisation and updating, including references to types of ships no longer in service. In November 1804, the Admiralty had sent a draft to the Navy Board and it had suggested amendments in March 1805.

Shortly after Lord Barham took office in May 1805, he wrote the Prime Minister, 'Our Naval Instructions will, I hope, be issued soon. It is an improvement of the first importance.'[48] In their earlier experiences in command, both Barham and Gambier had emphasised the importance and necessity of following regulations and both agreed on the need for revision. The other Lords Commissioners as well

---

46   Roger Knight, *Britain Against Napoleon: The Organisation of Victory, 1793-1815* (London: Allen Lane, 2013), p.227.

47   Great Britain. Admiralty, *Regulations and Instructions Relating to His Majesty's Service at Sea* (London, 1731). Reprinted in 12 subsequent editions 1734 2nd ed.; 1743-3rd ed.; 1746 5th ed.; 1747-6th ed.; 1757-9th ed.; 1766-10th ed.; 1772-11th ed.; 1787-12th ed. and 1790-13th ed. inclusive.

48   Laughton, *Letters and Papers of Charles, Lord Barham*, Vol. III; Publication of the Navy Records Society, Vol. 39, pp.8-82; Brian Lavery (ed.), *Shipboard Life and Organisation, 1731-1815. Publications of the Navy Records Society*, Vol. 138 (Aldershot, England: Ashgate for the Navy Records Society. 1998), pp.6-8.

as the First Lord fully approved Gambier's initiatives and the King in Council formally established and issued them on 25 January 1806.[49] These instructions remained in effect until revised in 1869 and superseded in 1879.[50] The new instructions consolidated and regularised practices across the entire naval service in much greater detail than before with a book of 440 pages, superseding the 186 pages of 1731.

One of the most notable aspects of the new instructions was an emphasis on cleanliness and health as well as the public expression of religion through the Church of England in the Navy, in line with both Gambier's and Barham's views. Through these regulations, Barham and Gambier gave new vitality to the liturgy of the *Book of Common Prayer* in the Navy and an officer-led and clergy-instructed presentation of Christian piety to the men of the lower decks.[51] In another notable change, the new *Admiralty Regulations and Instructions* quietly omitted the centuries-old English claim for foreign vessels to salute and strike their topsails to acknowledge British 'sovereignty of the narrow seas.'[52] When asked about it a decade later, Gambier replied that it was his initiative and that 'it was omitted solely on the ground of the absurdity of the practice and the certainty, if insisted upon, of involving the nation in disputes with foreign powers.'[53]

With the fall of the Ministry of All the Talents and the formation of the Duke of Portland's ministry on 24 March 1807, Earl Mulgrave became First Lord of the Admiralty and Gambier was again called to resume his seat as Senior Naval Lord on the Admiralty Board. He served in that capacity for just over a year from 6 April 1807 to 9 May 1808 and 'had direction of all the patronage in the Navy.'[54]

---

49   Great Britain. Admiralty, *Regulations and Instructions Relating to His Majesty's Service at Sea, Established by His Majesty in Council.* (London: W. Winchester and Son, Strand, 1806), reprinted 1808-2nd edition.

50   Great Britain, Admiralty, *Queen's Regulations and Admiralty Instructions for the Government of the Naval Service* (London: 1869); *The Queen's Regulations and Admiralty Instructions for the Government of Her Majesty's Naval Service* (London: HMSO, 1879).

51   Richard Blake, *Religion in the British Navy, 1815-1879: Piety and Professionalism* (London: Boydell Press, 2014), pp.3-8.

52   On this subject, see Thomas Wemyss Fulton, *The Sovereignty of the Sea: A Historical Account of the Claims of England to the Dominion of the British Seas, and of the Evolution of the Territorial Waters With Special Reference to the Rights of the Fishing and the Naval Salute* (Edinburg & London: William Blackwood & Sons, 1911) and Jakob Seerup, 'Danish and Swedish Flag Disputes with the British in the Channel', in N.A.M. Rodger, J. Ross Dancy, Benjamin Darnell and Evan Wilson (eds.), *Strategy and the Sea: Essays in Honour of John B. Hattendorf* (Woodbridge, Suffolk: Boydell Press, 2016), pp.28-36.

53   W.G. Perrin, 'The Salute in the Narrow Seas and the Vienna Conference of 1815', in W.G. Perrin (ed.), *The Naval Miscellany, Vol. III; Publications of the Navy Records Society*, Vol. 63 (London: Navy Records Society, 1928), p.326: Gambier to Croker, 21 Jan 1815.

54   Edward Hughes (ed.), *The Private Correspondence of Admiral Lord Collingwood, Publications of the Navy Records Society*, Vol. 98 (London: Navy Records Society, 1957),

Gambier continued to hold his appointment at the Admiralty when the Board entrusted him with command of the fleet in the North Sea then preparing for Baltic operations. For more than a year, British leaders had anticipated the contingency that Britain might have to go to war with Denmark. The previous ministry had seen the strategic danger and had begun to survey and to refit third-rate ships that could operate in the shallow waters of the Sound and Belts. When these officials left office in 1807, a dozen suitable ships were ready at Great Yarmouth. The new ministry continued the preparations and, by April 1807, 16,500 soldiers destined for Germany as well as the 8,000 men in the King's German Legion on the island of Rügen were available.[55] Some discussion had already taken place that Britain might occupy the Danish island of Zealand, but the impetus behind the operation came from an intelligence report in June 1807 that the Danish fleet was readying itself for action and another report in early July from Tilsit that Russia and France were contemplating an anti-British league. By mid-July, the Duke of Portland, with his ministers, concluded that the strategic situation seemed to be a replay of that in 1801 and decided to send both a fleet and an army to the Baltic.

On 17 July 1808, the ministry reached the conclusion that Britain must demand – or, if need be, seize – possession of the Danish fleet for the remainder of the war to prevent Napoleon from acquiring control of it and shutting down all British trade and commerce in the Baltic.[56] With 17 ships-of-the-line and numerous smaller warships, Gambier sailed on 26 July to Denmark with Vice Admiral Henry Stanhope, Commodores Sir Samuel Hood and Richard Keats, and Sir Home Popham as fleet captain. The military force of 25,000 men was commanded by General Lord Cathcart, with Major General Sir Arthur Wellesley in command of the reserve.

Gambier's mission was difficult and delicate. He would have to assemble a large joint amphibious force from several dispersed bases. Then, he had to use its presence as a latent force during diplomatic talks before taking any direct offensive action. To do all this, he needed firm command and superior leadership as well as effective coordination between the government at home and diplomats abroad as well as between the army and naval commanders.[57] Gambier carried this off

---

pp.248-249: Collingwood to sister, 25 June 1808.

55   Knight, *Britain against Napoleon*, p.202

56   Brenton, *Naval History of Great Britain*, Vol. 2, pp.169-80; James, *Naval History of Great Britain*, Vol. 4, pp.284-93; A. N. Ryan (ed.), 'Documents Relating to the Copenhagen Operation, 1807' in N.A.M. Rodger (ed.), *The Naval Miscellany*, Vol. 5, *Publications of the Navy Records Society*, Vol. 125 (London: George Allen & Unwin for the Navy Records Society, 1984), pp.297-329; A.N. Ryan, 'The Causes of the British Attack upon Copenhagen in 1807', English Historical Review, 68:266 (January 1953), pp.37-55.

57   Thomas Munch-Petersen, *Defying Napoleon: How Britain Bombarded Copenhagen and Seized the Danish Feet in 1807* (Stroud: Sutton, 2007), pp.97-116.

superbly, despite objections from senior naval captains Hood, Keats, and Stopford, who resented Gambier's delegation of authority to his First Captain, Sir Home Popham, who was junior to them but was experienced in Danish waters and had experience of joint expeditions.[58]

HMS *Victory* Leading the line into the Sound, painted by Captain Christer Hägg, Royal Swedish Navy, Rtd, for Lord Eric de Saumarez. (Permission of Lord de Saumarez)

Gambier's first task was to surround the island of Zealand, the largest of the Danish Islands on which Copenhagen is located, in a pre-emptive operation to prevent the Danish Army from concentrating there for defending the capital. As a neutral power, Danish authorities were entirely unprepared for an invasion. The Danes saw that Gambier and Cathcart had surrounded Zealand with warships, but they only had 13,000 troops to face the 25,000 British troops. Gambier and Cathcart tried to use the situation and jointly repeated the demands that the diplomats had already made. Repeating the statement that Gambier and Cathcart

58   Hugh Popham, *A Damned Cunning Fellow: The Eventful life of Rear-Admiral Sir Home Popham KCB, KCH, KM, FRS 1762–1820* (Twyardreath: Old Ferry Press, 1991).

had made several weeks earlier, they wrote the Danish commander, 'it is yet not too late for the voice of reason and moderation to be heard.'[59]

They now summoned the Danish officer commanding the defences of Copenhagen to surrender the Danish fleet, which 'shall be held on deposit for His Danish Majesty and shall be restored with all its equipment' at a general peace.[60] If the request was refused, 'the captured property, public and private, must then belong to the captors, and the city, when taken, must share the fate of conquered places.'[61] The Danes did refuse and declared war on Britain. Without hesitation, Gambier and Cathcart responded by attacking the city. The bombardment of Copenhagen involved the second use in wartime of Congreve's rockets, which caused fires in 38 places in the city and forced the evacuation of 20,000 people. About eight to nine percent of the central part of Copenhagen burned to the ground with severe damage in other areas of the city.[62]

Eventually, Denmark surrendered her fleet, which Gambier's ships towed back to Britain on 21 October, along with many naval stores. The Secretary of War, Lord Castlereagh, congratulated Gambier for 'carrying His Majesty's Orders and Execution for Preventing the Danish fleet and Naval Resources being placed in the hands of our enemies.'[63] On 9 November 1807, in recognition of Gambier's highly effective command, the king raised him to the peerage as Baron Gambier of Iver in Buckinghamshire.[64] At the same time, he was offered a pension of £2,000 a year, which he modestly declined.[65] In January 1808, both houses of Parliament voted their thanks to the commanders, but the opposition condemned the entire operation as an unjustified attack on a neutral. Among others who condemned it, Lord Erskine ranted, 'If hell did not exist before, Providence would create it now to punish ministers for that damnable measure.'[66] Upon completion of this operation, Gambier resumed his post at the Admiralty and served there until 9 May 1808, when he was appointed to the command of the Channel Fleet.

59 Joint Proclamation by Gambier and Cathcart, 16 August 1807, quoted in Marshall, *Royal Naval Biography*, pp.79-81. For a detailed study of the first phase of the operation, see Munch-Petersen, *Defying Napoleon*, pp.169-92.
60 Ryan (ed.) 'Documents Relating to the Copenhagen Operation': Gambier and Cathcart to Peymann, 1 Sept 1807.
61 Ryan, 'Documents ...'
62 Munch-Petersen, *Defying Napoleon*, pp.199-202. Congreve's rockets had been first used at Boulogne in 1806.
63 Quoted in James Davey, *The Transformation of British Naval Strategy: Seapower and Supply in Northern Europe, 1808-1812* (Woodbridge: The Boydell Press, 2012), p.32.
64 Centre for Buckinghamshire Studies, Archives: D 81/50: Copy of Royal Warrant creating Admiral James Gambier a Baron, 1807.
65 'Obituary', *The Gentleman's Magazine*, Vol. 103 (1833), Part 1, pp.599-600.
66 Quoted in Davey, *The Transformation*, p.32.

A primary strategic function of the Channel Fleet was to control the Western Approaches to the Channel and to maintain the blockade of the French fleet at Brest. This prevented a squadron based at Brest from getting to sea and joining forces with the major French Mediterranean Squadron based at Toulon to create a significant concentration of the French fleet. To British naval leaders, neither the threat of a French invasion across the Chanel, nor the opportunity for a major fleet battle in the Channel or Bay of Biscay seemed likely. Nevertheless, it was still prudent to remain on guard for such possible contingencies, so the dangerous and challenging work of maintaining the blockade continued. It was tedious and demanding work with little opportunity for personal gain and glory. Gambier saw the situation as an opportunity to introduce Christian piety to the fleet as a means to improve discipline and morale. Weekly church services returned to the fleet with regularity, as the regulations required, and Church organisations provided Bibles, prayer books, and tracts to seamen. His innovations in this area met with some success, but hardly eradicated the fleet's ingrained culture of licentiousness and drunkenness.[67]

Gambier had commanded in the Channel for nearly a year when a gale forced his blockading ships off their station, allowing French Rear Admiral Jean-Baptiste Willaumez to escape from Brest with eight ships-of-the-line. Sailing south, Willaumez took refuge at Basque Roads, near the mouth of the Charente River, where the Rochefort Naval Dockyard was located, to pick up troops and to prepare for a planned attack on British possessions in the West Indies. In anchorage, the French squadron enjoyed the protection provided by reefs, shoals, and the coastal fortifications on Ile d'Aix and Oléron, as well as a boom across the seaward approach to the estuary. Intelligence soon arrived that Vice-Admiral Zacharie Allemand had taken command of the forces and would soon attempt to escape.

British warships arrived on the scene on 17 March 1809, but Gambier faced a difficult, if not insoluble, problem in risking his deep-water warships to attack the French in this position. Gambier and several others realised that both the British and the French ships were vulnerable to attack by fire ships. Gambier took defensive measures and began to plan an offensive operation. In London, Lord Mulgrave and the members of the Admiralty Board saw the same opportunity and advised Gambier that they were sending fire ships from England for that purpose. As these preparations were in progress in London, Captain Lord Cochrane arrived home in the fifth-rate HM Frigate *Imperieuse* (38) from the Mediterranean. Cochrane's reputation was patchy. As an opposition Member of Parliament and a serving naval officer, he had unwisely attacked both the government and the Admiralty, in particular, for their inefficiencies. In the Mediterranean, Collingwood's attempt

67   Blake, *Evangelicals*, pp.202-03.

to use Cochrane at Corfu demonstrated his energy, but also his lack of diplomacy. Nevertheless, Cochrane's return to England at this time was opportune, as he had a well-earned reputation as an innovative tactician as well as a daredevil and aggressive commander. Lord Mulgrave thought him the ideal person to lead the fire ship attack under Gambier's overall command, although Cochrane suspected ulterior political motives designed to ruin him. Eventually, Cochrane warily accepted the appointment, on the condition that he also have 'explosion vessels,' a type of craft that he had designed for such operations.

When Cochrane arrived at Basque Roads on 3 April, several senior officers under Gambier immediately resented his presence, seeing him as an interloper, even though the First Lord had personally ordered Cochrane. Earlier, one of Gambier's flag officers, Rear Admiral Eliab Harvey, had volunteered to command a flotilla of fire ships in the attack. Unaware of Lord Mulgrave's intervention, Harvey blamed Gambier that he was not selected, publicly denouncing him with a string of epithets, calling him, among other things a 'Jesuit, Methodist, Psalm-singer.' In Harvey's anger, he told a captain to repeat his remarks to the commander-in-chief, which eventually resulted in Harvey's court-martial and dismissal from the service. After expressing his regret to Gambier, he was eventually reinstated but not employed.[68]

With the Channel Fleet blockading the estuary of Basque Roads, Cochrane carried out his attack. It was a successful attack, but not as complete as Cochrane would have liked. In the midst of the action, Cochrane signalled for Gambier to send in larger ships to finish off the French forces. Gambier and the fleet responded, but an unfavourable wind and tide prevented him from getting close enough to attack. Four French warships and an East Indiaman had been driven ashore or burnt, while the remaining French ships were all placed out of action and damaged. Several were forced to throw their guns overboard to seek shelter in the River Charente. Gambier ordered Rear Admiral Robert Stopford to use Congreve rockets to attack the French ships, but, Stopford's flagship grounded in the shallows and it became impracticable to continue the attack.

After the battle, the zealous Cochrane threatened to use his position as a Member of Parliament to oppose a planned vote of thanks to Gambier, accusing him of cowardice for not destroying all of the French ships. This led Gambier on 30 May to request that the Admiralty convene a court-martial to inquire into his conduct as commander-in-chief. But, the court martial honourably acquitted Lord Gambier, and a motion of thanks to Gambier for his service at Basque Roads readily passed in the House of Lords. Cochrane attempted to persuade the House of Commons of an alternative but was defeated and the Commons passed the vote

68   Tracy, *Who's Who in Nelson's Navy*, pp.174-75.

of thanks to Gambier. Gambier also received a medal as a reward for his skill and bravery at Copenhagen.[69]

The squabble that occurred between Cochrane and Gambier was of a type that erupted between officers from time to time in the eighteenth century Royal Navy. Personal disputes sometimes took the form of private duels and, on other occasions, broke out into highly politicised, major public rows. Such disputes had their foundation in a naval officer's concepts of personal honour and duty. In the period between 1660 and 1815, naval officers showed a general trend to shift their emphasis from honour to duty.[70]

The disputes that involved Gambier have an additional twist. His critics, such as Eliab Harvey and others, used a distinctively virulent rhetoric that focused on Gambier's religious beliefs and his central leadership role, along with Barham, in bringing public Anglican worship back into the Navy during the Napoleonic Wars. The virulent attacks on the Blue Lights were based on the different social values that they held, which were becoming serious threats to the conventional social life of naval officers who commonly exulted in gambling, womanizing, and drinking. Those who attacked the Blue Lights tended to dismiss them on the grounds that they were poor and ineffective naval officers, but as Gambier's career shows, they could also be highly competent officers. Such attacks on individual officers were representative of larger social tensions within the naval officer corps. They reflect the shift away from an emphasis on personal honour to a focus on personal discipline in carrying out one's duty to God and country. These values were ones that gave rise to the Christian reform movements in early nineteenth century Britain that eventually evolved into the social values of the Victorian era. The bitterness of the attacks on Gambier and others reflected a social struggle between two groups in the Navy that suspected – perhaps with good reason – that the other side had built networks that favoured individuals of their type when making professional choices for potentially rewarding assignments.

After the court martial, Gambier returned to the command of the Channel Fleet. He was promoted on 31 July 1810 to Admiral of the White and continued to hold command of the Channel Fleet until 1811, when the new First Lord of the Admiralty, Charles Philip Yorke, implemented the rule that admirals should be relieved from their stations at the expiration of a three-year tenure. At that point, Gambier returned to Iver Grove and returned to work with the Church Missionary Society. The Society elected him its first president in 1812 and Gambier

69   For Admiral Gambier's Bombardment of Copenhagen 1807 medal, see *Royal Museum Greenwich* <http://collections.rmg.co.uk/collections/objects/40473. html#GuTPC2RhKHkTP45Z.99>

70   N.A.M. Rodger, 'Honor and Duty at Sea, 1660-1815', *Historical Research,* 75:190 (2002), pp.425-47; Wilson, *A Social History,* pp.196-202.

retained the position for more than 20 years. In 1813, he added prestige to the Naval and Military Bible Society, joining along with Saumarez and eventually Wellington and Lord Liverpool. Gambier also became a patron of the British and Foreign Bible Society. Gambier outdid all his contemporaries in supporting such charitable activities, becoming a member of 39 of them, patron of three, governor of three, committee member of two, vice-president of 11 and president of another three in addition to his presidency of the Church Missionary Society.[71]

Gambier did not have to wait long for a return to public employment. On 4 June 1814, he was promoted to Admiral of the Red. A month and a half later, on 30 July 1814, the Prime Minister, Lord Liverpool, appointed Gambier to head the commission to negotiate peace between Britain and the US. The first meeting of the peace commissioners took place at Ghent on 8 August. The ministry in London expected that the American peace commissioners would push very hard for the recognition of American maritime rights, on which the ministry had no intention of yielding. For this reason, Liverpool was careful to choose men who could deal with this problem, and he selected Gambier as a senior flag officer, who knew Americans and American waters as well as maritime issues.

Lord Castlereagh and the ministry directly instructed the British delegation to treat the US as a defeated nation and to demand territorial concessions for its attack against Canada. Gambier and his colleagues held this opinion for the first three months of the negotiations. They developed a plan to carve out some 250,000 square miles of the present-day states of Michigan, Ohio, Illinois, Indiana, Missouri, Iowa, Wisconsin, and Minnesota – some 15 percent of the United States – to create an independent state for Native Americans. Designed to create a barrier for Canada that would prevent future American aggression, it would also hinder future development of the United States. When news of the British demands reached America, President James Madison quickly rejected them. The ministry in London was surprised that the United States could reject such terms while facing bankruptcy. The ministry soon changed its mind in pushing for punitive demands, not because of American opinion, but due to public opinion at home and to the situation of the war in Europe.

In London, Parliament made clear that it would not fund a continuation of the war in America. At the same time, the diplomatic situation in developing peace at Vienna became more complicated. The ministry and the negotiators began to soften their stance in October 1814. By December, there was a real possibility that Liverpool's government could fall if the war-time taxation continued at home. At the same time, it became clear to the negotiators at Ghent that the only quick and

71   Gareth Atkins, 'Christian Heroes, Providence, and Patriotism in Wartime Britain, 1793-1815', *The Historical Journal*, 58:2 (June 2015), pp.393-414, 407-08.

firm basis for peace was to return to the status quo ante bellum, both sides yielding nothing and agreeing to nothing that would in any way complicate or delay the peace. The two negotiating teams signed the treaty on Christmas Eve 1814 at the British residence, then sending the treaty off for formal ratification in London and Washington.

With the negotiations complete, the US ratified the Treaty of Ghent on 17 February 1815. Gambier returned to Iver Grove and resumed his life as a retired flag officer in the style of a modest country gentleman, occupied with his leadership and patronage of charitable organisations. On 12 April 1815, in the Great Council Chamber at Carlton House, the Prince Regent invested Gambier as Knight Grand Cross of the Most Honourable Military Order of the Bath.[72] During autumn 1823, Gambier was surprised to receive a letter from the Speaker of the US House of Representatives, Henry Clay, then one of the several candidates for the American presidency. At Ghent, Clay had shown no affinity or interest in religion – in contrast to the Bible-reading John Quincy Adams[73] – but on this occasion, Clay was writing to introduce to Gambier the Episcopal Bishop of Ohio, The Rt. Rev. Philander Chase.[74] A thousand miles from salt water, Ohio seemed an unlikely place to interest Gambier.

Consecrated as the first Bishop of Ohio five years earlier, Chase was deeply frustrated that he could find few clergymen willing to come west. After trying every possibility within his reach, Chase determined that he must create a college and seminary in Ohio, drawing on young men in Ohio to supply the needs of the church on the western frontier. There was no money to be found for such a project within his diocese, so Chase convinced the Ohio diocesan convention to fund a trip to England by which he might find support to realise his dream. Shortly after Chase arrived in England, Gambier invited Chase to attend an anniversary meeting in London of the Auxiliary Bible Society at which Gambier was to preside. Afterward, Gambier offered to bring Chase with him to Iver Grove, where they could talk.[75]

Gambier proved to be the key figure in the success of Chase's project. Gambier's influence brought Chase the support of the Church Missionary Society and with it, contacts and donations from many prominent lay figures, evangelicals and from within the Anglican Church itself. As Bishop Chase prepared to return to

72   *The London Gazette*, number 17004 (18 April 1815), pp.725-26.
73   Bickham, *The Weight of Vengeance*, p.245.
74   James T. Hopkins (ed.), *The Papers of Henry Clay*. Vol. 3: *Presidential Candidate* (Lexington, Kentucky: University of Kentucky Press, 1963), pp.470-71: Henry Clay to James Gambier, 20 August 1823.
75   Kenyon College Archives, Gambier, Ohio. Bishop Philander Chase Papers, Gambier to Chase, 24 Nov 1823.

America in the spring of 1824, the list of subscribers grew, and donations began to arrive. By 1826, they had raised £6,000, which Bishop Chase eventually used to purchase a tract of 6,000 acres of open land in central Ohio, which became the permanent home of the newly-named Kenyon College in the village of Gambier, Ohio. Today, that village still bears the names of Admiral Lord Gambier's friends and acquaintances on a number of streets and buildings.[76] With the accession of King William IV to the throne, the new king promoted Gambier to Admiral of the Fleet on 2 July 1830.[77] In 1832, King William presented Gambier with one of the only four batons that were ever made for a British admiral of the fleet.[78]

Gambier died at Iver Grove on 19 April 1833 aged 76. He was buried in the churchyard of St Peter's Church, Iver. Having no children, the peerage became extinct upon his death. His personal property at the time of his death was estimated to be under £30,000. Lady Gambier remained at Iver Grove until her death, when the final proceeds of their estate were divided between eight nieces and nephews. Long after Gambier's death, in 1860, Captain George Henry Richards, a hydrographer surveying the waters of British Columbia in HMS *Plumper* commemorated the Battle of the Glorious First of June. He named one of the islands Gambier Island, at the same time that he named the entire island group the Defence Islands, to commemorate Gambier's ship, and the adjacent water area, Howe Sound, to commemorate Gambier's commander in the battle.[79]

Taken in the context of a longer view of naval history, Gambier becomes a significant figure. He was a successful fighting captain, who rose very quickly to positions of high command and responsibility and through them had an enormous influence on the naval service that lasted for decades. His contributions to operational signalling and the Navy's Instructions and Regulations were notable steps forward. The attacks that Gambier experienced over religion quietly disappeared over time as the ideas he and Barham pioneered became accepted for what they were – a normal activity for individuals to pursue – and eventually

---

76   George Franklin Smythe, *Kenyon College: Its First Century* (New Haven, Conneticut: Yale University Press for Kenyon College, 1924), pp.16-58; George Franklin Smythe, *A History of the Diocese of Ohio until the Year 1918* (Cleveland, Ohio: Diocese of Ohio, 1931), pp.115-139.

77   *London Gazette*, number 18709 (23 July 1830), p.1539.

78   Curator's note on Admiral of the Fleet Lord St Vincent's baton at National Maritime Museum, Greenwich. <http://collections.rmg.co.uk/collections/objects/62081.html>

79   John T. Walbran, *British Columbia Coast Names, 1592-1906 to which are added a few names in adjacent United States Territory, their origin and history* (Ottawa: Government Printing Bureau, 1909), pp.134-135, 197-198, 253-256; Helen B. Akrigg, 'Richards, Sir George Henry' in *Dictionary of Canadian Biography*, Vol. 12, University of Toronto/ Université Laval, 2003 http://www.biographi.ca/en/bio/richards_george_henry_12E.html> (accessed 4 May 2017).

widening them to accommodate other denominations. The generations of naval officers who followed Gambier took for granted a role for religion in the Navy. Gambier's qualms over the use of weapons – like Congreve's rocket – that caused terror, would be echoed throughout the rest of the nineteenth century. Gambier's reactions seem to be early precursors of views that developed later in the nineteenth and twentieth centuries into the modern Law of Naval Warfare. Gambier's estimate of the situation at Basque Roads, and his reasons for not unnecessarily risking his force in those particular practical circumstances, after he had achieved the major strategic and operational purpose of his mission, is an equally modern and responsible military viewpoint. Admiral Lord Gambier's contributions to the Navy deserve much more appreciation than they have yet received. Since Gambier left no archive of his own, it will require extensive research in public and private records to plumb more deeply into the nature of his thought, character and prescient contributions.

17

Lieutenant William Pringle Green (1783-1846) – Halifax, Nova Scotia

Jeremy B. Utt

History often provides examples of people who, despite dedicated service to a nation, do not receive all of the recognition they deserved. Lieutenant William Pringle Green, a Royal Navy officer and an inventor, was one such person. He made significant contributions to the British Empire, both through active service in the Royal Navy and through his inventions and publications. He distinguished himself through his bravery, especially during the Battle of Trafalgar. He also distinguished himself through his practical and useful mechanical inventions, a number of which were adopted by the Royal Navy. Despite his contributions to his country, Green's Royal Navy service and the products of his practical ingenuity failed to translate into significant financial security. Green ended his service by resigning three years prior to his death, having risen in rank no higher than that of lieutenant; the rank he held for over 40 years after having been promoted to lieutenant for his valiant conduct during the Battle of Trafalgar.

Green was born into a family that was prominent in the provincial government of Nova Scotia, as well as in Massachusetts Bay, with possible roots in Lincolnshire, England. In his biography, *Fragments*, Green implied his family had aristocratic roots, and stated that his family was from Aulay Hall, near Boston, in Lincolnshire.[1] Green's third great-grandfather, Percival Green, immigrated to Massachusetts Bay

---

1 William Pringle Green, R.N., *Fragments from Remarks of Twenty-five Years In Every Quarter of the Globe, on Electricity, Magnetism, Aeroliths, and Various Other Phenomena of Nature* (Westminster: G. Hayden, 1833), p.iv.

Lieutenant William Pringle Green. (NMM)

in 1635 on the *Susan and Ellen*.[2] Percival Green's only son, John Green, Green's great-great-grandfather, was born in June 1636 in Massachusetts Bay, in an area that would become part of Middlesex County, Massachusetts.[3] John Green married Ruth Mitchelson,[4] a daughter of Edward Mitchelson and Ruth Bushell.[5] Edward Mitchelson had immigrated to Massachusetts Bay in 1635, and served as Marshal-General of Massachusetts Bay for 44 years, from 1637-81.[6] In his history

2   Levi Swanton Gould, *Ancient Middlesex: With Brief Biographical Sketches of the Men Who Have Served the County Officially Since Its Settlement* (Somerville, Massachusetts: Journal Print, 1905), p.145.
3   Gould, *Ancient Middlesex*, p.145.
4   Green, *Fragments*, p.iv. Green stated, 'This gentleman married Ruth Mitchelson, daughter of Edward Mitchelson, Esq. of Cambridge aforesaid, near Boston, New England, the *Marshal General* of the Colony.'
5   Gould, *Ancient Middlesex*, p.145. In his history of Middlesex, Gould spells Mitchelson as 'Mitchellsonn.'
6   Gould, *Ancient Middlesex*, p.145.

of Harvard College, Samuel Eliot Morison implied that Edward Mitchelson was an alumnus of Cambridge University, and mentioned Mitchelson's role as Marshal-General in Harvard College's first Commencement Ceremony on September 23, 1642.[7] John Green succeeded his father-in-law as Marshal-General, serving eight years, from 1681-87, and from 1689-91.[8]

Green's great-grandfather, Reverend Joseph Green, was born 29 November 1675.[9] He married Elizabeth Gerrish.[10] Paul Boyar and Stephen Nissenbaum, in *Salem Possessed: The Social Origins of Witchcraft*, provided an account of how Reverend Green, an alumnus of Harvard College, came fresh out of college at the age of 22 to serve as a Puritan minister in Salem Village, succeeding Reverend Samuel Parris in that capacity.[11] Boyar and Nissenbaum wrote, 'more experienced ministers were not clamouring to move into the parsonage Samuel Parris had finally vacated' and that 'Green proved a remarkably happy choice.'[12] They further stated, 'Joseph Green quickly made clear his belief that the witchcraft episode had been an unfortunate aberration, the sooner forgotten the better.'[13]

Green's grandfather, the elder Benjamin Green, was born in Salem Village (now Danvers, Massachusetts) in the Province of Massachusetts Bay on 1 July 1713.[14] Benjamin Green, Sr. worked as a merchant in Boston, with his brothers Joseph and John, and served Boston as an elected constable.[15] He married Margaret Pierce in November 1737.[16] He later took part in the 1745 seizure of what is now known as Cape Breton Island.[17] Benjamin Green, Sr. became secretary on 1 March 1745 to

7   Samuel Eliot Morison, *The Founding of Harvard College* (Cambridge, Massachusetts: Harvard University Press, 1963), pp.257-258. Morison wrote, 'Enters a small but solemn procession, headed by Edward Mitchelson, Marshal-General of Massachusetts Bay' and 'The Marshal-General, who was a Cambridge man, would have been the logical person to open the meeting.'

8   Gould, *Ancient Middlesex*, p.145.

9   Gould, *Ancient Middlesex*, p.iv.

10   Donald F. Chard, 'GREEN, BENJAMIN', in *Dictionary of Canadian Biography*, Vol. 4 (University of Toronto/Université Laval, 2003 <http://www.biographi.ca/en/bio/green_benjamin_4E.html> (accessed 29 December 2016).

11   Paul Boyar and Stephen Nissenbaum, *Salem Possessed: The Social Origins of Witchcraft* (Cambridge, Massachusetts: Harvard University Press, 1974), p.217. Reverend Samuel Parris was the Puritan minister in Salem Village during the Salem Witch Trials. Reverend Parris, whose daughter and niece were two of the afflicted girls, and whose slave Tituba was accused of practicing witchcraft, served as a prosecutor in the witchcraft cases.

12   Boyar and Nissenbaum, *Salem Possessed*, pp.217-218.

13   Boyar and Nissenbaum, *Salem Possessed*, p.218.

14   Chard, 'GREEN, BENJAMIN'.

15   Chard, 'GREEN, BENJAMIN'.

16   Chard, 'GREEN, BENJAMIN'.

17   James Burnley, 'GREEN, WILLIAM PRINGLE', in *Dictionary of National Biography, 1885-1900*, Vol. 23, <https://en.wikisource.org/wiki/Green,_William_Pringle_(DNB00)>

William Pepperrell, the commander of the expedition made by New Englanders against Louisbourg, Ile Royale (now Cape Breton Island).[18] This military action took place during King George's War (1744-48), the name of the North American theatre of operations during the War of the Austrian Succession (1740-48).

The beginning of the Green family's involvement in the political affairs of Nova Scotia began in July 1749 when Benjamin Green, Sr. 'sailed to Chebucto Bay and met Edward Cornwallis' expedition.'[19] He served on Cornwallis' first council as naval officer for Halifax and as judge of the Vice Admiralty Court.[20] In 1750, he became treasurer of the province, a job he held until succeeded by his son Benjamin Green, Jr. in 1768.[21] In 1760, he became a justice of the peace at Halifax.[22] Later, in 1766, and then again from 1771-72, Benjamin Green, Sr. served as Acting Governor of Nova Scotia. He died later in the year 1772. The city of Halifax named a street after him.[23] Benjamin Green, Jr. followed his namesake father in a life of public service in Nova Scotia, serving as the colony's treasurer from 1768 until his death in 1794.[24] In addition, Green's father was also a member of Nova Scotia's House of Assembly, and a justice of the Court of Common Pleas.[25]

Green was born in 1783 in Halifax, Nova Scotia.[26] He was the ninth child and sixth son of Benjamin Green, Jr. and Susanna Wenman.[27] Sources disagree on the year of Green's birth, and on the order of Green's birth relative to that of his siblings. Burnley mentioned that Green was born in 1785, and was the eldest son.[28] O'Byrne

(accessed 21 November 2016).

18   Chard, 'GREEN, BENJAMIN'. William Pepperrell was later made a baronet as a reward for his leadership in this endeavor, and thus became Sir William Pepperell, 1st Baronet.

19   Chard, 'GREEN, BENJAMIN'. Edward Cornwallis, then Governor of Nova Scotia, was given the task of founding a new British settlement. Americans might find it of interest that Edward Cornwallis was an uncle of Charles Cornwallis, 1st Marquis Cornwallis, the British general who surrendered after the successful Franco-American Siege of Yorktown (1781). The new settlement was named Halifax, in honor of George Montagu-Dunk, 2nd Earl of Halifax. Lord Halifax was, at the time, President of the Board of Trade. Halifax replaced Annapolis Royal as the British colonial capital of Nova Scotia.

20   Chard, 'GREEN, BENJAMIN'.

21   Chard, 'GREEN, BENJAMIN'.

22   Chard, 'GREEN, BENJAMIN'.

23   Peter M. Jangaard, *Some Descendants of John Green (1636-1691) and Ruth Mitchelson (1638-1728) of Cambridge, Massachusetts* (Halifax, Nova Scotia: Peter M. Jangaard, 2007), p.34.

24   Chard, 'GREEN, BENJAMIN'. Chard implies that the year of succession was 1768 by his mention of the elder Benjamin Green's resignation from the position of *provincial treasurer* two months after making his will in December 1767.

25   Burnley, 'GREEN, WILLIAM PRINGLE'.

26   Jangaard, *Some Descendants*, p.55.

27   Jangaard, *Some Descendants*, p.54.

28   Burnley, 'GREEN, WILLIAM PRINGLE' (1785-1846), '[I]nventor, born apparently at Halifax, Nova Scotia, in 1785, was the eldest son of Benjamin Green (d. 1794).'

suggested that Green was born in 1785, by reporting that he died in 1846 at age 61.[29] The National Maritime Museum, Royal Museums Greenwich mentions that Green was the third son.[30] The *Family Memoranda* section of Green's *Fragments* publication does not state the year of his birth nor give his relative birth order vis-a-vis his siblings.[31]

Green's naval service began on 9 July 1796 when he entered the Royal Navy at the age of 13[32] as a first-class volunteer on the third-rate HMS *Resolution* (74), a ship on the Halifax Station. Later in 1796 (or in 1797, depending on the source) Green became a midshipman aboard the fifth-rate frigate HMS *Cleopatra* (32).[33] From August 1797 to October 1801, Green served aboard another fifth-rate frigate, HMS *Topaze* (36).[34] While aboard *Topaze*, Green was reported to have been involved in actions in the West Indies and in Gibraltar Bay, and, perhaps most notably, to have 'accompanied the Duke of Kent from Halifax to England as his Naval Aide-de-Camp.'[35]

Green next served aboard the sixth-rate frigate HMS *Circe* (28), and then aboard the third-rate HMS *Sans Pareil* (80).[36] After the *Peace of Amiens*, Green served on the fifth-rate frigate HMS *Trent* (36).[37] The *Circe*, *Sans Pareil*, and *Trent* were all stationed in the West Indies.[38] Green served as a master's mate during his 14 months of service on these three ships, before returning to England in June 1803.[39] It was on Green's next assignment that he would be involved in the most important

29   William R. O'Byrne, *A Naval Biographical Dictionary: Consisting of the Life and Services of Every Living Officer in Her Majesty's Navy, From the Rank of Admiral of the Fleet to that of Lieutenant, Inclusive* (London: J. Murray, printed by William Clowes and Sons, 1849). 'William Pringle Green died in Nov. 1846, at the age of 61.'

30   'Lieutenant William Pringle Green', National Maritime Museum, Royal Museums Greenwich, MNT0118 <http://collections.rmg.co.uk/collections/objects/42066.html> (accessed 21 November 2016). 'Green was born in Halifax, Nova Scotia, the third son of Benjamin Green, treasurer of that Canadian province.'

31   Green, *Fragments*, pp.iii-iv.

32   O'Byrne, *Naval Biographical Dictionary*.

33   O'Byrne, *Naval Biographical Dictionary*. Burnley and the National Maritime Museum denotes the date as 1797. The National Maritime Museum gives 1797 as the year Green entered the Royal Navy.

34   O'Byrne, *Naval Biographical Dictionary*.

35   O'Byrne, *Naval Biographical Dictionary*. The Duke of Kent was King George III's fifth child and fourth son, Prince Edward Augustus, Duke of Kent and Strathearn, the father of Queen Victoria.

36   Burnley, 'GREEN, WILLIAM PRINGLE'. Burnley recorded the *Sans Pareil* as 'Sanspareil'.

37   Burnley 'GREEN, WILLIAM PRINGLE'. The Peace of Amiens was the brief period of peace between the United Kingdom and France between the French Revolutionary Wars and the Napoleonic Wars. The Peace of Amiens lasted from 25 March 1802 to 18 May 1803.

38   O'Byrne, *Naval Biographical Dictionary*.

39   O'Byrne, *Naval Biographical Dictionary*.

naval action of his Royal Navy service. After leaving HMS *Trent*, Green entered service aboard the third-rate HMS *Conqueror* (74) as a master's mate.[40] As reported in Green's obituary in 1847 in *The Gentleman's Magazine*, 'The Conqueror was one of the fleet which, under Nelson, pursued the enemy in the four quarters of the Globe, and ultimately fought the combined fleets off Trafalgar.'[41]

During the battle, *Conqueror* captured Admiral Villeneuve's flagship *Bucentaure*.[42] According to O'Byrne, 'Mr Green, we are informed, had command of the boats, which were twice sunk in their attempt to take the prize in tow.'[43] For his actions relating to *Bucentaure's* capture, Green was promoted to lieutenant. Green's obituary stated, 'For his services on that day Mr Green was selected by his Captain (Israel Pellew) as having merited the rank of Lieutenant, which he received.'[44] Green received his promotion on 8 January 1806 aboard the second-rate HMS *Formidable* (98).[45] Despite being a decisive victory that saved the United Kingdom from a serious French invasion threat, Trafalgar was not without commentary regarding proper military conduct on the part of the victors. James Davey, author of *In Nelson's Wake: The Navy and the Napoleonic Wars*, wrote, 'The crude arithmetic of the ships and men confirmed the British triumph, but in the aftermath of battle, doubts were still cast on the conduct of many of the ship's captains who had been in the very thin of the fury.'[46]

Green expressed opinions on the actions of some of his comrades years after the battle. According to Davey, 'Lieutenant William Pringle Green, writing seven years later, stated that "if the officers had done their duty in every ship" then "the whole of the enemy" would have been taken or destroyed.'[47] Vice Admiral Cuthbert Collingwood, second in command at Trafalgar, was reportedly disappointed about the conduct of British naval officers during the battle.[48] However, Collingwood would not permit the reputation of Trafalgar as a complete and glorious victory to be tarnished.[49] Davey writes, 'Collingwood's desire for silence won out while he

40   O'Byrne, *Naval Biographical Dictionary*.
41   Obituary of Lieutenant W. P.Green, R. N. 1847, *The Gentleman's Magazine*, Vol. 181-182, p.209.
42   Burnley, 'GREEN, WILLIAM PRINGLE'.
43   Burnley, 'GREEN, WILLIAM PRINGLE'.
44   Obituary of Lieutenant W. P.Green, R. N. 1847, *The Gentleman's Magazine*, Vol. 181-182, p.210.
45   O'Byrne, *Naval Biographical Dictionary*.
46   James Davey, *In Nelson's Wake: The Navy and the Napoleonic Wars* (New Haven, Connecticut: Yale University Press, 2015), p.103.
47   Davey, *In Nelson's Wake*, p.103.
48   Davey, *In Nelson's Wake*, p.103.
49   Davey, *In Nelson's Wake*, p.103.

was alive, participants kept their criticisms private. He had completed the perfect cover up: in Pringle Green's words, "all was hushed up."[50]

From HMS *Formidable*, Green served next on the former French fifth-rate frigate, HMS *Decade* (36) as her second lieutenant, on 28 November 1807. Apparently, this assignment was 'through the interest of the Duke of Kent.'[51] He was then assigned as first lieutenant to the sixth-rate frigate HMS *Eurydice* (24) on 4 June 1808, nearly four months after his marriage to Elizabeth Gilbert, whom he married on 22 February in Devon, England.[52] Elizabeth was the daughter of John Gilbert and Frances Hillman. Their marriage produced 10 children; three sons and seven daughters. Meanwhile, *Eurydice* was on the North American Station, and it was while on this assignment that Green proposed methods to the Commander-in-Chief of the American Station, Admiral Sir John Borlase Warren, for the improving of British gunnery vis-a-vis that of American frigates.[53]

Green took command of HM Brig *Resolute* in 1811 and held this command until 1815.[54] This command, which he also secured through the Duke of Kent, saw Green stationed off the coasts of Ireland and Scotland.[55] During this time, Green tested methods of training ships' crews; methods which proved successful and were later adopted by the Royal Navy.[56] After *Resolute* was paid off, Green occupied his time with his inventions until receiving his next appointment in 1829.[57] Between 1829 and 1832, Green served on the Falmouth Station.[58] He was appointed on 19 August 1829 to the *Astraea* packet, and on 3 November 1829 as commander of the *Frolic*, listed as another Falmouth packet, which he commanded until it was paid off on 26 November 1832.[59] Green was on half-pay until he received his final appointment as a lieutenant on HMS *Victory* (104) at Portsmouth on 10 May 1842.[60] Unfortunately for Green, 'he fell into embarrassments, had to resign a year later' from this position.[61] After *Victory*, Green was not employed on active service again, and he died nearly three years later on 18 October 1846 at Landport, Portsmouth.[62]

50   Davey, *In Nelson's Wake*, p.104.
51   O'Byrne, *Naval Biographical Dictionary*.
52   O'Byrne, *Naval Biographical Dictionary*.
53   'Lieutenant William Pringle Green', National Maritime Museum.
54   'Lieutenant William Pringle Green', National Maritime Museum.
55   O'Byrne, *Naval Biographical Dictionary*.
56   O'Byrne, *Naval Biographical Dictionary*.
57   Burnley, 'GREEN, WILLIAM PRINGLE'.
58   O'Byrne, *Naval Biographical Dictionary*.
59   O'Byrne, *Naval Biographical Dictionary*.
60   'Lieutenant William Pringle Green', National Maritime Museum.
61   Burnley, 'GREEN, WILLIAM PRINGLE'.
62   Burnley, 'GREEN, WILLIAM PRINGLE'.

In addition to serving the Royal Navy, Green made valuable contributions to the service, and to society in general, through his inventions and publications. O'Byrne mentioned, 'Lieut. Green was an officer of great mechanical powers.'[63] Burnley wrote, 'he devoted the greater part of his life to the promotion of inventions and improvements connected with the service, many of which were so valuable as to be introduced throughout the navy.'[64] It is through his inventions and writings that Green is best remembered by posterity. The earliest mention of Green is in his *Journal of Lt William Pringle Green, HMS Conqueror chasing the French Fleet, 1805-1808*.[65] Also, as previously mentioned, Green presented to Sir John Borlase Warren, Commander-in-Chief of the North American Station in 1808, 'the expediency of a change in the construction, armament, and discipline of British ships of war, in order that they might be rendered capable of more equally coping with the enemy.'[66]

While commanding the brig *Resolute*, Green wrote the manual, *Instructions for training a ship's crew in the use of arms in attack and defence*.[67] Within this manual, he included instructions, with illustrations, for seamen in the use of various types of small arms and tactics.[68] Green was twice awarded the *Silver Vulcan Medal* by the [Royal] Society for the Encouragement of Arts, Manufactures, and Commerce.[69] His first medal was awarded in 1823 for *Certain Improvements in the Rigging of Ships*.[70] In its citation, the Society observed:

The unfortunate issue of several naval actions with the Americans during the last war, in which British frigates were captured, first attracted Lieut. Green's attention to the subject. In analysing these, it appeared that a principal cause of the success of the enemy, was the rapidity with which he shot away the rigging, and consequently disabled the masts of his opponent.

63   O'Byrne, *Naval Biographical Dictionary*.
64   Burnley, 'GREEN, WILLIAM PRINGLE'.
65   'Journal of Lt. William Pringle Green, HMS Conqueror chasing the French Fleet, 1805-1808', National Maritime Museum, Royal Museums Greenwich, JOD/48 <http:// collections.rmg.co.uk/collections/objects/505830.html> (accessed 4 March 2017)
66   O'Byrne, *Naval Biographical Dictionary*.
67   Mark Barton and John McGrath, *British Naval Swords and Swordsmanship* (Barnsley: Seaforth Publishing, 2013), p.14.
68   Barton and McGrath, *British Naval Swords*.
69   This organisation is now known as the Royal Society for the encouragement of Arts, Manufactures, and Commerce <https://www.thersa.org/>
70   *Transactions of the Royal Society of Arts for the Encouragement of Arts, Manufactures, and Commerce* (London: T.C. Hansard, 1823), pp.198-200.

The masts of ships are secured in two directions; longitudinally, by means of long ropes called stays, and in a transverse direction by means of other ropes called shrouds, each of which has a loop in the middle which is passed over the head of the mast, while the two ends are fastened to blocks called dead-eyes, fixed on each side of the ship opposite the mast. Each pair of shrouds, therefore, may be considered as forming the sides of an isosceles triangle, of which, the apex is the mast-head, and being in pairs … that if one is shot away, its … opposite shroud becomes nearly useless. Lieut. Green … proposes that the shrouds should be single, and that each should be terminated at top in a strong iron hook, to take hold in an eye fixed in a strap or plate at the mast-head.

Another improvement proposed…is in the method of slinging the topsail-yards, by fixing to the yard where it comes in contact with the mast, a kind of clasp or crutch … that … serves to steady the yard … it has the farther advantage of saving the expense of rolling tackles, besides strengthening the yard…[71]

The Society further noted that Green, when in command of the *Resolute*, was given permission to erect a small mizzen mast (at his own expense), with his shrouds and yard slings that he designed, 'the result of which, as far as it went during the two years that the experiment lasted, was entirely to his satisfaction.'[72] Green's second medal was awarded by the Royal Society for the Encouragement of Arts, Manufactures, and Commerce in 1825 for similar work to improve ships' rigging. In 1833, Green began publishing his previously mentioned *Fragments*, which contains information on his family, as well as on several of his inventions. Green was later awarded two patents for his inventions. On 28 September 1836 he received a patent for 'Capstans, applicable to ships and to other purposes; method of reducing manual labour in working capstans used at mines.'[73] On 10 July 1837, he received a patent for 'Capstans; and machinery for raising, lowering, and moving ponderous bodies and matters.'[74]

When Green died 18 October 1846 at Landport, Portsmouth, he left behind Elizabeth as a widow, and his 10 children.[75] During his service in the Royal Navy, Green rose no higher in rank than lieutenant, and he did not acquire significant financial security for his family. When Green died, he left a pension of £50 per year

71   *Transactions of the Royal Society*, pp.198-199.
72   *Transactions of the Royal Society*, p.199.
73   Bennet Woodcroft, *Alphabetical Index of Patentees of Inventions* (London: Evelyn, Adams & Mackay, 1969), p.228.
74   Woodcroft, *Alphabetical Index*, p.228.
75   Burnley, 'GREEN, WILLIAM PRINGLE'.

to support his family.[76] Green's three sons, at the time of his death, were pursuing their careers, one as a medical student, and the other two in the service of the Royal Navy.[77] John Green served aboard *Victory* as a clerk.[78] Gilbert Elliott Green served as a master's assistant aboard the first-rate HMS *Hibernia* (100), 'flagship of Vice Admiral Sir W. Parker, in the Mediterranean.'[79] The citation accompanying the oval miniature portrait of Green found in the National Maritime Museum's art collection is a touching tribute:

> Green's life exemplified a general problem for competent men who lacked both the connections to rise in the Navy as far as their merits deserved, especially after 1815, and the access to capital needed to benefit from their enterprise.[80]

76 Obituary of Lieutenant W. P.Green, R. N. 1847, *The Gentleman's Magazine*, Vols. 181-182, p.210.
77 Obituary, p.210.
78 Obituary, p.210.
79 Obituary, p.210.
80 'Lieutenant William Pringle Green', National Maritime Museum.

18

Captain John Perkins (ca. 1750-1812) – Jamaica

Caitlin McGeever Gale

The expanse of the British Empire in the eighteenth and nineteenth centuries created the need for a large and powerful navy. As competition for empire increased between Britain, France, and Spain, more individuals found employment opportunities in the Royal Navy. One of these individuals happened to be a man whom most subjects of the Crown may not have expected to achieve such a high rank. John Perkins of Kingston, Jamaica played several roles within the Royal Navy, some specifically because of his mulatto status. Perkins has been considered a 'remarkable character' and a 'man ahead of his time' as possibly the first mulatto officer in the Royal Navy.[1]

Born in Jamaica, 'probably born in the parish of Clarendon in or before 1750 to an enslaved, or enslaved descendant mother and white father, John Perkins was socially classified as "mulatto"'.[2] In the eighteenth century it was possible for Perkins to have been lost to history; a name never recorded or remembered, due to the circumstances of his birth. However, as historian, Ray Costello, explained, 'sometimes the mixed-race sons of white men in positions of authority were acknowledged by their fathers and educated to occupy clerical and administrative posts in the West Indies.'[3] However, the expectation still remained that high-ranking positions were reserved for white subjects.

---

1   Ray Costello, *Black Salt: Seafarers of African Descent on British Ships* (Liverpool: Liverpool University Press, 2012), p.97.
2   Douglas Hamilton, '"A most active, enterprising officer": Captain John Perkins, the Royal Navy and the boundaries of slavery and liberty in the Caribbean', *Slavery and Abolition*, Vol. 39 (2018), pp.80-100. <https://www.tandfonline.com/doi/full/10.1080/014403 9X.2017.1330862> (accessed 21 October 2019).
3   Costello, *Black Salt*, p.97.

Jamaica's economy was important to the British Empire, with the colony containing half of Britain's investments in the West Indies. By 1803, total imports from the West Indies to Britain equated to £1.6 million, roughly one quarter of Britain's imports. The majority of British subjects in this region of the Empire resided in Jamaica and Barbados, and they would play an important role in protecting British Caribbean possessions as competition for empire between Britain and France intensified. Jamaican subjects, Perkins included, rose to fill leadership roles within the Royal Navy.[4]

Perkins' life at sea began in his youth. 'As a child he was sent to Kingston and Port Royal where he became a "servant" to a carpenter, William Young, who took him into naval service. On 22 June 1759, he joined the *Grenado*, a bomb vessel, as Young's enslaved servant.' He continued as Young's servant when Young transferred to the sixth-rate frigate HMS *Boreas* (28) on 7 March 1760. Aboard *Boreas*, the young Perkins was present at the captures of Martinique and Havana in 1762, during the Seven Years War.[5]

With the end of the Seven Years War in 1763, Perkins left Young and began to work as a pilot. By 1771, he had become so proficient as a pilot that he was employed by the Royal Navy and sent aboard the fourth-rate ship-of-the-line, HMS *Achilles* (60) commanded by Captain Richard Collins. Unfortunately, his assignment aboard *Achilles* did not last long, as he ran the ship aground when she approached Port Royal on 9 December 1771. He was found guilty at his court martial and judged as 'incapable' of serving as a pilot in any of His Majesty's Ships.[6]

Perkins continued as a civilian pilot for the next four years. But with the outbreak of the War for American Independence, he re-emerged in the Royal Navy in November 1775 as the pilot aboard the fourth-rate ship-of-the-line HMS *Antelope* (60), the flagship of the Jamaica Squadron. In this endeavor, Perkins displayed such

---

4   Martin Robson, *A History of the Royal Navy: The Napoleonic Wars* (New York: I.B. Tauris, 2014), p.76; James Davey, *In Nelson's Wake: The Navy and the Napoleonic Wars* (Wales: Gomer Press, 2016): pp.114, 121.

5   Hamilton, *Slavery and Abolition*. Hamilton cited the following: TNA ADM 1/2333 Captain's Letters: Perkins to W.W. Pole, Admiralty, 16 October 1808; ADM 36/5690 Muster Book, *Grenado* Bomb; ADM 36/5045 Muster Book, *Boreas*; ADM 33/606 Pay Book, *Boreas* 1759-1762.

6   Hamilton, *Slavery and Abolition*. Hamilton cited the following: TNA ADM 51/1/5 Captain's log of the Achilles, 16 April 1771 to 9 April 1772, Vols. 22–23, 9 December and 23 December 1771. The original document stated that Perkins was 'rendered incapable of servg. As Pilot in any of His Majtys Ships.'; Hamilton also cited David Syrett, *The Rodney Papers: Selections from the Correspondence of Admiral Lord Rodney*, Vol. 2, 1763-1780 (Aldershot, England: Ashgate, 2007), pp.71, 75, 86-87, 90: letters from Lord Rodney to Philip Stephens, 12 December 1771; Rodney to Stephens, 29 January 1772 and Stephens to Rodney, 17 April 1772.

competency that in 1778 he was placed in command of the HM Schooner *Punch*.[7] His service on this ship brought such acclaim that his accomplishments were often recorded in *The London Gazette*; several issues published between 1779-81 told the Empire of Perkins' great success by listing the names of foreign ships, both French and American, taken 'By the Punch, Tender to the Fleet' and the various locations of their capture.[8] As commander of the *Punch*, Perkins is recorded to have taken 315 prizes and over 3,000 prisoners of war. All claims were endorsed by the Jamaican House of Assembly. This remarkable start to his naval service earned Perkins the nickname 'Jack Punch'.[9] Of interest, none of the entries in the *London Gazette* referred to his race.

This success also earned Perkins a reputation that opened doors to several other opportunities within the Royal Navy. While the classification of 'mulatto' may have been a limitation in most sectors of society, it allowed Perkins to act as a spy for the Royal Navy, beginning in 1782. The 'stereotypical assumptions about the lowly position of black people' permitted Perkins to travel with little notice to Havana and Cape François where he observed Spanish and French defensive preparations and gained intelligence to pass back to Jamaica.[10] Governor of Jamaica, Major General Archibald Campbell recognized the success of Perkins' mission, noting that his skills were respected by the enemy, and recommended him for promotion. In 1782, Sir Peter Parker promoted Perkins to lieutenant and placed him in command of HM Schooner *Endeavour* (10), demonstrating his confidence in Perkins' abilities.[11]

While in command, Perkins captured a larger vessel that held important French officers. Gathering intelligence from this capture, Perkins relayed to Admiral George Rodney that the French fleet, under Admiral Comte de Grasse, planned to join with the Spanish fleet to drive the British out of the West Indies and capture Jamaica. Using this intelligence, Rodney's fleet met de Grasse's fleet and soundly defeated him at the Battle of the Saintes on 12 April 1782. In recognition of Perkins' success, Rodney recommended him to be promoted to commander.[12]

7   Costello, *Black Salt*, p.97; Andrew Jackson O'Shaughnessy, *An Empire Divided: The American Revolution and the British Caribbean* (Philadelphia, Pennsylvania: University of Pennsylvania Press, 2000), p.180; Gregory Fremont-Barnes, *The Royal Navy 1793-1815* (London: Osprey Publishing, 2013), p.17.

8   *London Gazette*, issue 11982, 27 May 1779, p.2; *London Gazette*, issue 12199, 16 June 1781, p.3.

9   Costello, *Black Salt*, p.97; O'Shaugnessy, *An Empire Divided*, p.180.

10   Costello, *Black Salt*, p.97.

11   J.J. Colledge & Ben Warlow, *Ships of the Royal Navy: The Complete Record of all Fighting Ships of the Royal Navy from the 15th Century to the Present* (London: Chatham Publishing, 2006), p.114.

12   Costello, *Black Salt*, p.97; O'Shaughnessy, *An Empire Divided*, p.180.

Whether due to destruction of or the lack of records, little is known about John Perkins between 1783 and 1790. However, it does appear that Perkins travelled to Britain on two occasions during this period, first in 1784 and again in 1786. In his correspondence to Admiral John Markham, he confided his experience that, 'I could not bear it…I felt the cold to such afect [sic] that I was obliged to quit England in the month of October, and beleve [sic] it would have been the death of me had I not left.'[13]

When he did return to serve with the Royal Navy, Perkins did so in a 'daring' manner.[14] In 1790, Rear Admiral Phillip Affleck recruited Perkins to conduct an espionage mission to the French Colony, St Dominique (Haiti), on the Caribbean island of Hispaniola. While the British may have used Perkins' mulatto status to their advantage in prior situations, it became detrimental to him as a slave revolt erupted in 1791. Believing that Perkins was supporting and possibly supplying the revolt, French officials arrested Perkins in 1792 at the port of Jéremie and sentenced him to death. Fortunately for Perkins, a British warship arrived at the port and, upon British orders, he was released.[15]

With France declaring war against Britain in 1793, the British saw an opportunity to intervene in the ongoing slave revolt. The British wanted to both encourage the revolt, yet contain the revolt so that it would not spread to British slave holdings in the Caribbean. The commander of the Jamaica Station, Commodore John Ford, in his flagship, the fourth-rate HMS *Europa* (50), together with three other frigates and a schooner, conducted a campaign against St Dominique.[16] On December 10, 1793, *The London Gazette* published a letter written by Ford that told of the capture of the French schooner, *Convention Nationale* (10), adding that he renamed her *Marie Antoinette*. Ford went on to write that he decided to give 'the Command of her to Lieutenant Perkins, an officer of Zeal, Vigilance and Activity.'[17]

As a result of the war with France, the Royal Navy's Jamaica Station was reinforced. By 1797, its size rose to 31 warships. With a new commander, Vice Admiral Sir Hyde Parker, Perkins was promoted to commander that same year.[18] Referring to Perkins as an 'old and deserving officer', Parker gave Perkins command of HM Brig *Drake* (14).[19]

13   Hamilton, *Slavery and Abolition*. Hamilton cited NMM, MRK 102/5/13 Markham Papers: John Perkins to John Markham, 8 May 1803.
14   Costello, *Black Salt*, p.97; O'Shaughnessy, *An Empire Divided*, p.180.
15   Costello, *Black Salt*, p.97; Laurent Dubois, *Avengers of the New World: The Story of the Haitian Revolution* (Cambridge, Massachusetts: Harvard University Press, 2004): p.54.
16   Robson, *A History*, pp.77-78, 110.
17   *London Gazette*, Issue 1360, 10 December 1793, p.1096.
18   O'Shaughnessy, *An Empire Divided*, p.180.
19   Costello, *Black Salt*, pp.97-98.

On 20 April, Perkins and the *Drake*, along with three other warships, sailed to the St Dominique port of Jean-Rabel for a surprise night attack. Launching during the first hour on 21 April, *Drake* and her consorts captured nine French ships in three hours.[20] Unfortunately, the claim for prize money was not fulfilled until years later. In February 1806, the *London Gazette* reported that *Drake*'s crew, 'who were actually on board at the Capture of the Corvettes *L'Egyptienne, Le Levrier, L'Elan*, and *Vengeur*, on 23 November 1799 ... will be paid their respective Proportions of Head-Money.'[21] Building on his success as *Drake*'s commander, Perkins took command of the fifth-rate frigate HMS *Meleager* (32) in September of 1800; unfortunately she was wrecked one year later in the Gulf of Mexico.[22] He was then given command of a former French frigate, the sixth-rate frigate HMS *Arab* (22) early in 1801.

Coinciding with the British Invasion of the Danish island of St Thomas in March 1801, Perkins was involved in a foiled attempt to capture the Royal Danish Navy brig *Lougen*. It was on 3 March, that Perkins, commanding *Arab*, together with the privateer *Experiment* (18) attempted to take the Danish brig commanded by Captain Lieutenant C.W. Jessen off St Thomas. Jessen put up such a fight that even the enterprising Perkins was forced to withdraw; such a rarity for Perkins. This action was the first between the Danes and the British before the Battle of Copenhagen on 2 April 1801. For his successful defence, Jessen received a ceremonial sword from the Crown Prince of Denmark.[23]

Perkins' last command at sea was the fifth-rate frigate, HMS *Tartar* (32). According to Rear Admiral Sir John Duckworth, his squadron in the West Indies was 'employed in the blockade of a French squadron at Cape François, Saint Dominique.'[24] During the night of 5 July 1802, Perkins on *Tartar* sighted two French ships attempting to escape from the Cape, one to the West and the other to the East. After 'heavy cannonading', he captured the eastward French ship, the *Duquesne*, which was bound for Europe under Commodore Pierre Maurice Julien Queranga.[25] Perkins continued to operate *Tartar* under Duckworth's command when the Admiral assumed command of the Jamaica Station in 1803.

20   William James, *The Naval History of Great Britain During the French Revolution and Napoleonic Wars, 1797-1799* (London: Conway Maritime Press, 2002) pp.100-101.
21   *London Gazette*, issue 15889, 11 February 1806, p.196.
22   Colledge & Warlow, *Ships of the Royal Navy*, p.222.
23   From an email sent by the former Historian of the Royal Danish Navy, Dr Hans Christian Bjerg, 20 October 2019.
24   Arthur William Alsager Polluck, *The United Service Journal and Naval and Military Magazine, Part II* (London: Harrison & Co., Printers, St Martin's Lane, 1840) p.469.
25   Polluck, *The United Service Journal*, pp.469-470.

BRIGGEN LOUGEN

(English Translation) The brig *Lougen* under the command of Captain Lieutenant Jessen. attacked near St Thomas by two British frigates, which after a stubborn cannonade roughly treated are forced to leave their positions. This took place on the 3rd of March 1801.

While Perkins continued to harass the French, he became increasingly embroiled with black revolutionary forces under the command of Jean-Jacques Dessalines in Haiti. Not all of the British leadership in the Caribbean were comfortable with Perkins' liaison position to Dessalines, particularly because of his mulatto status. There were concerns that Perkins' activities could inspire slave rebellions on British Caribbean possessions.[26] Perkins was accused by Edward Corbett of being 'unduly friendly with the black population of Haiti' and this could have been the cause for Perkins' career coming to an end.[27]

Nevertheless, Perkins held the respect and trust of Sir John Duckworth and Lieutenant Governor Nugent of Jamaica. He continued his interaction with Dessalines. With Dessalines declaring Haiti as a free republic in 1804, he ordered the massacre of the remaining white French population and French creoles remaining in Haiti. Perkins witnessed a massacre at Jéremie and recorded it in a

---

26   Julia Gaffield, 'Haiti and Jamaica in the Remaking of the Early Nineteenth-Century Atlantic World', *The William & Mary Quarterly* 6:3 (July 2012), pp.583-614; Costello, *Black Salt*, p.98.

27   Costello, *Black Salt*, p.98.

letter to Duckworth. Dessalines' actions and the reports of officers such as Perkins caused Britain to recalculate the moral implications of maintaining a relationship with Haiti against any potential economic opportunities.[28]

According to Hamilton, Perkins was relieved of command of *Tartar* early in 1805 and 'there is no record of Perkins continuing to serve in the Royal Navy after 1805.'[29] Hamilton continues:

> The initial problem was that the *Tartar* was redeployed to Nova Scotia, and Perkins refused to go. He suffered from asthma, which had afflicted him throughout his career, and he had been told that, 'going to a cold country in the dead of winter … would be the death of him'.[30]

By the time Perkins was placed on half-pay, he had become a well-known personality on Jamaica. As a senior naval officer with a stellar reputation, Perkins acquired a social status on his home island that very few free blacks could attain. He moved within the higher social circles on the island, to include that of the Lieutenant Governor's wife. Lady Marie Nugent often included Perkins in her invitations to naval officers to attend social functions at the Governor's residence.[31]

Perkins died in 1812 and was buried in Kingston, Jamaica. As Hamilton noted: 'The Jamaica Almanac for 1811 and 1812 recorded Perkins as owning the Mount Dorothy estate in Saint Andrews parish, along with…23 and 26 slaves…After his death…his estates passed to his children.'[32]

As a man of colour pursuing a life at sea, John Perkins was not unusual. Countless seamen holding positions aboard commercial and naval vessels were not caucasian Europeans. However, as a senior officer in the Royal Navy, Perkins was atypical; his status marked him as a member of the elite. His position within the elite afloat and ashore must be placed in context. As a free black man, it was his experience and performance that allowed him to enter and move about successfully in the white-dominated world of Jamaican society and that of the Royal Navy.

28   Gaffield, 'Haiti and Jamaica', pp.605-607.
29   Hamilton, *Slavery and Abolition.*
30   Hamilton, *Slavery and Abolition.*
31   Hamilton, *Slavery and Abolition.*
32   Hamilton, *Slavery and Abolition.*

Epilogue

Dr Judith E. Pearson

In the foreword to this book, Admiral Joe Callo asked, 'what was the extraordinary motivation that drew this special group from "The New World" to serve in a force dominated by the spirit of Admiral Lord Nelson?' You the reader, might recognise that each man's motivation was due to more than just being British and serving in a navy dominated by Nelson's spirit. Admiral Callo does address the motivation question further and sees a deeper reason why these men were attracted to serving in the Royal Navy. The deeper motivation can be attributed to shared attitudes and values between two nations of English-speaking peoples.

This time in world history experienced tremendous change involving a global conflict between ideologies. Many of the men in this book were much too young to decide which side they would take at the onset of the American War for Independence. In many cases, what ultimately decided their allegiance was that their families were facing danger – were coming out on the losing side. In his book *Tories: Fighting for the King in America's First Civil War,* American author and historian Thomas B. Allen characterised the Revolutionary War, as 'a civil war'.[1] The upshot of all this was that many of these men came from prominent families in colonial government; in commercial enterprise, or in the army or naval service. As Loyalists, they were forced to leave, many taking their wives and children away from the land of their birth.

Family connections to the Royal Navy were, for many of these young men, an avenue, if not the only avenue to a profession, open for them to take as they entered adulthood. For many, their families' relationship with influential men within the service facilitated their choice. Men with surnames such as Cochrane, Duckworth, Hood, Jervis, Parker and Nelson have been identified. Several were

1   Thomas B. Allen, *Tories: Fighting for the King in America's First Civil War* (New York: Harper-Collins Publishers, 2010), p.xxii.

friends of Nelson. Patronage certainly was a factor for John 'Jack' Perkins, who, being of mixed race, had a great deal to overcome. Ultimately, it can be seen in these biographies that patronage played an important role in giving many of these young men a leg up. However, patronage could only go so far. Successful performance in their duties was required for advancement in the service. The reader has seen that their performance in combat varied in scale, ranging from cutting out expeditions, land combat operations, and individual frigate actions to the great naval battles of the period, especially Nelson's greatest victory - Trafalgar.

However, performance in their profession of arms at sea rested on one common requirement: that each of these men were masters, or at least proficient in the technology of the day - sailing wind-powered ships. Such training required a level of formal education that many of them possessed prior to entering the Royal Navy as well as on-the-job training. That required almost all to enter the navy at the lowest possible rung as ship's boys, working their way up through the ranks of ordinary seaman, able seaman, master's mate, and finally as midshipman. From that point, for midshipmen, the combination of successful conduct of the day-to-day operations at sea, together with performance under combat conditions were requirements for advancement. Of course, luck played a role as well. Overall, the men selected in this book were a microcosm of the thousands of men from North America and the Caribbean who served in the Royal Navy during that part of the Georgian era selected for this book. Taken together, these North Americans did make a lasting contribution to the Royal Navy's successes during 22 years of almost continuous global warfare at sea. It can also be said that their contributions have rippled through history, helping to form a unique bond between the Queen's navies of Australia, Britain, Canada and New Zealand and the United States Navy today.

Thus, a central aim of this book has been to dispute the classic misconception that the late Georgian-era Royal Navy was largely a 'British-only' endeavour; that it was exclusively Britons who fought valiantly against Napoleon's navy at sea, while North Americans tended only to their distant part of the world, making only brief excursions into the global conflict during the War. Conversely, the subjects featured in this work demonstrate that North Americans played a vital role in the Royal Navy throughout the French Revolutionary and Napoleonic Wars. Moreover, the findings from this book challenge another popular misconception that the majority of North Americans who did serve in the Royal Navy during this era were pressed into service – specifically US citizens. While many US citizens were certainly victims of impressment, it has been argued here that an equally large number served semi-willingly or even enthusiastically, lured to His Majesty's Navy by dreams of riches and adventure. We have also seen that even some of the Royal Navy's most skilled post-captains and admirals were North American by birth. Ultimately, North Americans made a significant, meaningful, and until now, largely unknown contribution to Great Britain's victory over Napoleon at sea.

Connections Amongst Biographies

While this book covers an era that spans approximately two generations, and while the Georgian Navy consisted of hundreds of ships and thousands of sailors during the period covered by this book, with stations and squadrons operating across the globe, is it possible that some of the men profiled in these pages might have crossed paths with one another during their naval service? A crosscheck of these profiles, concerning 'who was where when' indicates that some of these men served together and/or knew each other, however briefly. Additionally, some of them knew and served with Nelson.

Of course, some of them knew each other through family relationships. The Brenton family of Newport, Rhode Island and Halifax, Nova Scotia, produced seven American-born Royal Navy officers who served during the Georgian era. Additionally, Isaac and Francis Coffin were cousins; as a midshipman, Francis Coffin served on the sixth-rate HM Frigate *Thisbe* (28) in 1788 under the command of his cousin, Captain Isaac Coffin. Admiral John Wentworth Loring began his distinguished naval service as a servant to his uncle, Captain John Loring. Yet, beyond such obvious connections, many of these men shared in the brotherhood of service in the Royal Navy itself, sometimes together in the same squadrons, the same naval operations, the same battles, and, occasionally, even aboard the same ships, all by coincidence. Here are two examples:

- When Admiral Sir John Duckworth assembled his squadron in the West Indies for the blockade of St Dominique, Haiti in 1802, Captain John Loring was there commanding the third-rate HMS *Bellerophon* (74) and Master and Commander John Perkins was commanding the fifth-rate HM Frigate *Tartar*. It was Duckworth who gave command of *Tartar* to Perkins.
- In 1812, Captain Robert Barrie left Commodore George Cockburn's Squadron off Cadiz to be transferred to Rear Admiral Francis Laforey's flagship, the third-rate HMS *Dragon* (74), operating in the Leeward Islands, during the War of 1812.

Nelson Connections

In 1773, a young able seaman, Nicholas Biddle, knew the very young midshipman Horatio Nelson when they both served aboard the *Carcass*. They became good friends. Biddle, however, left the Royal Navy to serve in the Continental Navy in America's War of Independence. Jahleel Brenton (the brother of Edward) was on the third-rate HMS *Barfleur* (74) at the Battle of Cape St Vincent in 1797. At the Battle of Trafalgar, William Carleton was in *Colossus*, William Pringle Green was in *Conquerer*, and Francis Laforey was in the third-rate HMS *Spartiate* (74). Of the men profiled in this book, each one who was present at Trafalgar made a unique contribution to the victory and each, undoubtedly, had a unique story to tell about the battle and its aftermath.

For example, the third-rate HMS *Spartiate* (74), commanded by Sir Francis Laforey, survived the battle with few losses and towed the crippled HMS *Tonnant* during the storm that followed. In Nelson's funeral procession on the Thames, Laforey carried the standard in the first barge behind the funeral barge. In another example, Sir Isaac Coffin, while not at Trafalgar, was one of six bearers of the canopy in Nelson's funeral procession.[2]

Of the 13,000 Royal Navy sailors and marines on the ships' books at Trafalgar, over 1260 were born outside of England, Ireland, Scotland, and Wales. The crew of *Victory*, in fact, was comprised of 22 nationalities.[3]

At the Battle of Trafalgar, over 500 names were listed on the muster books as coming from North America. Some were impressed and many had entered the Royal Navy voluntarily. Some were on the quarterdeck and some were below decks. It is not surprising, really, to learn that some of the people profiled in this book were at Trafalgar because the Ayshford Trafalgar Roll has been so thoroughly analysed and documented by historians. It is likely that Trafalgar veterans, particularly officers, would rise to the top of the heap when one searches for 'Americans in Nelson's Navy.' An association with Nelson is also the filter through which some of the profiles in this book were often chosen.

Naval historians have for two centuries maintained a fascination, and in some cases, an obsession, not only with Nelson, but with those who knew him and served with him – perhaps to decipher the extent of his influence on their lives through his example, leadership, and or patronage. Whether Nelson consciously surrounded himself with courageous, dedicated colleagues, or whether they were drawn to him through his charisma, or whether the Royal Navy simply attracted or developed such men, as a matter of course, remains a matter of conjecture. Perhaps this incident will explain Nelson's view of the matter. As Nelson was preparing to leave England for what would become the Trafalgar Campaign, Admiral Lord

2   Brandon Heubner, 'The Funeral and Burial of Admiral Lord Nelson, 9 January 1806', *On This Day in History* podcast, 9 January 2015 <http://maritimehistorypodcast.com/funeral-burial-lord-horatio-nelson-9-january-1806/>

3   Chris Pleasance, 'England Expects Every Foreign Man to do his Duty', How Nelson relied on more than 1,000 overseas-born Sailors at the Battle of Trafalgar', *Daily News*: 13 October 2013 <http://www.dailymail.co.uk/news/article-2457433/Nelson-relied-hundreds-foreign-sailors-Battle-Trafalgar.html>

Barham asked him to select his subordinate officers. Nelson replied, 'Choose yourself, my lord, the same spirit actuates the whole profession; you cannot choose wrong.'[4]

Directions for Additional Research

This book is intended only as a starting point to help advance our understanding of how and why this small but significant number of North Americans served in the Royal Navy during its wars with France. There are multiple areas within this field of study that require further research. For instance, the only naval battle where we have a clear picture of North American involvement is Trafalgar, thanks to the monumental research undertaking known as the Ayshford Trafalgar Roll. However, what of North Americans who served at the Glorious First of June? Or Copenhagen? Or the Nile? Future research will hopefully yield the identities of the North Americans who served in those other engagements as well, along with those who saw no battle but served honourably nevertheless. Further, while much is known about the senior officers born in North America who served in the Royal Navy, much less is known about the lower deck personnel.

Researching lower deck personnel further will also provide additional insights into why some were pressed while others served voluntarily. It will also allow us a useful lens into early nineteenth century America, a society that, despite having won independence, was still trying to forge its own unique identity following generations of British colonial rule. Thus, this book is not an end by any means to this important line of research, but only a beginning.

---

4   Nicholas Tracy, *Nelson's Battles: The Triumph of British Seapower* (Annapolis, Maryland: US Naval Institute Press, 2008), p.201, fn. Midshipman Henry Walker to Mrs. R. Walker, 22 November 1805, Logs II, 322.

References

Archives, Collections & Databases

American Philosophical Society, Yale University, and The Packard Humanities Institute, *Franklin Papers*, http://franklinpapers.org/franklin (accessed 30 March 2019).

Archive of Americana, Adams, Samuel (Amicus Patriae), 'Address to the Inhabitants of the Province of the Massachusetts-Bay in New England', in Evans, Charles, *American Bibliography*, in Readex Archive, Early American Imprints (originally published Boston: Rogers and Fowle, 1747). <https://www.readex.com/content/early-american-imprints> (accessed 12 May 2019).

Beinecke Library, Yale University, New Haven, Connecticut: OB MSS 35: E.P. Brenton Correspondence.

British Library, London: ADD MS 40543, Brenton Correspondence.

British Library, London, ADD 59004, Dropmore Papers.

British Museum. London, 1875, 0814.752, Print Collection: 'Commemoration of the Victory of June 1st MDCCXCIV'.

Brown University, Providence, Rhode Islan GB-N 1801, Anne S. K. Brown Military Collection.

Centre for Buckinghamshire Studies, Archives D81/50, Copy of Royal Warrant creating Admiral James Gambier a Baron, 1807.

Family Search <https://www.familysearch.org.> (accessed 3 May 2019), 'Rhode Island Births and Christenings, 1600-1914'.

Kenyon College Archives, Gambier, Ohio, KCL 231124b: Bishop Philander Chase Papers.

Library of Congress, Washington DC
- Acts of the Fourth Congress of the US.
- Acts of the Sixth Congress of the US.
- Manuscript Division: Biddle, Nicholas B. Papers, 1681-1933.
- Manuscript Division: Journals of the Continental Congress 1775 – 1789.
- The Declaration of Independence.

- Records of the Court of Admiralty of the Province of Massachusetts Bay, 1718–1747.

Loring Family Papers, Private Collection, United Kingdom.

London Metropolitan Archives, Board of Guardian Records, 1834-1906 and Church of England Parish Registers, 1813-1906.

Maryland Historical Society, Annapolis, Tilghman Family Papers, 1493-1940.

Massachusetts Historical Society, Boston, Graves, Samuel, *Samuel Graves Journal: 1774- 1776*, Vol. 2.

Massachusetts, Town and Vital Records, 1620-1988 [database on-line]. Provo, Utah: Ancestry Operations, Inc., 2011. <https//www.ancestry.com>.

Massey Library Archive, Royal Military College, Kingston, Ontario, FC441.B3A3, Barrie Letters from Kingston.

National Archives and Records Administration, Washington, D.C.
- Department of State Records Relative to Impressed Seamen.
- Microfilm M1839: Miscellaneous Lists, Papers and Protests Regarding Impressed Seamen, 1796-1814.
- RG 15, File no. 272: War of 1812 Pension Files.
- RG 45. Box 222 Subject Files 1775-1910: Bainbridge, William, Papers, 1775-1910, Bainbridge Battle Bill, Series 464.

National Maritime Museum, Royal Museums Greenwich, England
- ADM 354/229/20, 354/228/236: 'Almy, George'.
- BHC 0474: Nicholas Pocock, 'The "Defence" at the Battle of the First of June 1794.'
- BHC 3675: 'The Frigate Triton', by Nicholas Pocock, 1796. <http://collections.rmg.co.uk/collections/objects/15148.html>
- ED0012: Admiral Gambier's medal, Bombardment of Copenhagen <http://collections.rmg.co.uk/collections/objects/40473.html#GuTPC2Rh KHkTP45Z.99>
- MS 80/170, WQB/49: 'Robert Barrie'.
- MNT0118: 'Lieutenant William Pringle Green', <http://collections.rmg.co.uk/collections/objects/42066.html> (accessed 21 November 2016).
- JOD/48: 'Journal of Lt. William Pringle Green, HMS Conqueror chasing the French Fleet, 1805-1808', <http://collections.rmg.co.uk/collections/objects/505830.html> (accessed 4 March 2017).
- AD8791: 'The Battle of the Glorious First of June 1794; The "Defence" under tow by a frigate'.
- 'Research Guide B5: Royal Navy Dockyards', <http://www.rmg.co.uk/discover/researchers/research-guides/research-guide-b5-royal-naval-dockyards> (accessed 20 June 2016 and 9 July 2016).
- ZAZ3127, 'Ships' Plans', Admiralty Collection: http://collections.rmg.co.uk/collections/objects/82918.html

Naval History Division (now Naval History and Heritage Command), Washington, D.C.
- OCLC 42677: Naval Documents of the American Revolution.

Newport Historical Society, Newport, Rhode Island, Death Certificate of Edward Pelham Brenton.

Queen's University Archive, Kingston, Ontario, 2160.2 Robert Barrie Letters.

Rhode Island Historical Society, Providence, Rhode Island, Brenton, MSS 306, Jahleel, Papers, 1655-1732.
- Brenton, F., 'Descendants of William Brenton. Governor of Rhode Island.' Typescript (Spokane, Washington: C.F. Brenton, May 29, 1994).

The National Archives of the United Kingdom, Kew, London, England
- TNA ADM 1/480: Records of the Navy Board.
- TNA ADM 1/2012: Navy Board and Board of Admiralty.
- TNA ADM 1/3818: Governor William Shirley to the Admiralty.
- TNA ADM 6/89/229, ADM 6/96/6, ADM 6/104/246, and ADM 107/35/423-425, 107/6/314: Lieutenants' Passing Certificates.
- TNA ADM 36/7567: Admiralty Ships' Muster Rolls, 1688-1842.
- TNA ADM 45/15/518: Applications for Officer Examinations.
- TNA ADM 51/496: Lucius O'Brien's Logbook.

William L. Clements Library, University of Michigan, Ann Arbor, Michigan
- Barrie, Robert, Papers, 1812-1831.
- Medical day book of Surgeon Amos A. Evans, 1812-1813.

William Perkins Library, Durham, North Carolina, Duke University, Robert Barrie Correspondence.

Published Works

Admiralty, Great Britain, *Regulations and Instructions Relating to His Majesty's Service at Sea* (London, 1731 – reprinted in subsequent editions).

Admiralty, Great Britain, *Queen's Regulations and Admiralty Instructions for the Government of the Naval Service* (London: Her Majesty's Stationary Office, 1869).

Admiralty, Great Britain, *Queen's Regulations and Admiralty Instructions for the Government of the Naval Service* (London: Her Majesty's Stationary Office, 1879).

Admiralty, Great Britain, *Regulations and Instructions Relating to His Majesty's Service at Sea, Established by His Majesty in Council* (London: W. Winchester and Son, Strand, 1806).

Akrigg, Helen B. 'Richards & Sir George Henry', in *Dictionary of Canadian Biography*, Vol. 12, University of Toronto/Université Laval, 2003–, <http://www.biographi.ca/en/bio/richards_george_henry_12E.html> (accessed 4 May 2017).

Alden, John R, *A History of the American Revolution* (New York: Knopf, 1969).

Allen, Joseph, *The New Navy List and General Record of the Services of Officers of the Royal Navy and the Royal Marines* (London: Parker, Furnival & Parker, 1851).

Allen, Thomas B., *Tories: Fighting for the King in America's First Civil War* (New York: Harper-Collins, 2010).

Amory, Thomas C., *The Life of Admiral Sir Isaac Coffin, Baronet* (Boston, Massachusetts: Cupples, Upham and Company, 1886).

Anderson, Robert Charles, *Immigrants to New England, 1620-1633*, Great Migration Study Project (Boston, Massachusetts: New England Historic Genealogical Society, 1995).

Anon., 'A Table of Kindred and Affinity, wherein whosoever are related are forbidden in Scripture and our Law [in the Church of England] to Marry', *The Book of Common Prayer* (1662) <https://www.eskimo.com/~lhowell/bcp1662/misc/kindred_1662.html> (accessed 17 April 2019).

Anon., 'Carleton, Thomas', *Dictionary of Canadian Biography Volume V (1801 – 1820)*. University of Toronto/Université Laval, 2003 – 2016, at <http://www.biographi.ca/en/bio/ carleton_thomas_5E.html> (accessed 16 June 2016).

Anon., 'Daghee – Property of Commodore Barrie, Commanding British Naval Forces in Canada', *American Turf and Sporting Magazine*, Vol. 5, No. 5 (January 1834), pp. 225-227.

Anon., *Dictionary of American Naval Fighting Ships* (Washington, DC: Naval History Division, 1992), Digital edition: *Dictionary of Naval Fighting Ships* <http://www.hazegray.org/danfs/> (accessed 2 April 2019).

Anon., 'Ja'-le-el (yachle'el, "wait for God!")', *International Standard Bible Encyclopedia* (1915) <http://www.biblestudytools.com/dictionary/jahleel/> (accessed 3 May 2019).

Anon., The National Archives, Kew, London, 'Battle of Trafalgar, Nelson, Trafalgar, and Those Who Served', <http://www.nationalarchives.gov.uk/nelson/gallery7/trafalgar.htm> (accessed 17 June 2016).

Anon., 'Pedro Antonio Zia Martinez', *Guerres de 1792-1815: Quelques uns des derniers soldats de la Republique et de l'Empire*, <http://derniersveterans.free.fr/napoleon1.html> (accessed 16 June 2016).

Anon., '*Susquehanna* I (Side-wheel Steamer)', *Dictionary of American Naval Fighting Ships*, Naval History and Heritage Command, 2015, <https://www.history.navy.mil/research/histories/ship-histories/danfs/s/susquehanna-i.html> (accessed 20 May 2019).

Anon., 'That beautiful full bred horse ...' *American Turf and Sporting Magazine*, Vol. 5, No. 8 (April 1834).

Anon., 'The Importance of our Coast Fisheries', *Essex Standard* (1 August 1843), p. 4.

Anon., *The Services of the Late Admiral Sir John Wentworth Loring, K.C.B., K.C.H., in the two French Wars from 1789 to 1816, etc.* (Woolwich, Britain: Royal

Artillery Institution, 1900; originally published Bournemouth: Francis Nash, 1880).

Anon., 'Valuable Dogs' *American Turf and Sporting Magazine*, Vol. 5, No. 2 (November 1813), p. 150.

Arthur, Brian, *How Britain Won the War of 1812: The Royal Navy's Blockade of the United States, 1812-1815* (Woodbridge: Boydell Press, 2012).

Atkins, Gareth, 'Religion, politics, and patronage in the late Hanoverian Navy, c. 1780-c.1820', *Historical Research*, Vol. 88, No. 240 (May 2015), pp. 272-290.

Atkins, Gareth, 'Christian Heroes, Providence, and Patriotism in Wartime Britain, 1793-1815', *The Historical Journal*, Vol. 58, No. 2 (June 2015), pp. 393-414.

Ayshford, Pam and Ayshford, Derek, *The Ayshford Complete Trafalgar Roll* (Brussels, Belgium: SEFF, 2004).

Barnes, G.R. and Owens, J.H. (eds.), *Private Papers of John, Earl of Sandwich Vol. III* (London: Navy Records Office, 1933).

Bartlett, John Russell (ed.), *Records of the Colony of Rhode Island and Providence Plantations in New England,* 10 volumes (Providence, Rhode Island: A.C. Greene and Bros., State printers, 1856-1865).

Barton, Mark & McGrath, John, *British Naval Swords and Swordsmanship* (Barnsley, South Yorkshire: Seaforth Publishing, 2013).

Baugh, Daniel A., *British Naval Administration in the Age of Walpole* (Princeton, New Jersey: Princeton University Press, 1965).

Baugh, Daniel A., 'Great Britain's Blue-Water Policy, 1689-1815', *International History Review*, Vol. 10 (February 1988), pp. 33-58.

Bickham, Troy, *The Weight of Vengeance: The United States, the British Empire, and the War of 1812* (Oxford: Oxford University Press, 2012).

Biddle, Charles, *Autobiography of Charles Biddle: President of the Executive Council of Pennsylvania* (Philadelphia, Pennsylvania: E Claxton and Company, 1855).

Biddle, Nicholas, *Journal of the Andrea Doria*, 4 March 1776 in William Bell Clark (ed.), Naval Documents of the American Revolution, OCLC 426774 (Naval History Division, Dept. of the US Navy, Washington, DC: Government Printing Office, 1964)

Bienkowski, Lee, *Admirals in the Age of Nelson* (Annapolis, Maryland: US Naval Institute Press, 2003).

Bilder, Mary Sarah, *The Transatlantic Constitution: Colonial Legal Culture and the Empire* (Cambridge, Massachusetts: Harvard University Press, 2004).

Black, Jeremy, *The British Seaborne Empire* (New Haven, Connecticut: Yale University Press, 2004).

Blake, Richard C., 'Gambier, Baron James (1756-1833)', *Oxford Dictionary of National Biography*, Oxford University Press, 2004; online edition, Jan 2008 <http://oxforddnb.com/view/article/10321> (accessed 2 November 2015).

Blake, Richard, *Evangelicals in the Royal Navy, 1775-1815: Blue Lights and Psalm Singers* (Woodbridge: Boydell Press, 2008).

Blake, Richard. *Religion in the British Navy, 1815-1879: Piety and Professionalism* (Woodbridge: Boydell Press, 2014).

Blakeley, Phyllis R., 'Halliburton, Sir Brenton', *Dictionary of Canadian Biography*, Vol. 8, University of Toronto/Université Laval, 2003–<http://www.biographi.ca/en/bio/halliburton_brenton_8E.html> (accessed 17 January 2017).

Blanco, Richard L. (ed.), *The American Revolution 1776-1783: An Encyclopaedia*, Vol. I (New York: Garland Publishing, 1993).

Boatner, Mark M., *Encyclopedia of the American Revolution* (Mechanicsburg, Pennsylvania: Stackpole Books, 1994).

Börjeson, Hjalmar, *Biografiska anteckningar om Örlogsflottans Officerare 1700-1799*, edited by Karl Westin. (Stockholm, Sweden: Generalstabens litografiska anstalt, 1942).

Bosanquet, H.T.A., 'The Maritime School at Chelsea', *The Mariner's Mirror*, Vol. 7, Issue 11 (1921), pp. 322-329.

Boyar, Paul and Nissenbaum, Stephen, *Salem Possessed: The Social Origins of Witchcraft* (Cambridge, Massachusetts: Harvard University Press, 1974).

Boyd, Eva Phillips, 'Commodore Joshua Loring: Jamaica Plain by Way of London', *Old-Time New England Magazine*, (April-June 1959), <http://www.jphs.org/people/2005/4/14/commodore-joshua-loring-jamaica-plain-by-way-of-london.html> (accessed 2 January 2017).

Bradlow, Frank R., 'Five New Pictures by Sir Jahleel Brenton (1770-1844) with special reference to one of the Arniston Memorial', *Quarterly Bulletin of the South African Library*, Vol. 24, No. 2 (June 1970), pp. 247-254.

Breen, Kenneth, "Wallace, Sir James (1731–1803)," *Oxford Dictionary of National Biography*, (Oxford University Press, 2004; online edition, Jan 2008) <http://www.oxforddnb.com/view/article/28536> (accessed 30 December 2016).

Breen, T.H., *The Marketplace of Revolution: How Consumer Politics Shaped American Independence* (Oxford: Oxford University Press, 2004).

Brenton, Edward Pelham, *The Naval History of Great Britain, from the year MDCCLXXXIII to MDCCCXXII* (London: C. Rice, 1823-25).

Brenton, Edward Pelham, *A letter to the Rt. Hon. R.W. Horton: shewing the impolicy, inefficacy and ruinous consequences of emigration and the advantages of home colonies* (London: C. Rice, 1830).

Brenton, Edward Pelham, *Statement of the views and reports of the Society for the Suppression of Juvenile Vagrancy: upon the plan that has proved so successful in Holland, by providing agricultural and horticultural employment for the destitute children of the metropolis* (No location: no publisher indicated, 1830).

Brenton, Edward Pelham, *The Naval History of Great Britain, from the year MDCCLXXXIII to MDCCCXXXVI: A new and greatly improved edition* (London: Henry Colburn, 1837).

Brenton, Edward Pelham, *Life and Correspondence of John, Earl of St.Vincent, G.C.B. Admiral of the Fleet* (London: Henry Colburn, 1838).

Brenton, Elizabeth C., *A History of Brenton's Neck from 1638* (Newport, Rhode Island: John Sanborn, 1877).

Brenton, Jahleel, *Continuation of 'The Bible and the Spade', or, the History of Fanny Forsher, a moral tale, etc.* (London: J. Nisbet & Co., 1837).

Brenton, Jahleel, *An Appeal to the British Nation on behalf of her Sailors* (London: J. Nisbet & Co. 1838).

Brenton, Jahleel, *The Hope of the Navy, or, The true source of discipline and efficiency: as set forth in the articles of war provided for the government of the fleet of Great Britain: an address, etc.* (London: no publisher indicated, 1839).

Brenton, Jahleel, *Memoir of Captain Edward Pelham Brenton, R.N., C.B., with Sketches of his Professional Life and Exertions in the Cause of Humanity as continued with the 'Children's Friends Society,' &c., Observations upon his Naval History and Life of the Earl of St Vincent* (London: James Nisbet and Co., 1842).

Brenton, Jahleel, *Remarks on the importance of our coast fisheries as the means of increasing the amount of food and employment for the labouring classes, and of maintaining a nursery for seamen* (London: James Nesbit & Co, 1843).

Brenton, L.C.L., *The Septuagint with Apocrypha: Greek and English* (Peabody, Massachusetts: Hendrickson Publishers, 1986; originally published London: Samuel Bagster & Sons, Ltd., 1851).

Brenton, L.C.L. (ed.), *Memoir of Vice-Admiral Sir Jahleel Brenton, Baronet, K.C.B.* (London: Longman, 1855).

Brock, Thomas L. 'H.M. Dock Yard, Kingston, under Commissioner Robert Barrie, 1819 – 1834', *Historic Kingston*, No. 16, 1968.

Brock, Thomas L. 'Commodore Robert Barrie and his Family in Kingston, 1819-1834', *Historic Kingston*, No. 23 (1975), pp. 1-18.

Brock, Thomas L., 'Barrie, Robert', *Dictionary of Canadian Biography, 1836-1850*, Vol. 7, University of Toronto/Université Laval, 2003–, <http://www.biographi.ca/en/bio/barrie_robert_7E.html> (accessed 3 May 2019).

Brunsman, Denver, 'Subjects vs. Citizens: Impressment and Identity in the Anglo-American Atlantic', *Journal of the Early Republic*, Vol. 30, No. 4 (Winter 2010), pp. 557-586.

Brunsman, Denver, *The Evil Necessity: British Naval Impressment in the Eighteenth-Century Atlantic World* (Charlottesville, Virginia: University of Virginia Press, 2013).

Bunbury, Henry, *A Narrative of Military Transactions in the Mediterranean, 1805-1810* (London: T&W Boon, 1891).

Burchett, Josiah, *A Complete History of the Most Remarkable Transactions at Sea (1720)*, facsimile edition with an introduction by John B. Hattendorf. "Maritime History Series," John B. Hattendorf, series editor (Delmar, New York: Scholars' Facsimiles & Reprints for the John Carter Brown Library, 1995).

Burgess, Douglas R., Jr., *The Politics of Piracy: Crime and Civil Disobedience in Colonial America* (Lebanon, New Hampshire: University Press of New England, 2014).

Burnley, James, 'Green, William Pringle', *Dictionary of National Biography, 1885-1900*, Vol. 23, < https://en.wikisource.org/wiki/Green,_William_Pringle_ (DNB00)> (accessed 21 November 2016).

Callahan, North, *Flight from the Republic: The Tories of the American Revolution* (New York: The Bobs-Merrill Company, 1967).

Canney, Donald L., *Africa Squadron: The US Navy and the Slave Trade, 1842-1861* (Washington, DC: Potomac Books, 2006).

Cannon, Richard, *Historical Record of the Thirty-First or the Huntingdonshire Regiment of Foot* (London: Parker, Furnival, and Parker, 1850).

Capp, Bernard L., *Cromwell's Navy: The Fleet and the English Revolution, 1648-1660* (Oxford: Oxford University Press, 1989).

Carey, Harriet M., *Evenings with Grandpapa, or, the Admiral on Shore: Naval Stories for Children* (London: Dean & Son, 1860).

Carp, Benjamin L., *Rebels Rising: Cities and the American Revolution* (Oxford: Oxford University Press, 2007).

Carp, Benjamin L., *Defiance of the Patriots: The Boston Tea Party and the Making of America* (New Haven, Connecticut: Yale University Press, 2010).

Cavell, S.A., *Midshipmen and Quarterdeck Boys in the British Navy, 1771-1831* (Woodbridge: Boydell Press, 2012).

Chamier, Frederick. *The Life of a Sailor* (Annapolis, Maryland: Naval Institute Press, 2011)

Chard, Donald F., 'Green, Benjamin', *Dictionary of Canadian Biography, Vol. 4*, University of Toronto/Université Laval, 2003-<http://www.biographi.ca/en/bio/green_benjamin_4E.html> (accessed 29 December 2016).

Clarke, Samuel C., *Records of Some of the Descendants of William Curtis, Roxbury, 1632* (Boston, Massachusetts: David Clapp & Son, 1869).

Clark, William Bell, *John Barry, 1745-1803: The Story of a Naval Hero in Two Wars* (New York: Macmillan, 1938).

Clark, William Bell, *Captain Dauntless: The Story of Captain Nicholas Biddle of the Continental Navy* (Baton Rouge, Louisiana: Louisiana State University Press, 1949).

Clark, William Bell (ed.), *Naval Documents of the American Revolution* (Naval History Division, Dept. of the US Navy, Washington, DC: Government Printing Office, 1964).

Clowes, William Laird, *The Royal Navy, A History from the Earliest Times to 1900*, Five volumes (London: Chatham, 1997, originally published London: Sampson Low, Marston & Company, 1899).

Colledge, J.J. and Warlow, Ben, *Ships of the Royal Navy: The Complete Record of all Fighting Ships of the Royal Navy from the 15th Century to the Present* (London:

Chatham Publishing, 2006; Annapolis, Maryland: US Naval Institute Press, 2006).

Corbett, Julian S., *England in the Seven Years War: A Study in Combined Strategy* (London: Longman, 1907).

Corbett, Julian S. (ed.), *Signals and Instructions, 1776-1794, with addenda to volume XXIX,* Publications of the Navy Records Society, Vol. 35 (London: Navy Records Society, 1908).

Colburn, Henry and Bentley. Richard, *The United Service Journal and Naval and Military Magazine* (London: Samuel Bentley, issues 1829-32).

Collinge, J.M. (ed.), *Office-Holders in Modern Britain: Volume 7, Navy Board Officials 1660-1832,* (London, 1978), pp. 81-116. *British History Online,* <http://www.british-history.ac.uk/office-holders/vol7/pp81-116> (accessed 25 February and 20 March 2017).

Cordingly, David, *The Billy Ruffian: The Bellerophon and the Downfall of Napoleon: The Biography of a Ship of the Line, 1782-1836* (London: Bloomsbury, 2004).

Costello, Ray, *Black Salt: Seafarers of African Descent on British Ships* (Liverpool: Liverpool University Press, 2012).

Crawford, Michael J. (ed.), *The Autobiography of a Yankee Mariner: Christopher Prince and the American Revolution* (Washington, DC: Brassey's, Inc., 2002).

Crawford, M.J. (ed.), *The Naval War of 1812: A Documentary History, Vol. 3, 1814-1815* (Washington, DC: Naval Historical Center, 2002).

Curtis, Catherine P., *The Curtis Family* (Boston, Massachusetts: New England Historic Genealogical Society, 1876).

Dancy, J. Ross, *The Myth of the Press Gang: Volunteers, Impressment and the Naval Manpower Problem in the Late Eighteenth Century* (Woodbridge: Boydell Press, 2015).

Davenport, Charles Benedict and Scudder, Mary Theresa, *Naval Officers: Their Heredity and Development* (Washington, DC: Carnegie Institution of Washington, 1919).

Davey, James, *The Transformation of British Naval Strategy: Seapower and Supply in Northern Europe, 1808-1812* (Woodbridge: Boydell Press, 2012).

Davey, James, *In Nelson's Wake: The Navy and the Napoleonic Wars* (New Haven, Connecticut: Yale University Press; Greenwich: National Maritime Museum, 2015; Wales, Gomer Press 2016).

David, Andrew, 'The Emergence of the Admiralty Chart in the Nineteenth Century', Proceedings from the International Cartographic Association Symposium on 'Shifting Boundaries: Cartography in the 19th and 20th Centuries', Portsmouth University, Portsmouth, UK, 2008, <http://history.icaci.org/wp-content/uploads/2016/09/David.pdf> (accessed 3 May 2019)

Davis, Ralph, *The Rise of the English Shipping Industry in the 17th and 18th Centuries* (London: Macmillan & Company, 1962).

Delafons, John, *Treatise on Naval Courts Martial 1805* (Cambridge, Massachusetts: Gale, 2012).

De Roos, F. Fitzgerald, *Personal Narrative of Travels in the United States and Canada in 1826 with Remarks on the Present State of the American Navy* (London: William Harrison Ainsworth, 1827).

Douglas, W.A.B., 'Loring, Joshua', *Dictionary of Canadian Biography*, Vol. 4, University of Toronto/Université Laval, 2003–, <http://www.biographi.ca/en/bio/loring_joshua_4E.html> (accessed 6 January 2014).

Drescher, Seymour, *Econocide: British Slavery in the Era of Abolition*, Second edition (Chapel Hill, North Carolina: University of North Carolina Press, 2010).

Dubois, Laurent, *Avengers of the New World: The Story of the Haitian Revolution* (Cambridge, Massachusetts: Harvard University Press, 2004).

Dudley, William S., *The Naval War of 1812: A Documentary History, Volume II 1813* (Washington, DC: Naval Historical Center, Department of the Navy, 1992).

Duffy, Michael, *Soldiers, Sugar and Seapower: The British Expeditions to the West Indies and the War against Revolutionary France* (Oxford: Oxford University Press, 1987).

Duffy, Michael and Morriss, Roger (eds.), *The Glorious First of June: A Naval Battle and its Aftermath* (Exeter, England: Exeter University Press, 2001).

Durand, James, *The Life and Adventures of James R. Durand, From the Year One Thousand Eight Hundred and One, Until the Year One Thousand Eight Hundred and Sixteen* (Bridgeport, Connecticut: Stiles Nichols & Son, 1817).

Ehrman, John, *Pitt the Younger* (London: Constable, 1969).

Ferreiro, L., *Brothers at Arms: American Independence and the Men of France and Spain who Saved it* (New York: Knopf, 2016).

Field, James A. Jr., *America and the Mediterranean World 1776-1882* (Princeton, New Jersey: Princeton University Press, 1969).

Fitz-Enz, David, *Hacks, Sycophants, Adventurers, & Heroes: Madison's Commanders in the War of 1812* (New York: Taylor Trade Company, 2012).

Flannery, Tim (ed.), *The Life and Adventures of John Nicol, Mariner* (New York: Atlantic Monthly Press, 1997; originally published 1821).

Ford, Worthington C. et al (eds.), *Journals of the Continental Congress, 1774-1789* (Washington, DC: Government Printing Office, 1904-1937).

Fremont-Barnes, Gregory, *The Royal Navy 1793-1815* (Oxford: Osprey Publishing, 2013).

Frykman, N., 'Seamen on Late Eighteenth Century European Warships.' *International Review of Social History*, (2009), pp. 67-93.

Fulton, Thomas Wemyss, *The Sovereignty of the Sea: an Historical Account of the Claims of England to the Dominion of the British Seas, and of the Evolution of the Territorial Waters: with Special Reference to the Rights of the Fishing and the Naval Salute* (Edinburgh and London: William Blackwood & Sons, 1911).

Furber, Holden, 'How William James Came to be a Naval Historian', *American Historical Review*, Vol. 38, No. 1 (October 1932), pp. 74–85.

Gabrielson, Mark J., 'Enlightenment in the Darkness: The British Prisoner of War School of Navigation at Givet, France, 1805-1814', *The Northern Mariner*, Vol. XXV, Nos. 1 & 2 (January-March 2015), pp. 7-41.

Gaffield, Julia, 'Haiti and Jamaica in the Remaking of the Early Nineteenth-Century Atlantic World', *The William & Mary Quarterly*, Vol. 6, No. 3 (July 2012), pp. 583-614.

Gage, J., *J M W Turner: A Wonderful Range of Mind* (New Haven, Connecticut: Yale University Press, 1987).

Garitee, Jerome R., *The Republic's Private Navy: The American Privateering Business as practiced by Baltimore during the War of 1812* (Mystic, Connecticut: Wesleyan, 1977).

Georgina, Lady Chatterton (ed.), *Memorials, Personal and Historical of Admiral Lord Gambier, G.C.B.* Second edition (London: Hurst and Blackett, 1861).

Gilje, Paul A., *Free Trade and Sailors' Rights in the War of 1812* (Cambridge: Cambridge University Press, 2013).

Goodwin, Peter, *The Ships of Trafalgar: The British, French and Spanish Fleets, 21 October 1805* (London: Conway Maritime Press; Annapolis, Maryland: US Naval Institute Press, 2005).

Gould, Eliga, *The Persistence of Empire: British Political Culture in the Age of the American Revolution* (Chapel Hill, North Carolina: The University of North Carolina Press, 2000).

Gould, Levi Swanton, *Ancient Middlesex: With Brief Biographical Sketches of the Men Who Have Served the County Officially Since Its Settlement* (Somerville, Massachusetts: Journal Print, 1905).

Gradish, Stephen F., *The Manning of the British Navy During The Seven Years War* (London: Royal Historical Society, 1980).

Green, William Pringle, *Fragments From Remarks Of Twenty-five Years In Every Quarter Of The Globe, On Electricity, Magnetism, Aeroliths, And Various Other Phenomena Of Nature* (Westminster, London: G. Hayden, 1833).

Haggerty, Sheryllynne, *'Merely for Money?': Business Culture in the British Atlantic, 1750–1815* (Liverpool, England: Liverpool University Press, 2012).

Haley, John William, *William Brenton of Hammersmith* (Providence, Rhode Island: Providence Institution for Savings, 1933).

Hamilton, Douglas, '"A most active, enterprising officer": Captain John Perkins, the Royal Navy and the boundaries of slavery and liberty in the Caribbean', *Slavery and Abolition*, Vol. 39 (2018), pp. 80-100.

Harlow, V., *The Founding of the Second British Empire 1763-1783* (London: Longman, 1964).

Hattendorf, John B., 'The US Navy's Nineteenth-Century Forward Stations', *Talking about Naval History: A Collection of Essays* (Newport, Rhode Island: Naval War College Press, 2011).

Hattendorf, John B. (ed.), *Changing American Perceptions of the Royal Navy Since 1775* (Newport, Rhode Island: US Naval War College, 2014).

Headlam, Cecil (ed.), *Calendar of State Papers, Colonial America and West Indies* (London: His Majesty's Stationary Office, 1910), *British History Online*, <https://www.british-history.ac.uk/cal-state-papers/colonial/america-west-indies/vol5> (accessed 5 April 2019).

Heathcote, T.A., *The British Admirals of the Fleet 1734-1995: A Biographical Dictionary* (Barnsley, South Yorkshire: Pen & Sword Books, 2002).

Hohman, E.P., *Seamen Ashore: A Study of the United Seamen's Service and of Merchant Seamen in Port* (New Haven, Connecticut: Yale University Press, 1952).

Hopkins, James T. (ed.), *The Papers of Henry Clay. Vol. 3, Presidential Candidate* (Lexington, Kentucky: University of Kentucky Press, 1963).

Hore, Peter, *HMS Pickle: The Swiftest Ship in Nelson's Fleet* (Stroud, England: The History Press, 2015).

Hore, Peter, *Nelson's Band of Brothers: Lives and Memorials* (Barnsley, South Yorkshire: Seaforth Publishing, 2015).

Hughes, Edward (ed.), *The Private Correspondence of Admiral Lord Collingwood*, Publications of the Navy Records Society, Vol. 98 (London: Navy Records Society, 1957).

Irving, Washington, 'Nicholas Biddle', in Frost, John H. (ed.), *American Naval Biography* (New York: John Low, 1821).

James, William, *The Naval History of Great Britain, from the Declaration of War by France in 1793 to the Accession of George IV*, six volumes (London: Richard Bentley, 1837; originally printed for Baldwin, Craddock, and Joy, 1822-1825).

James, William, *The Naval History of Great Britain During the French Revolution and Napoleonic Wars: 1797-1799* (London: Conway Maritime Press, 2002;originally published London" 1837).

James, William, *The Naval History of Great Britain ... with an account of the origin and progressive increase of the British Navy and an account of the Burmese War and the battle of Navarino* (London: Richard Bentley, 1837, 1859, 1860, 1866, 1902, and 2002).

James, William, *A full and correct account of the chief naval occurrences of the late war between Great Britain and the United States of America: preceded by a cursory examination of the American accounts of their naval actions fought previous to that period* (London: Conway Maritime Press, 2002).

Jangaard, Peter M., *Some Descendants of John Green (1636-1691) and Ruth Mitchelson (1638-1728) of Cambridge, Massachusetts* (Halifax, Nova Scotia: Peter M. Jangaard, 2007).

Jones, E. Alfred, *The Loyalists of Massachusetts: Their Memorials, Petitions, and Claims* (Baltimore, Maryland: Genealogical Publishing Company, 1969).

Jones, George, *Sketches of Naval Life with Notices of Men, Manners and Scenery on the Shores of the Mediterranean in a Series of Letters from the Brandywine and Constitution Frigates*, Vol. 1 (London, Forgotten Books, 2017; originally published London: H. Howe, 1826).

Keppel, The Hon. Sir Henry, *A Sailor's Life under Four Sovereigns* (London: The Macmillan Company, 1899).

Knight, R.J.B. (ed.), *Portsmouth Dockyard Papers, 1774-1783: The American War: A Calendar*, Portsmouth Record Series, 6 (Portsmouth: City of Portsmouth, 1987).

Knight, Roger, 'Gambier, James (1723-1789)', *Oxford Dictionary of National Biography*, (Oxford University Press, published online January 2008) <http://www.oxforddnb.com/view/article/10320> (accessed 2 November 2015).

Knight, Roger, *Britain against Napoleon: The Organisation of Victory, 1793-1815* (London: Allen Lane, 2013).

Lambert, Andrew, 'Introduction' in William James, *The Naval History of Great Britain*, (London: Conway Maritime Press, 2002).

Lambert, Andrew, (revisions), 'Brenton, Edward Pelham (1774–1839)', *Oxford Dictionary of National Biography* (Oxford: Oxford University Press, 2004) <http://www.oxforddnb.com/view/article/3325> (accessed 21 December 2016).

Lambert, Andrew, *The Challenge: Britain Against America in the Naval War of 1812* (New York: Faber & Faber, 2012).

Laughton, John Knox, 'Journals of Henry Duncan, Captain, Royal Navy' in Laughton, (ed.), *Naval Miscellany*, Vol. 1. Publications of the Navy Records Society, Vol. 20 (London: Navy Records Society, 1902).

Laughton, John Knox (ed.), *Letters and Papers of Charles, Lord Barham, Admiral of the Red*, Publications of the Navy Records Society, Vol. 32 (London: Navy Records Society, 1907).

Laughton, John Knox. 'Marryat, Frederick (1792–1848)', revised by Andrew Lambert, *Oxford Dictionary of National Biography*, (Oxford University Press, published online 2004); <http://www.oxforddnb.com/view/article/18097> (accessed 27 December 2016).

Laughton, John Knox. 'Chamier, Frederick (1796–1870)', revised by Roger Morriss, *Oxford Dictionary of National Biography*, (Oxford University Press, published online 2004), <http://www.oxforddnb.com/view/article/5090> (accessed 27 December 2016).

Laughton, John Knox, 'Coffin, Sir Isaac (1759–1839)', revised by Julian Gwyn, *Oxford Dictionary of National Biography* (Oxford University Press: 1889; published online 2004), <https://www.oxforddnb.com/search?q=Sir+Isaac+Coffin&searchBtn=Search&isQuickSearch=true> (accessed 1 May 2019).

Laughton, John Knox, 'Gambier, James, Baron Gambier (1756 – 1833)', *Oxford Dictionary of National Biography* (Oxford University Press, 1889; published online 2004), https://www.oxforddnb.com/search?q=Gambier&searchBtn=Search&isQuickSearch=true (accessed 1 May 2019).

Lavery, Brian (ed.), *Shipboard Life and Organisation, 1731-1815*, Publications of the Navy Records Society, Vol. 138 (Aldershot, England: Ashgate for the Navy Records Society, 1998).

Laycock, Stuart, *All the Countries We've Ever Invaded: And the Few We Never Got Round To* (Charleston, South Carolina: History Press, 2012).

Lee, Sidney (ed.), *Dictionary of National Biography* (New York: Macmillan, 1909).

Lemisch, Jesse, *Jack Tar vs. John Bull: The Role of New York's Seamen in Precipitating the Revolution* (New York: Garland Publishers, 1997).

Lewis, Emanuel Raymo, *Seacoast Fortifications of the United States* (Annapolis, Maryland: US Naval Institute Press, 1993).

Lewis, Michael, *The Navy in Transition: A Social History 1814-1864* (London: Hodder and Stoughton, 1965).

Lews, Michael A. (ed.), *Sir William Henry Dillon, K.C.H., Vice Admiral of the Red, A Narrative of my Professional Adventures, (1790-1839)*, Publications of the Navy Records Society, Vol. 93 (London: Navy Records Society, 1953).

Linebaugh, Peter and Rediker, Marcus, *The Many-Headed Hydra: Sailors, Slaves, Commoners, and the Hidden History of the Revolutionary Atlantic* (Boston, Massachusetts: Beacon Press, 2000).

Mackenzie, Robert Holden, *The Trafalgar Roll* (London: Chatham Publishing, 2004).

Mahan, Alfred Thayer, *The Influence of Sea Power upon the French Revolution and Empire 1792-1812* (London: Sampson and Low, 1892).

Mahan, Alfred Thayer, *The Major Operations of the Navies in the War of American Independence* (London: Sampson Low, Marston & Company, 1913).

Malcomson, Thomas, 'Freedom by Reaching the Wooden World: American Slaves and the British Navy duing the War of 1812', *The Northern Mariner/le marin du nord*, Vol. 22, No. 4 (October 2012), pp. 361-392.

Mante, Thomas, *History of the Late War in North America* (London: W. Strahan and T. Cadell, 1772).

Marioné, Patrick; Pâques, Jean-Marie; and Rodger, N.A.M., *The Complete Navy List of the Napoleonic Wars 1793-1815* (Brussels, Belgium: SEFF, 2003).

Marshall, John, *Royal Naval Biography: or Memoirs of all the Flag-Officers, Superannuated Rear-Admirals, Retired Captains, Post-Captains, and Commanders* (London: Longman, Hurst, Rees, Orme and Brown, 1823).

McCrady, Edward, *The History of South Carolina in the Revolutionary War, 1775-1778* (New York: MacMillan and Co., 1901).

McCarthy, Matthew, *Privateering, Piracy, and British Policy in Spanish America 1810-1830* (Woodbridge: Boydell Press, 2013).

McCusker, John J. and Menard, Russell R., *The Economy of British America, 1607-1789* (Chapel Hill, North Carolina: University of North Carolina Press, 1985).

McDonald, Terry, '"It is Impossible for His Majesty's Government to withdraw from these Dominions", Britain and the Defence of Canada, 1813 to 1834', *Journal of Canadian Studies*, Vol. 39, No. 3 (Fall 2005), pp. 40-59.

McGrath, Tim, *John Barry: An American Hero in the Age of Sail* (Yardley, Pennsylvania: Westholme Publishing, 2010).

McKee, Christopher, 'Foreign Seamen in the United States Navy: A Census of 1808', *The William and Mary Quarterly*, Vol. 42, No. 3 (July 1985), pp. 383-393.

McKee, Christopher, *A Gentlemanly and Honourable Profession: The Creation of the US Naval Officer Corps, 1794-1815* (Annapolis, Maryland: US Naval Institute Press, 1991).

Morgan, William James, et al. (eds.), *Autobiography of Rear Admiral Charles Wilkes, US Navy, 1798-1877* (Washington DC: Naval History Division, Department of the Navy, 1978).

Moore, Robert J. and Rodgaard, John A., *A Hard-Fought Ship: The Story of HMS Venomous*, Third edition (St Albans: Holywell House Publishing, 2017).

Morison, Samuel Eliot, *The Founding of Harvard College* (Cambridge, Massachusetts: Harvard University Press, 1963).

Morriss, Roger, 'Charles Middleton, Lord Barham, 1726-1813' in LeFevre, Peter and Harding, Richard (eds.), *The Precursors of Nelson: British Admirals of the 18th Century* (London: Chatham, 1998).

Moultrie, William, *Memoirs of the American Revolution So Far as It Related to the States of North Carolina, South Carolina, and Georgia* (New York: David Longworth, 1802).

Munch-Petersen, Thomas, *Defying Napoleon: How Britain Bombarded Copenhagen and Seized the Danish Feet in 1807* (Stroud, England: Sutton, 2007).

Nash, Gary B., *The Urban Crucible: Social Change, Political Consciousness, and the Origins of the American Revolution* (Cambridge, Massachusetts: Harvard University Press, 1979).

Nicolas, Harris Nicholas (ed.), *The Dispatches and Letters of Vice-Admiral Lord Horatio Nelson* (London: Chatham Publishing, 1998; originally published by H. Coburn, 1845–46).

Noble, Dennis L., *The Sailor's Homer: The Life and Times of Richard McKenna, Author of the Sand Pebbles* (Annapolis, Maryland: Naval Institute Press, 2015).

O'Byrne, William R., *A Naval Biographical Dictionary: Comprising the Life and Services of Every Living Officer in Her Majesty's Navy, From the Rank of Admiral of the Fleet to that of Lieutenant, Inclusive* (London: J. Murray, printed by William Clowes and Sons, 1849).

Officer, Lawrence H. and Williamson, Samuel H., 'Computing "Real Value" Over Time With a Conversion Between U.K. Pounds and U.S. Dollars, 1774 to Present', *Measuring Worth* (2016).

O'Shaughnessy, Andrew Jackson, *An Empire Divided: The American Revolution and the British Caribbean* (Philadelphia, Pennsylvania: University of Pennsylvania Press, 2000).

Paine, Ralph D. (ed.), *Elijah Cobb, 1768 – 1848; A Cape Cod Skipper* (New Haven, Connecticut: Yale University Press, 1925).

Pappalardo, Bruno, 'Trafalgar Ancestors', *Nelson, Trafalgar, and Those Who Served*, The National Archives, Kew, London <http://www.nationalarchives.gov.uk/aboutapps/trafalgarancestors/> (accessed 17 June 2016).

Perl-Rosenthal, Nathan, *Citizen Sailors: Becoming American in the Age of Revolution* (Cambridge, Massachusetts: Harvard University Press, 2015).

Perrin, W.G. (ed.), *The Keith Papers: Selections from the Letters and Papers of Admiral Viscount Keith,* Publications of the Navy Records Society, Vol. 62 (London: Navy Records Society, 1927).

Perrin, W.G., 'The Salute in the Narrow Seas and the Vienna Conference of 1815', in W.G. Perrin (ed.), *The Naval Miscellany,* Vol. III, Publications of the Navy Records Society, Vol. 63 (London: Navy Records Society, 1928).

Phipps, Constantine John, Baron Mulgrave, *A Voyage Towards the North Pole Undertaken by His Majesty's Command, 1773* (Dublin: Sleater, Williams, Wilson, Husband, Walker and Jenkin, 1775).

Pleasance, Chris, 'England Expects Every Foreign Man to do his Duty: How Nelson relied on more than 1,000 overseas-born Sailors at the Battle of Trafalgar', *Daily News* (13 October 2013) <http://www.dailymail.co.uk/news/article-2457433/Nelson-relied-hundreds-foreign-sailors-Battle-Trafalgar.html> (accessed 3 May 2019).

Pocock, Tom, *Horatio Nelson* (New York: Alfred A. Knopf, 2013).

Polluck, Arthur William Alsager, *The United Service Journal and Naval and Military Magazine: Part II* (London: Harrison & Co. Printers, St Martin's Lane, 1840).

Popham, Hugh, *A Damned Cunning Fellow: The Eventful life of Rear-Admiral Sir Home Popham KCB, KCH, KM, FRS 1762–1820* (Twyardreath: Old Ferry Press, 1991).

Preston, Howard W., 'Rhode Island and the Loyalists', *Rhode Island Historical Society Collections,* Vol. 23, No.1 (January 1929), pp. 9-11; Part II, Vol. 22, No. 10, (October 1928), pp. 5-11.

Public Records Office, *Calendar of Treasury Papers, 1697-1701* (London: Government Printing Office, 1871).

Raikes, Henry (ed.), *Memoir of the Life of Vice-Admiral Sir Jahleel Brenton, K.C.B.* (London: Hatchard & Son, 1846).

Ralfe, James, *The Naval Biography of Great Britain: Consisting of Historical Memoirs of Those officers of the British Navy Who Distinguished Themselves during the Reign of His Majesty George III* (London: Whitmore & Fenn, 1828).

Rediker, Marcus, *Between the Devil and the Deep Blue Sea* (Cambridge: Cambridge University Press, 1987).

Rhoden, Nancy and Steele, Ian, (eds.), *The Human Tradition in US History: The Revolutionary Era* (Wilmington, Delaware: Scholarly Resources Inc., 2000).

Robinson, Hercule, *Sea Drift* (Portsea, England: Hinton & Co., 1858).

Robson, Martin, *A History of the Royal Navy: The Napoleonic Wars* (New York: I.B. Tauris, 2014).

Rodenbough, Charles D., *History of a Dream Deferred: William Byrd's Land of Eden* (Raleigh, North Carolina: Lulu, 2009).

Rodger, N.A.M., *The Command of the Ocean: a Naval History of Britain 1649-1815* (New York: W. W. Norton & Company, 2004).

Rodger, N.A.M., 'Honor and Duty at Sea 1660-1815', *Historical Research*, Vol. 75 No. 190 (2002), pp. 425-47.

Rodger, N.A.M., *The Wooden World: An Anatomy of the Georgian Navy* (London: Collins, 1986).

Rogers, Nicholas, *The Press Gang: Naval Impressment and its Opponents in Georgian Britain* (London: Continuum, 2007).

Roland, A.; Bolster, W.J. and Keyssar, A., *The Way of the Ship; America's Maritime History Re-envisioned, 1600-2000* (Hoboken, New Jersey: John Wiley & Sons Inc., 2008).

Rupert, Bob, 'Who Really "Crossed the T" in the Battle of the Saintes?', *Journal of the American Revolution* (Yardley, Pennsylvania, Westholme Publishing, 2015), p.312.

Ryan, A.N. 'The Causes of the British Attack upon Copenhagen in 1807'. *English Historical Review*, Vol. 68, No. 266 (January 1953), pp. 37-55.

Ryan, A.N. (ed.), 'Documents Relating to the Copenhagen Operation, 1807' in N.A.M. Rodger, (ed.), *The Naval Miscellany*, Vol. 5. Publications of the Navy Records Society, Vol. 125 (London: George Allen & Unwin for the Navy Records Society, 1984), pp. 297-329.

Sabin, Lorenzo, *The American Loyalists or Biographical Sketches of Adherents to the British Crown in The War of the Revolution* (Boston, Massachusetts: Charles C. Little & James Brown, 1848).

Sainty, J.C., *Admiralty Officials, 1660-1870*, (London: Athlone Press [for] the University of London, Institute of Historical Research, 1975).

Schroeder, Francis, *Shores of the Mediterranean with Sketches of Travel: 1843-45* (New York: Harpers & Brothers, 1846). Also found at *The Internet Archive*, Harvard University Collection, <https://archive.org/details/shoresmediterra-03schrgoog/page/n13> (accessed 31 March 2019).

Schroder, Walter K., *The Artillery Company of Newport: A Pictorial History* (Berwyn Heights, Maryland: Heritage Books, 2014).

Selby, John E., *The Revolution in Virginia, 1775-1783* (Williamsburg, Virginia: The Colonial Williamsburg Foundation, 1988).

Seerup, Jakob, 'Danish and Swedish Flag Disputes with the British in the Channel', in Roger, N.A.M., Dancy, J. Ross, Darnell, Benjamin and Wilson, Evan (eds.), *Strategy and the Sea: Essays in Honour of John B. Hattendorf* (Woodbridge: Boydell Press, 2016).

Shaw, William A. (ed.), *Calendar of Treasury Books* (London: His Majesty's Stationary Office, 1931), *British History Online* <http://www.british-history.ac.uk/cal-treasury-books/vol9/pp847-855> (accessed 16 June 2016).

Sibley, John L., *Biographical Sketches of those who Attended Harvard College* (Cambridge, Massachusetts: Harvard Press, 1881).

Slope, Nick, 'Discipline, Desertion, and Death: HMS *Trent*, 1796 – 1803', in MacDougall, Philip and Coats, Ann Veronica (eds.), *The Naval Mutinies of 1797: Unity and Perseverance* (London: Boydell & Brewer, Ltd., 2011).

Smith, Phillip Chadwick Foster (ed.), *The Journals of Ashley Bowen (1728-1813)*, Vol. 1-2 (Portland, Maine: Anthoensen Press, University of Maine, 1973).

Smythe, George Franklin, *Kenyon College: Its First Century* (New Haven, Connecticut: Yale University Press for Kenyon College, 1924).

Smythe, George Franklin, *A History of the Diocese of Ohio until the Year 1918* (Cleveland, Ohio: Diocese of Ohio, 1931).

Southey, Robert, *The Life of Horatio Lord Nelson* (no location indicated: reprinted by Astounding Stories, 2017; originally published 1813).

Stackpole, E.A., *Whales and Destiny: The Rivalry between America, France and Britain for Control of the Southern Whale Fishery, 1784-1825* (Amherst, Massachusetts: University of Massachusetts Press, 1972).

Stark, James Henry, *The Loyalists of Massachusetts and the other side of the American Revolution* (Salem, Massachusetts: Salem Press, 1910).

Steel, David, *Steel's Original and Correct List of the Royal Navy, and Hon. East-India Company Shipping, January-June 1813* (London: Steel's Navigation Warehouse, 1813).

Stewart, William (ed.), *Admirals of the World: A Biographical Dictionary 1500 to the Present* (Jefferson, North Carolina: McFarland and Company Inc., 2009).

Stout, Neil R., *The Royal Navy In America, 1760-1775: A Study of Enforcement of British Colonial Policy in the Era of the American Revolution* (Annapolis, Maryland: US Naval Institute Press, 1973).

Strong, John A., *The Unkechaug Indians of Eastern Long Island: A History* (Norman, Oklahoma: University of Oklahoma Press, 2011).

Sublette, Ned and Sublett, Constance, *The American Slave Coast: A History of the Slave-Breeding Industry* (Chicago, Illinois: Lawrence Hill Books, 2016).

Sutcliffe, Robert K., *British Expeditionary Warfare and the Defeat of Napoleon, 1793 -1815* (Woodbridge: Boydell Press, 2016).

Swanson, Carl E., *Predators and Prizes: American Privateering and Imperial Warfare, 1739-1748* (Columbia, South Carolina: University of South Carolina Press, 1991).

Talbot, John E., *The Pen and Ink Sailor: Charles Middleton and the King's Navy, 1778-1813* (London: Frank Cass, 1998).

Thomas, Admiral the Earl of Dundonald, *The Autobiography of a Seaman* (London: Richard Bentley, 1860).

Thompson, Frederic F., 'Gambier, James, 1st Baron Gambier', *Dictionary of Canadian Biography*, Vol. 6, University of Toronto/Université Laval, 2003–, <http://www.biographi.ca/en/bio/gambier_james_6E.html> (accessed 25 February 2017).

Tracy, Nicholas, *Nelson's Battles: The Triumph of British Seapower* (Annapolis, Maryland: US Naval Institute Press, 1996 and 2008).

Tracy, Nicholas, *Who's Who in Nelson's Navy: 200 Naval Heroes* (London: Chatham Publishing, 2006).

Trew, Peter, *Rodney and the Breaking of the Line* (Barnsley, South Yorkshire: Pen & Sword Military, 2006).

Tunstall, Brian, *Naval Warfare in the Age of Sail: The Evolution of Fighting Tactics 1650-1815* (London, Chatham, 1990; Edison, New Jersey: Wellfleet Press, 2001).

Vancouver, George, *A Voyage of Discovery to the North Pacific Ocean, and Round the World*. (London: G.G. and J. Robinson, Paternoster Row, and J. Edwards, Pall Mall, 1798).

Vickers, Daniel. 'The First Whalemen of Nantucket'. *The William and Mary Quarterly*, Vol. 40, No. 4 (October 1983), p.284.

Vickers, Daniel, 'An Honest Tar: Ashley Bowen of Marblehead', *New England Quarterly*, Vol. 69, No. 4 (December 1996), pp. 544-553.

Vickers, Daniel, 'Ashley Bowen of Marblehead: Revolutionary Neutral,' in Rhoden, Nancy and Steele, Ian (eds.), *The Human Tradition in US History: The Revolutionary Era* (Wilmington, Delaware: Scholarly Resources Inc., 2000).

Vickers, Daniel, *Young Men and the Sea: Yankee Seafarers in the Age of Sail* (New Haven, Connecticut: Yale University Press, 2005).

Walbran, John T., *British Columbia Coast Names, 1592-1906: to which are added a few names in adjacent United States Territory, their origin and history* (Ottawa: Government Printing Bureau, 1909).

Wareham, Tom, *The Star Captains: Frigate Command in the Napoleonic Wars* (Annapolis, Maryland: US Naval Institute Press, 2001).

Willis, Sam, *The Glorious First of June: Fleet Battle in the Reign of Terror* (London: Quercus, 2011).

Willis, Sam, *In the Hour of Victory: The Royal Navy at War in the Age of Nelson* (New York and London: W.W. Norton, 2013).

Willis, Sam, *The Struggle of Sea Power: A Naval History of American Independence* (London: Atlantic Books, 2015).

Wilson, Evan, *A Social History of British Naval Officers, 1775–1815* (Woodbridge: Boydell Press, 2017).

Winfield, Rif, *British Warships in the Age of Sail 1793-1817: Design, Construction, Careers and Fates* (London: Chatham Press, 2005; Barnsley, South Yorkshire: Seaforth Publishing, 2008).

Winfield, Rif, *British Warships in the Age of Sail, 1714 – 1792* (Barnsley, South Yorkshire: Seaforth Publishing, 2008).

Winfield, Rif and Lyon, David, *The Sail and Steam Navy List: All the Ships of the Royal Navy 1815 – 1889* (London: Chatham Publishing, 2004).

Winthrop, Robert C., *A Short Account of the Winthrop Family* (Cambridge: J. Wilson and Son, University Press, 1887).

Woodcroft, Bennet, *Alphabetical Index of Patentees of Inventions* (London: Evelyn, Adams & Mackay, 1969).

Woodman, Richard, *The Sea Warriors* (London: Constable Publishers, 2001).

Worthington, B., *Proposed Plan for Improving Dover Harbour* (Charleston, South Carolina: Nabu Press, 2010; originally published Dover, England: King's Arms Library, 1838).

Wroth, Kinvin L. and Zobel, Hiller B. (eds.), *Legal Papers of John Adams* (Cambridge, Massachusetts, 1965).

Wyon, William, *A Memoir of the Life and Works of William Wyon, Esq., A.R.A., Chief Engraver of the Royal Mint* (London: W. Nicol, 1837).

Young, Samuel, *Speech of Mr Young* (New York: E. Conrad, 1814).

Theses & Dissertations

Gabrielson, Mark J., 'Enlightenment in the Darkness: The British Prisoner of War School of Navigation, Givet, France, 1805-1814,' unpublished Master of Liberal Arts in Extension Studies (History), Harvard University Library, 2014.

Hubley, Martin, 'Desertion, Identity and the Experience of Authority in the North American Squadron of the Royal Navy, 1745-1812', PhD Dissertation, University of Ottawa, 2009.

Salmon, M., 'More Talk of Peace than Prize Money: The letters of common or 'lower deck' seamen from the Revolutionary and Napoleonic Wars 1793-1815', Master of Arts Thesis, National Maritime Museum, University of Greenwich, 2016.

Periodicals & Journals containing public notices (hardcopy, digitized, and online)

American Turf and Sporting Magazine
Annual Biography and Obituary
Anti-Monarchist and Republican Watchman
Bath Chronicle
Bell's Life in London and Sporting Chronicle
Maine Antiques Digest
Northampton Mercury
Rivington's Royal Gazette
Rhode Island Republican
The Athenaeum Magazine of Literary and Miscellaneous Information
The Edinburgh Gazette
The Gentleman's Magazine and Historical Chronicle
The Hampshire Telegraph
The London Gazette
The Naval Chronicle: The Contemporary Record of the Royal Navy at War

The Naval Chronicle: Containing a General and Biographical History of the Royal Navy of the United Kingdom with a Variety of Original Papers in Nautical Subjects
The Nautical Magazine and Naval Chronicle
The New Monthly Magazine and Literary Journal
The Northampton Mercury
The Royal Gazette
The Scots Magazine or General Repository of Literature, History, and Politics
The Spectator
The Virginia Gazette
The United Service Journal and Naval and Military Magazine
Transactions of the Royal Society of Arts for the Encouragement of Arts, Manufactures, and Commerce
Warder and Dublin Weekly Mail

Online Sources not published elsewhere

Abarim Publications' Biblical Name Vault, <http://www.abarim-publications.com/Meaning/Jahleel.html.> (accessed 4 April 2019).

Anon., 'Blockade of Saint-Domingue', *Wikipedia*, 2016. <https://en.wikipedia.org/w/index.php?title=Blockade_of_Saint-Domingue&oldid=755060401> (accessed 16 December 2016).

Anon., 'Barrie, Robert'. *Three Decks.org*, <http://www.threedecks.org/index.php?dis-play_type=show_crewman&id=3125> (accessed 9 May 2019).

Anon., *Colegio Almirante Reginald Carey Brenton*, <http://www.careybrenton.edu.mx/index.php?option=com_content&view=article&id=18&Itemid=16> (no longer accessible on 5 April 2019).

Anon., *Chronology of the On-Line Institute for the Advanced Loyalist Studies*. <http://www.royalprovincial.com/military/milit.htm> (accessed 8 July 2016).

Anon., 'HMS *Pomone*', *Maritime Archaeology Trust*, http://www.maritimearchaeologytrust.org/alumbay1. (accessed 2 April 2019)

Anon., 'James Gambier 1st Baron', *More than Nelson*. <http://morethannelson.com/officer/lord-james-gambier/> (accessed 3 May 2019).

Anon., '*Greyhound*, Pennsylvania Privateer Schooner', *American War of Independence at Sea* <http://www.awiatsea.com/Privateers/G/Greyhound%20Pennsylvania%20Schooner%20[Kemp].html≥ (accessed 22 May 2019).

Anon., 'Loring, John (Royal Navy officer, died 1808)', *Wikipedia*, 2016 <https://en.wikipedia.org/w/index.php?title=John_Loring_(Royal_Navy_officer,_died_1808)&oldid=721563750> (accessed 3 May 2019).

Anon., 'Mount Pearl', Wikipedia, <https://en.wikipedia.org/wiki/Mount_Pearl> (accessed 2 April 2019).

Anon., 'Naval Oceanographic Office', *Wikipedia* 2016. <https://en.wikipedia.org/wiki/Naval_Oceanographic_Office> (accessed 3 May 2019).

Anon., Photo of monument to Edward Brenton. *The Second Website of Bob Speel* <http://www.speel.me.uk/chlondon/chm/marylebonenewch/marylebone-brenton.jpg> (accessed 9 May 2019)

Anon., 'The Carey Family of Guernsey', *Carey Geneology History* <http://www.careyroots.com/hd2.html> (accessed 5 April 2019).

Anon., 'United Kingdom Hydrographic Office', *Wikipedia,* 2016. <https://en.wikipedia.org/wiki/United_Kingdom_Hydrographic_Office> (accessed 3 May 2019).

Bell, J.L., 'John Loring, Midshipman', *Boston 1775* (blog), December 3, 2008, http://boston1775.blogspot.com/2008/12/john-loring-midshipman.html (accessed 3 May 2019).

Bell, J.L., 'John Loring, Prisoner of War,' *Boston 1775* (blog), December 4, 2008, <http://boston1775.blogspot.com/2008/12/john-loring-prisoner-of-war.html> (accessed 3 May 2019).

Bell, J.L. 'The Ransom of John Loring', *Boston 1775* (blog), December 5, 2008, <http://boston1775.blogspot.com/2008/12/ransom-of-john-loring.html> (accessed 3 May 2019).

Finger, Jascin Leonardo, 'Do You Know This Building? The Admiral Sir Isaac Coffin Lancastrian School, Part One', *Nantucket Chronicle*, February 2, 2016 <https://www.nantucketchronicle.com/nation-Nantucket/2016/do-you-know-this-building-admiral-site-isaac-coffin-lancasterian-school-part> (accessed 14 September 2016).

Heubner, Brandon, 'The Funeral and Burial of Admiral Lord Nelson, 9 January 1806', *On This Day in History,* (podcast Jan 9, 2015) <http://maritimehistory-podcast.com/funeral-burial-lord-horatio-nelson-9-january-1806/> (accessed 3 May 2019).

Inglis-Arkall, Ester, 'The Dark and Twisted History of the Children's Friends Society', *Gizmodo* <http://io9.gizmodo.com/the-dark-and-twisted-history-of-the-childrens-friend-so-1677705809> (accessed 17 April 2019).

Phillips, Michael, *Ships of the Old Navy* <http://www.ageofnelson.org/MichaelPhillips/info.Php?ref=0341> (accessed 19 June 2016).

Index

From Reason to Revolution – Warfare 1721-1815

http://www.helion.co.uk/published-by-helion/reason-to-revolution-1721-1815.html

The 'From Reason to Revolution' series covers the period of military history 1721–1815, an era in which fortress-based strategy and linear battles gave way to the nation-in-arms and the beginnings of total war.

This era saw the evolution and growth of light troops of all arms, and of increasingly flexible command systems to cope with the growing armies fielded by nations able to mobilise far greater proportions of their manpower than ever before. Many of these developments were fired by the great political upheavals of the era, with revolutions in America and France bringing about social change which in turn fed back into the military sphere as whole nations readied themselves for war. Only in the closing years of the period, as the reactionary powers began to regain the upper hand, did a military synthesis of the best of the old and the new become possible.

The series will examine the military and naval history of the period in a greater degree of detail than has hitherto been attempted, and has a very wide brief, with the intention of covering all aspects from the battles, campaigns, logistics, and tactics, to the personalities, armies, uniforms, and equipment.

Submissions

The publishers would be pleased to receive submissions for this series. Please contact series editor Andrew Bamford via email (andrewbamford18@gmail.com), or in writing to Helion & Company Limited, Unit 8 Amherst Business Centre, Budbrooke Road, Warwick, CV34 5WE

Titles

No 1 *Lobositz to Leuthen. Horace St Paul and the Campaigns of the Austrian Army in the Seven Years War 1756-57* Translated with additional materials by Neil Cogswell (ISBN 978-1-911096-67-2)

* indicates 'Falconet' format paperbacks, page size 248mm x 180mm, with high visual content including colour plates; other titles are hardback monographs unless otherwise noted.